CW01096100

Democracy
Disfigured

Democracy
Disfigured

OPINION, TRUTH,
AND THE PEOPLE

Nadia Urbinati

Harvard University Press

Cambridge, Massachusetts
London, England
2014

Library of Congress Cataloging-in-Publication Data
Urbinati, Nadia, 1955–
Democracy disfigured : opinion, truth, and the people / Nadia Urbinati.
pages   cm
Includes bibliographical references and index.
ISBN 978-0-674-72513-3 (alk. paper)
1. Democracy.   2. Democracy—Public opinion.   3. Populism.   I. Title.

JC423.U774   2014
321.8—dc23   2013014795

To my students

CONTENTS

Democracy
Disfigured

Introduction

The figure is a shape that is externally identifiable, a composite of observable characteristics and the configuration of a person's distinctive features that enable recognition. Each of us has his or her phenotype thanks to which others recognize us. Our figure is thus precious to us because the traits composing it are meant to make our appearance unique, different from others. In this book I use the analogy with body figure to explore some disfigurements of democracy. The analogy of the "body" in political thought is as old as reflection on politics. Theories of political legitimacy have been developed as theories on the substance of the body politic, what makes it political. Thus, for instance, Jean-Jacques Rousseau famously argued that if citizens obey laws they do not make directly, the system in which they live is not political, although they may call it so, because the autonomy of their sovereign will is the substance that makes for a body politic. This is not the model I follow. I will not inquire into the substance of political sovereignty. Rather, I take "figure" or an observable configuration as indicative of a political order, a phenotype thanks to which we recognize it as distinct and different from other systems. A regime that is tyrannical is characterized by some traits or has a figure that makes an observer pretty much sure of its identity, like no regular elections, no division of powers, and no bill of rights. By the same token, a democratic society has certain traits that belong only to it and make it recognizable from outside. In relation to the figure that democracy exposes to the world I detect some disfigurations. This is the sense of the analogy I use in this book. In the first chapter I shall portray the main basic traits composing the democratic figure—the procedures and institutions and the public forum of opinions. In the subsequent chapters I will detect and analyze some disfigurations that, although they do not change the form of government, may be perceived as remarkable changes in what is externally observable of democracy. The word "disfiguration" implies a negative evaluation, not merely a description. The three disfigurations I will illustrate in this book are alarming mutations. In detecting and analyzing them I intend to alert readers to these forms of distress in view of amending them, and in the conclusion I advance some suggestions for legal innovations.

The analysis I propose pivots on the idea of democracy as a government by means of opinion. It particular, as I shall explain in Chapter 1, it relies on the premise that representative democracy is a *diarchic system* in which "will" (by which I mean the right to vote and the procedures and institutions that regulate the making of authoritative decisions) and "opinion" (by which I mean the extrainstitutional domain of political opinions) influence each other and cooperate without merging.[1] The societies in which we live are democratic not only because they have free elections and more than one political party competing but also because they promise to allow for effective political competition and debate among diverse and competing views; they promise that elections and the forum of opinions make institutions the site of legitimate power and an object of control and scrutiny. The conceptualization of representative democracy as diarchy makes two claims: that "will" and "opinion" are the two powers of the sovereign citizens, and that they are different and should remain distinct, although in need of constant communication. Based on this premise, I offer a theoretical and critical examination of three observable traits that have been recently put forth by actual democratic countries and theorized by scholars of politics in order to cope with the dissatisfying performance of democratic procedures: epistemic and unpolitical twists of deliberation; and the reaction of populism and of the plebiscite of the audience against representative democracy. Different as they are, epistemic views, populism, and plebiscite of the audience entail a view of the forum of opinion that is one-sided and disdainful of the diarchic configuration of democracy.

To be sure, dissatisfaction with democracy is part of the history of democracy and recurrent in democratic societies, and the right to free speech and freedom of association that citizens enjoy makes it public and frank. Thus, Demosthenes depicted Athens as a city permitting its citizens to praise the Spartan constitution over the Athenian one, Niccolò Machiavelli wrote against its critics that popular government allows everybody "to freely speak ill" of the people, and Alexander Meiklejohn argued during the Cold War that the Unites States must allow its communist critics to speak freely because "to be afraid of ideas, any idea, is to be unfit for self-government."[2] Tolerance and free speech made possible that Athenian democracy developed alongside with its "enemies," the oligarchs, and this proved the liberal character of its society, which denied neither its opponents nor foreigners freedom of expression, so as to make Euripides's Phaedra desire that her children lived there as "free men, free-spoken, honourable."[3] As for modern democracies, whose freedoms are protected by bills of rights and written constitutions, their stabilizing process in the last two and a half centuries has been dramatically interfered with, and in some cases stopped by its opponents. But with the end of the Cold War, this form of government was able to win global recognition. Today, democracy has no legitimate competitor; it would be hard to disclaim it in the name of a government that is more respectful of civil and political liberty.

Yet its planetary solitude does not make it invulnerable. Political theorists have recently pointed to the appearance of two concurrent phenomena that provide reasons for concern: on the one hand, the privatization and power concentration in the sphere of political opinion formation, and on the other, the growth of demagogical and polarized forms of consensus that split the political arena in factional and inimical groups. These are not extemporaneous characteristics but the signs of a transformation of the public sphere in mass democracies provoked by phenomena as diverse as the erosion of legitimacy of political parties in the managing of representation and the escalation of economic inequality. Both phenomena have a direct impact on the distribution of the opportunity of "voice" and influence in politics.

In the mid-nineteenth century, John Stuart Mill surmised that newspapers would be able to re-create in large societies that kind of immediacy and proximity in national conversation that ancient republics enjoyed by having their citizens gathered together in one assembly to directly interact in the agora or the forum. Modern means of communication, Mill thought, would rouse an immaterial forum of opinions by including issues of popular concern in the public arena and keeping politicians and the institutions under the judgment of the public of writers and readers.[4] Pluralism of the means of information would mirror the pluralism of ideas and interests, and both of them would be valuable obstacles to the growth of a new tyrannical form of power, coming precisely from public opinion. A century after Mill, Jürgen Habermas thus claimed the public forum essential to democracy on the condition it remains public, pluralistic, and autonomous from private interests of all sorts. With prescient words, already in 1962 Habermas depicted the acclamation style that can disfigure the public sphere in mass democracy.[5]

My primary concern here is opinion, not "will;" I am interested in the problems that arise from within the domain of opinion, although no longer or not simply in forms that raise the basic question of "how to protect freedom of expression from the power of the state." The issue is instead how the public forum of ideas can succeed in remaining a public good and play its cognitive, dissenting, and monitoring role if the information industry that affects politics so radically "in many different parts of the world belongs to a relative small number of private individuals."[6] In a political arena in which video power is so prominent an actor and an "acclamation-prone mood" tends to predominate, dispersal of mass media ownership, some scholars have suggested, should be able to prevent the "Berlusconi effect,"[7] the plebiscitarian disfiguration that has inspired me in writing this book.[8] Yet other scholars have expressed concern that dispersal of information is not in and of itself a sufficient condition for limiting homogeneity. The Internet produces a formidable dispersal of information but tends also to create the aggregation of millions around views that, as Cass Sunstein observes, are endorsed by imitation and tend to reproduce and radicalize old prejudicial and factional loyalties.[9] Even more than media concentration, online dispersal of information inclines citizens toward militant factionalism and the formation of self-referential and homogeneous niches of like-minded militants. The decline of electoral participation and the fragmentation of the public are intertwined phenomena to be treated as indications of metamorphoses of representative democracy or challenges from within to its diarchic nature. Within this actual scenario that belongs in various degrees to all consolidated democracies I situate the theoretical analysis of three forms of disfiguration of democratic politics—epistemic, populist, and plebiscitarian—as either a reaction against or an instrumental use of the fact that democracy is a government of and by means of opinion.

In past decades, populist and plebiscitarian forms of democracy predominantly appeared in nonconsolidated democratic states like those in Latin America or post-Soviet Russia. More recently they have emerged within consolidated or Western democracies. In some European countries, we have witnessed forms of plebiscitarian identification with publicized leaders whose popularity made them appear charismatic and directly authorized by their audiences, and forms of populist claims seeking to represent the whole people or the true meaning of a nation's values and history. Some scholars have coined the term "videocracy" to make sense of this new form of populist politics in *mediocratic* style.[10] Others have thrown skepticism on the democratic import of the Internet and pointed to "social cascade" and "group polarization" as two different yet overlapping processes that democracy seems incapable of containing without limiting freedom of expression and communication.[11] Others have finally proposed that democracy depoliticize itself by deflating the role of lawmaking (parliaments and voting) and of media alike and increasing the epistemic use of deliberative procedures so as to prepare for or promote unpolitical, less biased, and more competent decisions.[12] The phenomena these authors lament pose specific and unique challenges in comparison to earlier violations of democracy that require us to revisit the power and the role of the forum. The task of democratic societies consists in devising legal and cultural strategies that contain the threat of demagoguery at a time in which "demagoguery becomes scientific" without curtailing freedom and without obliterating the political nature of deliberation and the procedural and representative configuration of democracy.[13] In the conclusion, I will propose some general guidelines for these strategies that are consistent with democracy's diarchy.

The epistemic theory wants to bring rationality and knowledge into democratic politics in order to change its opinion-based nature. Today's myth of technical government (government by experts in financial issues) in European countries and the disparaging attitude toward parliamentary politics it provoked is an eloquent example of this epistemic metamorphosis. As I will explain in Chapter 2, the flourishing in recent years of epistemic views and practices testifies to a conflicting relationship between *doxa* and *episteme*. Defending truth against opinion imports a unilateral reading of the public as a process of enlightenment that should purify politics of ideological competition. Although for a noble cause and despite that it bestows wisdom to the crowd, the epistemic twist of the public sphere would deform democracy's distinctive cacophonic and imprecise character, which is essential to the enjoyment of political freedom. On the opposite side, populism represents an all-political transformation of the forum of opinions that repudiates democracy's diarchy. As I will argue in Chapter 3, populism fosters the polarization and simplification of social interests and political ideas, and thereby uses the world of opinion and critical assessment as a mere instrument for achieving the unity of the people above and against its parts. Finally, plebiscitarian democracy gives the public sphere a predominantly aesthetic function, and although it does not reject democracy's diarchy, it reduces the role of the forum to building the authority of the leader. As I will show in Chapter 4, the visual character of media communication and information facilitates this phenomenon of audience voyeurism, in which putting the life of the leader in public is primed to encourage spectatorial enjoyment more than control or inspection. Being "under the eyes of the people"[14] imports an aesthetic transformation of the public sphere that can have profound effects on representative democracy because it changes the very notions of citizenship and political participation.

That representative democracy is government by opinion entails that the citizens participate by voting and by knowing and seeing what the government does and by proposing alternative courses of action. The public forum of opinion means that state power is open to proposals and to inspection and is actually public, both because the law requires that it is performed under the people's eye (that is to say according to norms and open to scrutiny by justice and the press as well) and because it is not owned by anybody since appointment by elections means that the sovereign power has lost any specific location, embodiment, and possession. In the light of this, I identify three roles of *doxa* in the public forum of modern democracy: cognitive, political, and aesthetic. In relation to them, it is possible to detect forms of disfigurations—but it would be more appropriate to say of "radicalization" because they consist in exaggerating or stressing one character exclusively of the diarchic order. This is how I suggest we interpret epistemic, populist, and plebiscitary renderings: they are possible radicalizations of one of these three roles of the forum of opinions that spring from within representative democracy as its internal borders. Although these changes are not meant to bring about any regime change because they do not question the "will" or the democratic system, they modify the external figure of democracy in a way that is visible.[15]

Political philosophers see representative democracy from the perspective of the demagogy risk contained in partisan political judgment. They point to the biased distortion of political issues that electoral competition propels and argue that downplaying democratic procedures, like votes for representatives or in referenda, would emancipate democracy from the demagogy that political opinions inevitably create. To depoliticize democracy by enlarging the domain of impartial decisions with courts, committees of expertise, deliberative groups, and nonpolitical authorities in some key issues like the national budget is the answer given by what I propose to call *democratic Platonism*, or philosophy's appropriation of democracy, the most radical and resilient challenge to democracy, even when made in the name of democracy itself. Epistemic and unpolitical solutions seem to identify democracy with populism when they assume that political forms of consent seeking are impermeable to impartial knowledge. The predictable conclusion from this diagnosis is that limiting populism would require modifying the figure of democracy or taking away from it the "vice" of partisanship that electoral competition and representative institutions inevitably produce. The target is *doxa*. Yet amending democracy of its political nature by making it a process for the achievement of "correct outcomes,"[16] rather than outcomes that are procedurally and constitutionally valid, entails narrowing rather than rescuing democracy. The legitimate concern with demagoguery translates here into solutions that, if implemented, would change the opinion-based character of democratic politics and in fact disfigure democracy. This is what I propose to call democratic Platonism, or the persistence of the myth of the philosopher-king dressed in collective and egalitarian garb. A crowd that is made of people that, given some data and procedures of deliberation, achieve a correct outcome is still not necessarily a democratic gathering, although it is egalitarian. Equality in something, even when this "something" is relevant as in the case of knowledge, has nothing to do with democracy or political equality.[17]

On the other side of the spectrum, populism and plebiscitarianism propose no less radical restyling when they treat the sphere of public and political opinion as a terrain of conquest under the guidance of skillful leaders and comprehensive ideologies and the support of a crowd of spectators. Unlike with the theory and practice of representative and constitutional democracy, in these cases opinion is not a power that is meant to give voice to citizens' claims, monitor institutions, and devise alternative political agendas. As we shall see, populism and plebiscitarianism are not identical phenomena. Yet they overlap in scourging intermediary institutions like political parties and parliaments and in promoting personalistic forms of representation and the call for strong executive power. Both populism and plebiscitarianism make public opinion the game of words and images that transforms politics in a process of verticalization, all the while claiming they intend to bring politics to people and people to politics.

In all of these three cases, the opinion-based character of democracy emerges prominently. These interpretations put forth three different relationships to *doxa* that can be used as guidelines to understand their ways of construing democracy. Whereas Platonist or epistemic theory proposes to dislodge *doxa* from democratic politics and make it a diarchy of will and reason, populism takes advantage of *doxa* as an active strategy of hegemonic unification of the people that claims to be identical with the will of the sovereign; and plebiscitarianism, while it acknowledges the diarchic system and keeps the electoral moment separate from opinions, makes *doxa* the name of crafted images unfurled by video technicians to which the people react. Although for different reasons and plans, epistemic, populist, and plebiscitarian solutions disfigure democracy by intervening in the nature, role, and use of one of its two powers: the forum of opinions. Moreover, all of them propose to heavily revise or discard the procedural character of democracy upon which the diarchic figure rests.

In the end, I would say that there are two views of democracy that confront each other in contemporary political theory and practice: one that holds political proceduralism as the best *normative* defense of democracy, in fact holding it to be the figure of representative democracy because it is respectful of the diarchic character of this government, and the other that sees deliberative procedures and political contestation as instrumental to an end that transcends them in the name of truth or the construction of a hegemonic people or the creation of an ocular citizenship. Although different, epistemic, populist, and plebiscitarian visions are mirrorlike images that converge toward a view that denies the normative character of political democratic procedures and the form they take in representative democracy. The goal of their critique is the reconstitution of democratic authority either under the aegis of a process of decision making that is judged from the point of view of the correct outcome it produces or under the aegis of an homogenous sovereign people, whose voice is authoritative above the ordinary rules of the game, or under the aegis of "vision" rather than "voice," thus making the public a passive audience that watches leaders act with insatiable curiosity and no participatory aim. These three proposals of democracy's reconfiguration compete with representative democracy on the terrain of representation insofar as they challenge the meaning and function of the public, representation's most peculiar terrain.

In this book I unfold these interpretations and argue that we are able to detect them whenever we interpret democracy as government by means of opinion that operates through certain procedures and within a secure system of rights and the division of state powers, that is to say within an organization that is meant to diffuse, control, and break rather than concentrate and exalt power (and opinion as a form of power). This frame is also the premise that guides me to acknowledge the low profile and malfunctioning of actual democracy, whose planetary success makes it more vulnerable to its own problems.[18] In an unintended way, these disfigurations allow us to see better the risks awaiting contemporary democracy. Moreover, they make us aware of the fact that while democratic procedures have achieved full practical recognition in the late twentieth century, they became marginalized in democratic theory as a functionalistic method devoid of normative value. The simultaneous assault on them by epistemics, populists, and plebiscitarians speaks to their neglect by democratic theory, which bears responsibility for having made them the domain of realists who throw skepticism on their normative value and nature. In the conclusion I will thus propose that democratic theory re-achieve the normative value of democratic proceduralism as a demanding promise of protection of citizens' equal political liberties.

The figure that a democratic society exposes to the world and that makes it recognizable as democratic is first of all the individual right to vote, which entails its free, easy, and costless exercise and the counting of votes of equal weight according to the principle of majority. These foundational characteristics are consistent with the fact that all democratic decisions are subjected to change because they are "not simply a fixed outcome" of citizens' private interests or "nonpolitical" reasons, but the expressions of a political way that free and equal citizens have in acting in the public realm, something that has been identified with political deliberation in its broadest sense.[19] Political opinions make sense of the fact that democratic citizens are free to form and change their views and revoke their support to previously made decisions. The value and meaning of political equality and liberty rest on the persistence of this process. Opinion is the unavoidable starting point we must accept in countering the risk of demagoguery and the denunciation of the malfunctioning of established democracies. Thus, while philosophers insist we read democracy as evidence that a crowd (an unpolitical gathering), when led by appropriate procedures, is able to achieve correct outcomes, I argue instead that the actor of democracy is not a crowd but citizens who exist and operate through procedures that presume the changeability of their opinions, rather than truth or virtue. To restate John Rawls, "political liberalism views this insistence on the whole truth in politics as incompatible with democratic citizenship and the idea of legitimate laws."[20]

I develop my argument by making a critical analysis of the main contemporary objections to political democratic proceduralism in order to see whether they are on target in capturing the new risks coming from the domain of opinion formation. Philosophical attempts to make democracy a process that obtains correct outcomes resorts to the critique of democracy's endogenous lack of rationality. Their diagnoses suggest a limitation of the democratic element even if their declared intention is to make procedures that enable the many to produce good or correct outcomes, or to prove that the crowd is wise. Clearly, this new Platonist renaissance is not conceived so as to oppose the wisdom of the few against the irrationality of the many. We should not neglect the fact that what is today called "epistemic democracy" is rooted in the tradition of Enlightenment, a movement that brought philosophers to mobilize reason in defense of the collective as the only legitimate political sovereign. The problem with democratic Platonism, or the idea of neutralizing the wrong while at the same time avoiding making the few the only political experts, is that its good intentions are not enough to guarantee that democracy is honored. It is the epistemic perspective itself that needs to be revised, and in fact abandoned, because "a commitment to 'truth' in politics makes consent redundant."[21]

Against it I revive Alexis de Tocqueville's maxim that democracy is not good for the outcomes it produces, which sometimes are no better than those produced by nondemocratic regimes. Democracy's value rests on the fact that it allows citizens to change decisions and leaders without calling into question their political order. In no other political system is it crucial that means and ends are not in disagreement. Democracy is consistency of means and ends because it is both a goal and the process to reach it. And if it does not allow for shortcuts it is because it is not merely a functional way to reach some end or any kind of ends (even good ends). The goodness of the end does not justify the violation of the democratic process of decision making. This entails that the dualism between formal and substantive is wrongly posed because conditions for the correct work of procedures and procedures themselves must always be conceived together if a decision-making process is to be held democratically. Hence, this system of permanent change is not for achieving some truth, although citizens may think that this is the goal of their political activity, and although candidates in electoral competitions defend their platforms as the truest or the best. Rather, it is for making decisions with the contribution of all citizens, those who agree and those who disagree, with the results emerging out of the application of democratic procedures. Freedom of participation and the certainty that no majority will be the last one are the "goods" that democratic procedures provide. In this sense, democratic proceduralism is normative because it satisfies two essential conditions: equal political liberty and civil peace (peace entails both that citizens disagree in a climate of "tranquility of spirit" and that they consent to obey the law although in disagreement with the majority that backed it).

At first glance, populism seems to be more consistent with the characteristics I just described because it claims it wants to reclaim the democratic authority of ordinary citizens against the elites. "The key concept that lies at the heart of populist ideology is undoubtedly 'the people', followed by 'democracy', 'sovereignty', and 'majority rule', each defined through its links with the others."[22] The target against which populist ideology mobilizes is the government of temporality that elections establish, since elections promote party's elites, rather than the "will of the people." To be sure, populism has been met with dissimilar evaluations in Europe and in Latin America and the United States, where the language of populism is sometimes identified with the belief that "rule by the common people" is synonymous with virtue and lack of corruption, and the expression of more intense political participation that curbs the power of the elite and thus makes society more, not less, democratic.[23] I acknowledge this contextual specificity but nevertheless consider populism as a disfiguration of democracy. In the case of populism, contesting the political establishment is for the sake of making the opinions of a portion of the people (albeit the largest majority) the source of legitimacy with the consequence of debilitating dissent and threatening pluralism. Populist upsurges are primed to translate into an intolerant affirmation of "we the people" against minorities within the people and thus, fatally, against party pluralism and political competition itself. Constitutional and representative democracy is its true target.

As for plebiscitarianism of the audience, its disfiguring effect is even graver because although it does not question the diarchic structure of representative democracy, it questions the very idea of citizenship as an expression of political autonomy. While historically it was possible to adapt political autonomy to indirect participation through representation (modern democracy did it by making equal suffrage or the right to vote central), it is hard to reconcile democracy with a view of politics that makes the condition of "being ruled" and watching leaders act into a norm or the figure of "the People." Once rotation and lottery are no longer democracy's procedures, "there is far less reason for devaluing or ignoring the figure of the citizens-being-ruled."[24] Plebiscitarian democracy as audience democracy makes the given into a norm; it accepts the subjection of the citizens to the ruling creativity of the leaders and media experts when it insists that the core activity of the citizens is visual and spectatorial, not discursive or participation oriented. This vision of democracy can be taken to prove *a contrario* that the defense of democracy's diarchy passes today through the emancipation of proceduralism from the strictures of Schumpeterianism.[25]

The challenges awaiting constitutional and representative democracy are considerable, and the public sphere of opinion formation is the domain we ought to turn our attention to in order to see them. This is the leading thread of this book, which is motivated by the attempt to answer two intertwined questions: What is the nature of contemporary malfunctioning and dissatisfactions with liberal democracy, and what are the resources internal to it that can contain the absolute power of opinion without making politics a subdivision of knowledge and the people a crowd of militant followers or a passive audience? Representative democracy defends and benefits from the complexity of the public sphere of opinion: its critical and cognitive function, its political style and spirit, and its propensity to make power visible and also for this reason public. Yet none of these functions are sufficient alone; in fact, taken in isolation they may compromise the diarchic configuration of democracy.

Through its long and honorable history, democracy has shown great imaginative ability to devise institutions and procedures that are capable of solving problems that democracy's political process of decision prompts.

Just to mention a few well-known paradigmatic examples, ancient Athens dealt with the "tyranny of the assembly" by regulating the process of law proposal and promulgation with some sophisticated procedures known as *graphe paranomon*; in the eighteenth century, American colonies created constitutional conventions to give themselves a political order based on consent and the voting authorization of representatives; in the nineteenth century, European liberal states perfected representative government in a way that would make it capable of absorbing the democratic transformation of sovereignty in large territorial states; and after the debacle of totalitarian and dictatorial regimes based on consensus, post–World War II constitutional democracies succeeded in limiting the power of elected majorities with division of powers, the rule of law, and party pluralism, thus adopting a complex strategy of institutional innovations, juridical and political. In short, democracy survived in difficult times and circumstances thanks to its uniquely fertile institutional and normative imagination and capacity of innovation.

Today, the hegemony of *homo videns* and the radicalization of demagogical opinions are the symptoms of a malfunction that is dispensed by television and new, more sophisticated information technology. Of course the information and communication technologies give ordinary citizens extraordinary possibilities of more rather than less knowledge and participation (one of our modern myths speaks of a virtual republic and an Internet agora for new types of social drama and criticism).[26] Yet good does not come without some bad, and it is on this contradiction that democratic theory should turn its attention. Risks to democracy come today from within the complex world of opinion formation, that panoply of means encompassing the indirect power of ideas that free speech and freedom of the press and association create and reproduce. They come, as we said, both in the form of plebiscitarian identification of the masses with a publicized leader and in the form of populist claims seeking to represent the whole people as a homogeneous unity of values and history. These seemingly self-assertive acts of popular sovereignty assertion are in fact a worrisome phenomenon of political passivity and docility of the citizens that change democracy's physiognomy.

According to plebiscitarian theory, the passivity of the many is fatal in all forms of democracy, direct and representative, because democracy is a political system that is structurally made of active few and receptive many who learn how "to obey and accept the good intentions of those in charge."[27]

It is not election per se that makes democracy apathetic (the assemblies of ancient democracies were ruled by few rhetoricians and the citizens tended not to participate). Apathy or mass passivity belongs to this regime in an endogenous way since, as the iron law of oligarchy goes, politics is an art of the few, not the many. Yet people's habituation of "being ruled" reaches its perfection with representative democracy, because in this system is voice completely supplanted by sight and hearing, which are "the passive organs of sense" par excellence and the only expressions of citizens' presence in indirect politics. Contemporary citizens are an audience and representative democracy is an audience democracy.[28] To contemporary plebiscitarians, this trajectory represents democracy's perfection. Yet it would be bizarre to argue that the age of Silvio Berlusconi corresponded to the fulfillment of democracy's inner nature, unless we view democracy as identical with the audience imbecility of the many before the spectacle played by the few. Underneath the promise of an objective realism and dispassionate understanding, the plebiscitarian theory of democracy offers us an upside-down logic in which what happens becomes *eo ispo* rational.

This view, which relies upon an authoritative body of sociological and political literature pivoting on the works of Roberto Michels, Vilfredo Pareto, Max Weber, and Carl Schmitt, suggests we deem acclamation and mass democracy as both a description and a norm. It is the premeditated conclusion of a definition of parliamentary or representative democracy as an elected oligarchy or the mix of two predetermined and separated groups, that of the active few and the passive many. Beneath this view, in which democracy looks like a grand system of deception triggered through *doxa*, we may hear an echo of Plato's sarcasm at the lover of the demos. From Plato's times to ours, this view has never lost its attraction for philosophers and is periodically resurrected with new argumentative strategies and, alas, the complicity of the wretched performance of existing democracies and the help of technological innovation in the communication industry. This realist reading betrays the traditional and never-vanished aversion among the wise few for a government that relies, humbly and steadily, on opinion and for this reason on vote counting and majority rule. This reliance on majority rule requires no presumption of achieving correct outcomes but reflects the certainty of being the only political order that honors liberty not of some or the best, but of all, and not because they have some specific potentials but because they exist. In the diarchy of "votes" and "opinion" is thus the key to appreciate democracy as a government that pivots on equal freedom.

Opinion is a form of action and a form of power that has voice at its heart, not sight. If anyone, it is the all-too-active few who seek visibility and want to make *doxa* a matter of sight only. The few would love to make the people a gigantic eye, with no voice. But voice and hearing together, not one or the other, are the two complementary senses that ordinary citizens use when they form their views and listen to others' and change and express their opinions and seek through them to acquire a political presence, to watch and judge their elected politicians. Citizens' invisibility and silence are thus not spontaneous or natural to democracy but are crafted and constructed by the controllers of the means of information and communication and longed for by the political class, in their desire to remain unchecked and unchanged.

It would therefore be correct to say that representative democracy consists of a permanent struggle of representation or making public or an object of public debate issues that citizens deem central to their lives and interests, and at times (when they vote) transform into authoritative decisions. This is what makes *doxa* a power essential to democracy. It makes it a form of action, which is different from, but not less relevant than, the will or the conditions and procedures that organize votes and decisions. This is also what makes opinion the permanent object of desire (or scourge) of the few, who long to be surrounded by people who experience only the activity of being ruled and condescension, who do not express dissenting views and ideally do not even think of opinion as power.

1

Democracy's Diarchy

The identification of democracy with "the force of numbers" has traditionally attracted skeptics and detractors of democracy. After having derided the idea that government can be resolved as a numerical issue, Vilfredo Pareto wrote: "We need not linger on the fiction of 'popular representation'—poppycock grinds no flour. Let us go on and see what substance underlines the various forms of power in the governing classes. . . . The differences lie principally . . . in the relative proportions of force and consent."[1] For Pareto, number was simply a clever means to use force through consent, and democracy was the most effective way to achieve the goal all tyrants have longed for but could not get since they were unable to have the power of numbers on their sides. He did not add, however, the reason tyrants could not have numbers on their sides, and this made his view of democracy predictably truncated, prejudicial, and wrong: numbers work because liberty matters in the formation of consent. For leaders to have numbers on their sides citizens must have liberty on theirs. Yet what is the function of voting?

Revising Pareto's line of thought without renouncing his skepticism on democracy, Giovanni Sartori argued years ago that voting is what counts in democracy, although it cannot guarantee the quality of decisions because citizens do not learn how to vote by voting. No matter how rich and articulate, the open arena of discussion does not change the arbitrary character of voting and does not make citizens more competent or their decisions more correct.[2] It is not for the sake of achieving some desirable outcomes that democracy relies upon voting and an "uninhibited, robust, and wide-open" public debate, to use Justice Brennan's classic formula.[3] Rather, it is for the sake of citizens enjoying and protecting their liberty. Justifying political rights from the point of view of their consequences is a dangerous path toward democracy depreciation. We enjoy the right to vote not because this allows us to achieve good or correct outcomes (although we might go to the ballot with this aim in mind) but in order to exercise our political freedom and remain free while obeying, even if the outcomes that our votes contribute to producing are not as good as we had foreseen or as would be desirable. For this reason, the First Amendment "recognizes no such thing as a 'false idea'" and "cannot sustain, or even tolerate, the disciplinary practices necessary to produce expert knowledge."[4] As I will claim through this chapter and the book, the strength of a procedural interpretation of democracy (in fact, its normative strength) rests on this basic and simple assumption, which is as old as democracy itself.

Before getting to the central theme of this chapter, namely, the characteristics of the public forum (i.e., the meanings, conditions, and quality of *doxa*), in the following three sections I will elaborate three intertwined arguments: that the recognition of the role of opinion in the process of decision making is internal to a procedural interpretation of democracy; that representative democracy has a diarchic structure; and that the role of the political forum in democracy is essential, not optional. This preliminary clarification will lead me to situate *doxa* at the core of the democratic process and show the several facets it may take when made part of democratic sovereignty within representative government. Finally, it will take me to the central political claim of the chapter: that the diarchic and procedural perspective—the figure of representative democracy—contains the normative arguments thanks to which we can make the forum of opinion a public good and an issue of political liberty.

The Value and Maintenance of Democratic Procedures

Democratic procedures do not guarantee the improvement of citizens' decision-making capacities nor do they promise to guide them toward outcomes that are correct according to a criterion that transcends those very procedures. As I will have the chance to explain in the next chapter, what they do is ensure that citizens make decisions in a way that they can always be open to revision. A free and open forum is a sign of liberty and a good in and by itself: first, because the chance of contesting and controlling a regime rises to the extent that citizens' opinions are not confined within their inward minds or held as private opinions;[5] second, because it is consonant with the character of democracy as a political system that is based on and engenders the dispersion of power; and third, because it makes possible the formulation of multiple political opinions in relation to which citizens make their choices. "The democratic distribution principle is an end in itself, not a means predicted to lead empirically to some desirable result," and it holds both for the function of making decisions (voting) and the function of forming and questioning them.[6] Thus, while electoral power is no doubt the basic condition of representative democracy, the "substantial guarantee is given by the conditions under which the citizen gets the information and is exposed to the pressure of opinion makers. . . . If this is so, elections are the means to an end—the end being a 'government of opinion, that is, a government responsive to, and responsible toward, public opinion."[7] This is the leading idea that guides me.

Proceduralism in its standard definition comes to us with the mark of the author who made it famous, Joseph A. Schumpeter, who was very unsympathetic to democracy and conceptualized precisely that definition in order to tame the democratic element (political equality) and above all disassociate electoral participation from the achievement of a goal that goes beyond the aggregation of individual interests and claims to be instead inspired by or aim at the general interest. Severing procedural democracy from Schumpeterian proceduralism has been the project of several generations of scholars, from Hans Kelsen, Robert Dahl, and Norberto Bobbio just to mention the most representative of all. Gerry Mackie has recently proposed the following rendering of democratic proceduralism that amends Schumpeter's: "In a proper democracy, voters mostly control parliaments, and parliaments mostly control leaders, through prospective voting, public opinion between elections, and ultimately through retrospective voting in recurrent elections."[8] In sum, procedural democracy does not mean simply voting computation or institutional correctness but also using free speech and freedom of the press and of association in order to make the informal or extrainstitutions domain an important component of political liberty. Democracy is a combination of decisions and judgment on decisions: devising proposals and deciding on them (or those who are going to carry them out) according to majority rule. The character of democracy is diarchic and its nature procedural. This is its figure.

To go a step further, we may say that democratic proceduralism is in the service of equal political liberty since it presumes and claims the equal right and opportunity citizens have to participate in the formation of the majority view with their individual votes and their opinions; it is what qualifies democracy as a form of government whose citizens obey the laws they contribute in making, directly or indirectly. Democracy provides each of its citizens the conditions, legal and political, thanks to which they can, if they so choose, participate in a broad and complex sense: by forming, criticizing, contesting, and changing collective decisions in a climate of "tranquility of spirit," to use Montesquieu's effective words.[9] The normative value of the democratic procedures resides in the fact that they make inclusion and control by the included in the process possible. Suffrage and the forum of ideas are intertwined powers and essential conditions of democratic liberty. They are principled factors and do not need empirical evidence: the equal right to vote is essential even if we do not learn to vote by voting, and our equal chance to take part in a wide-open and robust public forum is essential even if this gives us no guarantee that we will achieve good or rational or correct decisions, that more information translates into knowledge. In this sense in the next chapter I employ the procedural interpretation of democracy to argue against the epistemic theory of democracy that procedures *(the rules of the game)* rather than content and achievement are the primary goods and what make a procedural conception of democracy normative. Democracy's normative value lies in its process's unmatched capacity to protect and promote equal political liberty. "Liberty and equality are the values that lay at the foundation of democracy . . . a society that is regulated in a way that the individuals who compose it are freer and more equal than in whatsoever other form of coexistence."[10]

Equal political liberty involves not only an equal distribution of the basic political power of making decisions but also participation in politics by freely expressing one's mind, and doing so under conditions of equal opportunity; the protection of civil, political, and basic social rights is essential to a meaningful equal participation.[11] Democracy promises liberty first of all and uses legal and political equality to protect and fulfill this promise. This was so since its ancient inception and is true today, although a robust tradition of liberal thought that grew in an anti-Jacobin climate has sponsored the belief that democracy is driven by the passion of equality rather than the love for liberty, that equality is inimical to liberty.

Yet in Athens, democracy began with *isonomia*, or "equality through the law," and *isēgoria* and *parrhēsia*, or their equal right to talk and vote in the assembly and moreover to talk freely and frankly.[12] Equality through the law means precisely political equality as the equal opportunity all citizens have, protected by the law, to exercise their power to take part in the decision-making process. Thus, Athens was conceived as a *politeia en logois* (a polis based on speech) and its citizens were defined as *hoi boulomenoi* ("whoever wishes to do so," namely, to address the assembly).[13] The electoral transformation of modern democracy did not change this principle.

If talking frankly and freely is a condition of participation it is because democracy promises social stability or peace through the participation of all (whether directly or indirectly) in lawmaking. Thus, liberty and peace together are the goals of the equal distribution of political power to make authoritative decisions upon which the democratic process of decision rests. This is what makes democratic proceduralism different both from a Hobbesian minimalist definition, which stresses the goal of peace but disregards that of liberty,[14] and from an epistemic interpretation, which situates the good as something that transcends the process itself, like the judgment on the content of the outcome, and laments that "the effort to rely on nothing but proceduralism" makes democratic authority not very valuable.[15]

As this chapter will show, if consistently embraced, a procedural interpretation of democracy is very demanding, although for reasons that pertain to its performance rather than the attainment of a specific outcome. Among the demanding conditions there is the open forum of opinion formation. This argument was brilliantly made by Hans Kelsen in 1945: "A democracy without public opinion is a contradiction in terms. Insofar as public opinion can arise only where intellectual freedom, freedom of speech, press, and religion, are guaranteed, democracy coincides with political—though not necessarily economic—liberalism."[16]

The case of ancient Athens shows that democracy pertains to the opportunity of both sitting in the assembly and being treated as equal by the law and voicing opinions in public.[17] Wherein it is clear that the procedures are distinct from the outcome, so that having equal opportunity to take part and a hospitable environment are good because they give each citizen the chance to make his or her contribution valuable.[18] Good outcomes, if and when they occur, are a reward for procedures, not what gives their normative value. Indeed, the Athenians enjoyed and praised their political right to talk in the assembly even if they only rarely used it and even if only some used it (and used it well). Democratic politics was like athletic competition in which all must start in line, wherein it is implicit that the conditions that allowed the citizens to start as equals were essential to make that political order recognizable as democratic.[19]

Concerning our contemporary societies, they are democratic because they have free elections and the opportunity to have more than one political party competing, because they allow effective political competition and debate among diverse and competing views, and finally because elections make the elected an object of control and scrutiny.[20] Bernard Manin has thus connected representative government's foundation on opinion to its egalitarian premise since its procedures entail that discord among opinions should not terminate "through the intervention of one will that is superior to the others" but through a majority decision that is open to revision.[21] Starting from similar premises, Noberto Bobbio came years ago to the conclusion that "democracy is subversive. It is subversive in the most radical sense of the word, because, wherever it spreads, it subverts the traditional conception of power, one so traditional it has come to be considered natural, based on the assumption that power—i.e., political or economic, paternal or sacerdotal—flows downwards."[22]

Clearly, institutions and procedures are exposed to distortion; in a democratic society distortions come from the violation of equality or the increase of inequality in the conditions that determine a fair use of them. "One could hardly take seriously one's status as an equal citizen, for example, if owing to a lack of resources one was precluded from advancing one's views effectively in the public forum."[23] The good work of procedures requires that the overall political system takes care not only of its formal conditions but also of the perception citizens have of its effectiveness and value. Attention to democratic procedures asks for a continuous work of maintenance. The criterion orienting this maintenance should be in agreement with the procedural interpretation of democracy: it should aim to block the translation of socioeconomic inequalities into political power.[24] As we shall see, this task is challenging because the insulation of the political system should be achieved without blocking the communication between society and institutions, which is one of the most important features of representative government, what makes it diarchic.

What Is Democratic Diarchy?

Diarchy of will and opinion applies in particular to representative democracy, a system in which an assembly of elected representatives, rather than citizens directly, is endowed with the ordinary function of making laws. The parliament, which is the core institution of a democracy based on election, presumes and entertains a constant relationship with the citizens, as single persons or political groups and movements, and opinions are the means through which this relationship develops. The conceptualization of modern democracy as diarchy makes two claims: that "will" and "opinion" are the two powers of the democratic sovereign, and that they are different and should remain distinct, although in need of constant communication. The terminology I use is an adaptation of the language of sovereignty, which in its modern codification has characterized the power of the state as the "will" of making authoritative decisions that obligate all the subjects equally. For Jean Bodin, Thomas Hobbes, Jean-Jacques Rousseau, and the theorists of constitutional government in the nineteenth and early twentieth century, "will" stands for *procedures, rules and institutions*, that is to say the normativized set of public behavior that gives birth to and implements the law.

Yet the classical theory of sovereignty, which was coined before representative democracy started its journey, did not contemplate judgment or the opinion by the subjects as a function of the sovereign.[25] But democracy, above all when it is implemented through elections, cannot ignore what citizens opine or say when they act as political actors, not electors. Thus, in representative democracy, the sovereign is not simply the authorized will contained in the civil law and implemented by states' magistrates and institutions but is instead a dual entity in which the decision is one component, the other being the opinion of those who obey and participate only indirectly in ruling. Opinion partakes of sovereignty although it does *not* have any authoritative power; its force is external to the institutions and its authority is informal (as not translatable into the law directly and not endowed with the signs of command). The representative democratic system is "one in which supreme power (supreme insofar as it alone is authorized to use force as a last resort) is exerted in the name of and on behalf of the people by virtue of the procedures of elections."[26]

It is important I make clear at the start that I use the words "opinion" and "political judgment" interchangeably. As we shall see in the next chapter, there are different kinds of judgment, and not all of them belong to the domain of lawmaking. Judgment by courts and tribunals and judgment by the citizens, the press, and representatives are different. Aristotle's idea of politics as it emerges in his *Art of Rhetoric* is the best perspective to grasp the specificity of political judgment (or deliberative discourse) as an opinion that is produced in the public forum among equal citizens, and that is not intended so as to produce true-false inferences like scientific judgment and judicial judgment. To anticipate in a few words what I will claim in the next chapter, it is important we distinguish political judgment from other genres of judgment if we want to appreciate the fact that political deliberation consists, properly speaking, in citizens making opinions concerning the course of actions it would be good for them to take or avoid taking. Free citizens make political judgment with the aim of convincing each other to decide on something that pertains to their future and has only a verisimilar or probable character.

Political judgment comes not only with agreement but also disagreement; it is a process of collective argument that needs a legal and procedural order that allows for people to know in advance they can change their minds and do so publicly and safely. The integration and communicative implications of political judgment are predictable. Indeed, democratic citizens use all the means of information and communication they partake in to manifest their presence, argue for or against a proposal, and monitor those who are in power, and they know this is no less valuable than the procedures and the institutions that produce decisions. The broad work of political life in a democratic civil society is what I include under the category of political judgment or opinion. The challenge awaiting representative democracy is that although "will" and "judgment" cannot be truly separated, they need to operate separately and be and remain different. Of course we are here talking of normative separation: we do not want the opinion of the majority to become one and the same thing with the "will" of the sovereign, and we do not want our opinions to be interpreted as passive reactions to the spectacle leaders put on stage. That representative democracy is government by means of opinion entails that the public forum keeps state power under scrutiny and is public, both because the law imposes that it is performed under the people's eyes and because it is not owned by anybody (in agreement with appointment by elections, which stipulates that political power does not belong in the category of property). The criterion deriving from the paradigm of diarchy that I will employ in this chapter may be rendered as follows: as a twin power, the public forum should be approached from the perspective of the "same egalitarian value that is embodied in people's equal right to be self-governing."[27]

Representative Democracy

I need to make a further clarification before I analyze *doxa*. Democratic diarchy pertains essentially to representative government, in which will and judgment do not merge in the direct voting power that each citizen holds but remain two different modes of participation, so that only the latter is in the hands of all the citizens all the time. But diarchy is not only a descriptive concept; most important, it designates both a separation of functions and a principle of equal opportunity as conditions that hold for both opinion and voting. Indeed, diarchy consists in keeping decisions and deliberations that occur inside the institutions distinct from the informal world of opinion, without, however, this distinction implying that only the former matters because it can be rendered in numerical certainty or, to the contrary, that only the latter matters because it is conceived as the genuine expression of the voice of the people above the strictures of the constituted power.

The idea of democracy as diarchy is equally distant from a pure electoralist conception of democracy (voting as a method to elect those who rule) and a conception that interprets government by opinion as a government in which sovereignty belongs to the majority that exercises it through acclamatory voice outside and above the voting procedures. On this premise political liberty acquires security not only in the legal system but also in the perception of the citizens. We may say that the world of opinion creates a buffer zone or a distance between citizens and political power and that this distance opens the floor to, on the one hand, citizens' judgments on power and, on the other, citizens' protection from power.[28] One of the consequences of the diarchic perspective, in fact the one that interests me, is that it makes the right to free speech and freedom of opinion an essential component of the political rights of the citizen, not only a right of the individual. The right to take part in the formation of opinions is a right that produces power, not only a right that protects from power.[29]

The *informal* nature of the power belonging to political opinion requires some specification. It is true that "by itself public deliberation decides nothing,"[30] that preparing for, and informing, decisions with a broad process of discussion offers no guarantee that voters will be influenced by good reasons. There can be no such guarantee because voting is arbitrary and unaccountable (we are not accountable to anybody when we cast our ballot, and this is the condition of our autonomy) and because the inequality between speakers and listeners is part of the political game. The formal equality that makes us citizens does not equalize the power that speech gives us to influence each other.[31] Representation does not change the opinion-based nature of democracy; if anything, it makes it even more pronounced. In fact, the representative system gives the forum a determinant role because it consists in putting politics in public, as citizens are required to judge and choose politicians according to what they say and do or exercise their prospective and retrospective judgment on them.

What makes the sphere of opinion share in sovereignty depends, therefore, on the form the sovereign takes. Voting for or electing a representative is what makes the forum share in sovereignty and the reference point in relation to which opinion plays its role. Democratic theorists have argued, rightly, that the centrality of decision in politics makes election the only truly democratic institution.[32] Votes are the most reliable public data at our disposal, and voting is the only formal way citizens have to punish and threaten their rulers. "Voting is an imposition of a will over a will," not a mere opinion; it is that which counts as a decision beyond reasonable doubt.[33] Yet the way in which will is imposed matters a lot, as differences between direct and representative democracy show. Because of its indirect form (citizens authorize lawmakers to decide in their names), modern democracy marks the end of yes-no politics and transforms politics in an open arena of contestable opinions and ever-revisable decisions. Thus, to scholars of representative government, the indirect power of opinion characterizes modern democracy no less than suffrage and does so in a *plurality* of ways that we do not immediately apprehend if we focus only on one component of the diarchy, the voting power.

As a matter of fact, if representative democracy is able to replace violence with counting votes (a capacity that scholars have defined as "miraculous"), it is because the weight of votes exceeds that of the numbers. When politics is structured according to electoral terms and the political proposals the candidates embody, opinions create a narrative through time. This makes electoral appointment of representatives a fertile terrain for ideological accounts, which purport themselves as visions of the entire society, its aspirations and problems, that link and divide citizens at the same time. This makes sense of the fact that the candidates are recognizable as different, and starting with this recognition they become objects of judgment on the part of the voters. On this ground I claim that political opinions never have equal weight, not even in the hypothetical case of two different opinions receiving the same number of votes. If the weight of opinions were equal, the dialectics of opinions, and voting itself, would make little or no sense. In representative democracy, voting is an attempt to give ideas weight, not to make them identical in weight.[34]

Thus, unlike direct democracy, in representative democracy voting compels citizens to be always more than electors, to transcend the act of voting in the effort to reassess the relationship between the weight of their ideas and the weight of their votes through the time between elections. Only in direct democracy are opinions identical with will because they translate immediately into decisions.[35] In direct democracy, sovereignty is *mono-archic*. But representative democracy breaks that unity because in it, opinions acquire a power that is independent from the voting act or will.

Opinions seek visibility and influence beyond Election Day, and although they cannot claim any legitimate hold on decision making, they give rise to an open and public forum of ideas, which generates a surplus of political activity and makes representative democracy more than electoral democracy and different from direct democracy. On the other hand, although elections (along with referenda) have become the only authoritative form of citizens' direct presence, electable candidates are not perceived nor meant to be solely appointed magistrates to rule instead of the people. They want to be (and actually need to be if they want to seek reelection) in communication with their electors.[36] Edmund Burke, the most prominent theorist of political representation as free mandate, had no doubt on the value of that communication, which, he added, must be frank and permanent.[37] Even more explicit were the American Founding Fathers, who derived the liberty value of the "chain of communication" between citizens and institutions from their experience of British domination, contending that the Parliament treated the colonists in exactly the same way as the vast majority of the British population because its authority derived solely from representation and not also communication.[38]

Following Burke and the Founding Fathers, one may say that it is precisely because representatives are legally not responsible to those who chose them that they must be made responsible to them by other means.

A free and permanent channel of communication between them and the citizens is essential in order for voters to perceive them as legitimate magistrates. Legal legitimacy constitutes only one side of the coin. Opinions work as a force of legitimacy by connecting and uniting people inside and outside the institutions (wherein connection may entail also dissent and breaking of trust). They do so because they do not only entail that people want to express them freely and openly but also that the people want to know what happens inside the palazzo. Their meaning is thus to be a burden upon the government precisely because government is founded on opinion.

The circularity of giving authority and checking on authority is what makes the power of opinion so hard to define scientifically and to regulate normatively, yet so indispensable practically. This complexity and elusiveness brought David Hume to define "public opinion" as a "force" that makes the many easily governed by the few and the few unable to escape the control of the many.[39] After the casting of "paper stones" one by one, it is the *circular movement* of opinions that links citizens among themselves and bridges state institutions and society.[40] This makes sense of representative democracy as diarchy. But it also makes sense of the risks this diarchic structure embodies.

The interaction between the people and their candidates and representatives may induce some to think that the most nosy citizens, or public debates on TV and lobbies of polls, are legitimate in vindicating a sovereign power. Populist and plebiscitarian phenomena are incubated within democratic diarchy as a longing to overcome the distance between will and opinion and achieve unanimity and homogeneity, an idealization that has characterized democratic communities since antiquity.[41]

On the other hand, because of its diarchic nature, representative democracy should be engaged in an extra effort to guard the opportunity citizens have to participate in the making of the *informal* sovereign. Since there is an unavoidable link between public opinion and political decision, concern about the disproportioned possibility that the wealthiest or the more socially powerful have to influence the electors and the governments is sacrosanct. Empirical research proves this concern is well posed when it demonstrates how economic inequality and political inequality "are mutually enforcing with the result that wealth tends to entrench, rather than distribute, power over time."[42] Theorists of democracy take this evidence as a justification to argue that in representative democracy citizens may suffer a new kind of corruption, a "duplicitous corruption," that consists in excluding those who have equal citizenship from a meaningful presence in the forum and doing so in a way that the excluded cannot prove their exclusion because they retain the right to throw a "paper stone" in the ballot box, which is factual evidence of their equal citizenship.[43]

The main argument of this chapter is thus that when opinion is introduced in our understanding of democratic participation, then political representation must attend to the question of the *circumstances of opinion formation*, an issue that pertains to political justice, or the equal opportunity citizens should have to meaningfully enjoy their political rights.[44] Citizens' equal rights to an equal share in determining the political will (one-person-one-vote) ought to go together with citizens' meaningful opportunities to be informed but also to form, express, voice, and give their ideas public weight and influence. Although influence can hardly be equal and estimated with rigorous calculation, the opportunity to exercise it can and should be. Although we can hardly prove beyond any reasonable doubt that there is a causal relationship between media content, public opinion, and political results or decisions (no data can prove that Berlusconi won three electoral competitions because of his media television empire), the barriers to equal opportunity to participate in the formation of political opinions should be kept low and their level permanently monitored. This is the salient meaning of political equality as liberty protection I am defending in this book, that is, the idea that the focus of democracy is on inclusion *because* its concern is "on the reasons for excluding individuals" and money is a powerful reason for exclusion even when exclusion does not take the radical form of suppressing suffrage.[45] The same principled reasoning that holds for voting holds for opinion, since although we can hardly prove that voting translates in some desirable outcome, we do not conclude that to distribute it equally is meaningless. As said, the normative character of democratic procedures rests on the fact that its practice is its value.[46]

Doxa, Politics, and Freedom

The Greek word *doxa* or the Latin word *opinio* combines two meanings, which became representative of two grand traditions in western political philosophy. On the one hand, *doxa* has a philosophical meaning as an idea that is impervious to truth, and on the other it has a civil meaning as

a kind of judgment that signals how a view or an act performed by someone is received by others. The former evaluates *doxa* from the perspective
of the cognitive outcome. The latter judges it from the perspective of the
conversation it brings about among persons who interact in a common
and public environment and moreover make laws. We can trace these two
traditions back to the two greatest philosophers of antiquity, Plato and Aristotle, and recognize a mediated strategy in Cicero's pragmatic solution
of separating philosophical *sermo* from civil *eloquentia* within the republic, so as to judge them from the perspective of two values that are different: truth in the former case, and liberty in the latter.[47] The conception of
politics as an art by means of which persons who are different and strangers to each other regulate their behaviors and relationships with agreed
upon norms belongs in the Aristotelian tradition. It is in this tradition that
political discourse is conducive of stability and liberty.

A Gray Zone

Opinion, wrote Plato, is the name of a view or a belief that cannot pass the
bar of philosophical analysis; *doxa* does not belong in *episteme* or the domain of knowledge. Opinion inhabits the gray zone in between the wrong
and the right, with the predictable consequence that in popular governments it opens the door to canny and ambitious leaders, who craft arguments and ideas in view of acquiring power with people's consent, without
necessarily pursuing people's interests. An intermediary between knowledge and ignorance, opinion entails permanent change, not because it
tends to approximate truth but because, given its uncertain and instable
nature, it induces individuals to try and experiment with different views
and styles of thought in order to make or remake their decisions with no
assurance that their search will stop sometime in the future.

Opinion is endogenously rooted in people's emotions and in direct communication with action. Its mediating function between passions and the
decision to act made Plato, and his countless followers, think of opinion as
dangerous to politics. Opinion is a disposition of our mind that makes us
see the same things from different angles and makes it hard to know what
the truth of those things is since most of the time the same things "appear to be beautiful in a way and also to be ugly in a way."[48] The *opinable*
is thus easily associable (and associated by philosophers) with biases and
prejudices; it is "the wandering intermediate grasped by the intermediate

power"; it is the irrational domain of "nonattitudes" that government should resist against by relying upon an autonomous class of experts or competent deliberation committees.[49] The opinable cannot be amended, nor can it be translated into truth, and when it becomes rooted in popular culture it acquires the character of a natural given endowed with the authority of a norm.[50] Opinion is for this reason able to become an invisible authority (a "yoke" in Tocqueville's vocabulary) that leads people to do or desist from doing by means of a compelling power that seems to be springing from people themselves, their ancestors, and traditions.[51] Opinion makes people actors and victims at the same time; it creates conformism or, as a way out of it, the withdrawal from the forum and the fall in "a spiral of silence."[52] For instance, Marcus Tullius Cicero conceived of virtues not so much as qualities of the individual but as qualities of a socially situated person that education shapes with the aim of producing habits of behavior that other people judge and evaluate.[53] Hence, reputation, or the reflection of oneself in others' minds, and honor, or our desire to be according to what others regard as desirable or convenient or proper, make opinion the source of a new kind of sovereignty that fits the character of popular government and can open the door to a new form of despotic domination, as Mill and Tocqueville argued.

In sum, opinion cannot generate truth, although it can be overcome only by truth. It is the enlightenment of knowledge that dissolves the density of prejudices, which look like opinions that reiteration through time has condensed and made in a residue, as Pareto would define the sediment of a given set of opinions that forms an all-embracing narrative or ideology. Looking for the reason of things in the domain of politics as well as philosophy and morality entails reaching that definition that apprehends "things themselves that are always the same in every respect."[54] Evidently, decisions concerning right and wrong cannot be a matter of voting, which is the reason why lovers of knowledge are hardly lovers of democracy. Thus, Terence Ball has observed, authority based on *episteme* conflates the distinction between "being in authority" and "being an authority" by assimilating the former to the latter.[55] It associates authority to qualities someone possesses and disassociates it from institutions and procedures.

Democracy, we may infer from Plato's premises, is disposed toward relativism precisely because it is based on opinions. The implication of this anti-*doxa* perspective consists in that it fosters a *critique of immanence* (a characteristic that springs instead, as I will explain at the end of this chapter, from a procedural interpretation of democracy), with the caveat that transcendence may be invoked in the name of different kinds of good, such as theological truth, philosophical reason, and also the authority of a charismatic leader. Regardless of the kind of good in whose name it is made, this critique of immanence manifests deep dissatisfaction with democracy, not because democratic politics does not make room for epistemic claims but because it threatens them as if they had no special authority and no permanence either. For people like Callicles, who epitomized the engaged citizen in Plato's *Gorgias*, to practice rhetoric means to live for politics, or have one identity only, that of the "public man," with no transcendent point of view that detaches him from the opinion of the forum.[56] It is changeability, or its procedural organization in view of making changes possible, that makes democracy a government based on opinion. Democracy is government by discussion because it is government by opinion.[57]

Public Discourse in the City

A slightly different position was expressed a few years after Plato by Aristotle, who translated Plato's view into a definition of opinion that could be accommodated with collective deliberation and freedom. According to Aristotle, opinion in the assembly was equivalent to what the Romans called "verisimilitude," a species of truth in its own right (*verum similes*, or that which resembles the truth), not a gray zone distant from truth and perilously tending toward falsehood; it was a process of knowledge that was "within the cognizance of all men and not confined to any social science."[58] More importantly, opinion was synonymous with a constitutional political order or a republic (in today's parlance a legitimate government) and thus with liberty. It was used to designate politics itself as "a dialogical activity practiced by citizens."[59] The link of opinion and freedom is a seminal idea in the rhetorical tradition that Aristotle inaugurated.

Aristotle distinguished three functions in the government, to which he associated different forms of judgment. The work of the "legislator" (*nomothéton*) was different from that of the "public assembly" (*ekklesia*) and of the jury (*dikastes*) in a very important way. The legislator (the lawgiver or founder or, in modern experience, a constitutional assembly) exercises a kind of judgment that "is universal and applies to the future"—it creates the conditions for subsequent judgments on what is "important or unimportant, just or unjust" on the specific cases that will become objects of decision. It sets the criteria, rules, and procedures that will guide the lawmakers ("public assembly") and the magistrate (the justice or the court), who have to decide on specific and actual issues and do so by applying those criteria or laws. In these last two domains (that of the assembly and of the jury), passions and emotions enter the scene since the issues under discussion are not written in the law (upon which unanimous consent is assumed) but need to be resolved by applying the law, which figures thus as the general premise of judgment, not the conclusion.[60] This "constitutional" conception of the polis entails that "disagreement" is not eliminable and that "when conditions are right, it is possible for an entire city to have a common and correct understanding about what human well-being is," which the fundamental law is in charge of transmitting from one generation to another so as to create the ethos of the polis and make people decide within the frame of the constitution.[61]

For instance, suppose the basic law claims equal inclusion of all adult persons in the citizenry. A specific legislation is then required that implements it and regulates its application when and on what conditions that general criterion applies—for instance, by deciding on the threshold of age. The decision that individuals should enjoy the right to vote at the age of eighteen is not an inference that can be judged in terms of correctness since it is the outcome of a conventional view or a legal and moral tradition (that individuals are to be held responsible for their deeds and punished accordingly) that meets with the acceptance by the large public: all this together (that is to say, the conventional view, the legal and moral tradition, and the general opinion) may be held as "evidence" of the *verisimilitude* of the decision on the majority age. But judging the majority-age threshold in terms of correctness or wrongness would make no sense. Indeed, the threshold of eighteen years of age is not more "correct" now that people accept it than it was when the people thought that the major age should be, say, thirty or forty years old. It is not an immutable truth but a verisimilar one, because it presumes a contextually based idea of what is right and wrong in relation to the basic law that claims equal inclusion.

The same can be said of questions that pertain to decisions on war or peace, an example Aristotle liked to refer to in order to explain the impossibility of judging political deliberation with the criteria of philosophical deliberation, although this would not entail that politics was not a reasonable art. "For some problems are useful to know with a view to choosing or avoiding, for instance, whether pleasure is to be chosen or not; others only with a view to knowing, for instance, whether the universe is eternal or not"; hence, the question "Should we go to war?" would be of the first kind, calling for political deliberation, and not the second, calling for epistemic truth.[62] On issues concerning "choosing" or "avoiding"—which for Aristotle were issues of utility and justice—questions of verisimilitude are in turn not questions of truth, which is why we entertain in pondering pros and cons and making arguments of prudence or convenience and why, finally, we need procedures for decision making that allow for disagreement to be expressed. The work of the *ekklesia* and that of the *dikastes* are thus a work of judgment. Yet they do *not* use the *same* kind of judgment, as we shall explain in the next chapter.

Clearly, discussion and disagreement are endogenous in a city whose government is based on opinions. This both requires and feeds a climate of freedom and public exposure of ideas. In *The Nicomachean Ethics*, Aristotle says that if a community had in its midst heroes it should let them rule.[63] But then he adds promptly that the political condition in which men live testifies to the fact that there are not superhuman beings in their midst; thus, the city ought to be built as the best possible city, given the assumption that men can be individually virtuous, but many are not really, and none is godlike. Given that the city is made of ordinary and diverse individuals, they need to decide together; their imperfection makes them all in need of cooperation and inclusion. Thus, all of them should be members of the assembly and the jury, and they should search together what is advantageous and just for all. Deliberation as a collective decision-making strategy entails the recognition of the uncertainty citizens have to cope with and the reality of their living together; it entails that the participants anticipate that decisions cannot always be unanimous, nor do they always have to be expected to be so.[64]

As one reads in his *Art of Rhetoric*, political deliberation makes sense precisely because things to be decided on are not the object of scientific knowledge and philosophical deliberation, and all decisions (even those on the constitutive laws) are open to revision.[65] An open trial of opinions and disagreement is endogenous to the political life of the city. It is on what is open to rhetoric or opinions that we are invited to measure political freedom, and thus distinguish among the forms of government. Thus, democracy is the government most friendly to public discourse.[66]

Aristotle wrote that "there are some states, especially those that are well administered," in which "there would be nothing left for the rhetoricians to say," and there are other states in which people are forbidden to speak "outside the subject" in court, where speech is required to follow procedures that are established so as to make the judges reach the truth on particular cases.[67] We have here two very different situations in which opinion should not be in place. This difference helps us to appreciate and understand better the link between *doxa*, politics, and freedom, or why free government is based on opinion.

The "well administered" polis in which "nothing is left for the rhetoricians" looks like an enlightened despotism or an epistocracy.[68] In this kind of state there is a radical denial of politics (and of liberty) because no room is left to public speaking since a ruler will take care of all decisions. On the contrary, the polis in which opinions are ruled out of the court looks like a constitutional government, in which the place of political opinion needs to be circumscribed, and this limitation translates into liberty protection. Indeed, in this city, if opinions must not enter the court it is because they are presumed to flow freely in the public sphere. Thus, laws must be made that keep opinions "outside the subject" of justice.

We call constitutional democracy a society in which a judge is required to silence his religious faith or ideological opinions when making authoritative judgments or verdicts in court. But we do not imply that this requirement is to be made of citizens and, to a certain extent, their representatives in the assembly. The crucial issue advanced by Aristotle is thus the existence of an endogenous link between government by opinion and freedom. Limitations and containment of opinions (separation of justice from politics and of court from the assembly) make sense because of that link.

Opinions entail searching for consent and acquire their authority on people's minds not by reason alone and above all not by a solipsistic kind of reason but by a kind of reason that is diffused in society in the forms of people's conformity to or acceptance of something they regard as reasonable in relation to the circumstances of their social and moral lives, their ethical culture, and the idea of well-being they have. The law of opinion and reputation that John Locke discussed in his *An Essay Concerning Human Understanding* as derivative of the faculty of judgment ("which God has given men to supply the want of clear and certain knowledge") as well as the general opinion, or what Immanuel Kant called *sensus communis*,

are the platforms of a society that relies upon people's basic views in relation to which they make inferences and reasoned arguments when they
make decisions or judge those who are elected to make them.[69] To be
united in political society and dispose of their united force (the law) does
not empty individuals of their "power of thinking well or ill" but makes
them more capable of making moral judgments.[70]

Opinions are interpretations of specific facts and events that result from
applying the ideas or values that the people at large share already as their
common beliefs. If appeal to basic principles occurs, this is not for epistemic goals, however, but rather with the aim of overcoming disagreement and making decisions that are legitimate or acceptable to those who
are to bear them. Arguments of political legitimacy are made in order to
secure acceptance and obedience of free citizens.[71] These arguments rely
heavily on a subterranean general opinion on which people agree to the
point of regarding it as a principled assumption that inspires inferences
people treat and regard as "truth" or "correct" or "sound." Aristotle's view,
which echoes in the work of authors as diverse as Edmund Burke and John
Rawls, suggests the existence of a notion of the public or political reason
that produces arguments of political legitimacy, yet not expert knowledge.

We may at this point capture the consequences of the two meanings
that *doxa* or *opinio* encapsulate. When judged from the epistemic perspective, opinion is the domain of the uncertain and the prejudicial, and
for this reason a condition of disorder and dispute that is primed to desta-
bilize authority. The goal of knowledge is to overcome it or pass from what
is a matter of opinion to what is a matter of proved and no longer contested evidence. Either *doxa* is transformed into *episteme* or it needs to be
expelled from the political sphere if this is to become a place of harmony,
as Plato and his followers wanted. Political liberty is wholly foreign to this
conception of the city and politics, whose main goal is order rather than
freedom. When judged from its social or communicative perspective
instead, opinion is a medium through which people create a space of
exchange of judgments and ideas, as in Aristotle's tradition. In this case,
liberty is a condition for peace rather than harmony. It is essential to the
life of the city, and the evidence of this lies in the fact that politics is the
home of opinions.

However, the division of labor between *doxa* and truth, as if the former
were for the general many and the latter for the few, does not spare opinion
from criticism; in fact, it makes philosophers conclude that all opinions

must be taken with great suspicion unless they become themselves a product of their (philosophers') critical work, unless the competent public dictates the correct line of interpretation of the political issues. In the next three sections I will show how the classical dualism between *episteme* and *doxa* transfers to the conceptualization of opinion in representative democracy. As it will appear, three functions have been attached to opinion: that of social integration or consensus that unifies public behavior and orients political decisions toward a goal that is common to all, that of the expression of interests and ideas that are partisan and send inputs to the political system, and that of exposure of politicians and policies to public judgment. The forum of opinions is meant to host and diffuse information, stimulate public reason, express political dissent and criticism, and keep politicians and institutions under people's eyes.

Integration and Consensus

In *The Structural Transformation of the Public Sphere,* arguably the most influential genealogical study of the formation and decline of public spirit into public opinion, and of general opinion into interested opinions, Jürgen Habermas has reconstructed the way in which opinion gained dignity in modern society, parallel with the formation of representative government and a market economy. These institutions need opinion to perform as mediums for exchange of information and knowledge, thanks to which products become commodities and needs are evaluated, sought, and priced. Thus, Locke was the first author who saw in the world of the verisimilar not solely a possible site of wrong and vices but also the condition for the creation of an informal network of social relations' and judgments' communication. Locke distinguished three kinds of law or sources of authority: God, civil government, and opinion. Opinion was to him synonymous with both coercion, as transitory views that impose their verdict like "fashion" on individual choices, and freedom, because clearly opinion runs and changes when individuals are free to interact and talk. Thus, as the site of judgment and feeling, it was the locus of freedom from the civil law, but meanwhile it was also the source of an indirect and invisible sovereign, that of the public that approves and disapproves "of the actions of those whom [persons] live amongst, and converse with."[72] Opinion goes along with agreement and has thus a connotation of public setting and consent, but it also goes along with law ("law of opinion and reputation") and has thus a coercive character, although Locke suggests, interestingly, that people can decide to listen more or less intensely to the opinion of society and put a certain distance between their minds and the general mind.[73]

Habermas's historical reconstruction reached its peak with the Enlightenment, the age in which public opinion acquired the nobility of a liberating authority from both "the *auctoritas* of the prince, independent of the convictions and views of the subjects," and the partial and prejudicial world of the flickering crowd.[74] It was Rousseau who gave the first codification of public opinion as the most basic authority upon which the system of decision making founds its legitimacy. In his *Social Contract*, *l'opinion* was the soul of the general will because it was able to take away from the law its mechanical character of coercion and make it felt by the people as their own voice.[75] The function of general opinion is to enforce and even create legitimacy insofar as it provides a basis for the difference between simply obeying and obeying with conviction and even enthusiasm. As a matter of fact, Rousseau's concern with not merely obedience to decisions made according to agreed procedures but moreover obedience with passionate spirit induced him to give opinion the thickness and pervasiveness of a civil religion. Yet what is important for me here is to stress that, in discussing the procedures and institutions of a legitimate government, Rousseau felt the need to introduce a power external to the will that would however serve to strengthen it. *L'opinion* was the place where Rousseau looked in order to prove that majority rule is the condition for political autonomy of all the citizens, including those who happen to be in the minority or disagree with the majority. This is what legitimacy is about, whose condition is not only *la volonté generale* (the sovereign power of the law) but also the *l'opinion generale*.

When a citizen casts his vote in the assembly, Rousseau explained, he is supposed to listen to his public will (the will he has as *a part of* the general will or the citizenry), not his private will. Each citizen has two selves (and wills), but only one ought to talk (with the voice of reason, not rhetoric) and be listened to in the public setting (the assembly) where decisions are made. When the citizen who casts his ballot feels it is not hard or problematic to make his public self talk and his private self silent, it means that the general will is operating easily and quasi-automatically, like an intuition (or a natural emotion) that guides judgment so that the individual *citizen* does not need to mobilize his censuring sense of the public *against* his private self. Rousseau's view inspired James Bryce to claim that the degree to which the general will corresponds with the general opinion that circulates in public is the thermometer that measures the strength and health of political freedom.[76] The deeper and easier the correspondence, the smaller the gap between "legal" country and "real" country, between the general will and the general opinion. Power is emancipated from the plague of being identified with a command-obedience relationship, which harbors conflicts and instability and becomes associated with consent. "Accordingly, the conflicting aspect of power—the fact that it is exercised *over* people—disappears altogether from view."[77] This protohegemonic conception of opinion represents the highest level of felt legitimacy, although unlike the legal or institutional authority it is not always identical to itself but may experience ups and downs, and thus be in need of permanent reinforcement by the citizens and the institutions (Rousseau contemplated the role of censorship as central to the stability and unity of the republic). These two *manifestations* of sovereignty are essential and in a mutual relation of sympathetic attraction and repelling separation, or of action and reaction. Their need of mutual reinforcement signals that the question of legitimacy or political freedom is a dynamic condition, not a static condition. It resembles an elastic relation of equilibrium between two poles (the general will and the general opinion) from a maximum of overlapping to a minimum one.

In book two, chapter twelve of the *Social Contract*, Rousseau lists *four kinds of laws* (wherein "law" is the legitimate form that the will of the sovereign can take), three of which belong to the same genre, while the last one is unique. The first three are properly speaking the laws: *juridical, formal, and procedural* (political law, civil law, and criminal law). The fourth one is in a class of its own and a strange kind of sovereign law. "I speak of morals [*moeurs*], customs, and above all of opinion; a part [of the laws] unknown to our politicians but on which the success of all the others depends." This "law" ("the most important of all") is what today we would call the general public or public opinion. It operates from beneath our individual reason like an invisible force (similar to Newton's gravitational force) and exercises indirect influence over decisions rather than direct authority. It is the voice of the sovereign (Rousseau uses the word "law," a term he applied only to denote the voice of sovereignty), although it is not like the will and does not operate in the presence of the institutional sovereign (the assembly) but underneath it and through sympathetic imagination rather than rational inference. However, without it the legal system would be a purely formal norm with no conscious acceptance by the citizens; the law would be *de iure* effective but de facto not supported by the people as a whole and thus felt by some as oppressive as an illegitimate law. For majority rule not to contradict political autonomy, these two levels of sovereignty must always be connected. The formal sovereign does not substitute for the absence of the informal one, the general will for the general opinion.

The majority and minority dialectics presume the *informal* as much as the *formal* sovereign and make the citizen feel nonetheless free when he or she obeys a law he or she disagrees with. A political body is held together by the fact that all the citizens agree on the ends of the political order, on the principles that allow those means to operate, and on the means by which the government and the deliberative processes operate (we might call this underlying agreement a constitutional ethos). Given this basic agreement, although the opinion of the majority prevails, the political community in its entirety should still be capable of *representing* itself as a free community because it is a community that is larger than the will of the majority and the numerical consent in general.[78]

Thus, *l'opinion generale* is the sentiment and the vision of a single inclusive discourse that unifies a country; all the while citizens may disagree on several specific issues on which they have to make decisions (which Rousseau treats at the end of the *Social Contract* as a religious kind of ethical unity because, when it works, it is capable of commanding obedience without need of rational persuasion). Precisely because its civil society is complex, conflicting, and plural, the political community requires this common grammar. Opinion is, as George Wilhelm Friedrich Hegel perspicaciously argued, the terrain on which the individual freedom of judgment and opinions meets and clashes with the "absolutely universal" good (the general interest of the state). This tension and conflict is the constitutive character of opinion and the justification of freedom of communication and the press; this dynamic registers the difference between the organic unity of the ancient city-states and the inorganic commonalty of modern society, which representation impersonates so well. Public opinion is thus modern, Hegel wrote:

> [It] is a repository not only of the genuine needs and correct tendencies of common life, but also, in the form of common

> sense (i.e. all-persuasive fundamental ethical principles dis-
> guised as prejudices), of the eternal, substantive principles of
> justice, the true content and result of legislation, the whole con-
> stitution, and the general position of the state. At the same time,
> when . . . [public opinion] enters the representative thinking . . .
> it becomes infected by all the accidents of opinion, by its igno-
> rance and perversity, by its mistakes and falsity of judgment. . . .
> Public opinion therefore deserves to be as much respected as
> despised—despised for its concrete expression and for the con-
> crete consciousness it expresses, respected for its essential basis,
> a basis which only glimmers more or less dimly in that concrete
> expression.

Freedom of communication and freedom of the press, Hegel concluded, are the conditions that make sense of the dual character of opinion.[79]

The crucial problem in contemporary democracies lies precisely in the actors that provide this inclusive discourse, which most of the time are private subjects (classes, groups, or media experts) although they exercise a public function. Reflecting on this conundrum, contemporary theorists have debated whether democracies should have an identifiable public broadcast (e.g., BBC) with the purpose of providing this inclusive common-ality of basic representation of the country as a whole, or whether the "inclu-sive discourse value has no logical, certainly no necessary, relation to a single form owning multiple 'media voices.'"[80] It is of course impossible to propose a universal prescription or a norm since the answer to this question is cer-tainly dependent upon the political and historical context. However, as a general maxim, I would suggest we consider that what we call "public opin-ion" (the name of an object that social and political scientists have not yet been able to define in an uncontroversial way)[81] is a plural space that is composed of several kinds of opinion. This plurality and diversity itself plays the role of a unifying and "inclusive discourse" that lies underneath democratic politics as the condition that keeps *doxa* and freedom related.

The Cognitive Role of Opinion

Yet Rousseau added to his analysis of the sovereign role of the general opinion that the unreflected opinion of the general will is *incompetent* to detect and recognize what has to be done and needs to rely upon the opinion of the wise few, because while the general opinion is always right, its judgment can easily be misguided by ignorance or prejudice.[82] The solution Rousseau proposed was, as we know, the institution of an assembly of citizens who voted yes or no directly and in silence on proposals coming from a council or a senate. Public opinion was held in secrecy (and in this sense in private) as a reasoning inference that lingered within the inner mind of each citizen with no external communication or publicity. It was written and jealously protected within people's hearts and minds, sheltered from "sight" and "voice," the two senses that were primed to make opinion truly public and also to mobilize emotions and rhetoricians and distort natural reason and sentiments.[83] "Speechless" nondiscursive events like festivals, parades, or the arithmetical harmony of music were the public forms of communication and action in Rousseau's republic. They were cultural rather than political. Contrary to spectacles based on imitative sentiments like the theatrical game of characters and words (a representative assembly belongs to the theatrical genre), they stimulated a unidirectional current of ideas and emotions whose terminus was the individual mind. The unacceptable alternative was the endless circularity and perennial changeability of opinions, two necessary factors in representative politics, which Rousseau, as we know, opposed radically. Public life should teach the kind of introspective reasoning (based on "the way things really are" rather than on "the opinions of other people") that enables citizens to vote in the assembly.[84]

To include all in the republic, Rousseau had to make all silent—this was the compromise he struck with Plato's epistemic view of the general will (the need of *l'opinion generale* to rely upon the wisdom and competence of the few). As we will see in the next chapter, Rousseau's injunction of silence, which was actually a *tópos* in the republican tradition before Enlightenment, returns in the contemporary epistemic theory of democracy as well as in the neorepublican theory of government in its attempt to narrow the role of representative assemblies because of the partisan character of its deliberation, its contamination of the republic of reason with passions and interests.[85]

Clearly, "opinion" and "general opinion" were quite different in Rousseau's depiction: the former retained Plato's stigma that only competence and knowledge could amend (hence, the citizens were stripped of the power of proposing laws), while the latter was in the form of a substantive faith or belief or sacred opinion (quasi-religious in kind) and so unreflected that only a lawgiver could interpret, decode, and translate it into constitutional principles.[86] Its unreflected character was the condition that made it genuine and inclusive, but also incompetent to detect problems and thus unfit to prepare for legislative proposals, a task that did not belong to people in the voting assembly. People "always love what is good," know instinctively the difference between right and wrong, and can make good judgments in the general interest, but somebody has to call to their attention the need for a specific law or policy because "it is in this judgment that they [the people] make mistakes." Keeping the heart and the brain separate thus penalizes the people, not the magistrates or the wise few, because belief is the language of the heart, and belief can be manipulated with much more facility than reason. In the end, the government *is* the "heart of the body politic" *because* it is its brain.[87]

This means that, although in theory it is everything, Rousseau's general opinion does not rule; reason does. *Doxa* and *episteme* remained as distant as *voluntas* and *ratio*. In Rousseau's distancing of *"l'opinion"* from public debates where decisions are to be made, we find the evidence of his strong opposition to political representation, which is the most important institution in the creation of the public or making politics an affair that is of the public and made in public because the citizens must judge what representatives propose to do and do in their names—thus talk and listen, not simply vote. The representative system overcomes all residue of Platonism in deliberation and legitimates an open and public performance of opinions, while on the other hand it can make use of competence without dethroning ordinary and "incompetent" citizens from their authorizing power. Even when needed, competent opinions would be endowed with no special weight in the state but would always be ancillary to political opinions, both when they converge toward law-making assembly and when they float in society. Speech, which Rousseau expelled from the place of political decisions, needs to be given full authority. Public opinion is thus public not only because it pertains to the judgments of "the occupants of public office" but also because it exists in the open, in the public space, outside of the state and nourished by the free speech that citizens enjoy, as Hegel observed.

The transformation of the source of authority from competent opinion that only few hold to political opinion that all indistinctly contribute in forming, and the enrichment of the meaning of the public as both state-based (what pertains to the legal and institutional order) and what is open to all and under public scrutiny, achieved their full manifestation in representative government. This came along with a mixture of the good and bad, because while on the one hand the public can become a tribunal of control and monitoring of the activity of the elected, on the other hand it fatally loses the critical and impartial stature that the enlightenment wanted to give to the public when it vindicated its legitimacy against the *arcana imperii* of the prince. This is also what contemporary theorists of epistemic democracy complain about when they point to the partisan nature of politics that electoral competition and representative politics engender. Yet it is interesting to observe that in the same few years in which the idea of a necessary connection between constitutional government, public opinion, and the principle of publicity was shared by the political philosophers of the continent, in Great Britain, the country in which the representative system was already implemented, an additional image of opinion and the public emerged, one that stressed instead the good of "divisions" within the political opinion of the public, the idea of party politics.

Political Divisions and Partisan Opinions

Political or partisan opinions started achieving legitimacy in Great Britain along with the defense of the Parliament, "essential of British liberty . . . freedom of elections, and the frequency, integrity, and independence of parliaments."[88] Henry St John Bolingbroke was the champion of political opinions as manifestations of judgment, good or bad, on the performance of the government, made by electors and Members of Parliament.[89] He thought it was essential to create (he himself contributed in creating) a political opinion as an oppositional or partisan kind of public presence, with the goal of shaping political programs, orienting citizens' views and decisions, and facing electoral competitions. Bolingbroke emancipated political division and partisanship from the traditional opposition it met in political thought, beginning with Aristotle, who, as we know, located in partisan contrasts or factions the most important factor of decline of constitutional government as the primary sign of immoderation. In *A Dissertation upon Parties*, which appeared weekly in the political magazine he founded, *The Craftsman*, from 1733 to 1734, Bolingbroke distinguished between three forms of partisanship, or, as he called them, "possible division," that can occur in a "free government" (or a government that is based on electoral consent): the first is that of "men angry with the government, and yet resolved to maintain the constitution"; the second of "men averse to the government, because they are so to the constitution"; and the third of "men attached to the government; or, to speak more properly, to the persons of those who govern; or, to speak more properly still, to the power, profit, or protection they acquire by the favour of the persons, but enemies to the constitutions."[90] Partisanship was declared not only legitimate but, moreover, a positive component on condition it did not question the constitutional pact and did not serve private or class interests. Sharing in a common grammar (being a partisan of the constitution) was the condition for critiquing political decisions and for actually making politics outside the institutions in a permanent "tribunal," as Jeremy Bentham would say few decades after Bolingbroke.

Within a representative government, thus, opinion acquired an additional meaning: it was not simply identified with what was sensed as just or good of the people—as in Rousseau and in Kant—but also with the citizens' reflections or judgments of the work of the government and their social conditions or needs or grievances. Bolingbroke's injunction not to be partisan for reasons of profit or favor entailed that elections made citizens reflect upon the interest of their country in light of their problems. Indeed, what Bolingbroke asked for was not patriotism without "divisions" but patriotism with good divisions, or divisions that would "promote liberty." The notion of opinion gets at this point complicated, since under the word "opinion" we may now detect three kinds of opinion: l'opinion generale as integrative force à la Rousseau (or Bolingbroke's people "resolved to maintain the constitution"); political opinion, or the unavoidable "divisions" among citizens in the name of political programs that combine together their interests as socially situated beings and the interest of the nation; and, finally, private opinions or personal interests that do not make any effort to meet the general interest but want instead to curb the latter to themselves. As we can intuit, private opinions and interests are lethally wrong (the sources of deadly factions according to Aristotle and Cicero) and the main factors of corruption when they claim representative hearing in the government ("Private motives can never influence numbers").[91]

But political opinion is good "division" that makes sense of voting and gives public legitimacy to the judgment of the citizens, not because they are the "acculturate public" or have special wisdom and knowledge but because they are voters. As Habermas observes, Bolingbroke even used different names to denote the two legitimate kinds of opinion: the "sense of the people," which retained the character of generality, and the "public spirit," which acquired the partisan character of political-as-party opinion.[92] Once elections were instituted, it would become more difficult to disentangle the former from the latter. This transformation that representation provoked would later be identified with the decline of the republican public spirit and the growth of interested public opinion instead. It might be useful to recall the critical evaluation of the bourgeois transformation of the republic from a city of virtue to one of interests and calculus of preferences as per Hannah Arendt (and Habermas along with her), who consequently expressed strong reservation on representative government.[93]

Edmund Burke was the theorist who captured in the most perceptive way the complexity and fatally conflicting composition of public opinion in representative government: on the one hand, the expression of a general sentiment that unites all the governed throughout the centuries and generations around some shared values (what Rousseau called *l'opinion generale*), and on the other hand, the political opinion that infiltrates through elections from society to the law-making assembly (which makes us understand why Rousseau rejected representation, or *political opinion*).[94]

It is precisely this kind of opinion—which is *political and public* although *not general*—that contemporary political theorists dismiss when they make accusations about the lack of impartiality in representative assemblies and citizens alike, and propose to narrow the domain in which democratic procedures operate in order to expand the room of competent knowledge and impartial reasoning, like experts' committees, assemblies of citizens selected in order to achieve nonpartial outcomes, juries who reclaim some superior authority over elected bodies. Moreover, it is *political opinion* that we have to refer to in evaluating populist and plebiscitarian forms that democracy can take, which represent the extreme manifestation of the commonsensical idea that elections inject political judgment and partiality in lawmaking. From this stance, political theorists from Weber to Mosca to Pareto have concluded somehow disparagingly that politics is war by other means—omitting that the "other means" makes all the difference in the world, so that politics is *not* war, and winning a competition by means of persuasion is *opposite to* getting rid of an enemy. I shall return to this argument in the next chapter.

The accusation that representative democracy allows neither for impartial opinions nor for competent knowledge in power resonates with the desire by contemporary philosophers to emancipate democracy from *doxa* in order to put it in harmony with truth (as according to the Platonist premise that is detectable in Rousseau).[95] On the other hand, as I am going to explain in Chapters 3 and 4, the realist claim of taking democracy as it is (namely, very imperfect because tainted with an endless game of interests) invites us to consider political competition not as an expression of autonomy or liberty but as a spectacle that is worthy of the Roman forum and the Coliseum, a television game that is played by the few for the amusement of the many and ends with the crowning of the leaders who have conquered the favor of the audience.[96] Although emancipated from "the *auctoritas* of the prince," opinion would not be in this case able to emancipate itself from the stigma of being untranslatable into truth. Platonist and plebiscitarian ideas of politics mirror each other and are somehow complementary as the epistemic deformation of politics leaves dialogical activity empty of value because it is devoid of technical knowledge, and within this emptiness the terrain of opinion becomes fertile for demagogical rhetoric.

The conclusion to be derived from this brief overview on the three functions that *doxa* acquires in representative government may be phrased in the following way: to rehabilitate *doxa* (and democracy), we have to question both the epistemic ambition of making public deliberation a terrain of competent knowledge, whose achievements have to be judged as science judges a technical task, and the realistic temptation of transforming political opinion in a warlike arena in which might makes its way through words and images and with the consent of numbers. In two words, the challenge is to disprove Pareto.

The Government Rests on Opinion

Sovereignty of opinion has been generally conceived as a euphemism because, after all, to opine is not the same as to want. Opinion has not been considered a power in and by itself but a "negative" power. Thus, it has been analyzed and treated as a prerogative of the liberty of the individual to pressure the government and seek protection against it (the assumption being that the state is the site of an untamed potential for arbitrary intrusion in the life of the individual). Its informal nature has militated in favor of the private identity of the right to free speech because trying to influence political actors is not, after all, the same thing as making them act authoritatively. As seen above, this bare fact has suggested to theorists of representative government to narrow participation to elections alone, which are the only institution that allows us to "prove" in an uncontestable way the democratic character of political decisions. But within this perspective it would be hard to devise criteria to detect (and contrast) the threat coming from the concentration of economic power and the corrupting practices within the domain of opinion formation. The very proposal to extend the meaning of democratic deliberation, so as to include the informal discursive character of a pluralistic forum of associations, political movements, and opinions, risks looking like an ideological refurbishment, functional to the new communicative strategies for elite selection, a view that has made theorists of plebiscitarian democracy doubt that opinion is a form of power control, while it certainly is a means for authority building.

Certainly, free speech can have unpleasant and even devastating effects, in particular when armed with the power of the press: it may spread gossip and create facts out of innuendos; it may violate individual privacy and damage a person's reputation. Moreover, precisely because of its hold on peoples' minds, the forum of opinions can be mobilized to unify millions of people under one banner.[97] Hence, Alexis de Tocqueville wrote of this freedom: "I love it more from considering the evils it prevents than on account of the good it does."[98] Yet he promptly added that control by the state cannot be justified because an authority with the power of sorting out the good and bad of information would become fatally tyrannical. In order to tame a freedom that divulges and spreads news, a censorial authority must be centralistic and monopolistic. There is no room for moderation when political power curtails freedom of speech and the press so that any remedy would be worse than the disease. Thus, Tocqueville concluded his analysis of the freedom of the press in the United States with the idea that the only legitimate strategy to control the power of the press is by promoting its "incredible dispersion."

Following Tocqueville, in the remaining part of this chapter I will be led by these criteria: that pluralism and a wide-open forum are at the same time conditions for government control and for an individual's protection against the "negative" power of opinion; that these conditions presume the equal distribution among the citizens of the authority of both judgment and the will; and that, finally, freedom of opinion cannot be justified based on its outcomes, no matter how good and desirable. As with the right to vote, its defense must be principled or not be at all. This means that any intervention by the law must go in the direction of guaranteeing and, if necessary, restoring the conditions of pluralism and of the equal opportunity by the citizens to participate with their votes and ideas in the political life of their country. In the last section of the chapter I will thus argue that a procedural interpretation of democracy contains the normative conditions that fulfill these criteria, namely, equal political liberty, immanence, and self-containment.

A Political Civil Right

Although the relationship between representative democracy and freedom of opinion "is not obvious," this form of government has shown the existence of an "intrinsic connection between freedom of opinion and the political role of the citizen."[99] From this perspective, I shall make the argument that the identification of freedom of speech and opinion with negative liberty, or a liberty that has no connection with the character of government, is dissatisfying because it says nothing about what makes citizens able to pressure and control their government or make it responsive. Yet when we say that representative democracy is government that rests on opinion, we imply that opinions play a political role. Paraphrasing Machiavelli, the prince has to "feel" to be affected by the people and the people have to "feel" it affects the prince.[100]

If we follow the traces of diarchy we realize that, contrary to other negative liberties, free speech is a kind of freedom whose protection may require an activist state (as a matter of fact, even conventional negative rights, like property for instance, require government action or "significant taxpayer support" and a complex institutional arrangement).[101] Owen M. Fiss wrote years ago that noninterference may not be the best policy with a right that is certainly individual but has direct political implications: "Protecting autonomy by placing a zone of noninterference around the individual . . . is likely to produce a public debate that is dominated, and thus constrained, by some forces that dominate social structures, not a debate that is 'uninhibited, robust, and wide-open.'"[102] Hence, an important implication of the diarchic character of democracy is that free speech is a Janus-faced right, with a negative or individual face (protection against power) and a positive or political face (formation of political opinions).

Certainly, the claim for freedom of opinion was born as a claim for the protection of individual freedom. In particular, it was born as a vindication of religious freedom or freedom of conscience from secular and cleric authority as well, the condition not simply of social peace but also of a free and sincere spiritual practice of faith.[103] The invocation of that right was for the sake of instituting a negative kind of liberty that would put limits on authority by declaring a portion of individual life to be exclusively under one's private jurisdiction or will. Yet the acquisition of that first negative liberty made society a place of many diverse opinions, religious and otherwise. The technological invention of printing amplified the effect of the individual freedom to hold, express, and exchange ideas on issue of religion, and otherwise.[104]

I do not need to rewrite the history of freedom of religion and freedom of speech to prove my argument. Suffice to recall that beginning with the English Civil War, the right to free speech and freedom of the press acquired a true political meaning precisely at the moment they were vindicated civil rights. Republicans and revolutionaries gave those rights the significance of political resistance against established powers, a means of denunciation and the unveiling of *arcana imperii,* as well as of inquiry and truth searching. Their negative or protective character gave rise to a power of control and pressure on government and became a political right of the citizen. John Milton, just to mention one of the most authoritative protagonists of the early battle for freedom of opinion, defended the liberty of unlicensed printing in the name of an open process of discussion that would change the nature of authority, political as well as religious, and thus also the nature of liberty.[105] In the *Areopagitica,* he framed the argument of freedom of speech within the republican paradigm of liberty versus slavery: "When conflicts are freely heard, deeply considered and speedily reformed, then is the utmost bound of civil liberty attained that wise men look for"; the opposite is tyranny, the suppression of public voice.[106] Milton's task was the defense of civil liberties, and although his narrative strategy was classically republican, his proposal was very modern: the defense of the dynamic of disagreement as both a condition and a sign of freedom and intellectual improvement, of the individual and the society as well.

Since then, civil rights have played a vivid political role, although they have never translated directly into political participation.[107] Their indirect or "negative" power was seen from the start as a quality that was antityrannical in character: this gave them the political feature of a vindication for a government that had to be checked and controlled, both by institutions and rules and by the inspecting power of the citizens. Some centuries after Milton, Hans Kelsen and later Habermas stressed the endogenous link between negative liberty and political liberty when they argued for an intrinsic relationship between individual rights and democracy.[108] Thus, classical civil liberties, from freedom of religious conscience to freedom of speech and association, are foundational to democracy because they are essential in the formation of the two conditions without which democracy could not exist: that the citizens have free access to political information, and that they are always free, not only during the electoral campaign or in coincidence with the exercise of their sovereign will, to express and divulge their opinions on their government (i.e., to criticize it and openly voice their dissent).[109]

The fact that representative democracy is government by opinion has two implications, one obstructive and one expressive: it makes government limited and it makes government based on liberty. Public deliberation renders the common interest a collective construction of the citizens and the outcome of ongoing persuasion and compromise that never ends in a final verdict (no matter how good or correct it might be). In this comprehensive process, dissent is equally crucial as consent; criticism works as a stabilizing force of political liberty as much as shared opinions on some basic principles, such as, for instance, those that are embodied in the Bill of Rights and the Constitution. Thus, the "negative" power of opinion may be depicted both as an invigorating force and as an indicator of the status of the "integrating force" linking the elected and the citizens. As Baker puts it, the role of the public forum of opinion in modern democracy is "both egalitarian dispersal" (which expresses the principle of pluralism and antimonopoly) and "inclusive common discourse."[110] This is the premise upon which the double meaning of public opinion, as a critical and controlling power and an integrative force of legitimacy, resides. It is also the premise that justifies legal interventions for protecting equal liberty in the forum.

Barriers, Opportunity, and Withdrawal

Democracy started with Solon stating that persuasion should be the way to win, not money or force or family relations. "Citizens come into the forum with nothing but their arguments."[111] In today's consolidated democracy, "we may take for granted that a democratic regime presupposes freedom of speech and assembly, and liberty of thought and conscience."[112] Taking them for granted may obfuscate their strength and fragility. In a now classic empirical-theoretical study on the place of unanimity and conflict in the functioning of small scale democratic organizations, Jane J. Mansbridge observed that the conditions in which equal power is seen as necessary are when they are in fact proved to be and felt as missing or deteriorating. Mansbridge added also that inequalities are not per se a problem if the perception exists among all the members and that each has the opportunity "to exercise equal power"—if, in other words, all members think that they have in their hands "equal power 'if they [want] to.'"[113] This is what makes procedures valuable and people perceive themselves as autonomous even while obeying laws that have been passed by the majority or by an elected parliament.[114] I propose we apply the distinction between "equal opportunity" and "achievement" of equality to the formation of opinions. As with the authoritative power of the will, citizens' valuation of their opportunity to participate in the forum seems to be strong in proportion as that actual opportunity is slim or felt as such.

It is not conflict or unequal power per se that is the problem. Much more worryingly, the problem is citizens' perceptions that they do not have "an equal chance to move their organization in the direction of their preferences," that they have no power, or that what they do does not impact the public in the same way as when others act.[115] Decline of electoral participation in consolidated democracies is an alarming sign that citizens might think they have no chance to impact the political life of their country; that they are unequal in managing the power of opinion, all the while enjoying an equal right to vote, talk, and print; and that, in other words, voting power is a futile power anyway if it is an isolated power.[116] Their quest is not of equalizing social conditions but blocking their *translation* into political voice and power. This is the lesson of democracy since its inception, when Solon, after he liberated his indebted fellow citizens from the subjection to their creditors, tried to make them equal in the chance to participate in political power, because he thought this the best way to make sure they would no longer fall under the domination of the well-off. It is thus on the obstacles to political equality and participation that democratic decisions should intervene, in order to disclose and remove them. In his 1910 address on the New Nationalism, Theodore Roosevelt restated similar ideas when, after stating that the right to property "does not give the right of suffrage to any corporation," he argued: "It is necessary that laws should be passed to prohibit the use of corporate funds directly or indirectly for political purposes. . . . If our political institutions were perfect, they would absolutely prevent the political domination of money in any part of our affairs."[117]

Barriers to participation, direct as well as indirect, must not be too high, although they do not need to be arithmetically equal; what is important is that people know and believe that with some efforts on their part they can overcome them (this is precisely what Rousseau meant when he argued that *l'opinion* written in citizens' "hearts" is the propelling energy of the general will, written in institutions and procedures). The voluntary character of participation should work as an incentive and a reminder of the power citizens have rather than a fatalistic disincentive to act. Certainly, inequalities of wealth must not be too big. But they do not need to be eliminated for political equality to persist—what is crucial is that the people know and believe that their unequal economic power is not a reason for making their political voice unheard. Using procedures must not be felt as futile; withdrawal from the forum and the ballot must not be felt as convenient.

The transformation of politics in a forum of opinions amplifies the meaning of citizens' political presence (or absence). Their power of influencing people's decisions makes opinions very appealing to political leaders, who are tempted to use the forum only in order to acquire popularity rather than also to reveal their deeds: the world of opinion can make publicity a strategy of concealment and a means to strengthen the ideological consent politicians enjoy beyond the weight of electoral consent. On the other hand, it can be an attractive power for social and economic groups, which hope to lead the political agenda, condition the debate inside of institutions, and influence lawmakers. The unavoidable disparity that presence through voice involves can gravely escalate as a consequence of the unequal opportunity citizens have to use the means of information and communication. Ronald Dworkin made this argument elegantly when he wrote that the issue at stake today is not that of free speech as the right of the individual but of free speech as participation in making democracy work. If we accept a view of democracy as diarchy, then legal interventions should be foreseen that lessen private money in politics so as to reestablish the rule of equality in political liberty by

preventing powerful individuals and corporations from having a disproportionate voice.[118]

Voice's Unbalanced Power

The existing socioeconomic barriers to diarchic citizenship clash with
democracy's principle of equal political liberty even if we cannot "prove"
beyond any reasonable doubt that they affect political decisions in this or
that way, because it is the "consent of the majority, and not debate, that
makes the law."[119] Despite their unbalanced attention to the threat to
stability posed by the have-nots, the Federalists clearly foresaw that wealth
disparity and cultural inequality can have an enormous impact on the
tenor of the republic, because representation relies structurally upon a diversity or inequality among citizens in oratorical skills and abilities. James
Madison expressed concern about the threat posed by the poor, yet he
also mentioned the danger the very rich posed to the health of the republic.[120] As a Republican, however, his main concern was about corruption,
not political inequality.

In democracy, though, protecting political institutions from corruption
is protecting political equality, which entails two things: protecting "the
integrity of the system of political representation" and ensuring "fair access to the public arena at each stage of political competition for those
candidates entitled to participate at that stage."[121] These are the indications
we may derive from the concern shaping the controversies over campaign
finance reform in the United States, when the Supreme Court and the federal courts use the argument of corruption to describe the "corrosive influence of corporate wealth" or the "undue influence" that an unequal "political presence" in the forum is primed to have, even though corporations
have no explicit plan or intention to exercise it and even though talking is
not identical to voting.[122] "Undue influence" refers to a disproportionate
inequality of resources that some candidates have per effect of a disproportionate inequality of resources that some citizens have. The sense of
futility that disadvantaged citizens may have of democratic institutions
should be interpreted not as a denunciation of the deficit of democracy
but as recognition of a lack of power, or the evidence that social inequality
does translate into an unequal political influence.[123] As Charles Beitz has
shown, the issue of inequality of political influence is complex and open

to interpretative controversies first of all because of the complexity of the principles of "political equality" and "political influence" and second, because it takes different manifestation when considered in relation to the citizens who want to express their voices and the candidates who claim for an equal condition of competition.[124]

If the U.S. Supreme Court has used the expression "undue influence," it is because it presumed that the basis of democracy is political equality, and not only in the domain of voting. The expression "undue influence" presumes in addition that there should be a *democratic influence maxim* that orients political judgments and decisions. Drawing on these premises, C. Edwin Baker has proposed a theoretically compelling argument to justify government activism for protection of pluralism in the domain of information and communication: "The same egalitarian value that is embodied in people's equal right to be self-governing and that . . . applies to the ballot box also applies to the public sphere."[125] This is the goal predicated in the democratic-influence maxim, which can be extended to evaluate the exercise of citizenship in the sphere of opinion formation in its entirety, both to protect pluralism of the media against property concentration and to protect political equality from "undue influence." "The media, like elections, constitute a crucial sluice between public opinion formation and state 'will formation.'" For this reason, "a country is democratic only to the extent that the media, as well as elections, are structurally egalitarian and politically salient."[126] The same can be said of financial contribution to political campaigns, or private money in politics, which are an attempt to monopolize opinion resources. The democratic-influence maxim is consistent with the diarchic character of representative democracy because it is attentive to the protection of the "chain of communication" between citizens and institutions that public and political opinion creates. This maxim has the task of making citizens and lawmakers recognize and unveil "undue influence," and claims that democratic government should command equal concern and respect by the laws and the magistrates and also equal concern on the opportunity citizens have to exercise their "influence" on the political process. Consistently with the assumption that opinion is a form of sovereignty, the democratic-influence maxim is guidance to judgment and decisions on issues that pertain to the circumstances of opinion formation and are issues of political justice.

Each country has a story of equality breach to be detected, denounced, and amended. The application of the democratic-influence maxim to the

United States would entail a change in the noninterventionist logic that springs from the "romantic view of the first amendment" as a "market-place of ideas."[127] This conclusion is not unwarranted if we consider the above-mentioned argument of the Court that an "undue influence" is a reason for corruption because it is a violation of an equal "political presence." Wherein corruption is detected and denounced in relation to the value of equal citizenship, not to virtue or any other good that exceeds the position of each citizen within the republic. In democracy, corruption is properly speaking a violation of equal political liberty.

Furthermore, unequal opportunity of political advocacy is primed to have negative impact on citizens' beliefs of their equal opportunity to participation. This may erode the value of democracy in people's opinions, as it may convince them that going to the ballot is futile or that voting for a candidate would not make them feel that their views have more visibility or strength. Erosion of trust in the work of the institutions may be alarmingly strong in representative democracy, which cannot rely on a "herald" as a means of information and communication but needs to rely on a panoply of intermediary actors. Because of the indirect form of political inequality (as a consequence of the indirect form of political liberty), socioeconomically marginalized and disadvantaged citizens may be stripped of that which the ballot is supposed to give them: a *point d'appui* in society and in the institutions in which laws are made.[128] Today, the number of people who are "necessarily mute" because they are "socially excluded" and politically irrelevant is large enough to make citizens worry about the future of democracy. What Robert E. Goodin has written in relation to disfranchised immigrants can be extended to poor and powerless citizens, a marginal periphery in their own political world as immigrants are in the larger world: "Those who are most in need of a voice—those who are most adversely affected by our actions and choices—are all too often least well situated to register their concerns with us. Action at a distance (our harming them) turns out to be considerably easier in the modern world than voice at a distance (their complaining effectively to us about those harms)."[129] The alarming fact in consolidated democracies is that many citizens are like disenfranchised immigrants with respect to the efficacy of their "voice at distance" and also of the "action at distance."

In representative democracy, therefore, political exclusion may easily take the form of not being heard and effectively represented, although the right to vote is equally enjoyed and the power of influence on lawmakers can be hardly "proved";[130] although, as Justice Anthony Kennedy has recently argued in the majority opinion in *SpeechNow.org v. Federal Election Commission*, there is no evidence that private money in electoral campaigns "give[s] rise to corruption or the appearance of corruption" because "influence over or access to elected officials does not mean that these officials are corrupt."[131] Yet "there is a considerable amount of systematic, if circumstantial, evidence that interest-group financial support is related to legislative performance on behalf of the group's interests."[132] Moreover, concerning Justice Kennedy's questioning the causal link between influence and corruption, one has to recall that replacing virtue and social and historical accident with normative principles and procedures was the great contribution of modern constitutionalism to democracy, a contribution that the opponents of campaign-finance regulation in the United States seem to underestimate when they ask for empirical evidence that affects elected officials in a corrupt way. *Post factum* remedies were not wise politics, and procedures were created to provide the political system with ex-ante conditions for neutralizing bad behavior. But these opponents have persistently denied—beginning with the landmark campaign-finance case *Buckley v. Valeo* (1976), followed by *Citizens United v. Federal Election Commission* (2010), and more recently *Speech Now.org v. Federal Election Commission* (2012)—that the conduct at issue in the case of money in political power leads to corruption.

This is Justice Kennedy's approach in *Citizens United*, whose arguments are, however, far from convincing when he asserts that large independent expenditures from corporations that create the appearance of special access to public officials "will not cause the electorate to lose faith in our democracy."[133] Yet the "threat of corruption resulting from dependence on private contributions is precisely the threat that performance of this important representative function [legislative deliberation] will be compromised. The fact (if it is a fact) that contributions effect legislative voting only at the margin, therefore, is hardly reason for complacency."[134] Dennis F. Thompson has thus proposed to understand these cunning ways of corrupting representatives without showing explicit evidence of corruption as "mediated corruption" in which political officials do not acquire personal gain but participate actively in serving private purposes while acting as representatives of the nation. The gain is devastating for the democratic process both at the stage of electoral competition (because it creates conditions for vitiating a fair race) and at the stage of parliamentary decision.[135]

Justice Kennedy cites no congressional findings or other sources of evidence to support his assertion; although, he concludes that the only reason corporations or anyone else would spend money to influence the public is because the public has "ultimate influence" over public officials. His conclusion is meant to be instrumental to make corporations equal in civil and political rights to individual citizens. Yet it is unable to prove that there is no evidence that Americans have lost faith in the democratic credentials of their political system in recent years and doubt their equal right to vote translates into having some perceived influence over their institutions and representatives.[136] Besides, it is shared historical knowledge that bills of rights and constitutions have been written and endorsed when the relationship between political power and civil society became constant and strong through time, and moreover a sign of the liberty of the subject to both influence and check the power of the elected magistrates.

The relationship between decision and deliberation that constitutes democracy's diarchy quite explicitly suggests that although only votes decide while "by itself public deliberation decides nothing," plenty of historical and empirical evidence is available to lawmakers and citizens who want to prove the connection between social power and political influence outside and beyond the formal event of elections. The U.S. Supreme Court's 2003 decision to approve Congress's campaign finance reform confirms the idea of the diarchic nature of representative democracy and the democratic-influence maxim. In Justices Stevens's and O'Connor's words, although the secret ballot prevents us from producing "concrete evidence" that "money buys influence," the secret ballot is not a sufficient indicator of the status of democracy because, presumably, it is not the only form the voice of the people takes. "Congress is not required to ignore historical evidence regarding a particular practice or to view conduct in isolation from its context." In a word, opinion is a power both when it is used to advance a political program or sponsor a candidate and when it is used by citizens to voice their dissent with the opinion of the majority or ask for more complete information on the government's practices. This makes equal opportunity in partaking in the sovereignty of opinion a sensitive issue, although no evidence can be brought to prove that the influence of opinion translates into decisions.

The democratic-influence maxim derives from the idea of representative democracy as diarchy. It acknowledges that political participation in representative democracy is complex and does not mean merely selecting lawmakers but counting upon effective representatives as advocates both outside and inside state institutions; in a word, enjoying an equal opportunity to participate in the public forum as electors and citizens.[137] Moreover, it iterates the normative value of democratic proceduralism in its impeccable ability to rely upon and reproduce equal liberty. Finally, it suggests that a democratic government should feel the responsibility to regulate the public forum of opinions so as to ensure that all have at last an equal opportunity to exercise some influence on the political system, even if:

a) not all intend to use that opportunity;
b) those who have more material power to affect political influence abstain from using it; and
c) elected politicians are virtuous enough to be deaf to the pressure of influential citizens.

Communicative Power

"If the public forum is to be free and open to all, and in continuous session, everyone should be able to make use of it. . . . The liberties protected by the principles of participation [namely, equal suffrage] lose much of their value whenever those who have greater private means are permitted to use their advantages to control the course of public debate. For eventually these inequalities will enable those better situated to exercise a larger influence over the development of legislation."[138] In these exemplary words, John Rawls rendered the idea of political justice in 1971. Rawls's argument rephrased a thought that was widespread in the early decades of post–World War II, and can be detected in Robert Dahl's discussion on the condition necessary to achieve political equality and earlier on in Jerome Barron's view that "there is inequality in the power of communicating ideas, just as there is inequality in economic bargaining power; to recognize the latter and deny the former is quixotic." If we recognize that political participation in democracy is made also of "communication of ideas," not only voting, Barron continued, we also have to recognize that "public information is vital to the creation of an informed citizenry" and that a democratic approach to freedom of information and the power of influence should entail not noninterference by the government but a politics of regulation or intervention to remove barriers to citizens' access to these means. Applying to media communication or the power of influence Rawls's principle that procedural rules are a value in and of themselves because as "pure process" they make possible equal liberty, Baker devises a democratic distribution principle for communicative power that requires a "maximum dispersal of media ownership."[139] This is a normative appeal that does not receive its validity from empirical evidence. Its justification "consists in what it allows, that is to say the formation of the public forum upon which democracy relies: the acknowledgment that money power is a factor that gives an unfair advantage in exercising political power, although and despite the fact that each vote has formally the same weight and each citizen has formally one and only one vote at his or her disposal. A democratic political order involves, *in part*, a struggle among different groups, each with its own projects and interests, its own needs, and its own conception of a desirable social world."[140] Egalitarian conditions pertain to the possibility that all citizens should have to participate in the formation, manifestation, and exposition of these views.

Regardless of their conception of democracy, whether merely procedural or constitutional or participatory, all theorists of democracy argue that competition of ideas and political visions is a fundamental condition for the citizens to have their opinions formed and make their choices. Granted that a democratic state should not have any interest in equalizing voices, it should have interest to make sure that "in a republic where the people are sovereign, the ability of the citizenry to make informed choices among candidates for office is essential."[141] What Walter Lippmann called disparagingly the "pseudoenvironment" that lingers "between man and his environment"[142] is a political good in democracy, the domain in which political participation happens; it is also a paradigmatic terrain of conflict between politics or the sphere of the public and private interests or the sphere of the social. On this terrain, rather than over the right to suffrage, the battle over political equality is fought in contemporary democracy.

Chain of Indirectness

We have thus clarified the political implication of freedom of speech, what makes opinion a political force in modern democracy, and why legal intervention for protecting equal liberty in the forum is justifiable. We can now turn our attention to the issue of the "quality" of *doxa*, or the means upon which opinions rely for their formation and communication. Contrary to its sister-sovereign power, the right to vote, the formation and expression of citizens' opinions requires more than simply their determination to act.

Although identified with voice and the choice of an individual to speak his or her mind, opinion does not rest merely on voice and the choice of the individual to use it. The rights to free speech and freedom of opinion are exercised with the help of technical tools, and this *material indirectness* is primed to become a new source of inequality.[143] Indeed, to make their opinion heard or influential, citizens have to make some extra effort beside choosing to refine their rhetorical ability or thinking freely and talking frankly and openly. These individual qualities have been traditionally referred to as evidence of some forms of natural inequality that the equal right to participation not only does not eliminate but moreover contributes in displaying and even exalting.[144] The classical description of democracy as a government in which individuals use *only* arguments is thus inadequate because although citizens cannot use money directly, the means they need in order to give their opinions public reverberation are costly and require money. Following Rawls's idea that enjoyment of freedom consists of both enjoying "basic liberties and the worth of these liberties," we may conclude that "without the financial means to exercise a free-speech right, the right might arguably have no real worth."[145]

Unequal personal qualities like good rhetorical skill or educationally acquired proficiencies in political performance pale in comparison to the unequal ownership and control of the means of communication. Although democratic citizens vindicate and acquire an equal right to participate, this does not ensure they will have an equal impact on political agendas and leaders if their voices are not uttered in view of being heard beyond the narrow circle of their friends and, moreover, if they do not have enough force to do so.[146] The technological medium that steps in between the right to free speech and the actual "visibility" of opinions is a crucial factor that adds to the uniqueness of representative democracy as a gov-

ernment by opinion.[147] The question of the geopolitical size of modern
states is an important factor that serves to explain this uniqueness; as we
know, Aristotle thought that a too-large city could not possibly be a political community because no herald would have such loud a voice as to be
heard by all the people. But the kind of indirectness we are talking of here
is not linked to size.

Uttering an opinion is not the same thing as making it communicative.
"Communication," Niklas Luhmann wrote, "only comes about when
someone watches, listens, reads, and understands to the extent that further
communication could follow up. The mere act of uttering something,
then, does not, in and of itself, constitute communication."[148] Opinions
do not pertain to speech alone, therefore, but to speech in common with
others, and when the community is large we need some extra help to make
communication possible. "We admittedly say that," Kant wrote, "whereas a
higher authority may deprive us of freedom of *speech* or of *writing*, it cannot deprive us of freedom of *thought*. But how much and how accurately
would we *think* if we did not think so to speak, in community with others
to whom we *communicate* our thoughts and who communicate their
thoughts to us!"[149] Kant's theoretical ground for communication found
further support in Justice Thurgood Marshall, who argued in *Kleindienst
v. Mandel* (1972) that "the freedom of speech and the freedom to hear
are inseparable; they are two sides of the same coin. . . . But the coin itself is the process of thought and discussion. The activity of speakers becoming listeners and listeners becoming speakers in the vital interchange
of thought is the means indispensable to the discovery and spread of
political thought."[150] A public forum is this means of communication,
and it presumes more than simply the will to talk and to listen. "If people
are not heard, and if they do not speak, both democracy and deliberation
are at risk."[151]

The right to free speech requires some external and material conditions
that make our opinions capable of being communicated, if communication is what we want to attain through speech, that is, if speech is meant
to serve a public aim, not simply to be among friends. (This was also the
sense of Cicero's difference between *sermo* and *eloquentia*.) The public in
a large polis needs some technical instruments in order to exist. Yet as
technical devices, the means of communication come with some heavy
burdens because they rely on and need money and technical expertise,
material factors that condition heavily the equal rights principle and

opportunity. In the above-mentioned decision, Justice Marshall surmised that that issue of communication ought not to overlook what "may be particular qualities inherent in sustained, face-to-face debate, discussion, and questioning."[152] No one helps us to grasp the relationship between autonomy of judgment and the "conduit," the means of communication and a constitutional government, better than Aristotle.

Aristotle argued famously that the small scale of the polis and direct relations among citizens in their everyday lives are crucial conditions of political liberty: a state "composed of too many . . . will not be a city, since it can hardly have a constitution. Who can be the general of a mass so excessively large? And who can be its herald, unless he has Stentor's voice?" A herald was considered crucial because the citizens' judgments, which were also crucial, depended on it. Ancient democracy was distinctive not simply because its citizens engaged in politics directly but also because they judged directly and made decisions according to their "ideological presuppositions and in the best interest of [their] state and of [themselves]."[153] Technical means did not interpose themselves between the people and their opinions. To paraphrase the words used by the Court in *Miami Herald v. Tornillo*, there was a "true marketplace of ideas" with "relatively easy access to the channel of communication." In contemporary democracy, instead, the "market of ideas" is not an open and truly free market. "Newspapers have become big business and there are far fewer of them to serve a larger literate population" with the consequence that these "means" are not simply vehicles that transport ideas and opinions but powers placed in "a few hands" that "inform" the citizens and "shape public opinion." The issue is not here simply that all do not have equal access to the "marketplace of ideas" but also that some have a louder voice than others because of the *material* wealth they have and can employ to amplify their voices and more easily pursue their agendas. Equality has been breached in a substantial way, and this is a challenge to political liberty.[154]

Aristotle's claim that population and territory had to be limited in size derived from his requirement that the citizens be socially and politically self-sufficient. This might explain why *isegoria*, "the universal right to speak in the Assembly, was sometimes employed by Greek writers as a synonym for 'democracy,'"[155] since both needed to be unmediated in their exercise. In Aristotle, the notion of self-sufficiency pertained to both the production of ideas and opinions and their expression in the assembly.

Citizens needed independent judgment as well as economic independence in order to act as self-sufficient subjects. They needed both material goods and knowledge in order to make free and responsible choices. According to Aristotle, citizens had to formulate their judgments individually and not en masse in the two public spheres that had the power to make decisions: the distribution of political offices and the execution of laws. Both the distribution of power (when citizens chose the magistrates) and the administration of justice (when judges judged people's deeds) required direct knowledge. Just as judges could not function with indirect or secondhand knowledge of their cases, citizens could not choose good magistrates or make good laws without firsthand knowledge of the candidates' qualities.

Whereas in ancient republics the only intermediary between the citizens and the institutions was the herald, in modern democracy, communication and information are a construction by intermediary actors, who run also the system for choosing candidates, developing political agendas, and forming opinions on the many issues that are primed to become an object of public judgment. In ancient democracy, the citizens could see and check over the leaders' or orators' personal qualities and judge them directly. In the modern one, the candidates' qualities and information about the behavior of elected officials are artificially constructed and transmitted to citizens. Moreover, they are made into a spectacle that is meant to amuse or distract or provoke or sedate an audience, which, for this reason, is made of reactive yet passive citizens.[156]

Thus, modern citizens are more passive not merely because they choose political leaders instead of deciding directly but also because they do not enjoy an equal opportunity to see and be seen, to have their ideas discussed and heard. In representative democracy, Mill complained in 1861, Themistocles and Demosthenes would have to win seats in Parliament in order to be heard, and would depend on the mediation of a party to be candidates.[157] Even more than that, they would need a media system friendly enough to make them pleasing to the audience, or powerful lobbies financing their electoral campaign in view of friendly laws. In modern democracy, political judgment, an indirect power in its own right, is indirect also in the conditions that make it effective. The chain of indirectness is what should make citizens alert to the quality of their equal rights when they assess issues of freedom of opinion in the public sphere of information and communication.

Two Concepts of Liberty

To paraphrase Aristotle, contemporary citizens lack self-sufficiency in gathering and interpreting information and obtaining effective communication. This lack of autonomy seriously curtails their opportunity to make autonomous political judgments and moreover exercise control over those whom they have chosen to govern. It is not solely their participation that suffers here. It is their liberty, which is weak and toothless. Violation of equal liberty in the domain of opinion is a checks-and-balances violation; it translates into concentration of power on the one hand and lack of counterpower that can stop or resist despotic or abusive power on the other.

In a democracy in which citizens' most important power is essentially a "negative" one—it is power of judging and influencing more than getting things done—the fact that their indirect power is operated through a chain of intermediation that relies heavily on money and thus is structurally unequal entails that it may not be an effective power of control any longer. Rather, indirect power appears as the source of a new and tremendously pervasive power out of citizens' control. In what has been defined "a landmark case," which became a precedent for a politics of government nonintervention as the better tool for countering monopolization in the media industry, Justice Byron White argued that "it is the right of the viewers and listeners, not the right of the broadcasters, which is paramount. It is the purpose of the First Amendment to preserve an uninhibited market, whether it be by government itself or by private licenses."[158]

Although arguments for countering monopoly may be made that propose an interventionist strategy by the legislative power, what interests me here is to call attention to the important recognition that the rule of the state is to protect the flow of information against concentration of powers and that the liberty of those who are in a condition of passivity, like an audience, is the first good to be protected by right. The indirectness that technology and money propel in politics worsens the unbalanced relationship between speaker and listener that the traditional rhetorical style of communication entailed, and makes the listener in need of more protection than the speaker. It moreover clarifies the existence of a clash between private property rights and the political right of the citizens to receive information or simply have access to communication.[159]

Thus, communication is the terrain of a new conflict within representative democracy between negative and positive liberty.[160] As a good that gives "substance" to the principle of self-government, it needs to be protected. This is, in the tradition of Brandeis, an important function of the First Amendment.[161] In the traditional liberal conception of free speech, protection of speech is viewed with an assumption of the individual as an autonomous sovereign against all other individuals and the society. Resistance to considering it *also* as a part of political right, or as the right to participate, relies on the assumption that free speech cannot be exposed to conflicting relationship with other goods such as equality in order to avoid risking curtailment or coercive interference.

Yet at issue here is not a conflict between liberty and equality but between two conceptions of liberty, one of which is construed as pure noninterference and the other as interactive or political. Intervention by the government should not be content oriented (against which noninterference or anticoercion has sacrosanct reasons) but rather should be attentive to guaranteeing the functioning of basic political rights: the purpose of freedom of opinion is *also* to allow citizens to participate in the debate on public issues in a way that does not privilege or penalize them on the basis of their material resources.[162] Constitutional democracy has overcome the nineteenth-century liberal approach in order to be consistent with the principle of self-government and its norms. The criteria of a democratic politics of communication are responsiveness and equal opportunity. Elected politicians and institutions should be responsive to the citizens, and in order for this to occur, an accurate rendering of political issues and interests is needed, not simply regular elections. Distribution of opportunity to speak and be heard is also central because it is the premise thanks to which citizens contribute both in the making of the political agendas and in the control and monitoring of politicians and institutions. These criteria are consistent with a diarchic view of democracy within which citizens play two roles: as participants in making their representative candidates and as "final referees or judges of political contests."[163] The goal is to fulfill democracy's basic promise, not to create a superlative democracy or any ethical view of the good society.

This adds to the argument that the domain of political opinion requires strategies of control similar in kind to those that constitutional democracy has adopted in order to regulate the actuating power of the will. In modern democracy, for a public forum to be open to all, opinion formation and communication require more than the protection of freedom of expression, more than the classical-liberal strategy of state noninterference. Constitutional politics (government nonintervention) is perhaps no longer sufficient, and democratic legislation may be needed that does not abstain from doing but adopts an active strategy of countering economic power in the public forum. A more active strategy is needed because, in appealing to the expressive rights of individuals, the classical-liberal approach fails to draw adequate attention to the political injustices that arise from the vastly unequal capacity to be heard.[164]

A New Issue

The awareness of the impact of technology in judgment formation and political influence was clear already in the eighteenth century, when progressive intellectuals and political thinkers proposed to extend education to all citizens by activating a national system of schooling so as to make them capable of using printed materials and participating in the democratic process of selection and judgment with responsibility and proficiency. The role of education in Nicolas de Condorcet's social philosophy of progress and political equality is one of the most impressive examples, although not the only one, of that novel attention to the conditions of opinion formation. They are examples of the fact that the right of citizenship is richer than the right to vote in a representative democracy. Condorcet thought that attaining mass competent participation through education was the most important task a republican government must pursue, along with the protection of freedom of the press and the advancement of scientific knowledge.[165] Training citizens to employ and engage with information and scientific education was a necessary premise for modern democracy to take roots. In the mid-twentieth century, John Dewey adapted this enlightenment and civic view to the exigencies coming from democracy in an industrial society and distinguished between knowledge and understanding. "I use the word 'understanding' rather than knowledge because, unfortunately, knowledge to so many people means 'information' . . . I do not mean that we can have understanding without knowledge, without information; but I do mean that there is no guarantee . . . that the acquisition and accumulation of knowledge will create the attitudes that generate intelligent action."[166] Based on this intuition, modern democracies have made education into a right/duty of the citizen, whose implementation requires state intervention rather than abstention from interference.

Today, the issues of opinion formation and communication seem to require a renewed cultural attitude because, on the one hand, the new means that technology dispenses to us are supposed to put in motion individual minds or critical understanding, not to indoctrinate or inculcate ready-made opinions, and, on the other hand, they require such a profusion of economic power that for the government to keep its hands off is simply self-defeating for democracy. The preservation of equal liberty requires strategies to be attentive to the social composition of classes, and the concentration of economic power is a circumstance to be considered in discussing liberty of opinion formation. The problem today is not declaring rights but implementing and protecting them, an effort that legislative assemblies do better than constitutional courts because this task requires state intervention in the form of institutional arrangement and money; it requires the will to make rights work and moreover work effectively and fairly for all.[167] Capitalist organization of society and the bureaucratic state make "the rule of law" a desideratum rather than a fact, not only because no state, no matter how liberal and democratic, "treats all citizens equally before the law" but also because social inequality impacts the application of the law: "Law can be highly predictable for the privileged strata while it remains maddeningly erratic for the less well-off."[168]

Dispersion versus Concentration

A society is democratic when people recognize inequality as an obstacle to their liberty and when they consequentially organize the legal and institutional system in the view of overcoming it, "when it extends rights to all members of a community to participate freely and fully, to vote, assemble, gain access to information, dissent without intimidation, and to hold office at the highest political levels."[169] Hence, government by means of opinion requires supplemental efforts to place citizens in the condition of easily accessing information and the means of communicating and developing critical habits of mind that train them to be alert on events of public concern and distrustful enough toward widely shared opinions to preserve their negative power of control over established beliefs, institutions, and public officials. Its effort is double: preserving equal rights as a condition for pluralism and resisting concentrations of power. Relying upon a similar train of thought, from the nineteenth century onward, liberal authors thought it necessary to reinvigorate the negative role of free speech by making it a shield against the potential for a new kind of tyranny, that of the opinion of the majority. They were suspicious of attributing a positive role to the state in protecting the equal condition of public dialogue because they located the source of this new pervasive power within the democratic state for its natural propensity to seek uniformity of ideas in order to form majorities.

As said, in the liberal tradition inaugurated by Mill, several generations of American judges, lawyers, and theorists have interpreted the text of the First Amendment according to the political value of the "marketplace of ideas" and the related "fortress model" of free speech, which the state protects by not interfering with. Accordingly, the preservation of this right, Lee C. Bollinger has commented, requires alternative techniques that "transcend the construction of seemingly unalterable legal authority" to tackle the problems posed to free speech from private money in politics and media communication.[170] But the role of the market in media technology, and of private money in buying television stations, providing means of information, and sponsoring electoral campaigns, are formidable challenges to the liberal paradigm of noninterference. As a matter of fact, because contemporary democratic societies are facing power concentration, interference by the state is needed that aims at reequilibrating powers so as to make the basic right to free speech more effectively guarded.[171] Media concentration, like any form of power concentration, is a threat to democracy because it is a threat to equal liberty.[172] Resisting the erosion of political equality is thus a liberty battle.

Already in 1947 the Hutchins Commission Report pointed out the intrinsic correlation between power concentration and the "decreased proportion of the people who can express their opinion and ideas through the press." The report ended by declaring concentration bad for democracy and a threat to freedom of the press.[173] There is no agreement on the interpretation of this phenomenon. Recently, American scholars of public opinion have dismissed the argument against ownership concentration as no longer an issue because of the fragmentation of information and communication that the Internet produces.[174] Moreover, there is no agreement on the means for the containment of the concentration threat (not all agree that the law should be used to reduce or contrast media concentration directly).[175] Yet it is an observable fact that concentration exists in consolidated democracies (although not all states have the same antimonopoly legislation on television media; some are more vulnerable than others to this rising power) and that this can be the site of a new form of "indirect despotism," to use a prescient expression coined by Condorcet in 1789.

Some scholars have questioned the argument of diversity protection by pointing to the fact that it is impossible to say how many views make for a pluralist society.[176] Yet this consumerist perspective is faulty because the issue is not quantity, since the democratic principle of power dispersion is not content based but procedural. As observed by Baker, from a content-based perspective, "the positive contribution of ownership dispersal—or, more generally, varying sorts of *source* diversity—must depend on the empirical prediction that this dispersal provides audiences with great choice among (desired) content and viewpoints."[177] But whether the dispersal will actually lead to such content is empirically not provable. It may or may not. Yet the issue, as I claim throughout this chapter and the next, is not one of outcome (or of intervention on the content) but one of democratic norms and procedures.

Democracy does not require that "speakers provide or listeners choose a maximum (or any particular, high level of) diversity in commodity content. On the other hand, an absence of content or viewpoint diversity that reflects independent but congruent judgments of many different people . . . differs fundamentally from the same absence imposed by a few powerful actors." The issue is a purely procedural one because source diversity is a "*process* value" not a content or "*commodity* value."[178] Relying upon a normative view of democratic proceduralism allows us to be more consistent in supporting the claim of counterconcentration politics in the domain of opinion formation. It is indeed fair to say that it is not a perfectionist view of democracy that may better guide us to see the gravity of the problem but a view that is rigorously based on what Bobbio defined as a "rules of the game" notion of democracy (*democrazia delle regole del gioco*).

Two Viewpoints

Democratic societies have adopted two strategies to resist media control by corporation and concentration: through competition laws such as anti-trust legislation and media specific legislation, and through subsidy arrangements, or policies of financial subsidizing of media diversity and newspaper pluralism.[179] These strategic differences are oriented toward the promotion of the same goal: protecting, or impeding the disappearance of, diversity in media communication. Diversity or pluralism is antithetical to concentration and monopoly while it is the character of an open society.[180] The right to vote and elective procedures are consistent with the principle of empowering citizens by means of distributing power among them and preventing social inequality from translating into political inequality. As I shall explain in Chapter 3, this principle is at the core of the antipopulist argument because it proceeds from the idea that the protagonist of democracy is the individual citizen, not the people en masse. Democracy empowers citizens by diffusing power among them.

This brings me back to the two viewpoints—one content-oriented and the other procedure-oriented—in relation to which I propose we consider opinion as the site of a "negative" form of political power that makes freedom of speech and of association not merely rights of the individual but of the citizen as well, that finally justifies legal intervention rather than abstention. What is the goal we want to achieve when we defend this freedom as political, not merely civil?

Consistently with a content perspective, democratic thinkers have argued that a free and diverse forum is good because it allows the achievement of a better decision through discourse or collective deliberation. In 1948, Alexander Meiklejohn advanced a pioneering argument in the direction of a perfectionist view of democracy. Meiklejohn thought that protecting free speech should be for the sake of creating a political environment in which citizens "as political equals" participate openly and publicly in devising the best decisions for their community. In a brilliant analysis of Justice Holmes's 1897 lecture "The Path of Law," he criticized the "mechanistic" conception of the law in the name of an ethical conception. Whereas Holmes invited his readers to see the law with the eye of the "bad man" or the law breaker, Meiklejohn proposed instead to see it first of all with the eye of the "good man" in order to understand the rights and the law as means for achieving a self-governing community. Contra the Federalists' philosophy, Meiklejohn thought that taking men as they are (potentially bad rather than virtuous) was not the better understanding of the Constitution. A better way was to see "a judge or a citizen" as "a good man, a man who, in his political activities, is not merely fighting for what, under the law, he can get, but is eagerly and generously serving the common welfare."[181] The Constitution as a means to implement a more perfect democracy was Meiklejohn's vision of the forum of opinion. His model was New England's town-meeting democracy, in which people met not to talk but "to get business done."[182] "Now, in that method of political self-government, the point of ultimate interest is not the words of the speakers, but the minds of the hearers. The final aim of the meeting is the voting of wise decisions. The welfare of the community requires that those who decide issues shall understand them. They must know what they are voting about. And this, in turn, requires that so far as time allows, all facts and interests relevant to the problem shall be fully and fairly presented to the meeting."[183]

Meiklejohn held freedom of speech in a causal relation with the achievement of a good: a wise and competent deliberation, which in his mind was the fulfillment of the sovereign authority of the people, in fact the promise of democratic government. To resume our previous analysis of the facets of *doxa*, I would say that he stressed only the integrating and consensus aspect and made free speech political insofar as it is functional to the formation of "public intelligence."[184] There was an epistemic-perfectionist vision in his view of self-government, so that he gave free speech an ethical value besides a political meaning insofar as it would allow a collective of diverse persons to perform together well and make decisions that were not simply valid or formally legitimate but also good. Meiklejohn's goal was proposing to achieve not merely a democratic society but a rational community and to bring about, he thought, better outcomes for all. In order not to be "mechanistic" he proposed a functionalist reading of the forum of ideas, the goal being the achievement a more perfect community.[185]

We may recognize in Meiklejohn's argument the echo of the eighteenth-century ideal of the authority of reason transferred to collective assemblies (what is today called the "wisdom of the crowd"): if good procedures and rules (among them free speech in a public assembly) are well devised and performed, the collective is not less capable of giving good reasons or correct decisions than a single expert or a philosopher-king is. As we shall see in the next chapter, an important component of contemporary democratic theory follows this rationalistic or epistemic path. Yet is this outcome-oriented view of democracy the only way to make the case for freedom of speech as a political right? What kind of answer can be devised that does not resume the liberal "private" paradigm and yet does not renounce having a political procedural conception of democracy that is not perfectionistic?

Let us revisit first the liberal objection to Meiklejohn's line of thought. Liberalism stages a dualism between individual liberty and political participation, within which the former is the locus of basic freedom, and the latter is a form of power or a method of decision making. As the liberal argument goes, whereas individual liberty is principled and fundamental, political participation is pragmatic and instrumental. Thus, while the right to basic liberty must be guaranteed to each equally, the exercise of political power does not require in principle being equally distributed in order for that basic liberty to exist. Within this liberal argument—which Isaiah Berlin made authoritative—the epistemic threat of democratic enlightenment is neutralized by reducing democracy to a method for selecting an elite, with a bill of rights and checks and balances that protect individual liberty by containing the power of political liberty.

Historically, it was Joseph A. Schumpeter who gave the best illustration of a liberal answer against the perfectionist interpretation ("the classical doctrine") of democracy, namely, the interpretation of the democratic method as an "institutional arrangement for arriving at political decisions which realizes the common good."[186] His argument featured a conception of freedom of opinion that relied upon the state's abstention from interference because he assumed that freedom to compete for political leadership was in and of itself a sufficient check on power since competition "will normally mean a considerable amount of freedom of the press."[187] Along the same line of thought, Sartori wrote that we should not invoke government by opinion on the assumption that by discussing freely in the public arena we can achieve better decisions. We should invoke it on the ground that an open and free competition is basic for the electoral method of selection to work. Instrumentality was at the core of this interpretation of democratic procedures, which was based on the assumption that people as a collective are unable to make decisions, let alone wise decisions. Freedom of opinion was necessary in order to solve democracy's weakness.

It is, however, possible to attempt another kind of counterargument to the perfectionist view that, although relying upon a procedural interpretation of democracy, does not consider the right to free speech as only an expression of negative liberty, and does not restrict the role of political participation to simply election. This is the frame within which I have situated the argument of freedom of opinion as a component of the political rights of the citizen, and in fact, the condition that justifies state intervention to block or dismantle power concentration in the public forum. The view of representative democracy as a diarchy supports this interpretation.

Back to Democratic Procedures

Because of the technological means that freedom of opinion requires in modern society, economic power enters politics and even occupies it in quite a direct and muscular manner. Political opinions can become, and actually have already become in many democratic countries, a commodity that money can buy and sell with the unavoidable consequence of making inequality in politics a consolidated condition. Inequality in the opportunity to exercise political rights and economic inequality tend to go hand in hand and reinforce each other.[188] Thanks to the ownership or the control of the means of communication, those citizens who dispose of more economic power may have more chances to elect the representatives they prefer and thus to facilitate decisions that favor their interests. This is a breach of legal and political equality that is primed to jeopardize democratic procedures by lowering the barriers against arbitrariness. To Jeffrey Winters, the power of media resources can foster the stabilization of an oligarchy in power, and this is the reason why it is so attractive to those who want to use their "personal charisma, status, bravery, words, or ideas to mobilize masses of otherwise powerless individuals into formidable social and political forces."[189]

Owen M. Fiss has elaborated perhaps the most effective argument for why the market is a constraint on equality and why the democratic state cannot simply be seen as the enemy on issues of opinion formation.

> The role of the state in protecting democracy becomes clear, however, once it is understood that the market is itself a structure of constraint. Although the newly privatized press might be

called 'free' because the state does not own or control the papers or radio and television stations, the media do not operate in a social vacuum. Owners will seek to maximize profits by maximizing revenue and minimizing costs. . . . These are the iron laws of capitalist economics; they hold true for the newly privatized press just as they do for any other business. The state might therefore be needed to counteract those constraints placed on the press by the market.[190]

The goal is essentially to protect the conditions that make democratic procedures work. In the last pages of this chapter I shall offer *three arguments* to sustain the idea that a consistent procedural interpretation of democracy offers a better answer to the perfectionist argument for legal intervention than the liberal noninterventionist conception. Moreover, I'll argue that it requires government intervention in the domain of opinion formation that removes barriers to an equal opportunity for political participation.

The first argument pertains to the recognition of political liberty as a condition of individual freedom. In past years, and in reaction to despotic regimes and populist forms of democracy, liberal theorists wanted to disassociate the enjoyment of individual liberty from the democratic form of government or political equality. Berlin argued, for instance, that liberty from interference can be equally respected or violated in an autocracy and in a democracy; indeed, he maintained that individual freedom can be enjoyed (or lost) both in an autocracy and in a democracy, and in this sense it "is not, at any rate logically, connected with democracy or self-government . . . there is no necessary connection between individual liberty and democratic rule."[191] However, he did not say that this holds true also in the case we take as our reference point, the *equal liberty* each person should enjoy of not suffering an *arbitrary* power of interference. To make his argument, Berlin had to circumscribe the notion of individual liberty to the factual case of an individual who is obstructed in his volition to act by an external and unqualified obstacle. Reference to the public relationship of an individual to his fellow citizens was extrinsic to the concept of liberty as noninterference, which was thus independent of any form of government.[192]

Yet if we are consistent with the principle of equal political liberty, if, in other words, we think that political liberty relies upon actions regulated by the law and the distribution of the legal opportunity to be free, then the character of the government becomes a very relevant issue. The conclusion that the political order is indifferent to the protection of individual liberty can no longer be sustained. Political liberties are "special" insofar as for them to be guaranteed in their "fair value" all citizens "must be sufficiently equal in the sense that all have a fair opportunity" to do what their political rights allow them to do: voting, competing for offices, and also participating in the "public forum" in a way that is meaningful.[193]

Liberty among equals in political power is a claim against despotism and oligarchy because it is a claim against concentration of power in the domain of will and opinion. Since ancient Athens, this is the democratic meaning of liberty: voluntary public relationship among equals, which may entail a sacrifice of one's will (for instance, obedience to laws) for a goal that is regarded as profitable to all *because* it does not result in an unequal distribution of the power to impose obedience, or the domination of some. A democratic citizen is thus ready to accept the republican distinction between "an unregulated action and an action regulated by the law," but on condition that it is completed with the specification that the action should be "regulated by an autonomous law (one accepted voluntarily)."[194]

This understanding of liberty, which considers the political order as a basic pact free citizens seal for resolving their disagreements on how to regulate their interactions, is apt to describe equal political liberty because it stipulates that in order for me not to be subjected to another's power I should somehow participate in making the decisions I am supposed to obey. This vision of liberty is mirrored in the second condition of procedural democracy and makes sense of the fact that democracy does not have an elsewhere, or some specific goals to aim at outside of the very process of decision making that is achieved by means of equal political liberty, for reasons that are peculiar to its nature.

The second argument pertains to the immanent nature of democratic legitimacy. The main contemporary theorists of democracy, from Dewey to Kelsen, Habermas, and Bobbio, have contemplated this condition of immanence by arguing that democracy does not need to conjecture the existence of a prepolitical nature as the site of inalienable rights in order to justify and respect them. To the contrary, democracy shows itself (its history begins) precisely when a community of men and women start claiming the existence of inalienable rights; that is to say, when it adopts the instrument of rights in order to solve its internal conflicts and disagreements and regulate their public relations.[195]

"The will of the community, in a democracy, is always created through a running discussion between majority and minority, through free consideration of arguments for and against a certain regulation of a subject matter. This discussion takes place not only in Parliament, but also, and foremost, at political meetings, in newspapers, books, and other vehicles of public opinion. A democracy without public opinion is a contradiction in terms. Insofar as public opinion can arise only where intellectual freedom, freedom of speech, press and religion, are guaranteed, democracy coincides with political—though not necessarily economic—liberalism."[196] Habermas rephrased this idea of Kelsen in a conception of deliberation that does not change the fact that "classical liberties are co-original with political rights" insofar as without those rights that "secure private autonomy" of each citizen there can be "no medium legally institutionalizing the conditions" under which citizens "can make use of their public autonomy."[197]

We cannot have democracy independently of individual freedom and what we call basic rights; we cannot have it without a legal system that is conceived so as to implement the rule of law. Both levels, that of individual rights and that of democratic politics, implicate each other if it is true that in a democracy, politics is made of a wide-open, plural, and public forum of opinions, a forum within which only political consent can emerge or change and dissent can have full right to exist and be made public; within which, finally, the distinction between political majority and political minority is presumed because of the democratic procedure that commands the opinions should be counted one by one and according to the rule of majority.

Hence, democratic decisions are legitimate (and, in fact, better than nondemocratic ones) because they tend to produce a more perfect self-governing community or approach more apt outcomes or outcomes that approximate correct decisions. This view, which belongs to a perfectionistic conception of democracy, seems to rest on a hidden aporia because it bases political legitimacy on a *post factum* logic that warrants justification for obedience on a proved outcome, which is absurd.

But democracy as diarchy gives the democratic process a normative value of its own precisely because no opinion can claim a substantive authority, not even one that has received a majority's support, since it is open to contestation and change. I use the word "immanentism" in order to convey the idea that democracy takes conflict channeled through procedures and political institutions as a norm of participation and not for the results it promises, because it gives all the citizens the chance to express freely and openly their opinions and to organize for the sake of changing or contesting existing laws and elected officials. Democracy *is* its procedures, with the caveat that there is nothing external to it that can evaluate "the substantive quality of its decisions." In this sense, it is "not a fact and never will be."[198] Its procedures have a normative value because they enable political competition for government to replace violence and do so by protecting and enhancing equal political liberty. It follows from this that the uncertainty of the result and the openness of the game of politics are the most precious "outcomes" of democracy, what make us free to voluntarily participate in voting and forming political opinions.[199] Claude Lefort very effectively stressed the nonfoundational and immanent nature of modern democracy, the fact that it disembodies power and makes it ubiquitous: "by virtue of discourse . . . [representative democracy] reveals that power belongs to no one; that those who exercise power do not possess it; that they do not, indeed, embody it; that the exercise of power requires a periodic and repeated contest, that the authority of those vested with power is created and re-created as a result of the manifestation of the will of the people."[200]

This brings me to the third argument, which pertains to self-containment and is intrinsically correlated to the previous two. In democracy as in no other political system it is crucial that means and ends are not in disagreement. Democracy is consistency of means and ends because it is both a goal and the process to reach it. And if it does not allow for shortcuts it is because it is not merely a functional way to reach some end or any kind of ends (even good ends). The goodness of the end does not justify the violation of the democratic process of decision making. Material and formal aspects should always be conceived together if a process of decision is to be held democratically.

Let us take some historical examples of what it means to use bad means (violation of equality) to achieve a good goal. Liberals have been the first to see that opinion can acquire the effective character of a positive power (oppressive and intrusive) while its nature remains unchanged (that is to say negative, invisible, and never directly coercive). They have also tried to devise possible solutions to this problem. For instance, Mill went back to Cicero's idea of an open ballot as a means by which the wisest, more competent, or more virtuous citizens could exercise their supposedly beneficial influence on ordinary and supposedly incompetent and unwise citizens.[201] More modern and less naïve, yet not less problematic from a democratic perspective, was the proposal advanced by Walter Lippmann in 1922: creating an independent class of experts on political and social questions (i.e., graduates and doctorates in Political Science) who "make the unseen facts intelligible and known to those who are to make decisions."[202]

Whereas Mill had proposed to intervene on the governed by inhibiting or taming their passions and prejudices through an electoral system that offered the more competent and virtuous more opportunities to exercise their influence on the elections (a proposal that lacks any empirical evidence and is itself the outcome of the prejudice according to which more scholarly culture translates into more political virtue), Lippmann proposed instead to intervene on the governing class by illuminating its job with the competent knowledge of a technocratic class. Skeptical about the possibility of inducing the large public to formulate wise or competent judgments without jeopardizing individual liberty, Lippmann turned his attention on those who held in their hands the means of power, as he himself wrote. Yet both Mill and Lippmann resorted to strategies that I would call "Platonist" because they were intended so as to exalt instead of counter political inequality. Their solutions were not in agreement with the circumstances of democracy because they tried to reach a legitimate end (controlling the power of the opinion of the majority) with illegitimate means (introducing elements of inequality among citizens). They broke the rule of democratic consistency essentially because they located the threats to liberty in political equality.

Contrary to these content-oriented strategies that presume democracy is unable to contain itself, I propose we give normative value to democratic procedures and judge them as Brian Barry did with the theory of justice as impartiality: it "must not only be done but must be seen to be done. And that means that the decision must be arrived at fairly. Even if the decision is itself perfectly just, it is still tainted if the method by which it was arrived at was unfair."[203] By the same token, democracy is a self-containing regime if interpreted as a set of procedures that a constitution seals, because it has within itself the condition of its own limitation. But correct procedures without the sustaining principles they rely upon—and not empty equal opportunity to participate in and influence decisions— may cost, as we saw, erosion of trust in democratic diarchy. To make this claim we do not need, as Kelsen explained, the Constitution to be seen as an "external" limit on the power that the people may legitimately exercise over themselves, but as a condition for the existence of this power in the first place, a condition that requires a persistent repairing and refurbishing.[204]

Thus, contrary to a traditional view, which was originally sponsored by its critics since antiquity, democracy is not an unbounded regime that needs to be tamed with externally devised strategies. As it was clear since its Athenian inception, it contains in itself the reasons for and means of its limitations, and also, of course, of its violations. This means that changes internal to democracy can occur—not by chance, Aristotle described six possible forms of democratic regime, ranging from a constitutional polity to a demagogical one. These changes can be explained as changes inside of the diarchic relationship between will and opinion, when one of the two parts gets supremacy over the other. They are primed to change the figure of democracy.

Keeping the democratic decision-making process in balance with the power of opinion is the task representative democracy should aim at in order to protect itself. It can be discharged not only by allowing the citizens to play the game of politics (thus participating somehow in making the laws they obey) but also by making them see that the game they are playing is fair, because it is made with rules and according to conditions that are equal to all and treat all equally.

These three conditions together—equal liberty, immanence, and self-containment—make sense of Tocqueville's maxim that democracy does not give us the certainty of excellent or good decisions (sometimes in fact its decisions are bad and unwise); what it gives us is the certainty we can amend and change all decisions without calling into question or revoking the political order, that is to say, without losing our liberty. In sum, democratic decisions require being amended with democratic means; they require being changed through direct and indirect strategies that are intended so as to reduce as much as possible the risk of being disfigured as means to ends other than equal political liberty.

Conclusion

In this chapter I have delineated the diarchic figure of representative democracy. I have also argued that democratic government promises citizens the guarantee that all of them enjoy equal rights to both vote and voice, and that this can require lawmakers to intervene in order to make sure that socioeconomic and cultural barriers are not so high as to jeopardize citizens' equal opportunity to an equal political influence. Unbalances in the diarchic structure of democracy are the most urgent problems to be solved by contemporary consolidated democracies. They testify to an exponential growth of social inequality and its factual translation into political power through the mechanisms of political influence, without revoking the constitutional rules of the game. This makes procedural correctness inadequate to fulfill the democratic promise of equal citizenship, and in fact, a stratagem that conceals the political effects of social inequality. Unbalances in democratic diarchy can be amended by reestablishing and patrolling the borders between the will and opinion, thus restoring the egalitarian conditions that a just work of democratic procedures requires. As a form of government, democracy needs to be a system of permanent self-maintenance.

In the following three chapters I will illustrate cases in which solutions to the unbalanced relationship among the diarchic powers have been proposed that blur the borders instead or change the function of one of its two components—namely, opinion. They do so by making *doxa* vanish in an unpolitical transformation of the public forum; by promoting the formation of a strong hegemonic opinion that aspires to embody the ruling power of the sovereign; or by transforming the role of opinion in an aesthetic spectacle performed by leaders to which citizens passively attend. These cases, which are represented by influential interpretations in contemporary political theory, are examples of a decline of the worth and value of democratic procedures. Indeed, the solutions they advance are not meant to restitute diarchic power to the citizens, which as a matter of fact they deem responsible for political system malfunction. They are meant instead to trade that dual power with one power only—be it the truth, the people, or the audience. In this way they weaken or disfigure democracy.

2

Unpolitical Democracy

The first source of the unbalance of the diarchic powers I detect and analyze is what I take to be an unpolitical reinterpretation of the procedural system of democracy. This phenomenon is not merely academic, although I do concentrate essentially on scholarly literature and treat it as a theoretical issue. Unpolitical democracy is the name of a complex family that includes both proposals of extending the domains in which nonpartisan decisions are made and proposals that advance a conception of democratic authority that receives legitimacy from the quality of the outcomes that its procedures allow. I list these approaches under the name of "unpolitical democracy" because they tend to neutralize that which makes democratic politics so characteristically associated with dispute, disagreement, deliberation, and majority decisions that are open to change. In the previous chapter I clarified that by politics I mean an art of public discourse in the tradition of Aristotle. Terence Ball has written: "politics is not essentially an instrumental or goal-oriented activity undertaken for the sake of some separately identifiable end, but is instead the medium of moral education of the citizenry."[1] The "medium" is the public activities regulated by rights, democratic procedures, and institutions; yet if it educates citizens morally it does so without premeditation. In this sense I have used and will be using the expression "democratic proceduralism"; that is, in order to stress that what makes it the spine of political legitimacy is the fact that it makes the process happen in the way it is supposed to, not that it delivers some substantive (or desirable) outcomes, which, if they come, come with no premeditation, although the actors

81

may want to use them to achieve some specific outcomes. The goals of the actors are legitimate insofar as they do not subvert the basic assumptions made in the common pact in which there is the respect of the procedures. It is in relation to this idea of politics that I examine unpolitical visions of democracy. Before proceeding, I need to say something of the context within which the unpolitical conception of democracy has acquired momentum in our times.

Arguments that invoke decisions at the governmental level that bypass partisan requests fostered by political parties reflect a current of opinion that is widespread in democratic states in these times of deep economic crisis, particularly in European states. They encourage us to think that electors and elected representatives are inadequate to make correct decisions because their judgments are endogenously tainted with strategic reasoning and not intended to deliver correct or desirable outcomes (wherein desirability is compliance with reasons that are independent of democracy's political authority). I do not suggest that unpolitical interpretations of democracy merge technocratic and epistemic interpretations, that in other words epistemic democracy is the same as technocratic government. As we shall see, the theory of epistemic democracy claims an equal distribution of basic potential of knowledge among the citizens and praises the wisdom of the crowd. Yet its focus on the outcome seems to imply that the work of democratic procedures is legitimate insofar as it is able to channel the knowledge of the many toward decisions that satisfy reasons that exceed their opinions or the principle of equal political liberty, which is the good that procedures reflect, promote and promise. In this sense I argue that, despite the differences among ways of employing *episteme* in politics, putting value in the achievable outcomes over or instead of the procedures may prepare the terrain for a sympathetic welcome to technocratic revisions of democracy.

It is remarkable that in a time of profound economic crisis, which democratic institutions seem unable to tackle in a resolute way, the value of *episteme* commands new attention as a desirable substitution of *doxa*, and that the issue of the optimum solution and obedience justified by knowledge attracts political scholars and democracy theorists in particular. Like in the 1920s when the then-weak European liberal states were put on trial for a crisis they seemed unable to solve, today's democratic states are facing a new wave of antiparliamentary spirit, with the argument that electoral and procedural democracy allows into politics partial judgments and electoral interests, which fuel a compromising and instrumental attitude at most and is least conducive of steady, just, and competent decisions.[2] The link of will and opinion that the diarchic system of representative government presumes appears to be at the root of the inability of democracy to deliver good outcomes. Diarchy is rendered as one between will and truth instead of will and opinion.

Different emergencies (war in the past and economic default in the present) call for different competences but propel remarkably similar unpolitical views, whether the claim is that citizens should aim to reach true outcomes or that only some few competent can do it. The recent substitution of elected executives with technocratic ones in some European countries is indicative of the pervasive belief that democratically elected institutions are incapable of achieving, or too slow in making, rational policy decisions in the domain of finance and the economy. Thus, they are judged destabilizing factors. Depending on the opinion of the citizens, this does not necessarily entail that austerity decisions are impossible, although it does demand that their proponents spend time to prove to the public that those decisions are necessary and to convince the citizens that they are good.[3] But once *episteme* enters the domain of politics, the possibility that political equality gets questioned is in the air because the criterion of competence is intrinsically inegalitarian. Today, it is actually the expansion of the domain of nonpolitical decisions that risks promoting this transformation, along with a reconfiguration of political judgment that is modeled out of the juristic method of truth-seeking. In recent democratic theory, political deliberation, when not driven by the goal of achieving consensual outcomes, has been countered with decisions by nonpolitical actors, like judges and juries or committees of experts, with the argument that this would protect the common good from the infiltration of prejudices, inaccuracy, and partisanship. The goal of these theoretical criticisms is, as we shall see, not to overcome democracy but to strengthen it. Yet the unpolitical road they walk leads to a devaluation of democracy, and finally its disfiguration.

In this chapter I analyze examples of the unpolitical attitude as they have emerged within democratic theory. As anticipated in the introduction, I suggest that from the theoretical point of view unpolitical interpretations of democracy and populist politics look like two sides of the same coin, at least because they are equally impatient with the democratic diarchy and want something else besides majority decisions, party pluralism, the art of compromise, and a wide-open public forum in which the citizens have the opportunity to participate, with their inaccurate ideas, noisy and diverse voices, and requests that reflect their social conditions and interests. The observation of contemporary politics in Europe adds to this theoretical insight and illustrates the codevelopment of populism and epistemic ambitions in government, each fueling the other while both devaluing democratic procedures unless they are capable of achieving some goals that are external to it, and to do so with premeditation.

The Myth of the Nonpolitical

Praise of the unpolitical is hardly novel among critics or skeptics of democracy and becomes particularly intense in times of crisis. In his *Reflections of a Nonpolitical Man*, a provocative critique of democracy written in 1918, Thomas Mann maintained that there is an intrinsic relationship between "politics" and "democracy." He was writing in the year Germany was close to adopting its first democratic constitution, and his goal was to inquire into the value of democracy, to him the name not merely of a form of government but of a comprehensive way of conceiving society. Democracy, Mann thought, makes all human reality invariably "political." "The political-intellectual attitude is the democratic one; belief in politics is belief in democracy."[4] Democracy was unavoidably political because it transformed all issues into objects of public evaluation and made people decide by voting. Democracy devalued values by making them a matter of opinion and consent. It was thus a method not simply for problem solving and decision making but for transforming all things into problems to be debated publicly and solved by majority rule. It made all social reality artificial and subject to the change of people's opinions.

Mann correctly associated democracy with *doxa*, and on this ground complained of its success in modern society. Democracy's chief and unamendable flaw was also the reason why people loved it as a regime open to permanent change and adjustable to their contingent interests or desires. Politics based on consent was a flaw because no unpolitical good could survive the corrosive power of government by discussion (certainly not the nation, a community of values, the decline of which Mann lamented as the effect of democracy).[5] It was unamendable because democracy could not exist without it. When critics of democracy, Mann explained, set out to denounce the corrupting effect of radical politicization of public ethos they are forced to behave politically; in order to promote their nonpolitical claim they have to become partisan, thus, democratic. "One is not a 'democratic', or, say, a 'conservative' politician. One is a politician or one is not. And if one is, then one is democratic."[6]

The argument Mann used to prove that the political attitude that democracy sponsored was a "nonvalue" recalled Max Weber's reflections on politics as a vocation and the ethic of responsibility. It was a "nonvalue" as it made all values dependent upon the opinions of ordinary citizens, with no specific competence whatsoever.[7] Yet only a political activity that is subjected to a superior good (like truth or an ethical value) would be able to achieve outcomes that served the community with independent spirit, above partisanship. To be in the service of the nation, Mann concluded, politics must be disassociated from opinion. As with Weber's criticism of the debilitating effects of parliamentary politics, Mann opposed "politics" as an ethics of responsibility and competence to the "political attitude" that electoral competition for office propelled.

Indictment of politicization is not new to critics of democracy.[8] As a matter of fact, the century that is known as that of democratic renaissance, the eighteenth century, was in fact the century in which the attack against the government of the many was harsh and radical. In that century two important criticisms of democracy were perfected: one in the name of rationality and one in the name of tradition. Both of them gained impetus as a result of the French Revolution. The centrality of an elected assembly and politicization went hand in hand and were the factors in relation to which both forms of criticism were devised.

The first criticism questioned the democratic principle of popular consent from the perspective of a priori superior goods, like truth or moral worth. From Plato to the contemporary theorists of epistemic democracy, "most lovers of truth [have found] democratic elections rather hard to stomach" because of their unavoidable partisan character, and have tried to envisage decision-making procedures that can approximate rationality and reconcile democracy with goals superior to the mere achieving of a political victory, whatever the competing opinions might be, sound or biased.[9] In this tradition that claims consistency with the value of equality, epistemic theorists seek to emancipate the crowd from condemnation by making it a gathering of decision makers who can, if assembled properly and led by good procedures and intelligent trainers, achieve results that are correct, in fact "better" than those achieved by nondemocratic procedures. The crowd is made capable of matching small groups of intelligent individuals, which clearly remain the standard model of good politics. It is emancipated by making it similar to the wise "few" (or the "one"), according to the assumption that knowledge is the foundation of political legitimacy. This democratic Platonism—or the persistence of the myth of the philosopher- king although dressed in collective and egalitarian garb—is an approach that, Jeremy Waldron has explained, follows in the template of jurisprudence, which when it talks about legislation is "most comfortable treating [it] on the model of a single individual."[10] As I shall claim in this chapter, the identification of judgment in the juristic mode with political judgment is among the most relevant signs of the epistemic infiltration in democratic proceduralism. This is the central argument I propose against the "good intention" of giving wisdom to the crowd in order to prove that democracy is superior to oligarchy from the point of view of knowledge.

To use epistemic equality as a political argument and moreover a democratic one is problematic, though, regardless of the good intention of making the crowd honorable like a king, because the epistemic paradigm locates the criterion for judging what is good or correct outside the political process, which plays one might say an auxiliary function, not authoritative. Not by chance, when Nicolas de Condorcet (one of the mentors of the theorists of epistemic democracy) wanted to argue in favor of the rationality of large groups of people deliberating, he took the jury as his model of collective decision, not the legislative assembly, so as to indicate that questions of truth and falsehood are at home in nonpolitical decisions, not all decisions—a corollary that is precious although neglected. But when Condorcet had to devise the constitution of the French republic, he did not choose the model of the jury. Having stated *disagreement* as the organizing principle of political decisions and foreseeing the possibility of dissent over the interpretation of both the constitutional articles and the legislative proposals, he tried to devise a set of rules that would enable the democratic process to reach a unified point (decision) without using nondemocratic strategies or keeping the door open to subversion. In his search, Condorcet started from the idea that democracy is a government by means of opinion, not truth. The rationale of his constitutionalism was that a legitimate law resembles a collective work that relies upon "general propositions" of independent validity (rights are "an independent truth") and seeks an outcome that is general in its substance and authority. The aim of the constitution is to make people agree at least partially on the interpretation of that "independent truth":[11] "These common rules cannot possibly accord with the view of every individual. They must therefore be determined by the view of the majority. The preservation of freedom requires each individual to make an equal contribution to the expression of that majority view."[12]

The second direction that the attack on democracy took beginning with the French Revolution was more radical, as well as fatal and explicit. In this case, the principle of popular consent was attacked by communitarians, antirationalists, and antiegalitarians, ideologues who countered the process of political emancipation in the name of historical continuity and tradition as criteria of social distribution of honor and power and conditions for moral stability, in fact, for authority.[13] Edmund Burke and Joseph de Maistre scourged democratically elected assemblies on the account that they dethroned honored competence, wisdom, and virtue from politics, but actually authority itself, which found its most friendly home in religion and tradition, ancestral sources of belief that commanded worship and deference, not discussion and consent. But the government of the assembly made politics a litigious arena of partisan battles, in which all issues were debated and became relative in value, because they were subjected to the opinions coming from society and translated into numerical majorities.[14] Democracy was accused of dethroning authority and legitimating anarchy and moral relativism.

In the two centuries that followed the Revolution of 1789, the theme of the incompetence of the masses and their crafty manipulation by ambitious politicians became topical and intertwined, because of course for manipulation to be discovered people should be not only able to recognize the difference between factual truth and ideas (a power that is hard even to the most expert minds) but also to be able to distinguish between rhetorical garb as different from objective perception. Behind the accusation that democratic politics manipulates reality because it is based on words and is thus conducive to rhetoric, there is the implicit assumption that in its pure form politics has (or should have) to do with "the-truth-and-nothing-but-the-truth political discourse" that dismisses politics altogether. The paradox being that tyranny is the best system because it is least exposed to manipulation since no public speech is allowed that orients actions and opinions as well.[15] Wherein it is clear that politics has nothing to do with the achievement of truth and should not be judged from this perspective, it has also nothing to do with ensuring liberty. Hence, it is not manipulation per se that is the problem but the distinction between democratic and undemocratic manipulation. The former makes sure that all can respond and look for emendation, criticism, and ratification, while the latter does not and moreover it institutionalizes the withholding of information so as to make the very critical inquiry impossible.[16] In sum, the distinction between manipulation and truth is in fact a distinction not between truth and falsehood, correct evidence and *doxa*, but between liberty and nonliberty, as we saw in the previous chapter.

The accusation that democracy manipulates truth because it is based on speech and rhetoric is vicious and alarming. It crossed a large spectrum of positions. It was developed in a variety of themes by authors as diverse as Hippolyte Taine, Gabriel Tarde, Gustave Le Bon, Carl Schmitt, Walter Lippmann, and Leo Strauss. Whereas epistemic democrats want to bring knowledge to the masses and make the many reason *like* one philosophical mind, the antidemocrats exclude the possibility that the many can achieve such a high score and refer to the need of majority rule as a proof of their deficiency. To prove, against this approach, that it is actually the case that the many can reason like one—that they can achieve the true outcome—is unsafe for democracy because it brings the defense of political equality onto the terrain of a source of authority that is external to compromise among opinions, or more precisely, superior, as reason is superior to *doxa*.

Although their goals are opposite, both rationalist critics and traditionalist critics of democracy as government by opinion share in the Platonist myth of a transcendent source of political competence as a prerequisite of legitimacy. Both of them give politics a mission that belongs to other endeavors, such as, for instance, philosophy or theology, and such as also the kind of achievement that justice pursues in tribunals. Their mistrust in democracy lies in that democracy *is* indeed the realm of opinion, which, although it may be defended in the name of approximation to truth, does not presume any unchangeable outcome or uncontested truth. Democratic procedures presume permanent reviewability, on which individual liberty to participate freely in the process of making and changing laws and policies rests. The value of democratic legitimacy, Robert C. Post writes, "causes First Amendment doctrine to construct public discourse as a domain of opinion because it prevents the state from maintaining the standards of reliability that we associate with expert knowledge. . . . The creation of reliable disciplinary knowledge must accordingly be relegated to institutions that are not controlled by the constitutional value of democratic legitimation."[17] Although for critical purposes, the identification that Mann proposed of "politics" and "democracy" was thus cogent. Indeed, this identification is the main object of blame, so that any attempt to make politics in agreement with truth results in depoliticizing democracy. This is the antidiarchy argument I shall explore in the chapter.

As for the two trajectories of criticism I have silhouetted, concern with politicization is more interesting than traditional antidemocratic lamentations. In fact, it is intrinsic to the process of democratic transformation of society, which pursues an ideal of justice as the elimination of privileges and in the name of equal consideration of all, above partial considerations and thus also political decisions. The desire of unpolitical as impartial reasoning is internal to democracy; in fact, it is its early claim against the justice of the few.[18] The expansion of bureaucracy and the domains of decision that are withdrawn from the political *agon* testify to an ambiguous relationship between democracy and opinion within consolidated democratic societies.

Within this perspective I critically analyze the renaissance of the ideal of emancipating democracy from the dominion of *doxa*. I will refer in particular to the work of three thinkers whose leading role in contesting the place of partisan politics and the political interpretation of the procedural work of democracy is hardly contestable. Criticism of democracy's vocation to politicize all decisions can be detected in David Estlund's epistemic emendation of procedural democracy, in Pierre Rosanvallon's proposal to extend the domain of nonpolitical decisions, and in Philip Pettit's call for a "republic of reason."[19] Certainly, the quest of these authors for the unpolitical does not share the same motivation as Mann's or traditional antidemocrats'. In fact, it would be a grave mistake to identify these critical trends as if their call for the unpolitical was voiced in the traditional language of antidemocracy and for the same sake.

Criticism from Within

The modern critique of democratic politics is complex. As in ancient Athens, it made its appearance along with democracy, accompanied its progression, and participated somehow in its making. As said, criticism of democracy does not involve only the irreducible enemies of the government of the many but, much more interestingly, also what I propose to call "critics from within."[20] Unlike antidemocracy critics, the latter testify to the dissatisfaction with certain aspects of democratic practice and institutions. They are an autochthonous expression of discontent, different in kind from the assault on democracy that springs from intrinsically antiegalitarian principles of political legitimacy. Distinctions among streams of criticism must be carefully made, and the parallel with Mann's thought may help us to appreciate them.

Whereas Mann wanted to censure the process of democratization, the intention of today's critics from within is to protect, as it were, democracy from its own weaknesses. Estlund questions the relativist or "nihilist" implications of a political interpretation of democratic proceduralism (which criticizes "the appeal to truth . . . as antipolitical") and proposes we care about the quality of the outcome, or "the substantive quality of its decisions," rather than the process per se as democracy's main value.[21] Rosanvallon observes approvingly that in representative democracy, ordinary political processes are happily complemented with and better discharged by unpolitical as bureaucratic practices and impersonal mechanisms of control (the realms of the "negative" power of judgment) designed to promote decisions that are more in tune with democratic principles and less partisan.[22] Finally, Pettit argues that "depoliticization of democracy" is needed in order to realize political deliberation: "if deliberation is really supposed to rule in public life, then there is no option but to depoliticize public decisions in various ways."[23]

These critics' concerns are also different. Mann's main concern was with the undermining of communitarian values such as the ethical "mission" of the German nation. Processes of domestic and international democratization, he thought, will make all individuals "free and equal," but they will also disintegrate the nation, which is not the sum of equal units. Contemporary critics from within have quite a different concern because their goal is different. Their goal is not protecting or restoring some communitarian goods but achieving decisions truly informed by and consistent with the principle of inclusion that democracy itself proclaims. Their concern is precisely with the disappearance of what Mann thought to be the main defects of democracy: rationality, humanity, and individual liberty. Estlund's, Rosanvallon's, and Pettit's concern points to the erosion of independent mind and impartial judgment, the sole bases for decisions that approximate truth and make democracy more legitimate and secure.

Yet despite these important differences, contemporary critics from within think, like Mann, that democracy (and particularly representative democracy, which fuels party competitions and biased propaganda) has an endemic predisposition to foster partisan views because of its politicizing nature. To recall Nancy Rosenblum's argument, the evolution of modern democracy belongs to the history of the "moral disdain for partisans" and partisanship.[24] The new attraction with the unpolitical in contemporary democratic theory is yet another chapter in that history.

How are we to judge the unpolitical temptation in contemporary democratic theory? Dissatisfactions with the epistemic transformation of political discourse in the deliberative theory of democracy are not new. In the form of devising competent assemblies or bureaucratic repositories of statistical knowledge or committees of nonpolitical experts that tutored inexpert parliaments, objections against ill-informed, prejudicial, and interest-driven opinion of the citizens are neither novel nor peculiar to our time and to modern society.[25] In recent years, they have resurfaced, and this phenomenon needs to be detected and studied.

As a matter of fact, scholars have already started detecting and studying it. Some political theorists have criticized the antirhetorical use of deliberation as a process of "constrained reason" as an erosion of citizens' political action.[26] They have blamed deliberative theory for making democracy a regime of consensus that expels antagonism and disagreement with the consequence of rendering the citizens politically apathetic.[27] My proposal in critiquing the unpolitical turn is different. I intend to question democratic Platonism from the perspective of a view of democracy that is strictly speaking procedural or, as I have already explained, one that is consistent with the diarchy of will and opinion that constitutes representative democracy. I intend to make my argument by discussing the unpolitical allegation that issues of public concern should be given depoliticized answers, all the while knowing that this patently conflicts with the character of democracy. Thus, in this chapter I treat the allegation of politicization raised from within democratic theory as an exemplary case of violation of the diarchic nature of democracy by annulling or narrowing the domain of *doxa*. This is "criticism from within" that, if actualized, would change the configuration of democracy, and moreover disfigure it.

I shall subject the actual trend toward unpolitical views of democracy to three main criticisms: the first points to the epistemic use of deliberation as an antidote against democratic politics itself; the second points to the expansion of the "negative" role of judgment that the temptation of the unpolitical makes visible; and the third points to the dissolution of opinion within a model of judgment that is tailored around jurisprudence and is forensic, rather than political-deliberative, in character. Estlund's, Rosanvallon's, and Pettit's idealization of the unpolitical and their critical reflections on the strategic competition of political views and on partisanship eloquently illustrate these critical trends.

These three authors belong to different intellectual traditions and pursue different agendas, yet their line of thought shows remarkable affinities. They are not alone in this battle against political democracy, but they are certainly pioneering authors and the most representative and challenging thinkers in this domain of political theory. Estlund identifies proceduralism mainly with the Schumpeterian interpretation or instrumental competition for election and brings the consequences of the deliberative critique to an extreme because he portrays proceduralist theory of democracy as a functionalistic method that is normatively empty and interested essentially in victory, that is, Machiavellian in the crudest sense. Rosanvallon frames his argument for the unpolitical within the dialectics between actuating politics (institutional *legitimacy* or the work of democratic procedures) and counterpolitics (exercise of *defiance* or the critical work of the public against parliamentary decisions) and locates the quest for nonpartisan politics in the latter, which is the domain of *the negative power of judgment.* Pettit sets up the terrain for a depoliticization of democracy by resorting to an old republican strategy that separates the two main functions of democratic practice: deliberation and decision. In his view, the former should entail competent and dispassionate judgment and the adversarial control on proposals and decisions, while the latter should consist merely in voting and majority rule, the two criteria of democratic decision making used by the citizens (suffrage) and their representatives.

As for the target of their criticism of the partisan and opinion-based character of democracy, Estlund's is a purely *political proceduralism* because it induces citizens to deem political decisions as content-indifferent; Rosanvallon's is *populism*, which is a predetermined destiny of representative democracy if precautions are not taken, such as countering the trend to make all issues objects of democratic decision; and finally, Pettit's target is the very "system whereby the collective will of the people rules" in representative democracy, namely, the *centrality of parliaments* or legislative bodies, which to him is in itself populist.[28]

Despite these remarkable differences, the reflections of these three authors on the nature and risks of democracy are exemplary and inspired by an ideal of deliberative democracy as a process of rationalization of collective decisions. This project of rationalization is meant to further a gradual but significant contraction of the sphere of democratic politics as a sphere that is inhabited by opinions, in which decisions are made according to majority rule because rational consent is structurally missing. They suggest that the value and worth of deliberation rest in the latter's ability to amend democracy of *doxa* and its politicizing inclination either by reducing the possibility of irrational (that is to say, partisan and biased or simply incorrect) outcomes (Estlund), or by interrupting the path toward demagoguery (Rosanvallon), or by narrowing the authority of representative bodies and citizens' votes in favor of the jury and a juridical strategy of control (Pettit). I will proceed as follows: first, I analyze each of these three interpretations; and second, I point to the common aspect of them all, which resides in the extension to political judgment of the character, model, and goal of judicial judgment.

Instrumental to Truth

The epistemic theory of democracy, which Estlund's work best represents, is a development from within the deliberative theory of democracy, but it goes well beyond that since it charges democratic procedures with the task not only of leading to autonomous decisions by democratic citizens but also of producing "true" or "correct" decisions.[29] The normative justification of procedures rests not on the fact that they rely upon citizens' liberties and treat them with equal dignity but in that they extract from their collective deliberation a valuable outcome. It consists in a revision of classical deliberative theory of democracy.

Deliberation in Jürgen Habermas's classical rendering argues that discursive social relations among citizens have the merit of producing decisions that are better because they are less partial than those produced by instrumental bargaining or simply majority rule.[30] They are held to be better because of the moral goods they produce, such as reciprocity, autonomy, and the inclusion of all the citizens. Thus, for theorists of deliberative

93

democracy, the issue of deliberation is not so much "correctness" of decisions as the moral "grounding" of its acceptance. It is because of this moral foundation of democratic practices that Habermas concludes that majority rule as a domesticated struggle for power is an inferior type of decision. Habermas praises democratic proceduralism for the morally correct disposition of the participants it educates and thinks that this goal does not come by chance. Indeed, although in his view not the consequences but the procedures matter, the intention with which the participants enter the deliberative trial matters because only on this condition can the deliberative process work to educate their behavior (thus, for instance, entering the trial in order to advance some predefined interests or achieve some assumed goods is opposed to a deliberative mental disposition because it precludes an open and frank exchange of reasons pro and con). Habermas suggests that we owe respect to democratic procedures because the process they enact consists in "practical discourse." This makes it legitimate. Thus, he distinguishes between a "balance of power" political process and one that consists in "practical discourse." While the former allows persons to enter deliberation in order to negotiate and compromise or "strike a balance between conflicting particular interests," the latter allows them to strive for a common interest through deliberation. Only the latter is a morally legitimate collective behavior in democracy, not the former, which Habermas identifies with the classical as Schumpeterian interpretation of proceduralism.[31] Thus, although he criticizes justifying and judging democratic deliberation from the point of view of epistemic outcomes, Habermas does invite us to praise it from the point of view of an evaluation that is moral and not solely political. "Thus in normative discourse reaching a rational agreement is replaced by something like achieving a mutual harmonization of feelings."[32]

The theory of epistemic democracy brings this approach to procedures (i.e., reasoning from the point of view of what using them would produce, apart from regulating political behavior in a condition of liberty) to its extreme consequence and concludes that classical deliberative theory itself is not satisfying because it is still inattentive to what deliberation delivers.[33] It is more radical than Habermas or the deliberativists in twisting procedures toward a concern with the epistemics' goal of correctness and does not simply admit that this may be an outcome that mostly occurs because democracy enables the revision and correction of previously made decisions.[34] Deliberative theorists accept proceduralism's main argument that "correctability" or "amendability" is the central aspect of democracy, although they aim at a moral justification of the use of procedures as in Kant's tradition. Epistemic theorists do not. According to Estlund, treating citizens and electors equally, as a normative view of what democracy requires, is not enough, because this implies focusing on the conditions ("the merit of democratic decisions are held to be entirely in their past") rather than the outcomes, which are instead a better test to evaluate democratic procedures. These procedures should bring citizens to produce correct decisions: this is the main purpose that democracy should seek; they should be designed in a way that decisions are or tend to be correct according to external (to procedures and political process) or "independent standards."[35]

Other democratic theorists who are close to the epistemic perspective have also expressed dissatisfaction with a purely political interpretation of democratic procedures because, they argue, they are too easily permeable with strategic rationality and thus structurally incapable of indicating a univocal path toward decisions that are morally correct.[36] Their concern is that this rendering of democracy lacks "substantive political standards," in fact, "independent standards" that constrain political choices in a way that attention to the conditions, in Habermas's vein, cannot do. Grounding legitimation to obey on moral standards is not sufficient to take away arbitrariness in political authority, because it is "difficult to see what evaluative standpoint might be adopted from which to criticize the very possibility of authoritative moral requirements."[37] Now, epistemic theorists seem to believe that correct decisions are a better path to justify authority and moreover that democracy can adopt it because, contrary to the aristocratic argument, a crowd of ordinary people can make correct decisions. The epistemic conception of democracy thus makes two important claims: that the "crowd" has dignity[38] and that there is a difference between epistocracy's call for truth (authoritarian because elitist or not egalitarian) and epistemic democratic standards (which can be followed by all because of the epistemic equality all enjoy). Only the latter position warrants the independence of judgment of those who produce them (antioligarchy assumption). The model epistemics embrace to make their case is the jury one: "When it is properly done, a jury trial seems to produce a verdict with legal force, but also with some moral force."[39]

Epistemic theorists are instrumentalist, although of a different kind than Schumpeterians, because they think that procedures should be seen as a method not to select a political class but to devise right decisions. They assume that democratic theory should pay more attention to the quality of the decisions than to the extent to which procedures protect autonomy or equal political liberty. Hence, Estlund criticizes Habermas's "deep proceduralism—his version of the no-truth arguments."[40] Estlund moreover claims: "Proceduralism is not the problem, but the effort to rely on nothing but proceduralism is. Democratic authority and legitimacy could never be understood without relying to some extent on the idea of retrospective or pure procedural value in certain way," without, that is, the "tendency to produce decisions that are better or more just by standards that are independent of the actual temporal procedure that produced them."[41]

At the end, epistemic democracy wants what deliberative democracy does not: objective standards for the evaluation of social choices that are above political communication and its procedures. Its goal is to have a standard of truthfulness that promises decisions (made by a collective of equals) that are not solely procedurally correct or valid because of consent with the principles and rules of the constitution. Estlund judges purely political proceduralism as a form of "nihilism" and thinks "its content-indifferent formalism makes democracy neither admirable nor valuable enough for citizens."[42] As for legal validity, this is no sufficient condition for a legitimate authority either; what is necessary is that democratic procedures operate "with a tendency to make correct decisions."[43] Hence, they have to be judged not simply valid but "correct by independent standards."[44] A purely political interpretation of democratic procedures cannot do so, which means that, clearly, a process that promises to treat citizens equally, regardless of the content of the decision, does not promise enough.[45]

The epistemic doctrine is a radical attempt to depoliticize democracy by making it a chapter in the search for truth; it brings to theoretical perfection the several empirical and pragmatic proposals of constructing *fora* for collective deliberation in which participants led by "good procedures" to achieve "just decisions" or "right answers" are a practical example of an epistemic interpretation of democracy.[46] Indeed, these experiments embody the ideal of deliberation as a supplement to elected representative bodies, whose decisions can hardly rely upon a large consensus and thus overcome the sense of injustice.[47] *Doxa* is the problem for both empirical deliberationists and epistemic theorists.

To sum up, the transformation of political decision making into an epistemic process clashes with democracy quite dramatically, first because it questions the diarchic structure of representative government and democratic proceduralism, and second because it refutes the condition of autonomy or immanentism that pertains to democratic authority. The first project challenges democracy's very political character and promise: equal political liberty, which is satisfied by means of the direct or indirect participation of all citizens in the making and judging of laws they obey; the second challenges its substance.

As for the first project, democracy does not promise decisions that are more correct or truer than, for instance, those achieved by some technocrats, nor does it demand that all citizens are competent or that they achieve a degree of competence that would allow them to make correct decisions. The condition of equality democracy presumes is one of opportunity, not substance. We ask: "Is the distinction of competence destined to disappear as democracy evolves or, conversely, does competence contradict democracy, as it may seem when theorists want to distribute it equally?" These questions reveal a Platonist interpretation of politics and a democratic flaw because the equal distribution of competence is not by itself enough to make collective deliberation democratic. A crowd that is made of people that, given some data and procedures of deliberation, achieve a unanimous outcome is still not necessarily a democratic gathering, although it is egalitarian. As a matter of fact, it is unclear who judges on the necessary degree of needed competence and on the correctness of the decisions, if not citizens themselves.

The second project violates democracy's autonomy as it violates the principle of immanence upon which this political system relies. According to Estlund, democratic decisions are better than nondemocratic ones because they tend to produce more apt or better outcomes: he makes the epistemic quality of democratic procedures the source of their legitimacy. This instrumental view seems to suggest that legitimacy to obey the laws rests on a proved outcome, which is a paradox because *post factum* logic would entail that citizens should have the chance to test the outcomes of the laws before obeying them. Further, epistemic authority assesses procedures with an external criterion for evaluating their outcomes, and this contradicts the principle of democratic autonomy: besides, who in a democracy can define the correctness of decisions if not the very people who use or nominate somebody to use them? And if such a judge existed "independently" of the actors, would not he or she be the sovereign? As I argued in the previous chapter, democracy is an immanent process in that it does not contemplate an external reference point for evaluating its authority.[48] Thus, both *doxa* and changeability of decisions are inherent to it, which means that democratic legitimacy cannot depend on the promise that it will provide correct decisions.

Democracy does not need to advance toward some truth to be legitimate. And although good outcomes are what candidates promise, citizens expect, and procedures allow, it is not because of them that democratic authority is legitimate. Both in the case that we get good outcomes and in the case that we get disappointing results, procedures are legitimately democratic because they deliver what they are made for: to protect the freedom of its members to produce "wrong" decisions.[49] In this sense, democracy is clearly not perfectionist. I would say it is virtueless. This idea was brilliantly formulated by Albert O. Hirschman when he wrote that the only truly essential virtue of democracy is *love of uncertainty,* which is not naïve love but a habit of the mind supported by an open process of public-opinion formation (open to discussion and new information that questions consolidated beliefs).[50] Hirschman added also that the maxim *errare humanum est* should be read as saying not merely that we humans can make mistakes but moreover that only humans make mistakes.[51] Democratic procedures assist our endogenous need to change previously made minds and decisions, with no deadline for the attainting of the correct outcome and no final outcome to attain.

This means that the likelihood of making "wrong" decisions (as I shall explain below in analyzing political judgment, "wrong" refers to decisions that do not deliver either what we have been promised or what we thought useful and good for our political community) need not be considered a weakness of democracy. Democratic procedures combine two conditions: some kind of homogeneity—all persons should have some sort of equality in sharing political power—and diversity—each citizen is specific (diversity in interests, opinions, and values); they presume moreover that dissent (which diversity can engender) is good as an injection of vitality and reviewability into the democratic process, yet not necessarily a means to truer outcomes.[52] While truth tends to overcome dissent, democratic procedures presume dissent always. In this sense, democracy should not be judged by its capacity to produce correct outcomes but by its capacity to allow all views or ideas to compete openly and freely for attaining the decisions they judge important to achieve the promises that democracy makes.[53] As Aristotle pointed out, politics is identifiable with liberty because it is a realm of opinion. Democracy promises to be the better condition for attaining this because it promotes an equal distribution of political power.

But once it is made the terrain of truth, politics becomes inhospitable to contestation and liberty and also to peace, since there is a risk that political conflicts assume a violent and intractable nature. When the political arena is inhabited by conflicting interpretations of what a true idea means, compromise between them looks difficult to achieve, and logically impossible. Since the opposite of truth is error, it makes no sense to tolerate an error unless those who hold it see it as a temporary error to be overcome. An excellent justification of this attitude has been given by Cicero, who is a valuable reference point for assessing the distinction between forms of dialogue, and in particular the philosophical and the political.

Cicero dealt with disagreement in relation to disputes within philosophical schools and among philosophers and in relation to the orators in the forum. He argued that when agreement of the former kind was not possible, the individual participant in a *sermo* (philosophical debate) could freely decide to follow his own judgment, if his philosophical school did not offer him any secure guidance on how to solve the conflict among basic assumptions. "But let everyone defend his views, for judgment is free: I shall cling to my rule and without being tied to the laws of any single school of thought which I feel bound to obey, shall always search for the most probable solution in every problem."[54] But suspension of judgment was highly undesirable in political contentions, in fact, impossible because decisions could allow for procrastination at most, yet not suspension and most of the time not even delay. Moreover, the city had secure guidance for conflict resolutions in the laws, both constitutional and ordinary. In sum, suspension of judgment was possible only with philosophical debates. Cicero did not, of course, intend to say that philosophers should be free in all their opinions or tolerant of all beliefs, any more than a citizen or a judge. His theory of disagreement, and the distinction between truth and probability, relied upon a basic agreement on what human reasonability was; at any rate, suspension of philosophical judgment was for the sake of resolution of uncertainty and the achievement of truth. Cicero did not practice what contemporary epistemics call "nihilism." His philosophical school was the Academy, whose basic moderate skepticism was equally distant from Platonism on the one hand and from Pyrrhonism or absolute skepticism on the other. Probability instead of total suspension of judgment, and arguing *in utramque partem* instead of dogmatic assertiveness, were the basic rules of the Academy and civil eloquence.[55] A moderate skepticism was for Cicero the key to the continuation of *sermo*: "The philosophers of the Academy have been wise in withholding their consent from any proposition that has not been proved . . . nothing could be more unworthy of the dignity and integrity of a philosopher than to adopt a false opinion or to maintain as certain some theory which has not been fully explored and understood."[56]

The rules of *sermo* were thus necessarily different from those of rhetoric because the former were dictated by truth and the latter by prudence (*decorum* or *propriety*), which contended that the orator should accommodate himself to the character of the audience and avoid imposing a standard of certainty on materials that had to do with conviction and persuasion among free citizens. The reference point of the orator was the republic's good—the preservation of liberty and civil peace: the law and the rights were his secure guidance. Cicero's position is not different from the one suggested by John Rawls, who also argued that disagreement in the name of truth has a natural propensity to degenerate into violence, since the parties take it as a duty to resist others' wrongs and convince them of the truth. An old but still evocative example of failed agreement among participants who entered deliberation with the intention of convening on some determinate truth is that of the numerous religious councils that were held in the early decades after Luther's protest, which not only jeopardized the humanists' irenic goal but moreover radicalized religious disagreements and opened the door to the wars of religion. Dialogue proved to be out of place because the views that caused disagreement could not be made objects of consent.[57] When truth is the topic of politics, proselytism takes the place of persuasion and deliberation, and persecution the place of tolerance. This was the source of the wars of religion. Its nefarious logic does not disappear because we create a democracy but only if we take away from political discourse the quest for truth.

As a matter of fact, the theologians (Catholic and Protestant alike) who in the seventeenth century set up to resolve their dogmatic disagreements through dialogue ended disastrously because they resolved to adopt Cicero's rules of *sermo*, not those of rhetoric.[58] Their choice was predictable because they wanted to achieve not peace in liberty but the kind of harmony *(concordia)* that only truth allowed and that commanded the overcoming of important differences (thus, "errors") and the suspension of decisions until truth was restored.[59] The rules of *sermo* were the recipe for intolerance and war because they were incompatible with pluralism.[60] But for the continuation of dialogue and the preservation of peace, the strategy would have been that of minimalizing the doctrinal content of religion and, in this way, deflating the ethics of coherence and strengthening those of respect.[61] But this position could be embraced only if dialogue would be moved outside of the domain of truth (theology in that case) in the domain of politics or civic rhetoric. Truth entrusts competence as authority, thereby making opinion pluralism transitory and only instrumental to the outcome. Furthermore, appeals to truth in politics are divisive because they do not allow for accommodation.[62] Clearly, epistemic theorists make the court or forensic judgment (achieving the truth on some fact) their model of collective decision making, not the political assembly or the work of legislators. As I will argue at the end of this chapter, the epistemic and unpolitical ideal rests on equating judgment in jurisprudence with judgment in politics.

Another objection that can be raised to the epistemic conception is the following: When should we stop testing the "correctness" of a decision? Contrary to a court, which is expected to produce, and produces, a definite verdict, democracy is an open game of political decisions and revisions of previously made decisions. It does not consist in a process whose aim is to fill a vacuum of knowledge at some point in the future and thus stop deciding. Its procedures are not meant to produce ultimate decisions. Democratic decisions, as all political decisions, occur in the time dimension of the present, but in contrast with other decision-making processes, they do not promise a final solution to a given political problem. The acceptance of legal change is a recognition that democratic procedures are meant to regulate conflicts and disagreements that arise persistently.

As said above, theorists of epistemic democracy claim to rely upon Condorcet's jury theorem when they argue that democracy should be a procedure that tends to generate correct decisions. Yet, this theorem is the least apt to explain deliberation in political assemblies.[63] The "mistake" in applying it to the those assemblies should be ascribed to contemporary theorists of epistemic democracy rather than Condorcet, who, when he set out to devise the constitution of the French republic (1792–1793), dropped the jury theorem and foresaw the possibility both of dissent over the interpretation of the constitution and of constitutional amendment. He actually offered a relevant contribution to democratic constitutionalism when he interpreted the law-making activity in the representative assembly as a work of implementation and interpretation of the principles and rights contained in the constitution, a work that was endogenously open to diverse opinions and disagreement. Consequently, Condorcet selected disagreement as the perspective in relation to which the performance of the democratic decision-making process should be judged.[64] Thus, he asked how the democratic process could be made less prone to instability without resorting to nondemocratic strategies. Although suspicious of parties and factions, Condorcet conceded that the object of democracy is opinion, not truth. He thus thought that the political work of an elected assembly and of electors should be seen as a process of permanent emendation. As he said, "Today's legislators are simply men, who cannot give to other men equal to them anything but laws that are transient like they are."[65]

This point does not deny that there should be limitations to what the democratic procedure can decide upon on an ordinary basis. This is the function of constitutionalism—the main object of justice in Aristotle's terms, as we shall see below. Democracy can be prevented from having "incorrect" outcomes by constitutionalized politics. But the evaluation of the "correctness" of decisions rests on a criterion that is internal to the mechanism itself, and thus an opinion itself.[66] As Frank Michelman has argued, law-making procedures produce "laws that are valid," not laws that are true: a "regime of lawmaking needs not, in order to be right, result in perfectly just laws; rather, it need only use procedures capable of producing laws that are valid."[67] Interpretations of the constitution are not only possible but allowed because diversity of opinions is the condition that democratic liberty values and beforehand provokes. The majority and minority divide is the basic rule that governs the world of public discourse on political issues, both when the constitution is at stake (and decision is made by referendum)[68] and when everyday policies are. To claim that there is or ought to be one correct interpretation of the values of equality and liberty, independent of the circumstances in which those values are applied, is questionable from within a democratic perspective. As per Condorcet, constitutionalism is needed precisely because dissent, rather than consensus, is to be foreseen. However, the epistemic doctrine seems to hold that this is the case, thereby denying or excessively reducing the scope of politics in developing normative values.

Epistemic arguments in the definition of democratic legitimacy raise two additional problems that pertain to the meaning of the epistemic turn and the appeal to Aristotle's authority, respectively. The attempt to prove that democracy is good, or better disposed toward true decisions, because the collective is rational, was a strategy devised in the eighteenth century to counter the popular antidemocratic argument that democracy is a bad regime because it relies on the many, who are incompetent and irratio-nal.[69] Jean-Jacques Rousseau and Condorcet answered to this classical criti-cism by switching the locus of political legitimacy from content and outcome to procedures ordering the work of collective gatherings. Willing to contest the aristocratic argument that virtue and competence were the requirements of ruling, they had to prove that political equality was able to meet the criteria of knowledge and competence. It is hard to figure out what is today's terrain of contestation in relation to which epistemic theo-rists bring the issue of legitimacy back to competence. Why do we need to make democracy resemble an aristocracy, and why do we want to dress it with the garb of the best one or the best few?

The second problematic argument consists in defending epistemic de-mocracy by endorsing Aristotle's critique of Plato's epistocracy.[70] Indeed, although Aristotle purported democracy as a degeneration of constitu-tional government, when he had to evaluate the role of the many, he ac-knowledged their deliberative proficiency in the public assembly *(ekklesia)* and the jury in law-courts *(dikastes)*. But this is not a complete depiction of Aristotle's position toward democracy. It is inappropriate to say that Ar-istotle thought the many were competent in making good laws if we do not make the crucial distinction he made between laws and decrees. This is what the epistemic theorists who invoke the authority of Aristotle disre-gard. To him the many were good (and actually better than the few) in making *judgments on individual cases*, which is what the assembly and the jury did in his mind because they judged in conformity with already exis-tent laws (constitution) made by the legislator *(nomothéton)*. As a matter of fact the assembly did not make laws but decrees *(psephismata)* and the jury gave verdicts on specific cases (civil and criminal). But according to Aristotle, the many were not good at making "the laws" and in this sense they were not given the authority of the *nomothèton*. Virtue, a quality much more easily found in single individuals, was the principle and condition for good government and lawmaking.[71] This is the perspective we have to situate ourselves when we want to present Aristotle as friend of the multitudes. In his view, the many used consent (not virtue) as the strategy for decision making, so they could not make political decisions that met with independent standards—they could not transform *doxa* into *arête*. Yet the reason for having citizens set in the assembly was not that.

According to Aristotle, the participation of the many in the legislative function was essential to attaining liberty. Citizens protected their liberty through participation in two ways: first, their great number was an important obstacle against corruption (not even the richest citizen could buy a majority in the court or the assembly); and second, they were able to act together, which showed that, while each was individually weak, the inclusion of all, regardless of their individual qualities (and knowledge), made them strong and able to govern themselves. While the government of the few relied on exceptional individualities, the many had the virtue of making decisions in concert (cooperation more than knowledge was their skill)[72]—which is what in fact the wisdom of the crowd consisted of. Small gatherings risked instability because they were too small a number to contain the egotism of great personalities. But the power of the great few would deflate in a large crowd. At any rate, according to Aristotle, the many did *not* compete with the few on the matter of correctness or goodness or wisdom of decisions. They competed with them on the matter of liberty, by claiming they were able to rule themselves although they had no special personal quality, virtue, or honor; and on matters of cooperation, which was harder to attain by great personalities.[73] This was the goal and the argument that led the Athenians' democratic revolution. The many reclaimed their liberty, not correctness, when they claimed to be included in the law-making assembly. Democracy is a regime of liberty, not *episteme*.

In sum, democracy pertains to liberty, not truth. It is better than any other regime not because it produces good decisions but because it allows us to feel directly responsible for the decisions we make and do so by using the same procedures in order to make decisions that all of us obey. And we are autonomous under democracy not only because we obey the laws we make but also because we "set the agenda" concerning the problems that we consider important and want to decide upon. Democracy is not simply a method for solving problems (as according to the epistemic approach) but also for naming problems, or transforming a given in a problem to be publicly discussed.[74] Thus to theorize the value of democratic competence is "to confront with a seeming paradox. Democratic *legitimation* requires that the speech of all persons be treated with toleration and equality. Democratic *competence*, by contrast, requires that speech be subject to a disciplinary authority that distinguishes good ideas from bad ones."[75] Democratic society has many authorities operating in different domains—from markets to the courts—yet the supreme one remains "public opinion" which freedom of speech and association concurs in making educated and informed, with no certainty of success.

A final objection can be made to the theory of epistemic democracy: when we speak of political "decisions"—right or wrong, correct or mistaken—we should avoid considering all decisions as if they are identical in kind. Political decisions are, most of the time, decisions on issues that are very controversial, not only or mainly on problem-solving kinds of issues. They are issues whose outcome is a law that imposes an obligation to obey on all the citizens, not only on those who regard it as just or correct. A scientist who acknowledges her mistakes and embraces the outcomes of her colleagues capitulates before the truth: she acquiesces; she does not simply obey it. A jury that achieves a verdict produces a definitive and no-longer-revisable decision and a decision that has the same interpretation for all; liberty to revision would mean compromising the value of justice. Hence, even the appeal to "correctness" takes different meanings in a political assembly. "The difference between the jury and the electorate is that while the jury is faced with an issue which has one answer which is correct for all individuals, different decisions may be correct for different voters."[76]

As I shall explain in the following section of this chapter, neither the domain of scientific knowledge nor the domain of juridical justice can make sure that liberty is a principle all the way through because the search for truth is supposed to come to an end. This is not the case with politics: issues such as "What type of health-care system should we have?" are objects of decisions that are hardly definable as "correct" because they are hardly solvable with one true answer now and forever.[77] Obeying them does not require accepting them as correct; it does not entail capitulating before them or no longer revising them. As Hans Kelsen showed, obeying a law entails accepting the constitutional and legal order, and moreover the procedures that made it possible: this is what we obey when we obey a law we do not agree with.[78] It is obedience not merely of this or that decision, but of the entire institutional system. This is the site of democratic authority and the place in relation to which issues of political legitimacy emerge.

The Negative Power of Judgment

The idea of the expansion of the unpolitical in contemporary democracy has been described by Rosanvallon as a peculiarity of representative democracy or an uninterrupted dynamic of the *reactions* of civil society to the actions by the political institutions. Democratic politics acquires thus both a positive and a negative meaning. The *positive* sense refers to the formal and authorizing sovereignty of the will that springs from citizens' suffrage along with the authorized work of the institutions. The *negative* sense describes all those informal public activities that provoke *impediment, surveillance,* and *judgment:* forms of participation by means of which citizens check the work of democratic institutions and peacefully subvert the established order. According to Rosanvallon, these informal public activities are more central in democratic legitimacy than direct or traditional positive actions because what citizens need most today is checking that procedures are used correctly. Thus, domains that were originally seen as external to and even a containment of democratic decision making, like bureaucracy or justice, are on the contrary essential components of democratic legitimacy.

A quick observation needs to be made on the meaning of Rosanvallon's overall project of rethinking democracy from the perspective of the stabilizing function of nonpolitical departments of collective action, like justice and, above all, bureaucracy. To the latter, which has been traditionally regarded as antithetical to politics and democracy, Rosanvallon ascribes two crucial functions: bureaucracy as a force of integration and solidarity in a society that is highly individualistic, and bureaucracy as a force that brings impartiality in a democratic polity, in which decisions are based on majority rule and deeply marked by partisanship and partiality. It is certain that a major factor in this shift from negative to positive acceptance of bureaucracy has to do with a change in the way bureaucracy operates in contemporary advanced societies, and also with the growth of European integration. Rosanvallon's resuming of bureaucracy thus reflects a trend in European democratic thought; it is internal to the stabilizing role of the European Union, which was achieved first of all thanks to a capillary system of regulations able to impose uniformity standards on the diverse national systems of administration. But the endorsement of the bureaucratic mind as internal to democracy has theoretical implications that go beyond these contextual reasons. The older nineteenth-century conceptions of bureaucracy, which focused on strict hierarchy, centralized state control, and homogenizing treatment of people and issues, have given way to a diffusive practice of regulation in the local, regional, and municipal administrations. The European Union contributed in emancipating bureaucracy from stigma while changing its character and making it a basic resource for democracy in its local self-governing expression. The impact of this new attitude toward bureaucracy is revealing what Rosanvallon thinks is an expansion of the negative power of judgment at the expense of the positive one: citizens ask for checking and monitoring of decisions more than to participate in making them. They thus play the role of judges more than that of political actors.

Of the three forms of public activities associated with negative power—impediment, surveillance, and judgment—the last one is certainly the most modern and important.[79] The role of judgment in politics acquired momentum in the second half of the twentieth century, in coincidence with the consolidation of constitutional democracy, the technological revolution of the means of information and communication, and the expansion of civil society, domestic and global, with movements of contestation and denunciation.[80] Civil society acquires the physiognomy of a large tribunal or the forum in front of which political leaders and magistrates are required to appear in order to be checked in their behavior and pressed to make or avoid making certain decisions. In representative democracy, however, the actor of this negative politics is not the citizen-elector but the citizen-judge, who operates through an uninterrupted work of public scrutiny that may have great influence on institutions, although it is informal and not authoritative. According to Rosanvallon, judgment is the site of counterpolitics or counterdemocracy (that is, counter to the decisions made by democratic institutions); it is located in civil political society as a permanent work of evaluation of the *politique politisée*. Negative power is the expression of citizens' distrust when distrust is not merely the symptom of a sentiment of dissatisfaction (which is permanent in democratic society and never completely satiated) but an active force of counterpower.[81] Counter- or negative politics, according to Rosanvallon, may be unpolitical in its forms but is not in and by itself a reaction against politics. Indeed, the citizen-judge may give birth to a frontal opposition against the established political powers, but it is not antipolitical in its outcome.[82]

However, the unpolitical character that judgment puts in motion to check on and monitor institutionalized politics may encourage distaste for politics and even democracy. Moreover, it may mobilize actors that are invisible to the people in whose name opinion is proclaimed. As Rosanvallon observes, the Internet has revolutionized the very notion of opinion because it claims the immediate representation of the opinion of the public by the users of the web, who overcome all intermediation, structural and organizational. The web destroys dissimulation and arcana by placing all information at our disposal, but it resists arithmetic measurement and aggregation of any sort. Regardless of whether traditional mass media concentrates, the web decenters, or of whether the former leads viewers according to a centralized plan, the latter demolishes centralized planning.[83] The web serves the public better than it does democracy, which needs a central moment of decision or a legitimate actor, like the voters who vote at the same time and according to the same rules all over the country.

Rosanvallon is aware of the risk of depersonalization and fragmentation when he observes that while the *démocratie impolitique* is an expansion of citizens' indirect influence on institutions and the representatives through their censorial judgment, it may rouse a "decline of the political" just in the moment it unveils democratic politics' inherent association with partial interests and even corruption, as Mann had also argued.[84] This explains why in contemporary democracy citizens' surveillance and criticism are not made in the name of more participation or of their direct exercise of power. Citizens' negative power conveys a message of *power avoidance* rather than power reclaiming, also because judgment is the power of the spectator, not of the actor. As we shall explain below, unlike the political actor, the judge needs to be disengaged from and external to the fact in order to judge competently.[85] In Rosanvallon's mind, this is or should be the attitude of the citizens when they monitor and evaluate their representatives' decisions.

Unpolitical democracy is a detached form of participation, as that of independent viewers or evaluators. It is, as it were, a form of passive presence with the pretense of disinterestedness. Indeed, the goal of the citizen-judge is to make power more transparent and impartial, not more accessible or widespread. Its goal is to devise institutions and rules that can in the long run make political participation less needed. Paradoxically, apathy as the drying up of passionate involvement seems to be the final outcome of an effective negative power.[86] This inference raises the legitimate doubt that counterpolitics or unpolitical democracy can actually foster rejection of politics, either as distaste for ordinary politics or as a populist quest for an exemplary disruption of ordinary politics.

As said, Rosanvallon acknowledges these potential risks. Yet he does not seem to worry about the latent antipolitical implications of the expansion of the unpolitical. Actually, he regards citizens' negative power as an effective barrier against too-much politics (and, moreover, populism), the pathology of democracy, and a true denial of politics, against which Rosanvallon proposes his idea of a counterdemocracy or resistance to the decisions made by political organs like parliaments.[87] As I shall explain in the next chapter, populism is to representative democracy what demagoguery was to the direct democracy of antiquity. It may be described as the militant use of political partisanship for the sake of overcoming pluralism in partisan views and creating a unified opinion, that is to say, by making one partisan view representative of the whole people.

In Rosanvallon's rendering, the broadening of impartial judgment is meant to be an antidote to populism because partisanship, in contrast to impartial or independent reasoning, is the natural nourishment of populism. Accordingly, deliberative *fora* of discussion and issue-based committees by experts (practices of public judgment that pervade today's domestic and international arena) should be welcomed as sites of negative power in modern democracy. They are a check on partisan politics *and* potentially tyrannical majorities, and moreover activate the reserve of defiance (*réserve de défiance*) that naturally exists in democratic society. They make the public attentive rather than mobilized, suspicious rather than faithful to a leader or an ideology. They make citizens diffident toward politics and in search of dispassionate judgment and impartiality.

The worth of deliberation is actually proved *a contrario* by populism's misuse of judgment: when an *audience populist leader* declares himself to be the true representative of people's will beyond and outside the electoral mandate, he puts in motion the destructive power of judgment and calls into question not simply a bad or corrupt performance of state institutions but electoral politics itself, its advocacy character.[88] But contrary to the populist leader's ambition of representing the purity of the people's will independently of the electoral mandate, the citizen-judge wants to restore, not vilify, the moral legitimacy of representative institutions. Thus, negative power respects representative democracy's positive power. Hence, Rosanvallon's conclusion that since populism is a threat contained in the genes of democracy's partisan nature, it can be neutralized effectively only by relieving democracy of partisanship. Impartial judgment would thus play a hygienic function.

The problem is that the border that separates unpolitical and antipolitical expressions of popular mistrust is very thin, although for a reason that Rosanvallon does not contemplate. If we pay attention to the recent fortunes of populism (both in its traditional form and as videocracy) in Europe, we may see that populism has found fertile soil precisely in countries in which the distrust of parties and partisanship has been very strong. The crisis of political parties may be counted as one important factor in the raising of new forms of populism. Take, for instance, the case of Italy. In Italy, the Northern League and Mr. Silvio Berlusconi's movement—two populist parties—emerged in the 1990s, during a time in which traditional parties had declined because of both corruption and the end of the polarized ideologies of the Cold War. Decline in partisan identifications translated into a decline in citizens' participation (both electoral and associational) and the broadening of the distance between citizens and institutions.[89] It did not, however, bring a more reasonable public sphere. Nor did it bring more numerous independent voters or the rise of nonpartisan and more objective sources of information.[90] Instead, it opened the door to new political actors and movements that built their ascendancy on a public arena that was emptied of partisan attachments and branded in the language of nonpartisan politics and free and private media against traditional forms of political aggregations. As I will illustrate more diffusely in Chapter 4, videocratic populism succeeded by making the citizenry an unqualified and undefined audience, a public of individual consumers of political commercials, with no party affiliation and loyalty and no claim to participation either.

What, then, is the antidote to the risk of a displacement of politics that negative power may foster, particularly if this power takes the feature of a distrust and suspicion for partisan leanings? Rosanvallon agrees that the antidote is not to be found in the myth of self-regulated markets, as neoliberals prophesize. Its site cannot be the instrumental reason of the private individual but the impartial judgment of the citizen. Its site can be, as anticipated above, the bureaucratic system and the judiciary system, because both are domains in which dispassionate judgment and impartiality operate within the institutional order. The protection of democracy from the risk of populism comes from extending the domains of nonpolitical decisions. This seems to suggest that politics, rather than populism, is on trial. The reason for that, as we shall see in the next chapter, may be found in the implicit identification of democratic politics with populist politics or, more accurately, in the location of the insurgence of populism in the process of political participation. Certainly, procedures do not give sufficient guarantee against populism because they are based on majority rule and the winning goal that drives political competition of political opinions. Democratic participation, even when made according to procedures, is based on opinion, and opinions are fatally plagued of partiality, prejudices, and partisan biases.

Along with the extension of the bureaucracy, another strategy that scholars of democracy have welcomed as a correction of the bad possible outcomes of political assemblies has been the creation of minipopuli or deliberative arenas, experiments that are growing numerous in all democratic societies and which are intended to supplement decision-making institutions with the wisdom of the crowd and rational advice.[91] Rosanvallon praises these experiments in selective participation as repositories of judgment as the true reserve of impartiality and reflexivity, two qualities that can amend the democratic politics of partisanship. Let us analyze this important phenomenon more closely.

Since the second half of the twentieth century (with the Nuremberg trial as a symbolic turning point in legitimating the role of judgment), the place of judgment in politics has become gradually more esteemed and pervasive. Meanwhile, the citizen-judge that emerged in the nineteenth century as the generating force of public opinion has gradually become more specialized and sophisticated, thanks also to the technological revolution of the media. Along with the traditional forms of judgment (surveillance and control that citizens' diffuse political action engenders), judicial forms of censure and adversarial initiatives have increased their influence. Their purpose is not simply that of monitoring ordinary political decisions (as constitutional courts may) or promoting new or different decisions (as public opinion and social movements may) but rather that of reaching impartial opinions on issues that, if left to the democratic political arena, would be exposed to citizens' biases. "From here comes the growing

importance we must recognize to the development of new modes of intermediary structuring of actions of surveillance by means of militant yet *not
partisan* organizations."[92]

Bipartisan committees rather than political assemblies or parliaments
are the strategies of discussion and agreement capable of compelling participants to polish their partial views and reason dispassionately as only
judges in the court can do. Thus, the ideal site of impartiality is the domain of justice, not of the market, because the former is more consistent
with the monitoring character of negative power and the diarchy of will
and judgment that makes for representative democracy. Deliberative *fora*
and gatherings of sorted or selected citizens and appointed experts in ad
hoc committees for the sake of problem solving or the critical assessment
of controversial issues are the new terrain in which the negative power of
the citizen-judge shows its compelling counterdemocratic effects.[93]

These are important sources of information on what citizens think, and
important strategies for devising solutions to controversial problems in
specific areas that pertain to administration more than lawmaking. Or, if
they are to contribute in lawmaking, they do so by devising competent
suggestions to be sent to decision-making bodies. The authority of judgment is subjected to the authority of the will as I have argued in Chapter 1.
The idea of diarchy rests on this basic assumption, which is meant to
make these two faculties collaborate rather than replace one another's
role. The question we should ask is thus whether these deliberative *fora*
are a true "redemption" of democracy from its inborn risk of populist potentials. I would like to raise four doubts about the ability of these new experiments of independent public reasoning to fulfill the role Rosanvallon and
other deliberativist theorists assign to them. It seems that while they do
not cure democratic societies of the possibility of populism, they do contribute in devaluing the work of democratic institutions.

First, deliberative committees reflect the idea that representative bodies
are mainly partisan and hence irrational or incapable of judging the public
good; they question the main institutions of modern democracy: elections
and representation. The "civic capacity" in collective actions is facilitated
by "civic intermediaries" that are not political parties but associations, focus groups, and the like. The goal is to avoid "a pluralism of mobilized interests groups" that leads to "a tower of Babel marked by polarized debate,
impasse, domination."[94] Take for instance the case of new deliberative
creations like "deliberation day" and the growing practice of nonelected,

carefully designed venues into which citizens are selected for representative (of the general public's opinion) purposes, such as recent experiments with citizen juries and panels, advisory councils, stakeholder meetings, lay members of professional review boards, representations at public hearings, public submissions, citizen surveys, deliberative polling, deliberative forums, and focus groups. These are all examples of self-authorized representational forms that Gene Row and Lynn J. Frewer have named "citizens representatives."[95] As the ideal of deliberative assemblies of this kind stands, citizens representatives are intended as supplements to elected representative bodies or administrative bodies in areas of functional weakness or highly contested issues, areas in which a large consensus would be desirable to overcome the sense of injustice that a decision carried out by majority rule may create. Although these deliberative assemblies have no power to substitute for authoritative political institutions or elected representatives (they are meant to offer advice, not make decisions), their "competent" and "impartial" outlook gives their opinion a moral authority that sometimes exceeds that of authoritative political bodies (the only ones that enjoy democratic legitimacy). In these cases, democratic legitimacy is felt as faulty because it is unable to deliver decisions that are truly above "the will of all," to paraphrase Rousseau, the theorist who is the hidden inspiration of today's critics of democracy from within.

A second critical reflection pertains to the fact that these committees are a challenge to the diarchic character of democratic sovereignty in another important way. Indeed, in the mind of their proponents, the results of these informal bodies of deliberation are not meant to be simply counterfactual but also a kind of statistically representative snapshot of the existing but latent preferences of citizens—something that power-holders seeking to represent "the people" need to know. This is the reason why governments increasingly constitute citizen juries and panels whose charge is to represent the views of citizens more generally on a given issue.[96] However, should these forms grow, they would bring new challenges to democracy because any randomly selected deliberative body will inevitably generate opinions that are different than public opinion and moreover than the opinion that elections register. Who is going to resolve the disagreement between positive power (elected law-making assemblies) and negative power (informal gatherings of citizens' representatives)? Is it not possible that this disagreement will have the unintended consequence of strengthening the power of administration and the bureaucracy?

Thirdly, these deliberative committees may encourage elitism, imper-sonating citizens' engagement while actually encouraging passivity. As Bruce Ackerman has noticed, randomly selected bodies may become tools that elites can use to legitimate their policies while bypassing elec-toral accountability, or substituting for broader citizen judgment and participation.[97] Moreover, if we judge these new forms of citizens' delib-erative *fora* from the perspective of democratic participation, we cannot neglect the fact that this surplus of representative participation mobilizes few citizens while making the many (in the name of whom the selected few are asked to express their deliberative opinion) even more passive. Jane Mansbridge has convincingly observed that since participants volun-teer, those who have most intense interest in participation or a louder voice often dominate.[98]

Connecting nonelected bodies to broader publics in the absence of an electoral mechanism would be in itself a challenge to democracy because participation would be from the start and by principle kept disassociated from decision. Democratic procedures, as we saw, settle avenues of behav-ior that regulate participation (both in forming and in making decisions) by projecting them to win a majority. But unpolitical democracy may very well entail relocating public action outside the places in which political decisions are to be made according to democratic procedures. It may in-stigate ordinary citizens to think their function is only one of monitoring and judging. It may thus prefigure a transformation of the meaning of politics according to goals and criteria that recall the nineteenth-century utopia of the rational power of the experts with the support of the ordi-nary many. It may finally suggest that politics is a cognitive practice for reaching true outcomes, solving problems, and moreover eradicating "politically-relevant reasonable disagreement."[99] Committees of experts or councils of wise and virtuous citizens, who are asked to advise rather than make decisions, are most of the time the means public administra-tors (elected officials in search perhaps of reelection) use for not simply getting advice but also conquering more popular support, taming popular dissatisfaction, and co-opting pressure groups most representative of im-portant interests; in a word, increasing their credibility and trust through citizens' "engagement."[100]

The fourth critical observation pertains to the lack of democratic legiti-macy of these new practices of selected participation, and points to a way in which they may contract democracy rather than enrich it.[101] Indeed, in the deliberative *fora* the formation of the agenda and the frame of the questions to be discussed by the selected citizens are not part of the political process. They are instead kept outside the forum as the task of the mediators and organizers of these deliberative experiments. In clear violation of the democratic principle of autonomy, both the issues to be discussed without prejudice and the procedures regulating the discussion are not decided and chosen by the participants. Deliberative *fora* are made up of *tutored citizens:* spectator-judges who apply rules and procedures that others have devised and come to judge on facts they did not contribute in choosing. Selecting problems, framing agendas, organizing discussion, sorting out the audience, and leading deliberation: all these decisions can be made without involving partisanship on condition they are not made by those who are supposed to judge or deliberate. If objectivity and impartial judgment are the content and goal of politics, citizens' participation may become irrelevant and actually undesirable, because, after all, a few competent or virtuous participants can perform better deliberative service than many ordinary citizens.

This is an old issue and in fact reflects the main objection against democracy as the realm of opinions and decisions of the majority, since at least the classical essay by the Old-Oligarch and Plato's dialogues. Its renaissance in modern democracy, while democratic institutions seem to enjoy an unmatched success, should worry us, but not come as a surprise, because deliberation has traditionally been the task of the competent few and a method for cooling passions and containing the democratic element.

In the rhetorical tradition to which it belonged, deliberation was prized as an activity proper to a *politeia* or *res publica* that belonged to the *genus demonstrativum* because it did not simply imply making decisions but also affecting the interlocutors' minds so that they could express their final say and decide together (although not necessarily agree). Both qualities (making decisions and affecting the interlocutors' minds) are directly correlated and entail that the exposure of interlocutors to other arguments is decisive if consent is to be sought through discourse. However, there is no necessary correlation between deliberation and publicity and deliberation and political equality.

In early modern states and principalities, for instance, the prince and his ambassadors deliberated about how best to wage a war or pursue a diplomatic mission, but they were careful to avoid publicity. Moreover, until the revolutions of the eighteenth century, deliberation was associated with a frank discussion among equals in wisdom, or the few, and with circumspection or discretion. Even in our democratic age, deliberation retains an ambiguous relationship with participation and publicity. In order for "democracy to remain deliberative," Pettit has written, electoral interests (that is to say, "personal, aspirational ideals") must be taken off the table. Otherwise, the advantage of the large number will necessarily become the norm of decision making, which is not necessarily good.[102]

All in all, the risk of the unpolitical as dispassionate judgment is that it can suggest the desirability of bypassing the legitimate authority of citizens' suffrage and the parliament (two essential components of modern democracy), or replace active or actuating politics with a negative politics of judgment. This is, as we shall see below, also the message of political theorists who criticize from within democratic decision-making institutions. Clearly, the political sites of decision produce partial opinions; as with any decision taken by a majority, it is somehow the expression of opinionated views. The solution that the critics of democracy from within advance is thus narrowing the role of democratic institutions (citizens' suffrage and parliaments) or, more precisely, making sure they are not the privileged sites of decisions. "Electoral interests," Pettit writes, "raise problems so far as they ensure that rather than letting the common good crystallize and rule, as deliberative democracy would require, they invest power in other sources of influence: popular passion, aspirational morality and sectional interests."[103]

The Republic of Reason

Contemporary theorists' longing for the unpolitical is rooted in interpretations of democracy that are essentially skeptical of the latter's capability of promoting just or reasonable policies and thus protecting individual liberty from the will of the majority. One interpretation, for instance, is the electoral theory of democracy, which sees collective practices of decision making, especially electoral behavior, as methods characterized by an endemic paucity of rationality. Another interpretation is the deliberative theory of democracy, which integrates and somehow amends the minimalist definition of procedural democracy by making discursive justification the central task of participation.[104] Different as they are, these two interpretations converge in acknowledging an intrinsic lack of dispassionate evaluation in the democratic game of competing opinions for the sake of electoral victory or majority decision. Not by chance, Pettit brings these two interpretations together when he wants to prove "how electoral interests can jeopardize the ideal of deliberative democracy."[105]

Both interpretations refer to democratic decision-making processes in the same way democracy's critics have always referred to it since Greek antiquity. They stress majority rule, a characteristic that is after all pejorative, and try to elaborate strategies that can emend, narrow in scope, or complement it. "In modernity, democracy is often constructed as being concerned, in the first instance, with a voting rule for determining the will of the majority. . . . This reductive definition leaves democracy vulnerable to well-known social choice dilemmas, including Downs' rational ignorance and Arrow's impossibility theorem: if democracy as a political system is reducible to a decision mechanism based on voting rule, and if that voting rule is inherently flawed as a decision mechanism, then (as critics have long claimed) democracy is inherently flawed as a political system."[106]

This seems to be Pettit's approach to democracy. Pettit's project is the offspring of a low-profile conception of democracy that is familiar to students of public choice. "Electoral democracy may mean that government cannot be wholly indifferent to popular perceptions about common interests . . . but it is quite consistent with electoral democracy that government should only track the perceived interests of a majority."[107] But Pettit's view of democracy is also, and much more interestingly, the descendant of the republican tradition, whose relationship to the government of the many has been traditionally very ambivalent to say the least.

There is no need to go back to Cicero or Polybius to detect the antidemocratic spirit of republicanism (Athens "was always linked, in Polybius' metaphor, to a ship without a captain, buffered by the winds of public opinion"[108]). Rome and Athens represented, and continue to represent, two different models of politics and society. Rome, as John Dunn has recently written, gave us a large portion of our political vocabulary, from citizenship and constitution to republic and federation, but it did not give us "the word democracy. . . . Not only is democracy not a classical Latin word. It is not a Roman way of thought. It does not express how the Romans (any of them as far as we know) envisaged politics."[109] The renaissance of the Roman tradition in early Renaissance, and then in the eighteenth century, has reaffirmed and perfected the republican disbelief in democracy.[110] As

Pettit observes, despite "later reconstruals of the tradition [of republican liberty] as Athenian in origin and as committed to one-eyed enthusiasm about democracy and participation, the tradition was essentially neo-Roman in character."[111] The renaissance of Rome is detectable also in contemporary political theory, as the critiques of procedural democracy I discuss in this book testify in quite a striking way.

Neo-Roman republican tradition, which assesses itself as rooted within the Roman tradition as Ciceronian, means first of all the rule of law as a corrective of the popular will; it means that politics is conceived in the negative, as checks and balances, rather than in the positive, as participation in the law-making process. Citizens, he writes in his recent *On the People's Terms*, should be "invigilators of government," thus ready to challenge, judge, and control, not to "serve in the production of public decisions."[112] In fact, Pettit quite rightly adds, republican "enthusiasm" for liberty coincides almost invariably with "distaste for the pure democracy represented in many minds by classical Athens."[113] Those who love liberty as both noninterference and non-domination (that is to say, liberals and republicans) cannot trust democracy because democracy is a political order fatally stuck between the proverbial rock of an oligarchic solution (representative system) and the hard place of plebiscitarianism (direct expression of people's will by referenda but also election).[114] Democratic institutions are fueled by the "politics of passion." Pettit sees one important remedy for narrowing this defect: containing politics altogether while expanding deliberative *fora* and committees of experts, and moreover instituting adversarial practices of judicial contestation—solutions that are not democratic in character because they do not give priority to lawmaking or, in other words, are not legicentrist. As Richard Bellamy has recently observed, Pettit offers a republican argument "for the substantive view of legal constitutionalism" as a counterbalance to political (as democratic) constitutionalism.[115] "Good law," not simply legitimate law, is the ideal of freedom as nondomination; responsiveness to the public and citizens' consent are not criteria of good law and do not make citizens secure in their liberty, not even if people's consent is channeled through democratic procedures.[116]

As I mentioned above, deliberative *fora* and committees of experts are meant to rectify democracy by reducing the function of parliaments to a final yes-no vote. When sensitive issues like crime, prostitution, drugs, and the like are under discussion, the politics of passion must be restrained, Pettit admonishes. This can be done by making parliament "appoint commissions" of "relevant bodies of expertise and opinion, as well as of people as a whole, to oversee criminal sentencing," so as to take away from politicians and political parties topics that can easily be used to exploit popular prejudices and manipulate "aspirational morality." Parliaments must retain the ultimate control, but their final voting power should be on proposals that political representatives have not themselves discussed.[117]

Pettit advances here two important strategies of democracy containment. The first one consists in divorcing deliberation and decision or narrowing the function of parliament to a yes-no vote, while the second consists in making forensic justice the main protective safeguard of individual liberty. As we will see, in both cases the participatory aspect of democracy is held responsible for the vice of majoritarianism and populistic tendencies. As with Rosanvallon, in Pettit's redefinition of democracy, the negative power of judgment is pivotal. However, it is a kind of judgment that belongs in the courts and tribunals rather than in political assemblies.

The first proposal Pettit advanced is in perfect agreement with the republican tradition to which it belongs. Indeed, it echoes the prescription of silence that Francesco Guicciardini, James Harrington, and Rousseau imposed on popular assemblies, which they thought should neither initiate law proposals nor discuss the proposals coming from the council or the Senate in order not to give voice to popular passions.[118] Divorcing deliberation from decision is Pettit's first important strategy of depoliticization. It suggests that making parliaments into simply voting bodies would have the effect of cleaning democratic institutions of their natural flaw, which springs from the fact that they are representative of the people, and thus also of their passions and incompetence. It is thus the public forum that is the source of the danger because it exalts what is most problematic of democracy, namely, the cacophonic and partisan world of opinions. How can we not recall Rousseau's famous argument that giving voice to an assembly of people would fatally entail setting the stage for rhetoricians, with the consequence of making reason (and the general will) mute and powerless? Pettit's republic of reason belongs to the tradition of political rationalism and the devaluation of a humanist politics. Although he deems Machiavelli a pillar of the neo-Roman tradition, Pettit's depoliticized democracy goes against both the role of rhetoric in politics and against Machiavelli's defense of the deliberative ability of the *multitudine*, "which all writers attack," to hold "well-ordered" public discussions before voting. Machiavelli praised Rome for allowing "a tribune or any other citizen" to "propose to the people a law, in regard to which every citizen was entitled to speak either in favor of it or against" so that "everyone should be at liberty to express his opinion on it, so that when the people have heard what each has to say may choose the best plan."[119]

The inspiration for Pettit's proposal of separating deliberation or discussion from voting seems to be Harrington rather than Machiavelli. Harrington thought that Sparta was a better and more secure republic than Athens because the Spartan Senate had the power of deliberating and the assembly only of resolving. "Pure democracy" was Harrington's name for a commonwealth that did not separate debating and resolving. Rousseau, who retained enough aristocratic spirit (his admiration for the Roman republic was essentially an admiration for the Senate) to question the deliberative capability of "a blind multitude," expressed a similar view, as we saw.[120]

The dualism between the republic of reason and the republic of passions traverses the republican tradition, ancient and modern. This may be rendered as a dualism between the republic and democracy, between a well-ordered system based on virtue and competence and a political order that seems to be structurally unable to protect the commonwealth from both partisan interests and great "storms" and anarchy.[121]

Pettit's second important depoliticization strategy consists in proposing a broad application of contestatory practices. These practices are like legal avenues through which citizens can monitor and challenge the outcomes of decision-making bodies through strategies that are purely procedural and nonpartisan, similar in kind to those that instantiate expertise decisions and judicial verdicts. Pettit applies the forensic form of reasoning and practice to political issues and reaches a conclusion that is consistently unpolitical. "In the legal case it is taken to be important, not just that judges be consistent, but that their judgments on the doctrinally prior issues dictate in consistency how they vote on the matter to be adjudicated."[122]

Collective inconsistency is a defect that democracy produces but cannot amend by itself. Indeed "contestability," Pettit argues, is not a democratic strategy but a strategy that the moderns have inherited from the republican tradition of constitutional discussions whose aim was that of rendering government's interference nonarbitrary.[123] Within Pettit's reading, liberty as nondomination does not belong to democracy, nor does the counterpolitics it promotes. Indeed, "to have more informal and more routinized procedures" of hearing and contestation is not for the sake of more participation or "heroic debates" because their purpose is precisely that of depoliticizing the public arena. Contestatory democracy entails that "complaints" by ordinary citizens "should be heard away from the tumult of popular discussion and away, even, from the theater of parliamentary debate."[124]

The issue of whether the negative power of the people is a chapter in the history of republicanism or of democracy would be an interesting topic to discuss but is not what I can or want to do here.[125] It is sufficient to observe that in relation to democracy, contemporary neo-Roman republicanism plays the same role as liberalism after World War II. Whereas liberalism in the tradition of Isaiah Berlin accused democracy (positive liberty) of violating liberty as noninterference, republicanism in the neo-Roman tradition (negative political liberty) criticizes it for not being able to make liberty as nondomination secure.[126] "Quentin Skinner and other historians have shown that the long republican tradition did not embrace the positive concept of liberty, despite what Berlin and [Benjamin] Constant may have suggested. In particular, they did not embrace a concept of liberty under which being free is just being part of a self-determining democracy; they did not embrace the liberty of the ancients, as Constant described it."[127]

The charge against democracy as a positive liberty regime (thus exposed to the potential for tyrannical majorities) extends equally to direct democracy and representative democracy. Pettit excludes the possibility that referendum can be a safe practice of control against decisions made by elected bodies because plebiscitarian and direct democracy are regimes under which "the most capricious of powers remains morally as well as legally uncontestable." But he does not think that representative democracy can be cured of its endogenous defect either, because while elections do away with the extemporaneous passions of the demos, they subject politics to fictitious opinions for the sake of electoral victory and turn the entire society into a battleground of ideological partisanship. The question is whether according to Pettit representation and elections are the forms of politics most consistent with the "ethos of democracy," which gives "people's voice a certain morally social status."[128] As for representative democracy, although elections are a valid stratagem to neutralize people's incompetence and irrationality, as Montesquieu argued early on, they fatally expose politics to manipulation and rhetoric. Much like direct popular assemblies, parliaments are unavoidably led by a majoritarian logic, poisoned by partisan passions and political parties.[129]

It is the "republic of reason," not "the people's voice," that is closer to competent deliberative and contestatory models of politics. In these models, liberty from domination is deemed more secure because the power of interference is stripped of its arbitrary potentials that both the collective principle of sovereignty (democracy's "people" is "with the article" and refers to a collective) and majority rule unavoidably entail.[130] Hence, while he acknowledges that promoting contestation is crucial in order to narrow the domain and power of elected bodies, Pettit cautions that contestation is not a democratic device and in fact can be better organized if it is held by individuals before a court rather than by spontaneous groups of citizens in society. "I am prepared to concede that where members are very small, as in the judicial case, contestability can be achieved in significant measure at the individual level."[131] Whereas democracy's legitimacy principle is consent, republicanism's is "non-arbitrariness of interference," from which the idea of contestability comes. "The non-arbitrariness of public decisions comes of their meeting, not the condition of having originated or emerged according to some consensual process, but the condition of being such that if they conflict with the perceived interests and ideas of the citizens, then the citizens can effectively contest them."[132] Judicial action is the model of the republic of reason, not parliamentary or assembly action. Judicial action is characterized by an unpolitical kind of impartiality and is a check on a specific behavior that translates into a specific decision. It is an action that operates case by case, and is not collective like democratic forms of political intervention by citizens (as both electors and representatives).

Juristic Judgment and Political Judgment

I must at this point return to the role of negative power or the power of judgment in democracy. As I said in Chapter 1, judgment is the other leg of democracy's diarchy, that which makes the decision-making power of the people active beyond the decision that has been made, although active as an informal power that checks, criticizes, controls, and develops new proposals and the like. Yet what kind of judgment should we refer to when we make this argument? The ideal of deliberation in contemporary democratic theory is more or less directly associated with a view of citizens as actors, who in their authoritative political activity (voting) should "express their impartial judgments of what conduces to the general interest of all citizens" in a like manner as judges and juries.[133] Deliberation prefigures not only a quest for objective and dispassionate truth (the committees of experts model) but also, and above all, a quest of impartial judgment on certain given issues (the court decisions or jury model). Yet judgment in the courtroom is not the same as political judgment or judgment in parliamentary debates, in political campaigns, and even in the mind of the citizens when they go to the polls. Political judgment has generality (the general interest of the political community at large) as its criterion. Judgment in justice aims instead at impartiality in evaluating a certain fact or a set of data or deeds.

One crucial difference between these two forms of judgment is that the jury in the courtroom is not involved in the case under consideration in the way electors or representatives are *(nemo judex in causa sua)*. But the actors who advocate their cause in casting a ballot or voting in a representative assembly are the same ones who pass judgment, and the political setting they belong to does not institutionalize or command impartiality like the court. Jury and the courts (models of the unpolitical) are asked to pass judgment as external to the case, and their members are legally compelled to reason and act qua institutions, not political actors (individual-citizens or representatives). The former wear the mask of the state (or the law) and must set aside their personal values and preferences. The latter wear the mask of the sovereign (the public) and are expected to be able to see their personal case through the lenses of the general interest in order to make laws that are not a direct expression of their private will or preference, yet not wholly opposite or indifferent to them either.[134]

One may say that in judicial judgment domains, impartiality is a factor of ignorance (as freedom from *opinionated knowledge*) and of emotional independence from the case under judgment. The more the judge's mind is empty of personal and partisan (i.e. non-legal) opinions, the more the judge is in the right condition to impartially evaluate the case under judgment, as the law asks him to do (people who serve in a popular jury are instructed not to read newspapers or get information on the case under consideration from sources external to those that justice procedures provide).[135] But political deliberation suggests the opposite. It presumes and actually requires that citizens and representatives are exposed to all different opinions, that they actually contribute to forming a great variety of opinions, and, moreover, that they listen to all views that a free public sphere produces before they make up their minds and decide. Impartiality wants not merely what a reasoned and good political deliberation requires.

In John Locke's formulation, judicial power is a true third power—it is impartial in the sense that it is independent from the judgment of the actors. This means that it must not be politically representative in order to be consistent with the idea of public reason as it is expressed impartially in the law. The judgment formulated by the judge is supposed to represent not the sovereign's political opinions but only the authoritative voice of the law. Hence, it is and must be unpolitical; it is truly a negative power because the judge depends on the will of the sovereign (the law), but should not depend on the opinions of the sovereign: as per Aristotle, opinions should not be allowed in the court.[136] On the fact that the judge depends on and obeys only the law but does not depend on the same source of the law as the lawmakers do (the opinion of the public), Montesquieu rested his case for justice as a third power and the condition for limited power. Moreover, he argued for the juridical power as truly negative and protective of individual liberty, precisely because it was disengaged from "the individual opinion of a judge" as well as of the executive and legislative powers.[137] Unpolitical judgment means disengaged judgment, not judgment as a general or medium assessment among different views.

Since independence and constraint on getting information do not belong in political deliberation as they belong in the court, what kind of checks can political judgment tolerate in order to make decisions that reflect the general interest? The answer to this question casts light on the role of constitutional checks on the legislative assembly: they are intended not to make lawmakers act impartially but to act legitimately and responsibly. As we saw in the section of this chapter devoted to epistemic arguments, law-making procedures are intended to produce laws that are valid, not laws that are true. Rawls himself acknowledged this difference when he specified that it is essential to liberty that citizens and their representatives, unlike public officers, have only a moral, not a legal, duty to reason impartially: "I emphasize that it is not a legal duty, for in that case it would be incompatible with freedom of speech."[138]

Thus, law-making procedures aspire to a kind of impartiality that can never correspond to either the transparency of pure reason or disembodied judgment, two qualities that the theorists we discussed in this chapter attribute to unpolitical modes of reasoning as peculiar to courtlike checking bodies and committees of experts or deliberative advisory bodies. In fact, to attach to it the adjective of impartiality is inadequate because this is not the goal at which political decisions aim. In political settings, constraint on opinions appeals at most to the representative's and citizen's conscience, constitutional ethos, principles of morals, or even prudential reasoning (party loyalty or political calculus, for instance, the desire of a representative to be reelected.) It appeals to the ethical culture of participation and the educational potential that practicing democratic politics may have on citizens' minds. Tocqueville's dictum that democracy gets amended by more democracy exemplifies the pragmatic and process-oriented character of democratic politics.

It is not news to say that, although procedures can head off conflicts and social disorder, their efficacy is largely dependent on ethical factors. This is true particularly in the case of representation, because the mandate linking the representatives to their constituencies is essentially voluntary and politically constructed, but it is not and cannot be legally binding. This makes representation a political praxis that "is not merely the making of arbitrary choices, nor merely the result of bargaining between separate, private wants."[139] Instrumental reasoning and compromise occur in the context of a common understanding about the political direction the country should or should not take, with the awareness that it is "not a reality that is objectively given to us in one way or another."[140] Political judgment gets shaped within this pragmatic context, not outside or against it.

This brings us to the core issue of the specificity of political judgment. Political judgment aims at the general more than the impartial.[141] Broadly conceived, it is impartial in a way that the judgment performed by the judge is not—although the goal of both forms of judgment is that they be consistent with the ideal of public reason. Yet the style in which the public reason speaks takes shape according to the institutional frame and task within which it operates. Certainly, no representative would dare to declare in public that his proposal supports or fosters some partial interests against the community's.[142] The presumption of generality is essential to the moral legitimacy of political decisions, although contrary to justice procedures no legal enforcement can be tolerated if political deliberation is to occur freely. Moreover, the presumption of generality belongs to a society in which political power is equally distributed and the political society is seen as superior to the partial societies (interests and groups) it comprises.[143]

Political judgment cannot do away with opinionated views; it actually makes sense because it is based on them. As we saw in the previous chapter, it cannot be framed independently of the opinions citizens develop in social life. It cannot exist without ideal (ideological) perspectives or situated views (views that are more or less distant from the ideal of the general or public reason), like any form of advocacy speech that pleads a cause in the name of democracy's "promises."[144] However, political judgment produces arguments that appeal to justice, and it does so in two senses: because it refers to criteria of public interaction that all citizens presume and accept (decision-making procedures and the basic rights and principles contained in the constitutional pact), and because it refers or appeals to moral principles and ethical arguments (like rights or equal consideration or liberty) that citizens recognize as part of their legal, political, and also private language.[145] A democratic constitution is both a written document and an ethical document that lives in and throughout the ordinary life of the citizens as a guide to their public interaction and political judgment. The ideal of the general interest is a goal that political actors promise to pursue, and they try to convince their electors that the strategy they propose is the best. Democratic elections require citizens to play a part, both when they have to judge proposals and candidates and when they themselves are candidates. The part they play is arranged according to procedures and institutions that constitute democracy. Acting according to them is the only truthful action citizens are expected to perform.[146] This is what makes the system work and keeps it open to an endless game of interpretation and mind changing in the effort to fulfill the promises sealing the democratic pact.

Conclusion

It may sound disturbing to conclude that partisan views are an essential component in political judgments that try to be consistent with or pursue the ideal of the general interest, rather than be an unfortunate accident that good deliberation should wash out. In what sense can partisan views contribute to making general interests? When theorists identify the work of the assembly with that of the jury, they overlook the important fact that while the trial's setting presumes that the final sentence is definitive, the deliberative setting is organized so as to produce decisions that can always be changed and revoked. Nothing is definitive in a political deliberation scenario whose presumption of legal changeability is its constitutive structure.[147] The permanent openness that any decision has in a free political community is the democratic answer to democracy's critics from within, who propose narrowing the domain of politics in order to make good and true decisions. Openness to revision, rather than the interruption or containment of democratic practices, is the democratic answer to unsatisfactory democratic decisions. This is the maxim coming from a procedural conception of democracy that is normative.

In concluding this critical analysis of the renaissance of the unpolitical in democratic theory, it may be useful to recall Aristotle's argument in *The Art of Rhetoric* on the difference between political deliberation and forensic decision. The former presumes that citizens holding different (and sometimes conflicting) views on public issues seek what is convenient or just for the whole community and argue for or against by referring to cases and bringing "evidence" that all citizens can understand and check, although they interpret them differently because their interests and opinions are different.[148] It is not by taking controversial issues and interpretations out of political debate and making them the issue of committees of experts or selected citizens that deliberation may serve the cause of democracy. The cause of democracy is served rather by keeping the processes of judgment and will formation open to scrutiny and revision and the political arena open to competing political visions and political groups.

3

The Populist Power

Whereas theorists of epistemic democracy give the "crowd" the virtue of wisdom, theorists of populism give it a mobilizing virtue. The former feature the citizen as a member of a jury who listens to the voice of reason, not opinion. The latter instead feature the citizen as a member of a "we" whose unity some leaders concoct as a hegemonic opinion that claims it speaks for the will of the whole. While in the former case the political process is deemed representative of the public insofar as it is disembodied from social interests or ideologies, in the latter the social and ideological unity of the people occupies politics' central stage and becomes the norm of true representation. Yet despite these crucial differences, both epistemics and populists criticize parliamentary democracy for making politics a terrain of bargaining among a plurality of interests and parties. They both question the diarchic structure of representative democracy, although for different purposes: the former because they aim at replacing *doxa* with knowledge and as a consequence give priority to deliberation of nonelected bodies; the latter because they make the opinion of one part of the people merge with the will of the state, and as a consequence are impatient with party divisions in elected bodies. Finally, both of them judge the legitimacy of democratic authority from a reference point that is external to the political process, like "truth" or a preprocedural "people." In the end, despite their differences, epistemics and populists deform the diarchic structure of representative democracy.

Populism is the name of a complex phenomenon. It is a certain political style or set of rhetorical tropes and figures, but it also seeks state power to implement an agenda whose main and recognizable character is hostility against liberalism and the principles of constitutional democracy, from minority rights, division of powers, and pluriparty system. Populism is a radical contestation of parliamentary politics and thus an alternative to representative democracy, as I have defined it in Chapter 1. Although "we simply do not have anything like a *theory* of populism,"[1] in this chapter I adopt the following generalization: a populist movement that succeeds in leading the government of a democratic society tends to move toward institutional forms and a political reorganization of the state that change, and even shatter, constitutional democracy. These forms and reorganization include centralization of power, weakening of checks and balances, strengthening of the executive, disregard of political oppositions, and transformation of election in a plebiscite of the leader. In this chapter I will try to detect and analyze these characteristics and present populism as a disfigurement of democracy. But before proceeding, some preliminary clarifications are needed that pertain to the current usage of the word "populism."

Social Movements and Populism

I do *not* treat populism as the same as "popular movements," movements of protest, or "the popular." Populism is something else and different, and the characteristics I am going to analyze are meant to show why this is so. As a preview of the distinction between popular movement and populism, it may be helpful to consider the two most recent movements in American politics, Occupy Wall Street and the Tea Party. The Occupy Wall Street slogan "We are the 99%" fits inside the formal sketch of populist discourse as polarization between the many and the few and contestation of representative institutions (two important components of populism). Yet it does not fit with the populist view of democracy I intend to criticize because it is headless and not organized so as to conquer political power at the governmental level. I do realize that empirical political phenomena operate on a shaky terrain and resist generalizations; it is also possible that there is fluidity between popular movement and populism so that clear-cut distinctions may be problematic and in need of a case-by-case analysis. However, without the presence of a leader or a centralized leadership that seeks control of the majority, a popular movement that has a populist rhetoric (i.e., polarization and antirepresentative discourse) is not yet populism.

The case of the Tea Party proves this by default. This is a movement that has many populist components in its ideology and rhetoric, but lacks a vertical and unified structure that, as we shall see, characterizes populism.[2] Yet this lack seems accidental more than premeditated since the Tea Party *was* in search of a unifying and representative leader able to conquer and change the Republican Party and the country, because since its inception it wanted to be more than a popular movement of protest.

We may thus say that there is populist rhetoric but not yet populism when the polarizing and antirepresentative discourse is made by a social movement that wants to be a constituency independent of elected officials, wants to resist becoming an elected entity, and wants to keep elected officials accountable and under scrutiny: this is the case of a popular movement of contestation and protest like Occupy Wall Street. And there is populist rhetoric and populism when a movement does not want to be a constituency independent of the elected officials but wants instead to occupy the representative institutions and win the majority in order to model the entire society to its ideology:[3] this is the case of the Tea Party, a movement with a populist project of power.

Thus, I would argue that for populism to pass from movement to a form of managing state power it needs an organic polarizing ideology and a leader that wants to transform popular distress and protest in a strategy for mobilizing the masses toward the conquest of the democratic government. Without an organizing narrative and a leadership claiming its people to be the true expression of the people as a whole, a popular movement remains very much what it is: a sacrosanct movement of protest and contestation against a trend in society that betrays some basic democratic principles, equality in particular. Yet populism is more than populist rhetoric and political protest. The distinction between *movement form* and *government form* is thus essential.

In my critical investigation I acknowledge these two levels but direct my attention to the examination of the characteristics and implications of populism as a conception and a form of power within a democracy system. In a democratic society, a popular movement of protest or criticism should not be confused or identified with a populist conception of state power. The former is consistent with the diarchic nature of representative democracy; the latter deems diarchy an obstacle that keeps the opinion of the people separate from the institutions. Populism is a project of power whose aspiration is to make its leaders and elected officials use the state to favor, consolidate, and extend their constituency.[4] In this chapter I will focus on this specific phenomenon.

Introducing Populism

Although it claims to sponsor and practice an antagonistic democracy, populism treats pluralism of conflicting interests as a show of litigious claims to be overcome by creating a polarized scenario that simplifies social forces and giving the people the chance to immediately take sides. *Simplification* and *polarization* produce *verticalization* of political consent, which inaugurates a deeper *unification* of the masses under an organic narrative and a charismatic or *Caesarist* leader personating it. The populist ideology of the people considers society to be ultimately split into two homogenous groups—the pure many (the people in general) and the corrupt few (the elite by electoral designation or bureaucratic appointment). Polarization is what makes populism an ideology of concentration (of power and opinion) rather than an ideology of distinction and dispersion or simply antagonism.[5] Thus, while the epistemic interpretation of democracy is headless, populism can hardly exist without a politics of personality; while the former aims at erasing ideology and all forms of sedimentation of opinions, the latter lives out of a strong ideological rhetoric. Populism reclaims the priority of the hegemonic unity of the people against both its rationalist translation into deliberative speech and its procedural rendering by means of electoral representation, participation through political parties, and constitutional norms that limit majority decisions. Thus, it contests all indirect forms of political action that representative government has created, although this does not make it identical with participatory democracy. Populism is not a call for participatory as self-governing democracy, although it praises and practices participation and even mass mobilization. This is the spirit of the argument I intend to make in this chapter: although populism claims a direct link between popular opinions and popular will, it is not consistently friendly toward democracy. This inconsistency is most obvious in democracy's representative form, but also holds in its direct form that involves diffuse participation by the citizens, because with populism this direct form is not a method of power dispersion but rather of power concentration.

Populism depicts and theorizes democracy as hegemonic conflict in the view of and for the domination of one largely majoritarian opinion over its components and over minority opinions. In Robert Dahl's words, it gives the demos "total" and "final control" over the political order, which means empirically the control of the majority.[6] This unifying project makes politics into a work of simplification that narrows the possibility of a space of communication that is open to all equally, as it does not belong to anybody. Although Ernesto Laclau claims that the populist occupation of the place of power is "partial" and never complete, the impression one has is that its incompleteness is more a limit that the human practice of consent formation cannot avoid or overcome than a normative principle. Populism takes advantage of government by opinion and makes it the expression of an opinion that belongs only to one public.

The author who better foresaw the populist risk contained within the government of opinion was Claude Lefort, who not by chance ended up describing totalitarianism in his attempt to grasp the extreme implication of a project that, while opposing pluralism, aims at materializing the collective sovereign as if it were a homogenous actor. Lefort described this process as "condensation . . . between the sphere of power, the sphere of law, and the sphere of knowledge."[7] Populism produces condensation and concentration of power and does so in the attempt to resolve the "paradox of politics"[8] that is "determining who constitutes the people."[9] Thus, whereas the proceduralist approach leaves this question always open, populism wants to close it, or, as Laclau argued in correcting Lefort's idea that proceduralization of politics makes the place of power in democracies empty, populism wants to fill that empty space by turning politics in the *production* of the emptiness through an hegemonic work of ideological realignment of social forces. Liberating the arena of its party components in order to refill it with one signifying narrative—this is the anti-pluralist aspiration of populism.[10] A consequence of this is the erosion of the symbolic domain of institutions, which are no longer used as a medium that relates and separates social interests and the state. On the contrary, the state becomes an instrument or a direct expression of the populist conglomerate of social interests. From the recognition that the symbolic framework of power is that which sustains a political regime, populism deduces its mission, which consists in occupying and conquering that symbolic framework. From pluralism of opinions to the production of a dominant narrative, this is the task of a political process whose goal is to merge the many publics that constitute public opinion in a democratic society.

I am aware that this is a bold statement that goes against a large body of literature on populism, critical and friendly alike, which represents populism as reclaiming politics on the part of ordinary people against an elected elite that concentrates power. I am also aware that theorists of populism have constructed their argument as counteranswer to the elitist theorists who, from Roberto Michels, Vilfredo Pareto, and Walter Lippmann, depicted the ideal of making the people the actor of politics either as a utopia or as a devious strategy that an emerging elite uses in order to achieve power with people's consent. However, things are more complex than they appear at first glance. The interpretation I am advancing may be useful to understand contemporary populist phenomena like videocratic forms of popular identification, simplified polarization of public opinion into niches of self-referential creeds, dogmatic radicalization of political ideologies, and finally, the search for a winning leader in the age of the public.

In what follows I will try to illustrate and analyze this complex set of ideas and present populism as a phenomenon that grows within representative democracy, its true and radical target. This rivalry, I argue, does not necessarily produce more democratic politics, although this is populism's claim. Populism has the people, more than the democratic citizen, at its core. Indeed, its polarized view resonates with the republican tradition in the Roman format more than it resonates with democracy. I regard this point as crucial (yet neglected) in order to grasp the anti-individualistic (as antiliberal) meaning of the appeal to the people and the reason for populism's profound antipathy to pluralism, dissent, minority views, and the dispersion of power, all of which are characteristics that democratic procedures intrinsically presume and promote.

Since populism is predicated on democracy, after a brief analysis of populism's attempt to appropriate representation, I will set out a parallel or comparison between it and demagoguery, which since classical times has been a permanent potential threat of disfiguring democracy. I take reference to classical political categories as methodologically pivotal in the analysis of populism, whose source springs from the archaic myth of the masses of equals as the source of political legitimacy and periodical renewal of a given political system. Subsequently, I will return to modern times with a brief overview of the interpretations of populism in those domains in which it is most studied: history and political science. I will propose a parallel between U.S. and Western European experiences and evaluations of populism and argue that although no unitary definition is available, populism has nonetheless some recognizable characteristics, and although it is not the name of a political regime and comes with different historical manifestations, it is not such an ambiguous term when compared to constitutional and representative democracy. The following sections will illustrate two of populist politics' more important characteristics: polarization as a means for creating a politics of identity, and Caesarism, or mono-archy, as its possible final destination. This will allow me to resume the reference to the Ancients and situate the structural sources of populism in the Roman republic template of politics and government. Based on these conceptual and historical examinations, I will conclude by restating the idea of populism as the oppositional alternative to representative democracy and the open door to plebiscitarianism, which is the topic of the next chapter.

The interpretation I advance is inspired by Norberto Bobbio's criticism of populism, Margaret Canovan's interpretation of its ideology, and Benjamin Arditi's analysis of its manifestation as representative democracy's "internal periphery." Like Bobbio, I situate populism within not simply democracy but representative democracy and argue that its critical and sometimes dramatic questioning of the procedures and institutions of liberal democracy hardly turns out to enrich democracy. Reference to classical political categories is crucial to grasp the implication of populism, which, as with demagoguery for direct democracy, may open the door to an exit from democracy if successful.[11] Like Canovan, I take populism to be ingrained in the ideology of the people in a way that, although it is in communication with the democratic language, is in sharp contrast with "practical democracy" or the political activity of ordinary citizens and, I would add, its procedural structure.[12] Like Arditi, I read populism as a permanent possibility within modern democracy because it is endogenous to the ideological style of politics that elections feed by promoting the struggle for votes and positions.[13] Populism competes with representative democracy on the meaning of representation, and although it is an expression and the sign of a vindication of democratic participation by ordinary citizens, it should be carefully distinguished from grassroots movements of protest, not the least because it longs for state power and by this means fosters a homogeneous unification of "the people," preferably under one leader or one ideology or both. The outcome, if actualized, would not be an expansion of democracy but the condensing of the majority opinion under a new political class. Its achievement would be an exit from representative and constitutional democracy.

Competing for Representing the People

How should we evaluate the normative character of populism? To which political family does it belong? These are daunting questions for scholars of populism, who have never been able to reach a consensus on the interpretation of this political phenomenon (and make it into a category) and its relation to democracy.

All populist movements, Yves Mény and Yves Surel wrote, exhibit a strong reservation and even hostility to the mechanisms of representation, in the name of one collective affirmation of the will of the electors or the people.[14] While democratic proceduralism acknowledges that citizens have the right to make bad decisions, populism presumes the people (in the singular) is always right—this makes it blur the diarchic structure and prioritize the domain of opinion (unified within one narrative). Populism is thus "parasitical" on representative democracy, by which I mean that it is *not* external to it and it *does* competes with it on the meaning and use of representation or the way of detecting, affirming, and managing the will of the people.[15] I also mean that if it succeeds in dominating the democratic state, it can modify its figure radically and even open the door to regime change. It may be useful to briefly recall the genesis of representation.

Representation was born in a confrontational environment. Its origins are to be found in the context of the medieval church and in the recurrent disputes over whether the pope or the Council of Bishops represented the unitary body of the Christians.[16] Representation was born both as an institution of power's containment and control (of the chief of the church or the king) and as a means of unifying a large and diverse population. These two aspects together presumed an active involvement of both partners because the representative, who was sometimes called "procurator" and "commissary," was supposed to speak or act for a specific group of people who endowed him with the power of representing their interests in front of an authority, secular or religious, that was recognized as superior.[17] When a given community delegated some members to be represented before the pope or the court of the king, with powers to bind those who appointed them, there lay the origins of representation. This technique was then transferred to state context.

In the form of a synthesis, thus, unification (of the multitude) and subjection (to the decisions made by the chosen delegates) merged in the institution of representation. Yet it was the institutionalization of elections by those "subjected" that injected a new factor of conflict and introduced the quest for accountability. With eighteenth-century constitutional states, representation started becoming the terrain of unresolvable tension between its traditional unifying and subjecting functions and the new ones that elections conferred upon it, namely, electors' advocacy and representativity (the expressions of the call for accountability). The state's relationship with civil society made electoral representation a terrain of political and social conflicts; it made it an institution that served to mediate among interests and the state more than solely create the unity of the state and make visible its sovereignty. Populism infiltrates this tension and reclaims the unifying and subjecting role of representation (Hobbes) against the bargaining role that the parliamentary form of electoral democracy has instead legitimized (Locke).[18]

Populism aims at a more genuine identification of the represented with the representatives than elections allow. Moreover, it is impatient with the dialectic between pluralism and unity that representation entails. The representative, Laclau writes, is an active agent who gives words and credibility to the represented unity; he is the actor of the homogenizing process who puts an end to the divisions of the electorate.[19] An agent, moreover, that no accountability is able to check, not even the political party he relies upon, because the party is most of the time his creation and instrumental to the acquisition and the preservation of his power. We need just to mention Carl Schmitt's argument in favor of presidentialism against parliamentarianism. The latter, Schmitt explained, is an assemblage of elected delegates who represent economic interests, political parties, and social classes, while the "President is elected by the entire German people." In the latter case, only elections would be a strategy for unity and subjection (versus divisions) and represent a truly visual reproduction of the whole nation at the symbolic and institutional level. The president embodied Schmitt's catholic view of representation as the process of making visible the invisible divinity, which was now the collective People. In his reading, electoral representation was the denial of that unity because it served to bring pluralism inside the state, which was the mortal sin in Schmitt's political theology, the equivalent of a religious schism. I will come back to Schmitt's conception of the form of authorization that his antiliberal conception of representation entailed in the next chapter. Here I would like to show how populism builds on a view of representation that aims at unification and subordination as in the premodern format, but does not aim at accountability and advocacy.

Clearly, since Schmitt thought of representation as a synthesis of identity and the presence of the sovereign, party pluralism and parliamentary competition were anathema to him. "The President, by contrast [to the fragmentation of parliamentary grouping] has the confidence of the entire people not mediated by the medium of a parliament splintered into parties. This confidence, rather, is directly united in his person."[20] In similar manner, populism uses representation to constitute the political order above the society and through the expulsion of pluralism. As per Schmitt, who thus gave populism an important argument, representation is political *insofar as* it repels the liberal calls of advocacy, control, monitoring, and a constant dialogue between society and politics, and narrows the distance between the elected leader and the electors so as to incorporate society within the state.[21] This antidiarchic project echoes in Canovan's words: "A vision of 'the people' as a united body implies impatience with party strife, and can encourage support for strong leadership where a charismatic individual is available to personify the interests of the nation."[22] The demagogical factor is thus part of populism, insofar as the ideological construction of consent is its instrument.

Demagoguery, Social Conflict, and a More Intense Majority

People unification versus pluralism is the structural trope of populism as it was of ancient demagoguery in relation to direct democracy. The impact of their appeal to the people is of course different, and the representative system is the key to understanding it. Indeed, while populism's upheaval develops within the nonsovereign sphere of opinion (the world of ideology) and may very well remain so if it does not get the majority to govern, demagogy has an immediate law-making impact because in direct democracy, the opinion of the people becomes law by raising hands (as I have explained in Chapter 1, direct democracy is mono-archic). Aware of the important differences that electoral appointment brings to democracy, I employ the ancient analysis of demagoguery in order to explain populism's conflicting relationship to democracy.[23]

Aristotle is the author who produced the most precise characterization and definition of demagoguery; his ideas are illuminating in understanding the nature of modern populism. First of all, he broke down Plato's identification of the demagogue with the tyrant and thus made the former part of the democratic style of politics. However, Aristotle also introduced a distinction among demagogues and in this way was able to emancipate demagoguery from disdain and moreover theorized the idea of a transition democracy can make from constitutional to unconstitutional. He thus found historical examples of both "good" democracy (constitutional) and "bad" democracy (demagogical). Cleisthenes was the popular leader who, "after the fall of the tyranny," gave to the Athenians "a constitution more democratic than that of Solon." Cleisthenes was a member of the elite and yet led the Athenians toward democracy by means of rhetoric and persuasion that mobilized the disenfranchised many and gave them a new constitution and new rules. By contrast, Pisistratus, who "had the reputation of being a strong supporter of the common people," wisely masked his intention to become a tyrant. He was a formidable demagogue who manipulated the bitterness of the enfranchised peasants to conquer political power with their support; in this way he "seized power" by "flattering on peoples."[24]

Much like populism with representative government, in direct democracy demagoguery was a permanent possibility as the waiting room for tyranny, although not in and by itself an exit from democracy or a regime in its own right. A disfigured democracy was still democracy, and according to Aristotle, demagoguery was certainly the worst among the forms democracy could take because it exploited the search for consent in the assembly by making the people's minds in tune with the plans of cunning orators; it exploited free speech by putting it at the service of unanimity, rather than a free and frank expression of ideas. Demagoguery could not exist without a leader because it was not simply horizontal mobilization of ordinary citizens. Like populism, when it aspired to getting power, it could not be headless.

Aristotle's analysis is pivotal for our argument. It suggests we focus on the use citizens and leaders make of their speaking abilities and political liberties in order not merely to win a majority vote but to over-win and reduce the opposition to a meaningless entity with no role in the po-

litical game. To grasp this majoritarian regime, Aristotle turned his analysis to social classes. "In democracies the principal cause of revolutions
is the insolence of the demagogues; for they cause the owners of property to band together, partly by malicious prosecutions of individuals
among them (for common fear brings together even the greatest enemies),
and partly by setting on the common people against them as a class."[25]
Aristotle offers a structural analysis of the conditions that prepared for
the insolence of demagogucry. The crisis of social pluralism and the narrowing of the middle class were the two intertwined factors that accompanied that transformation. Polarization (well-off/the poor) and
the erosion of the middle class were, and still are today, at the origin of
political simplification.

We should recall that Aristotle takes the presence of a robust middle
class to be the condition for any constitutional (or moderate) government
(also of "good" democracy) and its disappearance as the condition for constitutional changes or revolution. "And constitutions also undergo revolution when what are thought of as opposing sections of the state become
equal to one another, for instance the rich and the poor people, and there
is a middle class or only an extremely small one; for if either of the two
sections becomes much superior, the remainder is not willing to risk an
encounter with its manifestly stronger opponent."[26] The disappearance of
social moderation translates into the end of moderation in political decisions. We should read moderation as a politics of compromise, because
this is what makes the numerical minority always part of the democratic
game in a good way.

Then, under certain conditions, demagoguery transfigures democracy.
As we shall see below, this is also the case with populism, which takes
advantage of social distress to exalt polarization and nurture the political
winners' temptation to use state power in a punitive way against the minorities, thus in order to break class compromise (or, as for Laclau, to rearrange
the "formal" generality of *politeia* with a "true" one).[27] This twist of majority rule into the rule of the majority is particularly alarming. In comparison to the numerical majority of which democracy consists, demagoguery
exalts the opinion of the majority in order to promote policies that translate the interests of the winners immediately into law, with no patience for
mediation and compromise (Bernard Crick characterized populism along
these lines as "impatient of procedures").[28] Polarization helps this strategy.
From majority rule as a procedure for making decisions to the rule of the

majority: this is the radical transformation of democracy that demagoguery and populism inaugurate.

Is demagoguery the tyrannical rule of the majority of the people? Not entirely according to Aristotle, who is attentive to the game of words and the politics of consensus formation. Certainly, the demagogue needs the consent of the majority and uses speech to bring the assembly on his side. Yet manipulation by means of speech is manipulation nonetheless, however hard it is to measure and achieve a clear-cut distinction between what is straight and what is twisted when freedom of speech dominates a political order. Yet although it relies on the majority, democracy and demagoguery are different.

This means that to gain a large majority in an assembly is still not the same as having democratic politics. The same argument can be found in Rousseau's *Social Contract*, which tells us that when *the will* and *the opinion* merge, the republic enjoys stronger legitimacy because the will of the assembly is so little contested (decisions are made with a large majority of votes) that all the people or its largest majority feel themselves one body politic *de iure* and *de facto*. It is not unanimity or a large majority *per se* that makes a democracy demagogical but *the way* the unity of opinions is achieved. We should recall that Rousseau suggested that the assembly should not discuss in order to prevent orators from performing. Conviction by reason rather than by rhetorical persuasion was in his mind the safe condition for making the merging of *de iure* (general will) and of *de facto* (*l'opinion generale*) sovereignty a sign of political justice, rather than merely of numerical power. Yet the problem remains because it is possible to achieve that unison both by reason and by persuasion—demagoguery, as populism, is for this reason a permanent possibility in a regime that, like democracy, is based on opinion and speech.

Aristotle offers us some important suggestions on how to interpret the phenomenon of unification or, in Laclau's words, create the hegemonic unity. Recall that a good constitution is, in Aristotle's mind, an institutional arrangement that rests on a dynamic equilibrium between the two main social classes—the rich and the poor. Regardless of the form of government, this equilibrium is what makes a government moderate and the home of liberty (in modern times, this approach was resumed by Montesquieu). For social (and political) equilibrium to exist, a broad social medium is needed; in the case of democracy, this medium persists as long as the very poor are few in number and the very rich feel their wealth is safe even if they are a minority (the same idea inspired Tocqueville's conviction that a large middle class is the condition for a not-bad democracy). Uprooting the middle and radicalizing the social poles: this is what demagoguery makes explicit and exploits; this is when majority rule achieves an intensity that is unknown to a constitutional democracy. What for? Why is a more intense majority needed?

This question is relevant precisely because demagoguery is not identical to democracy even if the poor (which populism claims to empower) are the majority. Why should the poor, who are always in numerical majority, be in need at a certain point of a more intense majority? Why is simply a majority of votes no longer enough? These questions suggest that, presumably, the particular actor of demagoguery is *not* the numerical majority. As majority is the norm of the democratic decision making, demagoguery is not simply an expression of the numerical majority.

The social changes that Aristotle indicated as a factor of class polarization speak of an increase of poverty. Compromises that the poor were previously able to strike with the middle class and the rich became more difficult because a large number of impoverished people needed a more interventionist policy on the part of the state. They needed a policy that was more on their side as never before, and this was primed to upset or worry some among the well-off, who started "banding together" in order to better resist popular claims. Hence, it is not the presence of the multitude of the ordinary people (the nonwealthy) that explains the demagogical involution of constitutional democracy. What explains it instead is the *break of social equilibrium*, which entails an erosion of the generality of the law. Polarization and partiality are the characters of a more intense majority that demagoguery creates.

This is the important difference with democratic majority, and the reason why democracy and demagoguery (or populism) are not the same, although they both make appeal to the people and the majority principle, and although they belong to the same genre. Economic worsening or the decline in the well-being of the many can make the numerical majority more ready to pass laws that induce "the owners of property to band together" in order to resist, for instance, tax increases. This is the class factor at the origin of demagoguery. Aristotle tells us that a constitutional democracy risks a lot if society becomes poorer.[29]

Why call it demagoguery and not tyranny? As we saw with Pisistratus, Aristotle listed cases in which demagoguery can become a tyranny. Nonetheless, demagoguery operates within constitutional democracy, in which the assembly of freeborn citizens is the supreme organ and proposals must gain the majority of their votes to become laws. Until the equilibrium among classes persists, the weapon of words seems to be enough strategy and, moreover, a strategy that is still within the constitutional limits. Demagoguery represents in this sense a form of political language that is consonant with assembly politics, and thus democracy. Yet this "neutral" reading ends when a tyrant emerges.[30]

But it is not the oligarchs or the few in their totality (as if they were one homogenous class) that break with the rule and turn demagoguery into tyranny. It is a part among them, or some few among the few, who understand that they can, through the expediency of rhetoric and by exploiting the condition of social duress, acquire more power and use people's distress with poverty to turn them against the constitution, and first of all against those among the few that still uphold the equilibrium among classes and make the democratic constitution hold. The *third party* between the few and the many to which Aristotle referred in order to explain Pisistratus's tyranny is the key element to understanding not merely the social condition for the demagogical victory but also the role of the individual leader.[31] Social distress unleashes the immoderate desire for power among the few, who realize that the break of the social and political balance can be turned into a strategy for regime change, thanks to which they can make decisions without consulting the opinion of the people.

The demagogues represent a new class within the class of the wealthy, those who think they can obtain more power or enjoy more privileges with the very support of the many, and who break equality with the very support of the majority. They are "men ambitious of office by acting as popular leaders." They represent a split inside the class of the few and are able to gain the favor of the people to pass laws in their own favors, with the people's own support.[32] Aristotle's scheme seems timeless. As Joseph M. Schwartz writes in his merciless analysis of the erosion of equality in modern democracy, few reformist theorists would have predicted at the end of the 1970s that "the right (particularly in the United Kingdom and the United States) would build a populist majoritarian politics in favor of deregulation, de-unionization, and welfare state cutbacks, particularly of means-tested programs."[33]

Like demagoguery and regardless of its appeal to the "united body" of the people, populism is a movement that relies upon the cunning usage of words and the media in order to make the many converge toward politics that are not necessarily in their interests. Polarization is indeed for the sake of a new unification of the people, and is a strategy the few use to claim and acquire more power in order to achieve some results that an open, pluralist, and long deliberation would not allow. Clearly, populist policies are not merely the product of procedural majority. A more intense and large majority is needed and claimed. The people's collectivity as a homogenous whole, rather than an *ex post* result of counting of votes, seems to be, since Aristotle, one of the signs of a disfigured democracy, a democracy that is prone to host a demagogic leadership.

In a similar vein, Machiavelli made a distinction that added an important factor to the analysis of populist politics, that between *partisan-friends* and *partisan-enemies*, or party conflicts and factionalism. Conflict is oxygen to liberty on the condition it is managed by the people and the few in a way that neither of the two can use the other as a mere instrument (this is what the "buoni ordini" do). Conflict for the good of the city is thus the prerequisite—a norm of liberty because it does not allow a zero-sum game among the two parts of society.[34] As long as this persists, or as long as elections are an open game and not an instrument that de facto advantages one part although with the support of the majority, demagoguery is powerless. However, *demagogic speech may always emerge*, and freedom of speech makes it possible because democracy is an articulation of partisan views, a plurality of interpretations on the better way to realize the promises written in the democratic constitution. It is thus not demagogic speech (or populist rhetoric) but rather its victory that is the problem. Pluralism is the strategy that neutralizes the bad without repressing its expression.

Party politics, one may say, is both a way to channel participation and a way to make conflict work in the service of the whole system. Thus, in breaking with it, populism wants to make the entire people into one large party or identify it with one vision and one leader, while the minority is no longer honored as partisan-friend but treated as partisan-enemy. When this happens, the institutional order starts working as a strategy that functions for the power of a part against the other—the city becomes a city of two peoples.

The divorce of institutions and virtue was the argument Machiavelli devised in order to explain the decline of the republic, and in particular two things: first, that good rules produce the foreseen effects depending on the social and ethical conditions in which they operate; second, that a political system can change without its constitution changing. In the case of ancient Rome, for instance, Augustus did not revoke its republican institutions, which however became futile and no longer able to make the empire qualify as a republic. The same institutions that made Rome a great republic were able to mark its decline because the citizens were corrupt; that is to say, the social structure was changed and made virtuous behavior too expensive.

Cicero said something similar in his *Laws*, where he commented on the transition from open ballot to secret ballot. The open ballot was a good institution and served well the *res publica* until the senators did not use their leading role in order to accumulate their personal power against their peers and did not use people's mobilization that the institutions of the republic allowed to further their personal plans or ambitions. Within this new condition, the open ballot became a ruinous institution because candidates used it to blackmail the voters and "buy" consent rather than to make all—the few and the many—responsible toward each other through the means of publicity.[35]

Aristotle himself suggested the existence of a link between institutional change and social change when he observed that "when the magistracies are elective, but not on property-assessments, and the people elect, men ambitious of office by acting as popular leaders bring things to the point of the people's being sovereign even over the law."[36] Elections facilitate ambitious demagogues. Thus, it is not orators per se who define the change to demagoguery but orators who seek political posts in the leading functions of the state, and it is not majority itself that generates demagogy. Applied to contemporary populism, we may say that this is not simply a popular movement but a movement that wants to conquer power, thus leading the state and using it as its own constituency or in order to distribute favors and posts. Reaching power through mobilization, a populist leadership can consolidate and perpetuate it through patronage or clientelism. A democratic Machiavelli would say that in that case, it would not be the people sovereign "over the law" but the leaders who conquer people's consent to their plans. This is what populism does as a style of politics through words and the goal of conquering consent for changing or disfiguring the procedures of democracy.

A Complex Phenomenon

The United States and Europe

The historical and political context is an important variable in the evaluation of populism, which is one of those phenomena that serve to highlight significant differences between the United States and Europe. American historian Michael Kazin considers populism a democratic expression of political life (a movement rather than a regime) that is needed from time to time to rebalance the distribution of political power for the benefit of the majority. Through the vehicle of populism, American citizens "have been able to protest social and economic inequalities without calling the entire system into question."[37] Ralph Waldo Emerson wrote famously "March without the people, and you march into the night."[38] Consistently with this maxim, the historians Gordon Wood, Harry S. Stout, and Alan Heimert interpreted the Great Awakening of the mid-eighteenth century as the first example of American democratic populism, a "new form of mass communication," thanks to which "people were encouraged—even commanded—to speak out."[39] Jonathan Edwards's followers, Heimert explained, translated the abstract language of both liberal and republican intellectuals into their own language, one made up of religious symbols and biblical allegories, against professional theologians and political leaders as well.[40] Populism was born as a denunciation of the newly implemented Madisonian republic. In that early denunciation the basic populist language was de facto coined and its characteristics defined.

A powerful allegation of that early form of populist movement was that democracy (but in fact "popular government") holds an instinctive anti-intellectualist vocation insofar as it rejects linguistic styles and postures that are distant from those that the people share and practice in their everyday lives. *Intellectualism* or *indirect language* was thus opposed to a *popular* or *direct style* of expression. The same dualism was applied to politics as a collective action that was made either by indirect means (institutions and procedures) or direct expressions of popular opinions. These dualist couples resurfaced periodically (not only in the United States) and became the *primum movens* of populism. The platform of the People's

Party of 1892 was forged out of the binary logic opposing the plain language of crop producers to the sophisticate language of the financiers and the politicians.[41] *Polarization* as a *simplification of social pluralism* into two broad factions—the *popolo* and the *grandi*—was since its inception the main character of populism, its Roman feature.

American history seems to show that populism, both as political rhetoric and as a political movement, has been seen as a viable form of collective expression of resentment against the domestic enemies of "the people."[42] Its hidden force was contained in the belief of an alleged purity of the origins of popular government and its adulteration by the artificial complexity of civilization and the sophisticated institutional organization of the state.[43] As the participants in the First Awakening aimed at an emancipation of religion from the established churches in the name of a religious purity, so the People's Party of the late nineteenth century claimed the emancipation of the nation from "money power" *(artificial)* in the name of property and labor *(natural)*. Directness versus indirectness paralleled nature versus artifice, tradition versus modernity, popular movements versus institutional politics.[44] When and if politics takes indirect modes it risks becoming antipopular: in American history, this was, since the beginning of the republic, the basic message of populist ideology, and the reason for its attraction among Democrats. It is interesting to notice that populism as a positive movement of elite containment was born within the ideological and institutional frame of a *republic*.

This line of thought deserves to be pursued: in the last part of the chapter I will argue that populism can be seen as an interpretation of democracy made from within a republican structure of government and politics. This allows us to say that popular government, rather than democracy, is its reference point.

Based on the American experience scholars have proposed to distinguish between "good" and "bad" populism by distinguishing a sincere democratic faith and an instrumental faith—like a thermometer, populism would measure the tenor of democracy in a given society. This scheme returns in the work of the most representative scholars of populism (supporters and critics as well). Peter Worsley proposes populism and elitism as the two extreme poles of the continuum of politics, whose democratic tenor is like a pendulum from the former (more democracy) to the latter (less democracy).[45] Canovan suggests we read populism as a "politics of faith" that aims at emending normal politics of its unavoidable skeptical and pragmatic mood.[46] The same insight shapes Laclau's interpretation of populist movements in Latin America as processes of hegemonic rebalancing within the power bloc attained through the incorporation of the popular democratic ideology of the masses. Laclau goes further and identifies populism not simply with "political action" but with a democratic kind of political action that gives the class of ordinary or working people a central role. Populism, he claims, is a more egalitarian or democratic politics than the one obtained through representative procedures, which is its true direct adversary.[47] In sum, according to a consolidated reading, populism belongs in the democratic family not merely because it relies upon speech and opinion—which is certainly the case—but more importantly because of its two structural characteristics: polarization (the many versus the few) and the alliance with the democratic side (the many), in fact, the incorporation of the vision of the largest majority in one collective actor.

This reading is not fully convincing though, because polarization makes the ideology of the people less inclusive than democratic citizenship. As it appears in the work of John McCormick, populism's concept of the people is endogenously sociological and identified with a portion of the population (the less affluent), although it is not necessarily Marxist, or based on a classist reading of history and society, or progressive.[48] Populism is a politics not of inclusion but primarily of exclusion: this is what polarization is for. It is not by chance that "the people" is its sovereign core, not "the citizen" as in democracy. Incorporation is not the same as isonomic equality, so if equal liberty is what characterizes democracy, populism is a poorer, not a richer, signifier of it.

This critical diagnosis is confirmed by European political history after the eighteenth century. Indeed, the extension of American historians' positive judgment to European societies and politics would hardly be defensible. Europe is a much more interesting laboratory of populism, though, because in Europe this phenomenon was able to clear the floor of all ambiguity and unveil its most peculiar potentials and characteristics. In Europe, national or popular unity (a collective whose members were presumed equal, not merely normatively or as juridical persons) was the pillar upon which democracy was constructed. In addition, whereas the United States was a democratic project since its inception (regardless of the intention of its most representative founders, which was not democratic) because it was a political order born out of consent, in European countries democracy sprung from within a society in which philosophers and political leaders (intellectuals in the broader sense) tried systematically to stop democratization or tame it by subjecting it to a bureaucratic state and a hierarchical society, in which consent would be imposed from above. The political experience of continental Europe shows two things: that populism was born in the representative and constitutional age, and that its role was devastating for democracy.

Napoleon was the first leader to "manufacture" consent through public opinion, to use the means of opinion formation and propaganda that his society offered to mobilize the people on his behalf, with an increasing number of printed materials and political clubs.[49] Napoleon, facing the opposition of the public (the presses and the acculturated few) to his imperial ambitions and politics of reconciliation with Catholic clergy, excited people's antielite sentiments to condemn his critics as "ideologues" and "doctrinaires."[50] His demagogic strategy has been recurrent in Europe. Just to focus on the Italian case (which is far from unique), Benito Mussolini exploited post–World War I economic distress of the middle class and the impoverishment of the already poor in order to polarize political life and transform Italy's liberal government in a mass regime against the political minorities. Although he never suspended the constitutional charter of the liberal state, Mussolini created a populist regime that made regular appeals to the people and used propaganda to mobilize the many and mold their opinions, while repressing pluralism and the opposition.[51] As for recent history, new versions of populism have been exemplified in Italy by the secessionist movement led by the Northern League and Silvio Berlusconi's Caesarist politics. Their main rhetorical strategy consists once again in portraying their respective movements as "true" alternatives to both the existing political parties and parliamentary democracy. They attack parliamentary politics as elitist and antidemocratic because of its attempt not to be absorbed by popular opinion. Moreover, they make a systematic use of propaganda—and in some cases own half of the national television stations and printing industry—in order to create a uniform way of thinking and talking in public. New populists exploit *doxa*, which is their creation more than the citizens'.[52]

To conclude this brief parallel between the Unites States' and European experiences of populism, I would say that European populism, in its recurrent resurrections, has more ordinarily followed right-wing kinds of politics, or a politics that did not aim at implementing the promises of constitutional democracy but at disfiguring them instead.[53] If social scientists and political theorists judged populism from the perspective of the historical experience of European authoritarian and populist movements, past and present, their evaluation would be less positive. Although it is the symptom of a malaise in representative democracy and economics, and although it regularly appeals to more popular politics, populism would, if successfully realized, upset constitutional democracy and the politics of rights it represents.[54]

This allows me to comment on the vagueness of the term: if populism is a vague term, it is because it is not the name of a regime but of both a movement and a form of democracy (sometimes so extremely majoritarian and hostile to division of powers and party-pluralism as to become a new regime altogether). It is an assault on representative and parliamentary politics in the name of a unitary collective affirmation of the will of the people, wherein this will is not assessed through certain criteria but uttered and declared by crafty orators or a class of ambitious politicians. Moreover, if it is hard to give populism the status of an analytical category, it is because of the very normative status of representative democracy, which allows us to categorize only a break in the constitutional order (for instance, per effect of a "push" or a tyrannical coup), not its internal changes. A disfigured democracy is still a democracy after all. Thus, while a tyrannical break is visible and detectable, this may not be the case when populism disfigures democratic institutions in ruinous ways because it makes the dialectics between minority and majority opinions hard to manage, and in fact it uses the state power to penalize and discriminate against minorities, and because it uses the state to distribute favors and positions in order to stabilize its power. Populism represents an escalation of discrimination and corruption.

A Nonambiguous Politics

If populism is an intractable theoretical category, it is because it does not denote a political regime of its own. It is thus both a style of politics and a way of making a democracy more intensely majoritarian and less liberal. In particular, it is a critique that questions the centrality of the parliament, that wants to narrow as much as possible the distance between the people and their representatives, and that dismisses division of power and constitutional control on lawmaking. Moreover, it unleashes a quite explicit critique of liberalism as a culture that recognizes rights and pluralism as pivotal in democratic society. Populism may actually be described as a recurrent attempt within democratic societies to disassociate democracy from liberalism, and may simplify the meaning of democracy by adopting a politics of immediacy.[55] "What populists are necessarily against is liberal checks and balances . . . minority rights, etc., because their view of politics has no need for them at best—and, at worst, they obstruct the expression of the genuine popular will."[56]

Political theorists have thus stressed the role of people's mobilization as a *symptom* of political discontent with ordinary party politics, regardless of the outcomes it attains, as characteristic of populism.[57] As Newt Gingrich has said about President Barack Obama and the Democrats, "they are a government of the elite, for the elite and through the elite."[58] Protest against intellectuals, high culture, and college people, and attacks against the cosmopolitan "trash" of "fat cats" in the name of "the common sense of the common people" who live by their work and inhabit the narrow space of a village or a neighborhood are the components of an ideology that is everywhere recognizable as populist.[59] Yet populism is a more ambitious project than discontented anti-intellectualism. As Laclau has very effectively explained, it is a vivid expression of the democratic imaginary, but above all a strategy to merge together the various claims, discontents, and demands that political parties fragment and filter in the moment they provide for the institutional personnel, or occupy the state.[60] Canovan has thus advanced the idea that people's mobilization works as a redemptive force of democracy because its meaning is "bringing politics to the people" and taking authority away from intermediary bodies like political parties.[61]

These observations suggest we add a further characteristic to populism, namely, that it is not a revolutionary movement because it does not create people's sovereignty but intervenes once people's sovereignty exists already and its values and rules are written in a constitution.[62] Populism represents an appeal to the people in a political order in which the people are formally the sovereign. It would be wrong thus to employ it in order to describe a democratic revolution—the French and the American Revolutions were not populist but could not exist without people's mobilization. Populism does not create democracy. It can be, however, a movement that expresses the ambition of a new leader to quickly get into power without waiting for the political temporality that a democratic constitution regulates. It grows inside an existing democracy and questions the way in which it works yet with no certainty that it will make it more democratic.

Populism is more than a form of denunciation as we saw at the start, and endeavors also to be a project of political renewal. It wants to redress democracy by taking it back to its "natural" roots—this is what its appeal to the unity of the people is for. It thus denotes a way of being of a political movement or a party that is characterized by a recognizable set of ideas that are unanimously shared by a large group of people and work like a conceptual map in orienting people's political judgment and evaluation. As Canovan argues, not the people themselves but the ideology of the people is people's populism.[63]

Michael Freeden has explained that an ideology is a way of "converting the inevitable variety of options into a monolithic certainty which is the unavoidable feature of a political decision, and which is the basis of the forging of a political identity."[64] For sure, all political parties have a more or less strong ideological kernel that manages the interpretation of social and political complexity in order to be a guide to win a majority and make decisions. Yet not all parties are populist even when they are popular or their claims are widely representative of people's grievances and meet with large consent. As I argued above, populist and popular are not the same things, and when this distinction is neglected, populism ends up becoming identical with democratic politics or movement politics. Ideological simplification, which Laclau makes the core of populism, is a crucial component, but not in and of itself a sufficient one for populist politics to become populist power.

Populist ideology contains some themes that are detectable in all populist movements: a) the exaltation of the purity of the people as a condition for politics of sincerity against the quotidian practice of compromise and bargaining that politicians pursue; b) the appeal to, or affirmation of, the correctness and even the right of the majority against any minority, political or otherwise (populism feeds strong discriminatory ideologies against cultural, gender, religious, and linguistic minorities); c) the idea that politics entails oppositional identity or the construction of a "we" against a "them"; and d) the sanctification of the unity and homogeneity of the people versus any parts of it.

To wrap up these observations on the history, the meanings, and the characters of this concept, I propose the following interpretation: populism is more than a historically contingent phenomenon and pertains to the interpretation of democracy. Both the character and the practice of populism underline, and more or less consciously derive from, a vision of democracy that can become deeply inimical to political liberty insofar as it dissolves the political dialectics among citizens and groups, revokes the mediation of political institutions, and maintains an organic notion of the body politic that is adverse to minorities and individual rights. The ideology of the people displaces equality for unity and thus resists social and political pluralism. Its extreme consequence is to transform a political community into a corporate household-like entity, where class and ideological differences are denied and mastered in the attempt to fulfill the myth of a comprehensive and corporate totality of state and society. Hence, in spite of its proclaimed antagonism against the existing political order and the elite, populism has a deeply statist vocation; it is impatient with government by discussion and with parliamentarianism because it longs for limitless decisionism.

A Mono-archic Emendation of Democracy

The difficulty of considering populism a regime of its own has brought scholars to conclude that precisely because the "populist 'dimension'" is "neither democratic nor anti-democratic," it can be compatible with democracy insofar as it serves to make sure that the rights of the majority are not "ignored."[65] Yet, if populist rhetoric can play a democratizing role by mobilizing the excluded majorities (people outside the institutions) against existing elites and by demanding better forms of representation (this is what Occupy Wall Street wanted to be), it can have negative effects on an established democracy when it acquires governmental power because its criticism of representative institutions translates easily into plebiscitarian forms of participation (crowning a leader). This results in a paradox whereby the people end up playing more the role of a reactive audience than of a political actor, as we shall see in the next chapter.[66] In effect, as Norberto Bobbio and Pierre Rosanvallon argued convincingly, populism is the most devastating corruption of democratic procedures.[67] It radically ruins representation and transforms the negative power of judgment and opinion from one that controls, monitors, and influences politically elected leaders to one that rejects as "formality" electoral legitimacy in the name of a deeper unity between the leaders and the people; it vindicates ideological legitimacy against constitutional and procedural legitimacy, or turns opinion into a power that reclaims the power of the will, to use the vocabulary of diarchy.

Despite the democratic intention of reversing the passivity of ordinary citizens, populist mobilization does not deliver what it promises. When *a populist leader* declares himself as the true representative of people's will beyond and outside the electoral mandate, he puts in motion the destructive power of judgment and calls into question not simply a bad or corrupt performance of representation and state institutions but the electoral procedure itself, its advocacy, and its authorizing and mediating character. Despite the democratic intention of reversing the passivity of ordinary citizens, populist mobilization produces a militant kind of passivity as it groups people's opinions under a homogenous ideology that a leader impersonates by declaring himself to be the true representative of the people, above and against the elected representatives. It is true that not all populist movements converge in the creation of a strong leader who seeks to exercise state power based on direct support by large majorities.[68] While Latin America and Europe produced personalistic kinds of populist movements, North America shows, as I explained, that populism can also take the form of leaderless movements, in which ideology does the job of unification.[69] However, one of the most frequent experiences of populism (in its most successful form) is that of converging toward one representative leader. The search for a leader is, one might say, one of populism's most specific characteristics.

Power verticalization and the politics of personalization together result in what I would provocatively propose to call a *mono-archic emendation of democracy*. Populism's appeal to the people is primed to lead to Caesarism. I will articulate this argument through a critical analysis of the ideas of Laclau, the author who has devised the most consistent and challenging theory of populist democracy. Laclau argues that populism does two things that are democratic: it polarizes society by creating two fronts of confrontation, and through polarization, it produces a new unification of the people (a hegemonic politics) around issues that are on the side of the many. I shall discuss polarization in the following section. In his works on Peronism, Laclau relied upon Antonio Gramsci as the leftist author who more explicitly tried to make room for Caesarism when he introduced the distinction between progressive and reactionary forms of dictatorial solutions. Here I would like to explore these peculiar leadership implications of populist ideology.

Based on the idea of politics as constituting the people, Laclau maintains that populism and politics are interchangeable terms because they denote the process of creating a political narrative that can make sense of the many expectations and claims existing in society by integrating them in a hegemonic ideology, which explains but also mobilizes the people, describes social reality but also prescribes objectives.[70] My objection to this rendering is that if applied to populism, this unifying project entails something that Laclau cannot explain with his theory (nor above all, neutralize or avoid), namely, Caesarism. The reason Laclau prefers "populism" to "class" as a unifying strategy is presumably in order to give this neutral tool and the project it serves a name that appeals to a large spectrum of interests.[71] He does with populism what Gramsci did with hegemony: he makes it a nonevaluative category. Yet this scientific neutrality is achieved by forcing Gramsci's category in a way that is unwarranted.

Laclau relies on Gramsci's notion of ideology as a unifying narrative for collective identity constitution. But Gramsci was explicit in bringing to the floor the risks that the politics of hegemony contains. He thought, for instance, that unless it was anchored in a party organization with a collective leadership and entrenched in a conception of history and social progress that did not leave any interpreter the liberty of making it into a rhetorical tool of persuasion, hegemonic politics would be dangerously prone to becoming a vehicle for a reactionary Caesarism that uses populism to make itself victorious. In his *Notes on Machiavelli*, in which he analyzed the two forms Caesarism can take, progressive and reactionary, Gramsci revised the classical Marxist doctrine in which all forms of government figured *de facto* as dictatorship of the dominant class. Gramsci's articulation of Caesarism is an interesting reformulation of Aristotle's analysis of the emergence of demagogical leadership in a situation in which social equilibrium is broken.

Gramsci reinterpreted Marx's category of Bonapartism so as to make sense of a progressive function of leadership politics (i.e., the case of Caesar and Napoleon I) in a revolutionary scenario. Given a social deadlock or "catastrophic equilibrium" (*equilibrio catastrofico*)[72] that prepared for a revolution, a Caesarist leader could play a progressive role when his victory *unintentionally* helped the victory of the progressive force by compromising with it. The outcome, Gramsci thought, could be that the exit from a "catastrophic equilibrium" would open a political scenario that might help the progressive force to fulfill its agenda in the future.[73] As Benedetto

Fontana acutely observes, Gramsci's method is dyadic or shaped by antin-omy, as, for instance, civil society as opposed to political society, consent as opposed to coercion, and hegemony opposed to violent revolution and also dictatorial or coercive power.[74] In Gramsci's work, thus, Caesarism was primed to break out in a revolutionary situation, not a situation that he defined as "war of position," in which not Caesarism but cultural hege-mony would be needed to advance a gradual social and political change.

It would be wrong to transplant Gramsci's reflection on Caesarsism ("war of movement," or revolution), which does not need the politics of hegemony because the social situation is already ripe for change, into a situation in which gradual or molecular change ("war of position") is needed: where the politics of hegemony is in place, Caesarism is out of place and vice versa (although in moments of crisis, a party leader in a parliamentary system can succeed in unifying a large coalition under his or her representative figure).[75] But Laclau inserts Gramsci's interpretation of Caesarism within his project, which consists in proving that the populist regime of Peron was based on consensus (hegemony), not essentially on Peron's personal power. Here, however, hegemony serves a very different cause than it does for Gramsci: it serves to distinguish corrupt Caesarism from populist Caesarism, and then to include Peronism in the latter.

Making the party a *collective Prince* was Gramsci's strategy to prepare for the gradual work of hegemonic change (in a situation of "war of posi-tion") and to do so by countering the *risk* of personalization (which can reasonably be born in a revolutionary situation). Indeed, unifying the people through an ideology was not in and by itself a sufficient condition for making hegemonic politics into a progressive or democratic politics. In addition, it would be important to block the possibility of making the hegemonic project a fertile tool for plebiscitary and Caesarist leadership. In fact, the unifying politics of hegemony contained a dangerous risk of power concentration that needed to be preempted. Gramsci thought that civil society should be made of a plurality of aggregations in all domains, from the working place to culture, and society at large. He surmised that pluralism was essential precisely *because* the hegemonic politics was *not* naturally open to pluralism; it was a strategy of concentration and unity, or consensus.[76]

Thus, by default Gramsci's theory of hegemony shows how populism has an endogenous vocation to create a strong leader not only in a situation of individualist domination as in classical dictatorship but in a modern, or one might say Weberian, kind of society made of organized incorporation and bureaucracy; when this happens, the hegemonic project loses its progressive character.[77] Personalization of politics is *not* an accident in populism, but rather its destiny. Gramsci situated the solution to this problem in ideology itself, the way in which it was constructed and managed. His solution consisted in taking away pluralism from the world of opinion, not by censuring ideas and repressing freedom of speech but by conquering people's consent to a narrative that was held together by a philosophical view that would permeate people's minds and orient their behavior. Both party leaders and ordinary citizens would share in this ethical and political frame, which must have been impermeable to subjective interpretations. The hegemonic project would succeed in proportion as it neutralized the growth of the politics of personality. Thus, Gramsci's hegemonic project was meant to block any individual leader from succeeding in acquiring domination by intervening on the meaning and instrumental implementation of ideology. Relying on an immanent philosophy of history (Hegelian-Marxist), which was endowed with a self-propelling motion, Gramsci thought it possible to expel subjective interpretations in the domain of consent formation. His critique of Stalin pointed to precisely this risk of personalization as never completely tamed and neutralized. Stalin was the example of a leader who succeeded in appropriating the interpretation of the "Modern Prince's" doctrine.[78] On the other side of the spectrum there was Mussolini's Caesarism.

According to Gramsci, Mussolini represented the populist version of the degeneration of the collective Prince (the party) in despotic dogmatism; his project was not hegemonic but despotic.[79] Fascist movement was Mussolini's personal creation; he concocted an ideology that was completely instrumental to his project of power, or created *ex arbitrium*, without a philosophy of history that warranted it. His populist project consisted in linking together people's various claims and forms of dissatisfaction with liberal government. His goal was that of polarizing opinions by mobilizing the large number against the established institutions and norms in the name of a truer representation of the sovereign people, that is to say, his own representation (Gramsci does not fail to observe Mussolini's admiration of Le Bon).[80] This model was what Gramsci absolutely rejected, and what Laclau de facto resurrects when he injects Caesarism into a politics of hegemony in order to make the case for populism as the most radical alternative to constitutional democracy and representative institutions.[81]

Populism is a call for concentration of voice and power, will and opinion, and to overcome diarchy by blurring the border that keeps the people and the state, the opinion and the will, separate although in communication. This concentration is achieved by making opinion the Trojan Horse that conquers state power. This is achieved thanks to a strong leader. As a matter of fact, impersonation of political power in a leader is not avoidable when representation occurs in a void of political parties (or intermediary bodies) and when procedures are manipulated for the sake of identifying representation with a visible collective sovereign. This observation proves by default the nature of democracy as a form of political participation that tends to disperse power and be headless or many-headed. Citizens acquire more voice as long as power is diffused and nobody can legitimately claim to represent them as a whole: this is the golden rule of democratic proceduralism that populism rebuffs.[82]

Personalization, or the Caesarist factor, makes populism close to and on some occasions intertwined with plebiscitarianism because it makes the people a reactive mass of followers. We might say that in a representative democracy, populist politics might become *a way toward* a plebiscitarian democracy. Thus, although it starts as a phenomenon of mass discontent and participation, populism is a strategic politics of elite transformation and authority creation. As Gramsci saw, it is a project for the promotion of a new leader (and sometimes the creation of his charisma) that is, however, unable to protect itself from him. Populism may thus turn out to cheer a new leader who uses the ideological battle to achieve his or her goal, which is, as we have seen with Aristotle, hardly the same as that of the people. In modern democracy, this occurs through the strategic employment of mass media as instruments of propaganda. If populism emerges in democracy it is because of the role that opinions and opinion formation play in this regime.

Laclau tackles the criticism that populism is primed to create Caesarism or dictatorial leadership with the argument that, although it may take personalized forms and sometimes is identified with the name of a leader (e.g., Mussolini, Peron, or Chavez), it is not personalization that qualifies a populist politics. What qualifies it instead is the kind of thought it puts in motion: "through dichotomies such as the people versus the oligarchy, toiling masses versus exploiters, and so on."[83] Populism would thus be not simply "political action" but a democratic kind of political action that gives the working class or the poor or the ordinary people central stage in the forum. Populism would be the same as politics and moreover the same as a more egalitarian or democratic politics. Yet if this identification were true, then populism would lose its specificity. Laclau concludes thus that if personalization emerges, this is not what makes populist politics what it is; identification of the movement under a leader is a means that populist politics may find convenient in order to make polarization succeed, but it is not what characterizes it. The problem with this argument is that amending personalization with polarization does not help in making populism the same as democratic politics.

Polarization, Simplification, Acclamation

Polarization is the other basic characteristic of populist politics. As in the case of Caesarism, in this case too Laclau's ideas are the most interesting and challenging because they are the most theoretically oriented. Laclau locates polarization within a defense of populism that aims at overturning the traditional argument that identifies populism and democracy in order to prove that they are both an expression of the endogenous irrationality of the masses. I explained in the previous chapter how epistemic theory offers an answer to this objection. The populist answer takes a direction that is diametrically opposite to the epistemic one. Laclau argues that the identification of democracy and populism is indeed correct, and moreover is politics at its best. But we have to "invert" our analytical perspective, and instead of starting from a view of rationality that excludes collective forms of mobilization and endorses an economic or a problem-solving kind of reasoning as the template for politics, we have to start by assuming populism is "a distinctive and always present possibility of structuration of political life"; this is what makes it a rational politics.[84]

Laclau's interpretation can be rephrased as follows: instead of approaching populism as an abnormality or deviation from the norm of rational behavior, we should consider it as the norm of political action, which shares nothing with the individual model of rationality; politics is, like populism, the domain of the collective, which exhibits a kind of rationality that is rhetorical in character and instrumental, yet not according to an economic vision as one might find in an aggregative theory of democracy.

Rather than starting from units of preferences to proceed toward aggregation, we should start, as Georges Sorel and Carl Schmitt have, from the ideological nature of political discourse, which is made of linguistic strategies that rely on myths and symbols, not costs and benefits calculus. A rhetorical rationality entails a rationality that operates according to dichotomous or oppositional strategies ("we"/"them"), whose language is not that of preference and a linear aggregation of interests but that of identification, and its goal is eminently political and consists in achieving large consensus for redesigning the meaning of the whole society. Politics uses reason to mobilize passions and actually creates them artificially by means of myths or imagination. Politics is a work of regime or power creation through ideas: a work of ideology at its highest or as hegemony.

Laclau has good reasons to mock social choice's criticism of populism, which rests on the assumption that voting as a method of preference aggregation demonstrates democracy's endemic irrationality that appealing to the general interest cannot cure, since counting votes does not bring us to determine any rational or general will. Voting does not take away from democracy's arbitrariness; what makes it superior to other methods lies in the fact that it delivers social peace. As Canovan puts it in questioning William Riker's critique of populist democracy, "if Riker expected his dissection of 'populist democracy' to kill it off, he might just as well have saved himself the trouble," because both the idea of people's sovereignty and the idea of the will of the people retain an "unimpaired" power in democracy theory, aside from and beyond the populist form.[85] The fact that populism is "inconsistent with social choice theory"[86] is completely irrelevant to the success of populism; moreover, it is an inept argument against the identification of democracy with populism.[87] Yet rational choice is not the only way of interpreting elections and voting, nor is it the only language of democratic theory. And refuting this interpretation does not demand that we turn to populist ideology and reject a procedural interpretation of democracy.

In countering social choice interpretation of voting, Laclau claims instead that populism is a radical way of reinterpreting electoral competition because it makes society a battlefield that is sharply divided into two fronts of confrontations, the outcome of which would be a truly majority victory. Populism uses democratic institutions and procedures essentially as means to obtain power rather than to limit power; it thus empties them of any normative value. This is the reason why political conflict and party competition within an electoral democracy are not a safety net when used by populist strategists. Thus, polarization is a process that unifies the people and simplifies pluralism so as to give it a clear antagonistic structure that is consistent with the electoral structure of modern democracy. But the populist confrontational character of electoral competition is a condition not for pluralism but for concentration or unification of the competitors, which look like granitic strongholds. Once again: polarization seems to be a denial rather than a manifestation of pluralism.

Now, because populist politics disdains indirectness, its most congenial method of selection seems to be the investiture of the leader, rather than election. Indeed, its expressive language is acclamation more than discussion. A populist leader is not properly elected but acclaimed, as I shall explain in the next chapter. Consequently, Schmitt forcefully wrote that the "will of the people" is detectable only through voting because "[e]verything depends on how the will of the people is formed." But then he promptly added that "the will of the people can be expressed just as well and perhaps better through acclamation, through something taken for granted, an obvious and unchallenged presence, that through the statistical apparatus" of vote counting.[88]

Thus, another crucial aspect that underlines the friction between democracy and populism is the meaning that each of them gives to the institutions and norms that render the "will of the people." According to populist democracy, these institutions and norms have essentially an instrumental value. It is the people directly—in fact, its majority—that legitimizes them with no other mediation beside the people's actual and expressive will. "Against the will of the people," wrote Schmitt, "especially an institution based on discussion by independent representatives has no autonomous justification for its existence." Populism denies autonomy to political institutions, but in particular to the legislative branch. One can say that it aims at an actual assimilation of the level of sovereignty with that of government, of the "will" and its actuating "force," to paraphrase Rousseau's distinction.

The People

"The people" is among the political categories that is perhaps the most abused. The origin of the term is Latin. In the Roman tradition, *populus* held the meaning of opposition/distinction in relation to another group of

Romans that was not *populus* although shared with it the sovereign power of the republic: aristocracy or the patricians, and the Senate as its political organ and site. Since its origins, the term "the people" had a collective connotation as the opposite of an aggregation of individuals. It was a whole that existed in opposition to another organic but smaller group, that of the noncommoners.[89] It was because of its antagonistic character and exclusionary nature that, when the French delegates of the Third Estate had to decide, after July 14, 1789, how to name their Assembly, they decided not to adopt the adjective "popular" and opted instead for "national."

In the meeting of June 15, Thouret criticized Mirabeau, who had proposed the adjective "popular," with the argument that the employment of the term would engender two inferences equally problematic: that of identifying the people with the *plebs*, thus presuming the existence of superior orders, and that of identifying the people with *populus*, thus presuming a political actor that was collective in its sovereign meaning and opposed to another one. The solution would be in both cases impracticable: in the former, because it would entail a breach of equality, and in the latter, because it would entail dividing sovereignty into two corporate entities, a solution that would prefigure a mixed government.[90] On these premises Thouret convinced the assembly to adopt the adjective "national" instead of "popular."[91] The incorporation of the people in modern state sovereignty and its identification with the nation were perfected during the nineteenth century, along with the birth of the political movements of national self-determination.[92] The nation, Giuseppe Mazzini wrote in 1835, "stands for equality and democracy." On this condition only, it is "commonality of thought and destiny." In Rousseauian language, Mazzini believed that without "a general and uniform law," there were not people but casts and privileges, inequality and oppression; at most a "multitude" of interest-bearers bound together by convenience.[93] The nation entailed thus the equal weight of each in the voting power and the solidarity of all in the distribution of costs and benefits.

Following Thouret's precious indication, it is precisely the Latin origin of "the people" and thus its singular-collective character that is the source of the ambiguity that produced populist ideology. In most European languages, except for English, the terms *popolo*, *peuple*, and *Volk* designate an organic, collective entity, a single body with a collective name and meaning that has one will and is not separated in multiple units. Rousseau (to whom the origin of totalitarian democracy has been wrongly attributed) foresaw the risk of rendering the "all-body" as one plebiscitarian voice. When Rousseau described the popular assembly as the only legitimate sovereign, he clarified with great acumen that the citizens would go one by one to the assembly and then preferably vote in silence, reasoning each with his own mind, without listening to any orator (which is precisely what we do when we go to the polling booth). It would thus be appropriate to call Rousseau's assembly democratic, not only because it includes all the citizens as equal but also because it relies upon each of them as they reason and then cast their votes individually and separately. The individualistic aspect is crucial, and it is the condition that makes the collective people a composite unity, rather than an organic whole. This is where the people of procedural democracy and the people of populist democracy diverge (and the reason why Rousseau cannot be made into the forerunner of either totalitarianism or populism). As Thouret specified, both the principle of equality and the principle of the unitary source of legitimacy militate against the modern endorsement of the Roman notion of the people.

Clearly, the way consent is collected and votes are counted is essential to take away the ambiguity from the term "the people." Indeed, although in some European languages the term may be rendered as a singular-collective name, the rules of the game and the voting procedures are in charge of making it plural, composite, and even conflicting. The populists' ideology of the people is meant to erase this pluralistic aspect and make the people a crowd with one voice, leader, or opinion. For this reason this ideology opposes democratic proceduralism. This view has a direct impact in the way a collective decides; for sure, it betrays the character of the assembly in a democracy. For example, pre-Periclean Athens cannot be consistently categorized as a democracy in spite of the fact that its assemblies did not exclude the Athenian male population. The same can be said of fascist gatherings in Piazza Venezia in Rome during the 1920s and 1930s. This is because there is a clear perception that it is not *simply* the presence of the people *en masse* that characterizes a democracy.

Before voting was a distinct individual right, in pre-Periclean Athens people were assembled to listen to the speeches of their eminent leaders, but they had no voice as individual citizens. They could certainly act and make visible their presence, but only as an indistinct unity; "they expressed their sentiments only collectively, by voting and presumably shouting."[94] Individual expression was held as a privilege of the few, not the many. Indeed, the Athenian democratization coincided with the extension of that privilege to all citizens, and in particular with the institution of the *equality of speech (isegoria)*, which made the nonnobles (or bad or coarse or ignorant) equal to the nobles in the right to speak and vote in the assembly. Hence, in his "Funeral Oration" Pericles called Athens "a democracy" because its government was "not for the few but the many" and also because each citizen individually was granted equal expression in the assembly and equal consideration before the law.[95]

Consequently, one might say that the main political character of a democracy is not so much that the people are collectively involved but that they are involved as individuals, that they have an *equal political liberty.* After all, this was the main difference between Sparta and Athens. The Spartan assembly was a disciplined mass of indistinct members characterized by both lack of free speech and the endorsement of equality as uniformity: its members were *homoioi* not *isoi,* that is to say, they were alike not simply fairly equal in their consideration *uti singuli.*[96] In Athens, the egalitarian principle "one citizen–one vote" was actually employed and hands were counted or "estimated," while in Sparta the method of "open voting by shouting implicitly denied that principle and was thus the polar antithesis of Athenian sortation."[97] Spartans voted by acclamation and were supposed to either approve or disprove, but without articulating their assent or dissent. "The people then being thus assembled in the open air, it was not allowed to any one of their order to give his advice, but only either to ratify or reject what should be propounded to them by the king or senate."[98]

Both in ancient and modern times, the conquest of political democracy has coincided with the conquest of individual rights to vote, according to the crucial idea that democracy means not mass mobilization or mass organization but equal freedom of expression of each individually, not of the totality. No doubt, democratic politics means also collective action, but in this case too collectivity implies the actual cooperation of individuals in a common project. John Dewey was thus accurate when, in 1939, he defined democracy as "a *personal* way of individual life," in thought and action, in private and political life.[99] The definition of democracy contemplates always both equality and individual expressiveness or liberty; for this reason, beginning with the ancients it was Athens that was perceived as a democracy, not Sparta. "The argument," wrote Aristotle, "is that each citizen should be in a position of equality,"[100] which means that it is the "position" of the citizen that helps to define a democracy, not that of the masses. As I have claimed throughout this book, democracy *is* its procedures. To treat the latter as a means to something—be it truth or the unification of the people under one hegemonic leader—is thus to betray, rather than honor, democracy.

To pay attention to the meaning and character of the collective is thus very important. As we have seen in the previous chapter in mentioning the antipathy of republicans in the Roman tradition for popular assemblies engaged in disputations and rhetoric, the manifestation of social conflicts has been traditionally the main reason for mistrust in democracy. James Harrington acknowledged discussion and the individual freedom of expression only in the Senate, where the wisest were gathered,[101] while Rousseau, who contemplated only one assembly, thought of it as a laconic place. Precisely because unanimity should be the goal of the assembly—or at least the largest majority possible—Rousseau linked the existence of a few good laws to a simple language and the simplicity of the mores: the less sophisticated the people, the less inclined they were to rhetorical controversies and debate: "the common good is clearly apparent everywhere, demanding only good sense in order to be perceived. Peace, union, equality are enemies of political subtleties. Upright and simple men are difficult to deceive on account of their simplicity."[102] When a new law is proposed, if it is a just law, there is no need for discussion, because it expresses what "everybody has already felt, and there is no question of either intrigues or eloquence to secure the passage into law of what each has already resolved to do." The health of the republic, concluded Rousseau, is proportional to the absence of debate, to the silence of its assembly. "But long debates, dissension, and tumult betoken the ascendance of private interests and the decline of the state."[103]

As we said, it would be highly inaccurate, if not absurd, to list Rousseau (not to mention Harrington) among the founding fathers of populism. Rousseau did not blur individual citizens into the anonymous totality of the assembly, at least because he thought, as we said, that citizens would fly to the assembly one by one and would make up their own minds autonomously. It is the definition of the general will as uncontroversial truth that guarantees the right outcome of the final deliberation. Reason is what unifies the citizens, not a demagogue. Moreover, it is the obedience to public reason that makes for political autonomy; to be subjected to the will of a demagogue would mean for the people to become slaves. Thus, it is reason (which speaks through institutions and procedures) that protects Rousseau's republics from becoming populist, not so much the character of its assembly. For this reason, although decisions are made according to majority rule, the general criterion that validates this method is unanimity.

But clearly, an assembly of individuals who do not interact is not more democratic than an assembly that is monotonic in its opinion, at least if by democracy we mean *also* disputation, disagreement, and opposition: in a word, pluralism, not unanimity. Rousseau focused essentially on one of the two powers that compose sovereignty (the will), and for this reason his analysis of political institutions is insufficient to represent democracy. From this perspective, I portray epistemic democracy and populist democracy as mirror images rather than alternative views of democracy. Indeed, alternative to both of them is the view according to which democracy ought to be seen from both the perspective of the winner (the majority) and of the defeated (the political minority).[104] What distinguished it from populism (which is an extreme expression of majoritarianism) is that populism is essentially cross-eyed. Thus, it can be maintained to be consistent with the democratic principle of sovereignty once democracy has been stripped of its *isonomic* character. Hence, if one does not want to renounce a notion of democracy that incorporates the limitation of power, a bill of rights, and discussion as the peculiar form of political life, one is forced to conclude that populism is not an expression of democracy.

It is reasonable and meaningful to claim that democracy does not only and simply entail a constitutional frame and the rules of the game. Indeed, to take seriously this claim it would require not to confine democracy solely to a quest for political power, like populism does. Democracy is also a claim for an extension of the values of equality and nondomination to those sectors of social life where those values are still impotent. In other words, the project of democratization should orient itself also outside the space of political power and toward civil society at large.[105] But this project does not look at all like disclaiming the procedural nature of democracy. The opposite is true, because when we contest relations of domination in our social relations, we claim to have our voice heard and our will counted, and moreover that the environment within which we operate functions according to procedures we can monitor and check. Whenever and wherever we claim for the respect of some conditions and rules that treat us as morally autonomous beings, who are free and equal in respect and opportunity, we claim for democracy.

Attention to procedures does not entail that the existing distribution of power should remain unchallenged or unquestioned. More consistently, it means, first of all, that domination is not only a political phenomenon and the political sphere is not its only niche, and finally, that a democracy that incorporates the liberal constraints can become an instrument for pursuing a wider project of democratization. Far from being an indication of impotence, those constraints give to the democratic state the legitimization to encourage a consistent politics of democratization insofar as they put the state under control. But in the hands of a populist democracy, that very politics would actually become a frightening strategy of social incorporation and homogeneity. In conclusion, a "secured" and institutionalized democracy allows for a broader range of political resources and initiatives than populism does. Populism does not seem to be able to solve the riddle of either being minoritarian or becoming despotic. Being in the minority is not safe in a populist regime, and this is enough reason to mistrust it.

Populus and the Plebs

Let us now return to Thouret's intuition concerning the incompatibility of the populus and the plebs with a people of citizens-electors. The populist imagination portrays the people as a political actor that asserts its sovereign authority by remaining in a permanent state of mobilization. It does so by propelling ideological polarization. As I stated, its leading scheme is the dualism between indirect and direct politics, which relies on a meaning of "the people" that does not properly belong in the democratic tradition. In this section I try to explain the meaning of the populist people by situating it in a different experience than democracy, namely, republicanism.

It is Laclau himself who reminds us quite appropriately that populism's genealogy is in the Roman tradition. Laclau clarifies also that "the people" as a political category envisions the return of the populus, yet that of the Roman forum, not of the voting assemblies. "In order to have the 'people' of populism, we need something more: we need a plebs who claims to be the only legitimate populus—that is a partiality which wants to function as the totality of the community."[106] Populism and polarization merge thus as forms of energizing and permanent conflicts between the two sides of the city. "The reasons for these are clear: political identities are the result of the articulation (that is, tension) of the opposed logics of equivalence and difference, and the mere fact that the balance between these logics is broken by one of the two poles prevailing beyond a certain point over the other, is enough to cause the 'people' as a political actor to disintegrate."[107] The stipulation of this view is that none of the two poles should prevail, that the struggle should go on without an end: this is, according to Laclau, what makes populism, democracy, and political action one and the same thing. The prevailing of one of the two poles—as with the cases of Robespierre versus the Girondins or of Mussolini versus the liberals and the communists—would entail the interruption of polarization and of democracy.

Populism is the longing for a totalizing unity of society, but without its achievement, states Laclau, it is a permanent antagonism. It cannot end with one party occupying society or declaring that all social strata are unified within its view of the society. In this, it is not identical to nationalism.[108] Laclau's populism could actually be described as the collective sovereign in a permanent *status nascendi*—this permanent mobilization is the most radical antidote against the crystallization of politics in institutions, and perhaps the most secure guarantee that populism does not subvert democracy. To resume the Roman parallel, thus, for populist politics to exist and persist, the plebs should never become *populus*. Despite the philological origin of the term, populism denotes only the people in the forum, not also the people in the sovereign assemblies in which decisions were made. The process that makes the pleb conscious of its power to shape the totality of society occurs outside the institutionalized space of the republic. How different were "the people" in the forum and "the people" in the voting assemblies or the *comitia?*[109]

The *populus* in the forum was a receptive interlocutor of political leaders, who performed before a gathered group of people to seek ideological support for their plans for power. It was not the people in the voting power, or when the citizens gathered to speak through voting procedures. The *populus* in the forum was made of the free crowding many who acted outside the institutions and without the regulation of procedures, people who spent some of their daily time in the forum in order to attend the show performed by political candidates and rhetoricians. It was not the people in its decision-making capacity but the people in the act of cheering or booing those who competed for a political post or tried to conquer people's support to their cause. Opposite to that populist gathering was the Senate, whose building was located at the end of the forum: contrary to the people in the forum, the Senate was always structured as a visible body and place, and its members did not mix with the plebs. As I said, the people and the Senate were the two components of the republic. Their visibility was essential to the political life of the Roman state, which did not acknowledge individuals or *isotes* but citizens within the two predetermined groups that made for the republic—that is to say, when they acted as sovereign bodies. The dualistic paradigm was an essential feature of both the Roman style of politics and of republicanism through the centuries: noninstitutionalized people en masse versus institutionalized magistrates; the organized few versus the crowded many; and inclusion within polarized institutional domains versus equal inclusion of all or an equal chance to participate in the process of political decision or compete for magistracies.

I will analyze the power of the crowd and the differences between the people in the *forum* and the people in the *comitia* in the next chapter, when I shall focus on the plebiscite of the audience in contemporary democracy. Here, I will concentrate on another aspect of the Roman experience that is directly related to Caesarism and polarization.

As anticipated in the previous section, populism and democracy are not as close, or still less identical, as populists pretend, not even when democracy is performed in direct form. I have illustrated this difference by examining the character of voting and showed how the democratic right to vote presumes the centrality of the individual citizen, who is the true sovereign actor. From this opposition its hostility to both a politics based on rights and pluralism derives. The anti-individualist roots of populism explain also its resistance to political equality as citizenship status disassociated from socioeconomic status. This too makes polarization different from political pluralism. McCormick, a representative author in the contemporary renaissance of populism, states quite explicitly (and correctly) that populism is part of the republican tradition, more than the democratic one, and as such it claims the unity of the people not in abstract legal terms but as citizens grouped in socioeconomic clusters by virtue of their wealth, social status, and political power. McCormick agrees with Laclau that institutions are needed to defend the weak class from the abuses of the elite, and on this ground criticizes democratic proceduralism. This argument, which mixes normative and descriptive levels, relies upon Bernard

Manin's theory of representative government as a mix of oligarchy and democracy, a theory that pivots not on representation but electoral selection, which Manin reads as a break in political equality so that some will only rule (acting as full sovereign actors) while the large majority will only assent or judge. Representative government would thus replicate the ancient Roman republic, with the Senate proposing and leading the stage and the *populus* discussing (in the forum) and voting and promulgating by plebiscite (in the *comitia*).

Not by chance, Manin resumes the republican idea of mixed government, which does not contemplate merely the constitutional mechanics of the division of powers like a mixed constitution but also the procedural embodiment of two different portions of the citizenry in the management of political institutions. Political equality is dramatically violated according to Manin's interpretation of elections because the latter reproduce in modern society the *populus/senatus* division of the Roman republic. This reading, which relies on Schmitt's *Constitutional Theory*, is the locus we ought to look for if we want to find the justification of most of the recent literature on populist and plebiscitarian democracy. The next chapter will explore this idea.

Conclusion

I started this chapter with the argument that there is an unpredicted proximity between a populist and an epistemic rendering of democracy insofar as both of them contest the diarchic character of representative democracy and moreover treat democratic procedures as a means to a superior value that is extrinsic to the very procedural ordering of opinions and will formation. I have also made some reference to the historical context and situated the sources of populism in the age of democratization. Whereas its ancient terminological and conceptual sources are to be found in the Roman republic, its contemporary sources are rooted in the antiliberal reaction against parliamentary and party politics that, beginning with the French Revolution, resurface periodically to counter the institutionalization of popular sovereignty through political representation based on electoral consent and an open forum of opinions, which are two domains that pivot on the individualist foundation of political right. Although it claims to support an antagonistic democracy, populism mistreats the pluralism of conflicting interests as a show of litigious claims, which it proposes to overcome by creating a polarized scenario that simplifies social forces, so as to give the people the chance to immediately take sides. Simplification and polarization produce, however, not more popular, direct participation but instead a verticalization of political consent, which inaugurates a deeper unification of the masses under an organic narrative and a charismatic leader personifying it. I have thus concluded that if it succeeds in dominating the democratic state, populism can modify its figure radically and even open the door to regime change.

4

The Plebiscite of the Audience and the Politics of Passivity

W hen coupled with mass society and mass media communication, appeal to the people can facilitate a plebiscitarian transformation of democracy: "plebiscitarianism promises to restore the notion of the People as a meaningful concept of collective identity within contemporary political life" and does so by rendering it in its collective capacity "a mass spectator of political elites."[1] Yet when leaders go to the people directly they radicalize issues and make parties' bargaining more difficult; this makes the terrain of politics naturally fertile for leader activism, which does not, however, entail people activism.[2] "Certainly, when the representation of the parliament collapses and no longer finds supporters, [when there is an argument of 'nonrepresentative democracy'] the plebiscitary process is always stronger"[3] and democracy may become a call of legitimacy via audience over legal institutions.[4] The myth of unanimity or a deeper unity than that achieved by the arithmetic aggregation of votes gives plebiscitarian politics the aura of a stronger and more sincere democracy.[5]

Being *under the eyes of the people* is a plebiscitarian view that seeks to replace accountability by means of procedures and institutions with popularity while giving the public sphere a new meaning and configuration as it makes the public play mainly an aesthetic, theatrical function. As Jeffrey Edward Green writes in presenting his theory of plebiscitarian democracy as an application of Hannah Arendt's celebration of political life, this vision of democracy breaks with the "automatic and repetitive process of nature" and welcomes the idea that "eventfulness is a value to be enjoyed, not simply by the political actors who perform the event, but even more by spectators who behold them."[6] This is where populism and plebiscitarianism diverge, because although they both oppose theories of democracy that are suspicious of the People as an entity prior to the political process and that locate the source of authorization in the individual right to vote, populism gives the People a political presence, whereas plebiscitarianism gives it a passive one endowed with the negative function of watching. The former invokes participation; the latter wants transparency.

Plebiscitarian democracy in the audience style I will discuss here is a postrepresentative democracy in all respects because it wants to unmark the vanity of the myth of participation (i.e., citizenship as autonomy) and to exalt the role of mass media as an extraconstitutional factor of surveillance (in fact, even more relevant than constitutional checks). It declares the end of the idea that politics is a mix of decision and judgment and makes politics a work of visual attendance by an audience in relation to which the basic question is about the quality of communication between the government and the citizens or what people know of the lives of their rulers.[7]

Whereas populism has been throughout the decades the recipient of a rich analysis, with the end of totalitarian regimes plebiscitarianism had lost attraction among scholars of politics. Things have somehow changed lately. In the United States political theory is also witnessing a renaissance of interest in and sympathy for plebiscitary democracy as a result of a more favorable inclination toward majoritarianism and an idea of democracy that is less concerned with institutional limitations and more attentive to fostering forms of popular activity, either as direct populist action or as vindication of the visual transparency of power. In some European countries, parliamentary democracy is witnessing a plebiscitarian transformation because of several concomitant factors, on the top of which there is the decline of traditional parties, the role of television in constructing political consent, and the increasing weight of the executive as a result of the economic and financial emergency.

The aim of the critical examination I devise in this chapter is to bring to the fore this new enthusiasm for plebiscitary democracy and present it as an illustration of the intriguing role of the public as a power that, while making democracy look at first sight different from authoritarian regimes, can transform its features quite radically and in ways that are remarkable.

To anticipate in a nutshell my argument, plebiscitary democracy is, like populism, a possible destiny that representative democracy incubates and mass media facilitate. Audience democracy in the age of mass communication takes a plebiscitary form. Contrary to unpolitical and epistemic democracy, it rejects any attempt to amend opinion with truth; contrary to populism, it does not blur democracy's diarchy by making one hegemonic opinion the ruling power of the state. The plebiscite of the audience accepts the diarchic structure of representative democracy and is ready to endorse a Schumpeterian rendering of democratic procedures as a method to select leaders, yet it reinterprets the role of the public forum in a way that stretches and exaggerates one of its functions. Indeed, we can detect this form of plebiscitarianism whenever we consider the sphere of opinion in its multifarious functions—cognitive, political, and aesthetical—or as a complex activity that pertains to production and diffusion of information, to formation of political judgments, and to the claim for public exposure of the deeds of the leaders. As I have argued on several occasions through this book, the complex nature of the forum is one important reason for democracy's strength. It is also the domain in which changes in democracy's appearance are most observable. In what follows I will first analyze the meaning and theorization of plebiscitary democracy through the works of its classical scholars, namely, Max Weber and Carl Schmitt, and then turn to its contemporary renaissance as a plebiscite of the audience in consolidated democracies.

The Appeal to the People

In its classical meaning, plebiscitarianism entails an electoral form of leadership creation that seeks popular approval (in the next section I will explain in more details its historical origins in the Roman republic and its renaissance in the nineteenth century, along with representative government). In Schmitt's vocabulary, it entails a claim of legitimacy (this is what approval is for) that relies on the people directly as the sovereign that is "outside and above any constitutional norm."[8] Yet a cumbersome sovereign is not necessarily a sovereign that is democratically active. The passivity of the people figures in the instrumental rendering of procedural democracy. So Joseph A. Schumpeter famously wrote: "Democracy means only that the people have the opportunity of accepting or refuting the men who are to rule them."[9] *Approval* is the core theme of the plebiscite as a sign of investiture and confidence. Unlike populism, which embodies the ideal of mobilization, plebiscitary democracy narrows the role of active citizenship to stress instead people's reactive answer to the promises, deeds, decisions, and appearances of the leader(s). The other face of the appeal to the people is *transparency*: if the leader goes to the people for approval, the people are entitled to ask for the leader's public exposure. Transparency is the price of approval. These two phenomena attract each other and make sense of the plebiscitarian blurring of "popular" and "public." I will elaborate on this crucial aspect in discussing the ideas of Schmitt and show that in following them, contemporary plebiscitary Democrats put transparency first and give a theatrical feature to the opinion leg of diarchy. They argue that in modern democracy the paradigm of political autonomy gives way to that of spectatorship, which makes the "exposure of the leader" the first goal of democratic politics.[10] Plebiscitarian democracy is a celebration of the politics of passivity.

Like populism, plebiscitarianism has a Caesarist vocation. Weber thought that when the masses are democratically activated, a plebiscite is the instrument a charismatic leader may want to use in order to seal his charisma in people's eyes and with people's formal approval.[11] Representative institutions and constitutional rules enter the scene at this point as strategies for stopping the plebiscitarian democratic leader from becoming a plebiscitarian dictator. Parliaments and the formal constitution, in Weber's view, are thus important not because they regulate consent and control legitimacy but because they provide for what the charismatic leader cannot: institutional stability, the preservation of the legal order, and a gradual succession in leadership. Legal constraints are ancillary to leadership; they are important in the foreseeable event that the leader loses the trust of the masses, an event that can never, of course, be excluded.[12] Thus, Peron, Chavez, and, to a certain extent, Berlusconi are populist leaders and also Caesaristic leaders in Weber's sense, who seek trust and faith by the masses but want also the people's approval with a formal vote and do not disdain having a parliament. What they disdain is the check on their decision-making power by nonpolitical institutions, like a supreme court or a constitutional court. What they seek is the direct contact with the audience ("Chavez spent more than 1,500 hours denouncing capitalism on *Alo Presidente,* his own TV show;"[13] Berlusconi was for years a daily attraction in both state and his private national television stations). Plebiscitary democracy is a presidential mass democracy that downplays a liberal conception of power limitation and the division of powers. According to Weber, the American presidential system was a step ahead of parliamentary democracy because it entertained a direct relation with the people outside the procedures of election, and meanwhile succeeded in remaining within the track of constitutional democracy.

Weber thought that the democratization of an electoral regime consisted in the transition from a time in which a political leader is declared or chosen by "a circle of notables" and tested before the parliament (this was more or less how representative government functioned in pre-democratic Germany) to a time in which the leader "uses the means of mass demagogy to gain the confidence of the masses and their belief in his person."[14] Within this reading, as we shall see below, some theorists argue today that the media seem to play a more effective role of control than the legal strategies of checks and balances and the division of powers. But as Jeffrey K. Tulis has observed in his classical study on the rhetorical presidency, when the primary interlocutor of the president is the people rather than Congress, the quality of communication or speech by the president changes because his goal is not that of transmitting documents or special messages to the assembly, but of moving public feelings "where the visible and audible performance would become as important as the prepared text."[15] For a plebiscitarian president, delivering visionary speeches is more important than giving information or exchanging reasoned arguments to the other branches of government.

Populism is primed to be the open door to a plebiscitarian transformation of democracy insofar as it makes the role of personality essential in representing the unity of the People and elections a plebiscite that crowns the leader.[16] For this reason, presidential democracies are more exposed to both the populist style of politics and a plebiscitary kind of relationship between the leader and the people. Leadership is moreover offered as a cure for, or a preemptive strategy or gridlock, in Antonio Gramsci's words, against a "catastrophic equilibrium" of powers. The idea that a leader should be plebiscitarian thus adds to the idea that he or she is better capable of governing. Some scholars have thus distinguished Caesarism and plebiscitarianism with the argument that while the former is a category that belongs in the authoritarian genre of government, the latter belongs instead in the genre of democracy.[17] Yet much like the "bad" and "good" demagogues described by Aristotle, Caesarism too can have different connotations, so we can interpret the popular presidency as a kind of democratic Caesarism, a category that fits, for instance, the Wilsonian presidency.[18] However, regardless of the energizing factor a strong leader may have, it is certain that Caesarism is dangerously open to solutions that stretch the Constitution and the division of powers. In extreme cases, when the leader proposes authoritarian solutions, the government he or she leads does not even need to rely on electoral consent, let alone the communication or appeal to the parliament, and most of the time ends up inaugurating a police state with propaganda that orchestrates popular consent. The Caesarist solution shows that starting with people's trust or approval is not enough of a guarantee to qualify a regime as democratic because it is not sufficient to guarantee control and accountability. Other institutions and procedures are needed, which plebiscitarians neglect. A crucial factor is the *form* of people's approval. I will now explain what the people do when they vote in a plebiscite.

What Is a Plebiscite?

The Roman *plebiscitum* was a yes-no decision by the plebs to a proposal that came from the tribune of the plebs. Through the centuries, this form of decision has been used to give the mark of acceptance to a fact or to a course of action that was already decided in the state or by a leader. The meaning of plebiscitary consensus is popular *pronunciation* more than popular *decision*. Hence, Green insists correctly that plebiscitary democracy is opposite to citizenship activism and in fact the proclamation of the "citizens-being-ruled" principle.[19] As a pronunciation for or against, but not according to procedural normality like referendum or voting for a representative, this form of popular involvement has meant to sanction an exceptional event, to be a quest of trust, more than an election that seeks to limit power or to hold the elected accountable.[20] A few historical examples may be helpful to clarify the difference between plebiscite and election.

A plebiscite was held by Napoleon Bonaparte on several crucial occasions of regime change that he initiated: for instance, in 1800, when he sought people's approval for his new constitution, after the coup d'état on the Directory of 19 Brumaire 1799, by which means he "terminated the revolution" and made himself a military dictator in the role of consul for life, a decision he then wanted to be sanctified with a plebiscite (1802),[21] as he did with the designation of himself as emperor (1804).[22] A plebiscite was used by the king of Savoy in 1861 to seek popular approval by the inhabitants (with large male suffrage) of northern Italian regions that were previously military incorporated. A plebiscite may also have a democratic use. Its most democratic use is when it decides on a regime change, as in the case of Italy with the popular decision between the republic and the monarchy on June 2, 1946, or with the 1992 decision concerning secession in Czechoslovakia. In these and similar cases in which the vote is meant to open a new democratic phase and not to crown a leader, a plebiscite is identifiable with a constitutional referendum or, to use Václav Havel's apt words, a radical decision made in "a civilized manner."[23]

These different examples have in common the following: they show that what a plebiscite seeks is a leader's or a proposition's direct support by the people and the bypassing of any institutional intermediation. Besides these technical meanings and usage, a plebiscite is supposed also to have strong symbolic meaning and emotional impact on the people because it is an act of belief in the future, a trust or a pledge on something that a leader or a new regime promises to be. Thus, Ernest Renan used it to signify the commitment of a nation toward its own past and future, a pledge by which means a nation selects from its historical past what to retain or drop in the view of defining its cultural identity and strengthening its will to promote and protect it always. A plebiscite expresses a kind of religious consensus, thus, or a solemn recognition of a beginning or a renewal.[24] When rendered as the approval of a leader it is an act of identification with his deeds, words, and promises. This explains why the main concern the leader has is with abstention more than rebuff; indeed, it is high participation in the plebiscite, rather than the majority of the votes in and by itself, which seals the impressive adhesion of the people with his plans.[25] Counting suffrages does not count as much as the spectacle of showing consensus.

Let us return to the Roman meaning then, and the reason why since Roman times the plebiscite has been used as a strategy for strengthening obedience or devotion or faith by strengthening the solidarity of the plebs with their leader, their unity under and through him. Created in 494 BC as a concession by the patricians to the plebeian soldiers when they refused to combat and seceded to the Aventine and asked for the right to elect their own official, the tribune of the plebs represented the most important protection of liberty in Rome. The tribune did not come from the aristocratic or senatorial class, where from Roman magistracies must originate, and thus was not voted on by all the people of Rome (plebeians and patricians) but only by the plebeians. This entailed that the Tribune was not properly a magistrate, a condition that explains why he had to be made "sacrosanct." For the tribune to be sacrosanct meant that he needed to be protected against the aristocratic family "by divine interference, or popular vengeance."[26] The tribune acquired his sacrosanctity by the people's pledge to kill whomever harmed or interfered with him while in Rome and during his term office. His sacrosanctity sealed his unity with the plebs by making any offense against him an offense against the plebs (as a matter of fact, to harm a tribune or disregard his veto or obstruct his function translated de facto into a curtailing of the right of the plebs to resist abuses by the magistrates). Sacrosanctity entailed at the same time a protection of the tribune and of the prerogatives of the plebs insofar as the tribune was the guarantor of the civil liberties of the Roman citizens against arbitrary state power.[27]

A plebiscite was thus an act that signified the unity of the plebeians, because they sanctified their trust and faith in their leader. This is the aspect that best illustrates the difference between a plebiscite and the right to vote in a modern democratic sense, which stresses the judgment of each citizen in the act of making a decision and the aggregative aspect of the outcome of his or her vote.[28] Voting in a political election divides the people into parties and interests, but voting in a plebiscite creates a unity of the people beyond its internal divisions.

Vote versus Plebiscite

Voting in a political election is a matter of preference and trust together; the paradox is that the more votes are about trust, the less their function is that of a checking device. Ideological alignment or faith and individual choice are in a tense relationship, and this is what makes elections divisive. Election relies upon several factors, like wide dissemination of information, interpretations and opinions that both the press and intermediary associations, from parties to civil associations, contribute in prompting. It is thus also based on belief (for the additional reason that information comes to electors though means they do not produce and control, as I have shown in Chapter 1), which means that cognition is not always the determinant factor that motivates electoral decisions. Certainly, as Bolingbroke made it clear in 1734, without trust in the Constitution, partisan "divisions" are destructive.[29] Moreover, as an impressive literature in electoral behavior has explained in a century-old empirical body of research, citizens should expect that the candidates and then the elected will perform according to their promise in order for elections to operate as a valid system of appointment of representatives. Without this belief they cannot predict how the candidates will behave and thus judge them accordingly. But if this belief plays prominently they have little control over the elected.[30] In sum, information is a partial component that belief integrates. Belief is essential because the future is the perspective in relation to which voters choose a candidate, since they do not have all the information they would need to make a perfectly rational choice (supposing this kind of choice is feasible). Belief or trust thus applies to all social relations as the condition without which citizens who are strangers to each other and with limited information cannot coordinate their behavior.[31] For this reason trust has been considered as the fabric of society and its destruction as the most disastrous occurrence—destroying it, Thomas Schelling wrote, is to "spoil communication, to create distrust and suspicion, to make agreements unenforceable, to undermine transition, to reduce solidarity, [and] to discredit leadership."[32]

But voting in a plebiscite entails only one of the two components of voting because it operates for the purpose of proving the intensity of people's faith in a proposed leader; here, accountability is wholly out of place, and voting is acclamation rather than election.[33] Confidence and popularity rather than information is what counts, President Woodrow Wilson said. "Persuasion is a force, but not information; and persuasion is accomplished by creeping into the confidence of those you would lead."[34] Contrary to the election of a representative, thus, the plebiscite does not condition the deeds of the elected but confirms or accepts his leading role. Plebiscites are not for making the leader accountable but for making him popular. Hence, Weber stressed that a plebiscite can also be used for sanctioning a dictator: "Either the leader arises by the military route—like the military dictator, Napoleon I, who then has his position confirmed by plebiscite. Or he rises via the civil route, as a non-military politician (like Napoleon III) whose claim on the leadership is confirmed by plebiscite and then accepted by the military."[35] We should keep in mind these two aspects—the "plebian" approval and the antielectoral character—because they are, as we shall see, the pillars upon which modern rendering of plebiscitarian democracy rests.[36]

In sum, if the plebiscite is included within democracy, it is because of the formal modality of the popular consent it imports. Yet this is not enough to make an acclaimed leader a democratic leader.

Form and Matter

Weber was the author who first welcomed the transition to plebiscitarian politics as one toward democratization. He was also the author who radically dissociated democracy from the Constitution. Control and stability came from state institutions, not democracy, which for Weber, as for subsequent plebiscitarian theorists, meant essentially mass action external to the legal order, like pure and protean energy.[37] Weber's political conception rested on a polarized view of form and matter: the life in the cage of legalism and rationalism and the life of the extraordinary that gives politics new energy and even the poetry of heroism.[38] On that unshaped matter the leader put his mark.[39] Within a mass-democracy scenario, the parliament played an important function, yet not as a source of political legitimacy (which was vested in the people's plebiscitary consent) but as a means of control (on the plebiscitary leader) and stability (of democracy).[40] According to Wolfgang Mommsen, Weber thought that the leader and the parliament should work in tandem in order to neutralize the worst of them taken separately and face the challenge coming from the growth of bureaucracy, the true target of Weber's plebiscitary democracy.[41] The Machiavellian view of political conflict as a mechanism that both empowers and creates great personalities is one possible and legitimate reading of Weber's critique of parliamentary bureaucratism.[42] Yet Weber's appeal to the leader as rejuvenation of democracy was meant to overcome the strictures of parliamentary democracy and the legalistic constraints of the Constitution. A charismatic leader who lived for politics had the capacity (and people gave him the strength he needed) to break through the normality of legalism and overturn the limitation on decision-making power that constitutionalism created.[43]

Weber's understanding of leadership passed through a stylized reflection on the ancient states, certainly Athens and Rome. It was an understanding that "remained trapped within a view of the masses as essentially to be warded off or worked upon. The distinction is inherently cast in a tragic mode: the statesman can only control or remake the masses to a certain extent, and for a certain amount of time, before they break out of his command and he becomes their victim."[44] In fact, it was Theodor Mommsen's depiction of Julius Caesar as the chief of the "new monarchy" that was able to put an end to the conflicting and corrupt "old republic" that inspired Weber. Like Pericles, Caesar was a demagogue who was able to transform people's support into a creative source of energy that changed the character of his state, domestically and internationally.[45] This was Weber's model of a plebiscitarian leader, a "genuine statesman," Mommsen wrote of Caesar, who "served not the people for reward—not even for the reward of their love—but sacrificed the favour of his contemporaries for the blessing of posterity, and above all for the permission to save and renew his nation."[46]

Within this model, plebiscitary politics was identical to democracy, once democracy was rendered not as consent by "regular election" but as "popular confession of belief in the vocation for leadership" through acclamation.[47] This identification was inescapable because democracy was for Weber either en masse or it was not. Indeed, in order to be capable of any functional or instrumental or rational kind of action (to produce any effect whatsoever that was not simply anarchy), the masses needed a leader—as a leader needed the masses to reveal his character to the world. Charisma was a destiny, not a choice: for this reason electoral representation was out of place, because, although it may be staged, charisma cannot be pretended or be a fake artifact that cunning leaders and propagandists make.[48]

After Weber, the dualism between matter and form has become the paradigm of plebiscitarianism as democracy in action; its opposite was electoral and parliamentary democracy as lethargic democracy. In this sense, a plebiscitarian element is present in all electoral theories of democracy that regard elections as a confession of the masses' impotence to act without leaders.[49] Schumpeter called his anticlassical doctrine of democracy a "theory of competitive leadership," even if he resisted the conclusion that the government should depend for its ordinary acts directly on the people.[50] But it is precisely the government's direct dependence on the opinion of the people that plebiscitary democracy stresses. Within this scheme, the radical dualism it poses between state apparatuses and the masses fosters an ideology of antiparliamentarianism. Indeed, from the idea that parliamentary politics is inimical to demagoguery it is possible to jump to the conclusion (as Weber did not do) that true democracy means downplaying the function of electoral suffrage and the institutional control it generates.[51]

For sure, according to Weber the parliamentary organization of politics was more antagonistic to plebiscitarianism than it was to military Caesarism or even dictatorship. As a matter of fact, the latter could enjoy the support of the masses as in the case of Pericles or Napoleon, but parliamentary politics would kill demagoguery altogether. "Every parliamentary democracy, too, assiduously seeks for its part to exclude the plebiscitary methods of leadership election because they threaten the power of the parliament."[52]

Weber can be made our guide for understanding the following factors as the starting points of any plebiscitarian form of democracy: a sharp dualism, and actually a conflict between the legal order and the order of the masses, and the assertion of the masses are the sources of authorization of the leader, outside or beyond representative procedures that like elections institute a claim of accountability (but the irrational nature of the masses excludes both electoral authorization and accountability). The transition to plebiscitary democracy is thus more than simply rhetorical; it is a change in the figure of democracy because it is a downfall of democracy's procedural form. It is a change that is primed to occur more easily in a presidential system than in a parliamentary one, and in a society that relies on a pervasive system of mass media. The idea of the president as a popular leader has become "an unquestionable premise of our political culture. Far from questioning popular leadership, intellectuals and columnists have embraced the concept and appeal to a constant calling for more or better leadership of popular opinion. Today, it is taken for granted that presidents have a *duty* constantly to defend themselves publicly, to promote policy initiatives nationwide, and to inspirit the population."[53] Being popular is the virtue that makes accountability less important.

We can of course question the effectiveness of the claim for accountability. The point is that the very existence of a form of election that entails this claim introduces something that is crucial: it separates the people from the elected and positions the elected to question and control them. The elected are held responsible for "the manner in which they make and implement" the public choices.[54] For a president to communicate to the people via parliament or Congress entails avoiding the style that direct communication allows, hence being more attentive to the deliberative character of his rhetoric than to its emotional character and more cautious in supporting his talk with evidence. Talking to the parliament is making issues public; talking to the people is making them popular, wrote Tulis effectively.[55] As Schmitt made adamantly clear, plebiscitarianism consists in eliminating all distance (of judgment and opinion) between the leader and the people, thus merging "public" and "popular" and bypassing procedures and regulations that constitutional democracy has devised in order also to tame the few (the demagogues), not only the many. But as an act of acclamation or faith, a plebiscite does not contain any quest for control, regulated speech, and accountability. Moreover, electoral accountability intends to remove arbitrariness and regulate political temporality by linking decisions to the future (promise) and the past (reckoning) of their actualization, beyond the moment of their initiative. "The distinguishing characteristic of modern democratic political accountability is the attempt to control such hazards not at the moment of (or in advance of) public choice, but on the basis of subsequent assessment and initiative."[56] Responsibility of the leader and a regulated temporality are the two characteristics that representative democracy impresses on politics, and that plebiscitarian democracy opposes.

The Ocular Public against the Secret Ballot

Pivoting on the difference between election and acclamation, Schmitt radicalized Weber's plebiscitary argument and added a crucial specification that would derail plebiscitarianism from the track of liberal constitutionalism and parliamentary checking functions altogether: he attacked the secret ballot, the foundation of representative democracy, against which he opposed the plebiscite as the truest expression of the voice of the people.[57] Whereas Weber criticized the weak and debilitating effects of party politics and parliamentary democracy on national politics, Schmitt went to the heart of the problem and questioned the procedural organization of electoral democracy in its eighteenth-century foundation: *the individual right to suffrage in the form of the secret ballot.* Not by chance, he criticized the French Revolution of 1789 for its liberal character, which produced a "bourgeois (constitutional) democracy" based on the rights of the individual citizen.[58] "Under the current regulation of the method for secret individual votes, however, he [the individual] transforms himself precisely at the decisive moment into a private man. The electoral secret is the point at which this transformation occurs and the reshaping of democracy into the liberal protection of the private takes place. Herein lies perhaps one of the *arcana* of the modern bourgeois democracy."[59] *Arcana* as opposite of publicity paralleled *secret ballot* as opposite of plebiscite.

Arguments against the secret ballot were largely widespread in the nineteenth century, and not only among critics of liberalism.[60] Schmitt persisted in defending the open ballot in the twentieth century and did so explicitly in order to dissociate democracy from liberalism and pit one against the other. His project remained constant throughout his life and pertained to a definition of the public that was radically antiliberal. "Equal rights make good sense where homogeneity exists" and does not mean that an "adult person, simply as a person . . . *eo ispo* [is a] political equal to every other person."[61] Hence, to make it the voice of the People the vote must be disembodied from the "person" (the individual citizen) and rendered as the public expression of the will of the masses.[62] The form of the manifestation thus plays a central role.

In his assault on the secret ballot Schmitt advanced a new conception of *the public* that was not anchored in individual rights and their guarantee against the abuses of state power but was meant to render the aesthetic or visual and theatrical representation of the sovereign. His assault was thus not on *arcana imperii* as in Kant's tradition of the public but on the private as individual rendering (through secret ballot) of sovereign authority. Schmitt's appeal to visibility was for the sake of eliminating the anarchical or dissenting counterpower that the individual right to suffrage incubated. His move was perfectly rational since his objective was restoring state authority, not making government responsible to the electors. "The belief in public opinion," he wrote in *The Crisis of Parliamentary Democracy*, "is less a question of public opinion than a question about the openness of opinions."[63] This antiliberal view, which has the visual at its core rather than the articulation of ideas and interests in a communicative practice among equal citizens, resurfaces in the contemporary plebiscitarian renaissance.

Schmitt devised the most complete antiliberal definition of the public when he identified it with the visual. This is the sense of his attack against the secret ballot. Whereas to nineteenth-century critics of the secret ballot—among them liberals like John Stuart Mill—that form of voting epitomized a decline of political virtue and the license to use political power for the promotion of private interests (or, as in Benthamite vocabulary, "sinister interests"), Schmitt criticized it from a perspective that had nothing to do with the civic or republican tradition, but had instead one basic concern: *the restoration of the state's authority.* The theological dogma of Catholicism offered him the paradigm for fulfilling his objective. Schmitt's move acquired the meaning of a critique of liberal as Protestant modernity.

Similarly to Catholic theologians in post-Reformation debates on the dogma of transubstantiation, or the presence of Christ in the Eucharist, Schmitt argued that the sovereignty of the People was one thing with its appearance in the plebiscite: just as the symbol of the Eucharist was the very body of Christ, the acclamation by the People was the body of the People. The form was the substance. The particle was the symbol that revealed the presence of a mysterious entity that escaped all rational understanding.[64] As for politics, it would not be through discussion that the People could attain the unity of its parts. That unity must be simply seen in action, prior to any discursive strategy. There were no words that could convey what the People thought, any more so than in the case of the mystery of the flesh and the body of Christ that became bread.[65] The symbol served to reveal, not explain. To apply to Schmitt's notion of sovereignty, in Pierre Bourdieu's words, we may say that sovereignty represents in all respects a struggle "to produce and impose one vision of the word."[66]

Thus, elections, instead of creating a distance between the citizens and the leaders (on which distance, as we saw, the quest for accountability is meaningful), should serve to unify them and erase all difference. Elections are democratic insofar as they annul individual reasoning. Control and limitation are totally out of place because the symbol is identical to the matter, not a procedure by which means individuals advance their interpretative views or interests. It is evident that Schmitt's rejection of the secret ballot and its replacement with the public exposure of the voice of the people (*seeing* the voice through the show of votes) is the locus of the most radically antiliberal formulation of the public in the twentieth century.[67] The ocular is the public.

Public in Schmitt's vocabulary did not mean the "public interest" or the "general interest." It meant the form of the manifestation of the sovereign. It did not even entail a counter-power against the tendency of state power to conceal its intentions and deeds. Schmitt opposed the ocular public to the enlightenment (and in particular Kant's) idea of publicity of state power against the absolute state. The enlightenment used publicity to tame the Leviathan. Schmitt used it to make the Leviathan stronger and more absolute in its authority because it was affirmed by the voice and face of the masses themselves, rather than by the outcome of an agreement among individuals. Hence, Schmitt's public meant that which was visible, or made in public. The opposite was *arcanum*, which had nothing to do with the nature of the issue and in this sense was not opposite to private interests per se—indeed, if a private interest was able to receive the support of a plebiscite, it became immediately public. *Arcanum* entailed not-done-in-public, or covered and concealed.

The form, not the content, was thus crucial. What the sovereign decided was in and of itself public, and at that point no judgment was justified that inquired over the content of the state's decisions because no normative perspective existed outside the expressed and visible voice of the sovereign. The content of what was made in public was irrelevant. For instance, foreign ministers pursue state interests in secrecy because they do not want to be seen or heard by the enemy. Schmitt would not object to *this* arcana, nor to the vast realm of discretionary decisions that the executive made far from people's eyes. He excluded secrecy only in elections or in the expression of the opinion of the sovereign.

The secret ballot was in Schmitt's rendering the veil of privatization that liberalism put on democracy; it was a violation of the principle of publicity that the popular sovereign instead entailed. Publicity thus meant not so much or only the legal or what the civil authority put under its mantel and made an object of sanctioned decisions under state jurisdiction. It meant instead the action of the sovereign as staged in the open, similar in kind to the public executions in the squares of monarchical absolutist Europe. "The public execution is to be understood not only as a judicial, but also as a political ritual. It belongs, even in minor cases, to the ceremonies by which power is manifested."[68] In Schmitt's analysis the people were much like the crowd that attended spectacles of punishment in the ancient regime.

Deeds made in front of the people so that the people have the impression (illusion?) that they are the judge: this is the underlying logic of the visual meaning of the public, which opens the door to propaganda more than to control or surveillance precisely because it is not based on rights and freedom of interpretation and contestation, and seeks publicity not to protect the subjects from the state's arbitrary decisions but to show and prove the authority of the public. "Freedom of opinion is a freedom for private people" that serves for electoral competition but not, however, for making the public rule.[69] Thus, if Schmitt attacked secret ballot it was because secret ballot takes the people away from the visual scene, more or less like with the modern state decision of bringing trials inside the tribunals and subjecting the defendants to a judgment that is performed behind closed doors, although pronounced for the public and according to public (as state) procedures and by publicly appointed magistrates. The secret ballot followed the same path as the eighteenth-century conceptualization of justice: in the voting booth as in the jury, the judgment or individual reason was performed *within* (the mind of the elector or behind closed doors) and *away* from the eyes of the public, while its performance was held according to procedures that were *public* (going to the ballot or pronouncing the verdict). Cesare Beccaria and the Marquis de Condorcet, just to mention the name of two theorists who most contributed in defining the character and procedures of those public acts (and who were Schmitt's target), proposed the notion of the public against which Schmitt launched his radical critique. Beccaria and Condorcet identified the public with open discussion (hence, freedom of speech and the press) and with individual deliberation (hence, the right of each citizen to an equal voice) and surmised that "this" publicity would be "the most effective protection against political abuses."[70] Kant famously declared this to be the mark of both modernity and freedom: "And the freedom in question is the most innocuous form of all—freedom to make *public use* of one's reason on all matters."[71]

To get rid of this idea of the public use of one's reason (the individual judgment as essential for public opinion), Schmitt attacked the secret ballot for transforming judgment into a matter of calculation and its results into an object of aggregation. In this sense, individuals exercising their political rights were acting as private persons and only the counting of their decisions was made public. The substance was private although vested in public garb. And it was precisely that substance that Schmitt wanted to make public, because only in this way would voting be purged of its aggregative implication and be an act of acclamation. The form that the opinion took in the diarchic structure of representative democracy was the issue against which Schmitt mobilized plebiscitarian consensus.

To Schmitt, thus, the form of the presence (the garb) was that which made the nature of the actors and of their deeds. *Public as made in public*: this was the garb or the form that gave substance to the political. The

"People" as the sovereign could only be conceived in public. Hence, voting in secret and in silence was a guarantee of the private individual and a free ride for his social and economic interests, not a guarantee of the power of the People, which was simply displaced in the very moment citizens voted individually and secretly. The People as a mass could not be rendered through the will and opinion of the individuals going to the ballot. Public appearance and the masses were two essential and intertwined aspects of what Schmitt thought democracy consisted in. In his view, starting from this notion of the public would allow us to see the paradox of representative democracy: secrecy as the substance of the sovereign. The sovereign becomes the *arcana*, a not-seen entity that receives the mark of the public by constitutional law and procedures that regulate the actions of associated individuals.

Schmitt invites us to think that the form or the way the sovereign acts is what characterizes a regime. If public as theatrical is the form of the political, then plebiscitarian democracy is the best kind of democracy. Clearly, the opposite of democracy would not be monarchy or any other regimes held by the few. Its opposite would be instead representative as parliamentary democracy, which replaces acclamation with suffrage and stimulates a kind of public opinion that is anchored on the individual rights and freedom, thus playing the role of information, knowledge, contestation, and advocacy, not only of aesthetic reaction to public appearance of the elected leaders.[72] But to Schmitt, democracy consisted in expelling the private mind of the voter from public opinion, and with it, liberty. We have to consider that to him politics was not the home of liberty but of authority, and consequently it was the place of acclamation not dissent, of unity not diversity or plurality of opinions.

The identification of the people with the public that Schmitt promoted makes sense of the fact that democracy means "government by public opinion," but in a new (and I would add, disfiguring) way. "No public opinion can arise by way of secret individual ballot and through the adding up of the opinions of isolated private people. All these registration methods are only means of assistance, and as such they are useful and valuable. But in no way do they fully encompass public opinion. *Public opinion is the modern type of acclamation.*"[73] Of course, no rational voice is detectable in this view of public opinion because no individual opinion is allowed. Schmitt's public opinion is not the expression of many publics but the popular support by acclamation and without dissenting voices of a leader or a regime, an act of faith and identification.

A Question of Faith

The Roman republic is the template that better fits the view of democracy as mass democracy in which the forum rules. Thus, parliamentary democracy is the primary target of *democracy in public and of the public.* Since the making of modern representative democracy, in fact, since Napoleon's plebiscitarianism, Schmitt explained, two antithetical views of government by means of opinion have been opposing each other: one in which decision by suffrage is kept separated from the opinions in the forum (diarchy of will and opinion) and one in which the distinction remains but the two domains change their form and meaning, in particular opinion that acquires the simplicity of the people's expression in the forum. Opinion no longer performs the complex function we said above, but rather has only the function of testifying visually to the acclaiming people. "The genuinely assembled people are first a people. . . . They can acclaim in that they express their consent or disapproval by a simple calling out, calling higher or lower, celebrating a leader or a suggestion, honoring the king or some other person, or denying the acclamation by silence or complaining."[74]

We can thus appreciate why Schmitt thought that the form of election in plebiscitarian democracy is acclamation. Acclamation is the action of an assemblage of people that react to a proposal or a view or a fact it does not produce or initiate. Schmitt is very candid when he says that the act of petition or law proposal is always the work of a minority or even of one person. Yet it is irrelevant the way in which a proposal is made. What makes it popular is not the participation of the people in formulating it but the people's reaction to it: a petition that does not receive the people's approval remains simply a private fact, while a petition that receives majority support is *ipso facto* public. In Schmitt's positivist formalism, it is the majority victory that makes an issue a public act. Thus, the people do not govern, represent, or exercise any specific political function: "the peculiarity of the word 'people' lies in the fact that it is precisely *not officials* who are active here" but the people, who sanction with yes/no what the officials do.[75] The People is a mass and acts as a mass or as an indistinct unity of identical parts; it cannot be asked to reason or act the way in which individuals do; its activity consists in sanctioning or reacting en masse.

The mass is the judging agent. The fact that its judgment is not a rationalizable kind of presence (not the base for aggregating votes, like interests or preferences) is what makes the people en masse the only master and an absolutely arbitrary sovereign. The government by means of opinion and the will, the diarchic character of indirect democracy, changes its appearance in quite a remarkable way in order to comply with the plebiscite as a public *fiat*. In a word, Schmitt radicalized both the domain of the will and that of opinion. He made the former the expression of one and only one procedure—the rule of majority, and he made the latter the expression of one and only one form of opinion—the public show of consent.

We have seen in the previous chapter how the assembly by acclamation mimics the Spartan assembly more than it does the Athenian one; in fact, it mimics the Roman forum and the comitia. Its model is the Roman forum because of the public in action through opinion uttered in mass, and it is the Roman comitia because in those assemblies the citizens voted in public and together by shouting "yes" or "no" or raising their hands on proposals coming from the magistrates. No less important is the majoritarian character of the plebiscites. Except for Athens, in Sparta and Rome what counted was the assessment of the majority vote. In the Roman comitia, the counting stopped as soon as the majority was reached because what the assembly was expected to do was reveal the opinion of the people or the majority opinion, not account for each opinion.[76] In Schmitt's jargon, plebiscite versus "bourgeois" individual suffrage meant precisely to convey the perfunctory value of voting, which was indeed a shout or acclamation because it was not expected to make each individual (let alone the minority) public, but only the majority. Voting counted thus not as an expression of the equal right of each but as an expression of the incorporation of all in the collective public. Public voting versus secret ballot was for the obliteration of the individual, his or her participation in the making of opinions, and his or her decision. Indeed, in plebiscitary democracy the individual citizen has no place and no power: he or she simply does not exist. As a matter of fact, thinking has no place in politics because, as I argued, it retains a private garb and the form of judgment insofar as it occurs in one's mind (for this reason Rousseau wanted a silent assembly). But politics consists in showing of opinions, making the will of the people visible. Thus, within plebiscitarian democracy politics has an endogenous irrationality that the arithmetic of counting tries in vain to sedate while the plebiscite accepts and exalts.

A similar point has been recently made by Laclau when he objected to the rational choice interpretation of voting. As we saw in the previous chapter, similarly to the epistemic theorists' own proposal, Laclau introduces his populist view by attacking the classical argument of the irrationality or political incompetence of the crowd. Like they do, he wants to rescue democratic politics from this classical and periodically resurrected aristocratic argument. Yet his answer is opposite to that of the epistemics. Laclau resumes Gustave Le Bon's classical study on the crowd in his analyses of the psychological effects of rhetorical politics on the mind of individuals when acting en masse. He drops Le Bon's antidemocratic ideology but retains some central themes of his argument. Gathered and assembled peoples, Laclau agrees with Le Bon, introduce an element of irrationality that is new and different from individual irrationality insofar as it cannot be opposed with the rationality of each individual composing the crowd or the sum of individual opinions. Thus, Laclau questions, with Le Bon, the "ideal," which was born along with representative government, that "a large gathering of men is much more capable than a small number of them coming to a wise and independent decision on a given subject."[77] Even supposing each member of the crowd is rational, their acting together as a homogenous whole makes their decision what it is: an act of power, which has nothing to do with the judgment of an individual kind of rationality or irrationality. For sure, this new kind of irrationality can be employed to serve rational plans or goals and be thus instrumentally very rational (as for instance, when leaders seek people's support for political programs that are patently unpopular).

In substance, in both populist and plebiscitarian thinking, the defense of the crowd does not pass through the claim of the rationality of the crowd and is not identical with that of the best and most informed individuals. This is what makes them different from the epistemic revision of diarchic democracy. Populism and plebiscitarianism are an assault on parliamentary democracy for a reason that is opposite to that of epistemic theorists because it is based on a radical rejection of individual judgment in politics. But the denunciation of rationalism is not for the sake of procedural democracy either, or in order to support a system of norms that serves to regulate conflicts and compromises in a scenario that can never be wholly rational or purged of irrationality. Proceduralist democracy recognizes or does not exclude the possibility that the irrational is part of politics, not a vice to be purged but a source of energy that procedures channel so as to make it capable of generating decisions. This is what ideological partisanship is about. But denunciation of rationalism makes plebiscitarians and populists change the relationship between the domain of opinions and the domain of the will. Indeed, in procedural perspective the recognition that opinion is the content of political discourse in democracy goes together with the recognition that the authoritative will of the people must follow rules and procedures that are meant to respect or reflect individual judgment, although not to purge it of its irrational elements. This is what makes democratic rules capable of governing the temporality of politics without subjecting it to the will of the majority. The role of political parties as intermediary bodies that mediate between the plurality of political opinions and their translation of transitory majorities is crucial. But it is not in plebiscitarian forms. Indeed acclamation presumes a kind of opinion that speaks through myth and propaganda rather than arguments and dissent, acclaim rather than vote, and identifies with the elected leaders rather than asking for their representative accountability. Acclamation wants directness and a shortcut, not a regulated temporality. Plebiscitarian politics is about success (winning the majority) more than a political process of participation that only partially identifies with the elected majority; it is about the victory by a leader with the seal of people's support and consent.

We may at this point bring to a conclusion our parallel between procedural democracy and plebiscitarian democracy. The latter entails a form of people's approval that is opposite to the suffrage form of consent that characterizes the right to vote in representative democracy. This is so because beforehand it shares in a notion of the People as a pure affirmation (theatrical show of opinion) of power that an external agent only can guide or shape. Transcendence, which the argument of the appeal to the People conceals, is the theological aspect of Schmitt's theory of mass democracy insofar as, without the shaping quality of the acclaimed leader, the power of the People is mute.[78] This contrasts strongly with a liberal, constitutional conception of democracy, which declares a consistent immanent foundation of political legitimacy or authority. Procedures themselves give form to the citizens' voice. The difference between these two views of democracy is enormous because while one engrafts democracy within a notion of politics as authority celebration, the latter recognizes disagreement (even on the interpretation of the foundational pact) as not only possible but moreover a structural condition of the democratic system of decision making. In the authoritarian format, the agent that holds the thread of politics is external to the People, although plebiscitarian propaganda may convince the people that the contrary is true. But without a set of impersonal legal instruments (Weber) or a charismatic leader (Weber and Schmitt), the people is nothing. To Schmitt, as to Weber in his later work, a leader is actually the better solution precisely because a leader is confirmation of the endogenous irrationality that belongs to the masses.[79] This is the premise of a politics of faith and trust, or the searching for a religious kind of consensus that can unify the leaders and the masses and put a stop to the otherwise fatally conflicting nature of politics.

The Crisis of Parliamentary Democracy

Faith or confidence is meant to sustain or restore authority or national harmony and does so by overcoming or silencing dissent or disagreement. As an act of trust, faith consists in an active exercise of confidence or adhesion with the ideals or precepts of the authority in which the source of trust is located. When politics is a matter of faith, belief, and trust, the person of the leader is naturally a better source of guidance than citizens' autonomous deliberation. On the other hand, the formal mechanism and procedures upon which constitutional and representative democracy relies presume a kind of behavior on the part of the people that is invariably also private and does not as such exclude instrumental rationality and calculus of interests. In a procedural view of democracy, the social is never completely cast out, although its entrance in the sphere of the state is limited by legal restraints, filtered through intermediary organizations like political parties, and subjected to the rules of parliamentary deliberation. And, although electoral campaigns aim at building trust and creating confidence in a candidate or a leader, procedures are meant to dissociate trust and consent, to let mistrust and criticism in, insofar as no elected politicians can be endowed with trust to the point of dispensing with control (and new elections). The substitution of the ethical character of the leader with procedures, of faith and trust in a leader with norms and regulations of the deliberative process, was the important contribution of eighteenth-century constitutionalism to the construction of the government by opinion. Beginning with the late nineteenth century's critique of parliamentary government this has become the main target of plebiscitarianism. Its renewal in contemporary democracy signals a decline of the party system and parliamentary democracy that is chronic and cannot be ignored.

Starting with the dualism between legal constraints and constraints on opinion (which is what plebiscitary democracy does) it entails envisaging a radical opposition between a procedural regulation of the government by opinions and the visible and extraconstitutional manifestation of the opinion of the people. This is the strategy that populism and plebiscitarianism share in common. Constitutional democracy, not only representative democracy, is their target then, both because of its individualistic rendering of popular sovereignty (as the right to vote) and because of its identification of political liberty with institutional intermediation between leaders and society, and finally with the division of powers. But if representative politics replaces trust with procedures, it is not because it does not hold trust important. Elections and representation entail trust. Yet precisely because ethical and psychological aspects are central in electoral politics precautions must be taken that introduce a healthy sense of disbelief or distrust, a distance between the citizens and the institutions or political actors.[80] This implies that opinion, although it is what makes power public or under the eye of the public, is not a secure controlling power if some additional specification is not made. This additional specification pertains to a considerable amount of freedom of the press and the plurality of the means of information and communication without which the creation of trust in a leader in the view of seeking people's support turns out to be another name for despotic domination.[81]

In a pivotal text written in 1789, the first theorist of representative democracy threw on the floor some seminal concepts that would help to grasp the meaning of plebiscitarian disfiguration. Condorcet proposed a distinction between *de iure* and *de facto* arbitrary power, which corresponded to that between *direct* and *indirect* despotism. Contrary to the ancient form of "direct" despotism, "indirect despotism" renews the classical theme of domination ("that is to say, whenever they are subjected to the arbitrary will of others") in new forms, which fit a government based on opinion and a market society. Condorcet was not content with the individualistic character of the classical definition of despotism (which largely dominated in his time among the *philosophes*)[82] because he understood that any discretionary power needs to rely on a class of people or an elite that supports it and makes it last. Individual leadership as individual despotism "exists only in the imagination," since any ruler needs the cooperation of a certain number of acolytes.[83] Reference to the form of indirectness is paramount. Indirectness pertained to a kind of despotism operating through "influence," which can be compatible with a public sphere and freedom of speech and association. It can develop in a free society when social classes (constituted by honors or nobility, by economic and financial power, by religious prejudices, and by ignorance) hold an unequal power to influence the law. "It is easier to free a nation from direct despotism than from indirect despotism," because it does not rest on mobilization but on individualistic dispersion. Thus, indirect despotism, Condorcet thought, may grow more easily in modern territorial states because of geographical concentration of masses of people in big cities and commercial centers and, I may add, with the unintended help of the mass media.[84]

> In countries in which intermediary organizations are few, distant from politics and most interested in the exclusive pursuing of their social objectives, while public opinion, largely atomized, is heavily exposed to the influence of televisions (as in the cases of many modern democracies), a wide room is open to a leadership that is created through plebiscitarian mechanisms. Video-politics favors the emergence of political outsiders who capture attention by exalting emotions that cross public opinion and translate into an electoral consent that is decisive to conquer power: what is 'ephemeral' becomes the right channel to reach government. If, in addition, controls on leadership are scarce and weak and the exercise of his power substantially unlimited—except for the fact he can be dismissed in the next elections—then the risks, present and future, of plebiscitarian democracy are relevant.[85]

What we witness in contemporary scholarship and actual politics is a decline of awareness of the risks that these transformations incubate.

The plebiscitarian renaissance meets with a realist rendering of politics that pretends to unmask the ideology of democratic autonomy and states candidly that in politics the people play simply a role of support for and visual check on a leader they want to watch acting from afar. "Whereas traditional democratic theories oriented around the ideal of autonomy seek to give the People control of the means of lawmaking, plebiscitarian democracy, in pursuing candor, seeks to bestow upon the People *control of the means of publicity*," a control that, however, "is negative, since it involves wresting control from leaders rather than the People."[86] Scholars of Weber have reacted to his enthusiastic rendering of plebiscitarian democracy by proposing to use Weber's thought in reverse or in order to detect and call attention to "the risk of a charismatic-authoritarian overturning of plebiscitarian-democratic power."[87] This risk rests on plebiscitarian democracy's endogenous instability, because the crowning by people's acclamation gives the leader a strong incentive to escalate rather than moderate his power. Trust and faith are thus not safe strategies of power limitation, whereas they are extraordinary resources for the support of the leader. Because of his direct appeal to the people's sentiments and emotions, the plebiscitarian leader wavers toward an incremental concentration of power unless strong counterbalances in the constitution and the institutional organization of the state are in place and work autonomously from the world of opinion: until, in other words, the diarchic structure of democracy is recognized.

The American Renaissance of Plebiscitarian Democracy

Beginning with Weber, several generations of scholars from Mosca and Sartori to Lintz and Ackerman[88] have suggested viewing the United States as a successful example of moderate plebiscitarianism because it is a case of a realistic or pragmatic view of democracy and because it is a presidential system that, while relying on a bottom-up relation with the masses, makes room for a more energetic executive activism than a headless, parliamentary democracy. Recently, some works have been published that propose an enthusiastic interpretation of plebiscitarian politics as a revitalization of democratic governance against the ideology of constitutional checks and balances and a supine subjection of the executive to the Congress and the interests there represented, against finally the parliamentary centrality in representative democracy. Whereas to past generations of democratic scholars (within Schumpeter's tradition), the theory of elites served to express dissatisfaction with the functionality of the theory of democracy or to lament the ruling power of the few despite the proclaimed triumph of the masses,[89] contemporary plebiscitarian theorists detect and prize at the same time the role of leadership in democracy,[90] while blaming the crisis of authority on constitutional legalism and parliamentary politics.[91]

Trust in Popularity

Eric A. Posner and Adrian Vermeule's *The Executive Unbound* proposes a description of the present political course and of transformation of the balance of powers in American government that aims to be also a prescription for how American democracy should work. The "is" and the "ought" merge. These authors complain that the dualism and tension between legal constraints and political opinion constraints are detrimental to the efficacy of political decisions in times of distress, like a war or international instability. They criticize the "Madisonian model" of the republic with the argument that "liberal legalism has proved unable to generate meaningful constraints on the executive."[92] They discuss the diarchic character of representative democracy in order to show it is more a problem than a guarantee for a secure liberty. Deliberative institutions along with bureaucratic strongholds that the social role of the state has produced through the years are held responsible for paralyzing decisions and jeopardizing the national interest. "Rather than deliberate, legislators bargain, largely along partisan lines."[93] Emergencies coming from international politics, the authors claim, put to the fore the poverty and weakness of a headless and collective approach to political decisions. The problem is as old as at least constitutional and representative government, although Schmitt is the author who personifies it with renewed authority. "When emergencies occur, legislatures acting under real constraints of time, expertise, and institutional energy typically face the choice between doing nothing at all or delegating new powers to the executive to manage the crisis."[94]

Posner and Vermeule seek to moderate the role of legalistic constraints and intensify another kind of constraint: public opinion, which seems to be a better force because it can be mobilized to monitor and control the established power without debilitating its decision-making proficiency. Whereas the legalistic checks and balances tie the political actor to the point of making it frail and inoperative, public opinion with its transparency requests is a better controlling agent because it makes the government more willing to act and take control than more timid and contained. In times in which international conflicts challenge national security and the very image of the nation, Posner and Vermeule show an empathic sympathy with the ideas of Weber and Schmitt, who also dealt with issues of patriotic honor and national pride. Like their German mentors, contemporary plebiscitarians denounce the parliamentary style of politics, the game of compromise, and the extenuating debates that enervate and debilitate the government. Crisis, military or economic, highlights the powerlessness of the liberalism of moderation while making emergency an ordinary politics that demands constitutional democracies "to hand over vast open-ended authority to executive and administrative bodies widely seen as best suited to tasks of quick and immediate action."[95] This argument has achieved great momentum also in Europe in coincidence with the financial crisis that, in a few weeks, swiped away elected governments and replaced them with technical executives that parliaments supported with quasi-unanimous vote of confidence. Economic emergency blurred parliamentary politics and the very majority-minority dialectics, but showed also that it is possible for headless democracies to have strong executives without becoming presidential or directly plebiscitarian.

Posner and Vermeule deem deliberative and representative democracy as time-consuming and "ill-fitted" to quick and dramatic decisions. A muscular presidency or a Caesarist leadership is better able to keep together strong decisionism and popular support. Reelection constraints and the need to appear in front of the public in a captivating way are regarded as the most effective and in fact sufficient methods for making the executive act in and for the interest of the country without jeopardizing democracy. "Indeed, the greater the president's power becomes, both through delegation and other de jure mechanisms and through the debilities of oversight institutions, the more essential popularity and credibility become, as the public focus of the presidency goes."[96] Thus, since their primary concern is that of recognizing and propagating the interest of the nation, the means of information and communication aim at inspiring or creating a supportive public that trusts the system more than it wants to generate dissent. This makes the mass media a natural resource for an audience democracy because they are naturally attentive to steer the identification of the people with the ideal of national interests, and meanwhile set up the horizon of public discourse through a continuous production of information that makes those interests appear to be always in the making.[97]

Niklas Luhmann explained years ago that the mass media set the standard of what is acceptable and what is not, and in this way they generate a background reality—factual and normative at the same time—that constrains people's opinions without directly coercing them.[98] Moreover, their autopoietic structure makes them an autonomous and stabilizing system of control, which is even more effective than the traditional legal one. Based on similar assumptions, Posner and Vermeule oppose the Madisonian liberal republic with the plebiscitarian presidential one. "Even between elections, the president needs both popularity, in order to obtain political support for his policies, and credibility, in order to persuade others that his factual and causal assertions are true and his intentions are benevolent."[99] Their optimistic view of the public role of the media seems to underestimate that "newspapers and televisions have little incentive to monitor politicians and statesmen on an ongoing, issue-by-issue basis. Such reports will overwhelm the information-processing capacities of the *private* citizenry that constitutes the mass audience. What this public wants is " 'news'. . . . If 'news' is what they want, 'news' is what politician/statesmen will give them."[100] An additional risk with video politics is that it turns a presidential election into "a very chancy event."[101]

Plebiscitarian democracy gives public opinion one function only, that of building authority, which is building trust on government and creating popularity for the president. It has two main ingredients: the leader's direct relation to the public for acquiring or increasing popularity and building trust, and the strengthening of the role of the leader by giving him more autonomy from the legal constraints with people's support. The *judgment* coming from the people competes with the system of legal control. With all the carefulness that any analogy commands, it is no exaggeration to recognize in this criticism of liberal constitutionalism the echo of Weber's disapproval of the uninspiring legal restrictions that the Reichstag imposed on state power as leadership, and finally to recognize in this proposal of an executive-centered government rooted in popularity the echo of Weber's call for a Caesarist leader with plebiscite approval.[102] In fact, Posner and Vermeule are more radical than these analogies suggest, since they invoke the authority of Schmitt's dictatorial leadership and never quote from Weber.

After questioning the republican "tyrannophobia," the authors of *The Executive Unbound* conclude their peroration for a strong plebiscitary executive by pointing to the anachronism of the negative myths of Caesar in Rome and Cromwell in the English civil war that inspired the American Founding Fathers. In fact, their quarrel is with the eighteenth-century tradition of constitutionalism. Thus, whereas Condorcet warned about the new form of despotism that can emerge from electoral consent, Posner and Vermeule assure us that tyranny is a risk of the past. Whereas Condorcet surmised that a market economy and public opinion could prompt new forms of domination, they think instead that these modern forces have liberated us from the risk of tyranny. Posner and Vermeule argue that the complexity that a market economy naturally creates and the unstoppable flow of information that the modern system of opinion formation activates do not justify the worrisome appeal to those ancient tyrants that motivated eighteenth-century constitutionalism. "Modern presidents are substantially constrained, not by old statutes or even by Congress and the courts, but by tyranny of public and (especially) elite opinion. Every action is scrutinized, leaks from executive officials come in a torrent, journalists are professionally hostile, and potential abuses are quickly brought to light. . . . Modern presidencies are both more accountable than their predecessors and more responsive to gusts of elite sentiment and mass opinion. . . . On this account, presidents already receive close public scrutiny."[103] Because the costs of acquiring political information have fallen steadily in modern economy, and because a wealthy, educated, and leisured population has the time and technical tools to monitor presidential action and state institutions, it might seem that the moderns have achieved the ability to monitor their leaders without weakening them. The creation of a public sphere of opinion that media technology and the market would provide seems able to allow the modern republic to be plebiscitarian without risking tyrannical involution.

Democracy without Autonomy

The second contribution to the renaissance of plebiscitarianism in political theory I am going to analyze is even more pertinent to the theme of democracy as government by opinion since it welcomes a radical revision of the way to conceive democracy and the plebiscitarian perspective itself. In this new rendering that Green proposes, plebiscitarian democracy mirrors the visual transformation of the power of opinion as a result of the technological revolution of the means of information and communication that started in the twentieth century. Green replaces the plebiscitarian masses acclaiming the leader in the crowded squares of fascist Europe with the People's eyes that compel the leaders and other high officials "to appear in public under conditions they do not control."[104] In 1930s plebiscitarianism the leader controlled the crowd through orchestrated propaganda; in contemporary demo-videocracies the crowd (the taste of the audience) controls the leaders by imposing publicity on their behavior.

Unlike Posner and Vermeule, Green has no interest in asserting the centrality of the executive over the legislative (although this is the unavoidable result of plebiscitarianism); instead, he wants to reconfigure the relation between the power of the will (decisions, voting, electing, and voicing consent or dissent in the public forum) and the power of opinion or judgment (surveillance and watching supervision) so as to redefine the meaning and role of the People and moreover of political autonomy, which is the most important principle of democracy.

Relying on Weber's reading of plebiscitarianism (but sympathizing with Schmitt's theory of the public), Green surmises that, although born in the early twentieth century and then disappearing because of the bad reputation that totalitarian regimes cost it, a leadership democracy is destined to come to life again and is in fact "a nascent theory that has yet to mature."[105] The reason for this is that the age of television and the large diffusion of the use of the Internet have contributed to restoring democracy in what, according to Green, is its original figure: a regime based on a direct relation of the masses to the leaders. Once again, the individualistic foundation of political legitimacy—the sovereign of the citizen—is the eighteenth-century legacy under attack.

In the tradition of antidemocratic thought, beginning with Joseph de Maistre, who started the assault on democracy in the name of a strong personal sovereign, the mono-archic correction of political equality has been used to demonstrate the incapacity of ordinary people to act effectively as a headless collective. It is worthwhile to remember that Thucydides depicted Athenian democracy in its hegemonic moment as a principality and constructed a relationship between the leader and the masses that became paradigmatic in the theory of elites and plebiscitarian democracy. In the tradition of Montesquieu (to be soon revived by Hegel), Emmanuel-Joseph Sieyès saw monarchy as an ethical institution that embodied the unity of the nation beyond the partial interests of its members, and served as the model of political profession in that it was shaped by virtue, honor, and competence, rather than only ambition and interest.[106]

Green recovers the paradigm of democratic principality and elite emendation of the government of the many but overturns its antidemocratic meaning and argues that a leader democracy is the most consistent figure of popular government. Democracy without demagogues is less of a democracy, rather than a bad democracy. As we saw above, in the tradition established by the great Roman historian Wolfgang Mommsen, Weber explained the reasons of Athens's greatness with the greatness of its leader and his harmonious relationship with the demos. "Pericles, because of his position, his intelligence, and his known integrity, could respect the liberty of the people and at the same time hold them in check. . . . So, in what was nominally a democracy, power was really in the hands of the first citizen."[107] This representation of democracy enjoyed robust success in the second half of the nineteenth century in coincidence with the mounting critique of parliamentary government, and had in Weber a strong supporter, whose greatest heroes were, as said, Caesar and Pericles.[108] "But the major decisions in politics, particularly in democracies, are made by *individuals*, and this inevitable circumstance means that mass democracy, ever since Pericles, has always had to pay for its positive successes with major concession to the Caesarist principle of leadership selection."[109] Today, it is technology that leads the plebiscitarian mutation of democracy: the Internet and the transformation of political language with popularized messages and easy commercials mark the decline of politics as deliberation and the growth of politics as leader-making. In this sense, Green reasons convincingly that plebiscitarian democracy may have the future in front of it.

Plebiscitary democracy joins with populism in proving the renaissance of a Roman style of politics both in modern practices and in theoretical analysis, and in particular the ideal of candor (where from the name "candidate" and "candidacy" come) or the public exposure of the leader as a person to the people in the forum that judge him, and thus the people's role as an audience that visually controls the appearance and performance of the leader.[110] The model of the forum, as we shall see below, changes the style of politics quite dramatically because it makes vision, not hearing, the core sense of participation. What is surprising is the conclusion that Green derives from this: the ocular transformation of public opinion makes plebiscitarianism less vulnerable to possible abuses by leaders. Indeed, whereas direct democracy made the people of ancient republics identify with the words of their leaders, the mass media naturally create a certain distance that is itself a reason for a more secure relationship of critical adhesion by the people with their leaders.

Like Posner and Vermeule, Green shows great confidence in the constraining power of the market economy and the modern system of information and communication, which are two conditions that allow a large
and diversified society to function as one society with no need to seek
deeper incorporation and cultural and social homogeneity. Moreover, in
making vision, rather than hearing, central, television is said to have contributed in purging the opinion of the masses of all pretense of rationality
upon which the power of persuasion of the orators relied. In the television
era the eighteenth-century ideology of the progress of rationality through
political participation can hardly be sustained. Video democracy confirms the fact that the politics of the masses belongs in the domain of
aesthetic and theatrical, not cognitive or deliberative; it actually has nothing to do with rationality. This point is crucial.

Television, Luhmann explained, is the quintessential counterargument
of the eighteenth-century idea of the public, because "the more 'that
which is perceived', say, television, plays a role in this [creating the public],
the more communication is based on implicit knowledge which cannot
even be communicated."[111] The aesthetical function of the ocular public
is meant to convey the idea that participating in watching occurs without
the viewers' intention of using what they perceive as a means for acting. A
"visual knowledge" is incapable of being controlled subjectively insofar as
what viewers acquire in common (the same images) makes them and the
fashion according to which they see things. "Whereas the Enlightenment
assumed that commonality consists in a communicable interest based on
reason," communication through the mass media is changed into an
identification process of the viewers.[112] The ocular public is thus a public
whose identity consists in judging according to the parameters of fashion
within which the subjective point of view becomes an embarrassing sign
of anachronism. "*Homo sapiens* is or has developed into a reading animal
capable of abstraction . . . *homo videns*, a television-made animal whose
mind is no longer shaped by concepts, by abstract mental constructs, but
by images. *Homo videns* just 'sees' . . . and his horizon is confined to the
images that he or she is given to see, thus why *homo sapiens* is entitled to
say, in all innocence, 'I see' to mean 'I understand', *homo videns* sees un-
assisted by understanding."[113] Yet if this is the case, as also Green seems to
imply, it is unclear how the ocular public with such an impoverished critical potential can have a surveillance authority.

Green argues that along with its cognitive role, the public sphere of opinion with the new system of media also loses its political role since, as I shall explain below, it does not make the citizens more competent in self-government, nor does it make them a mobilizing mass that claims sovereign power. On his account, epistemics (but also deliberativists) and populists are equally unwarranted. According to an aesthetic function of the forum, the public does not need to inspire participation in order to be political. It is political insofar as it makes the people capable of imposing visibility on their leaders, and *images* are more effective in achieving that than words. Since visibility, not "understanding," is the weapon of control, video politics is a more proficient system of control than even voting. Moreover, images contain more egalitarian implications and are more democratic than words. The parallel Green proposes between a logos-oriented form and an ocular-oriented one is interesting, compelling, and full of potentials in a society that like ours is based on and moreover made of images and visual inspection of distant leaders.

The bad side of rhetoric comes from its foundation in both speech and reason (*logos* was the Greek word to denote both of them), which makes the intentionality of the speakers a factor that is totally discretionary and remains unchecked, because it can never be made transparent to the listeners. Green makes the argument against words and for the primacy of vision by claiming that words and hearing live with (although react against) a system of power opacity; this would explain why the "public" was born along with the birth of large states that needed centralized systems of organized behavior and information, and with the birth of video technology. Accordingly, Green suggests, face-to-face democracy is primed to be more opaque than media democracy because it is most exclusively based on words or speech, and rhetoric entails concealment rather than transparency. Yet once politics operates in a forum made of images, the intentionality and even manipulation of the speaker cannot go along undisturbed for too long and without the inspecting interference of people's eyes. Green thinks that Machiavelli's maxim that the good leader should say without meaning works better in a politics that is not based on images because it does not require the leaders' actions to be exposed to the public. But images are fatal to popularity (and concealment), much more than words are. And although leaders of all times and places are driven by the temptation of manipulating people's consent, it is the use of words that gives their intention more chances of success. Images are, after all, much more at the viewers' disposal than are words. The leaders feel the influence of fashion like everybody else, and this is what makes the power of images more egalitarian and its constraining power more effective.

Green wants to unmask the rhetoric of deliberative democracy, according to which voice or dialogue or words represents a form of democratic participation in the decision-making process. He argues instead that candor, or the plebiscitarian revelation of the person of the leader to the audience, is much more democratic, although it does not cultivate any participatory ambition. In effect, the theory of deliberative democracy with its abstract scholasticism conceals the bare fact that the few rule without giving the many any real power of influencing the political game, since the game of politics falls outside the norm of deliberation. But plebiscitary politics starts from the recognition of those bare facts and wants to make sure that "those who do have massively disproportionate authority and power in a democracy in some sense be compelled to *recompense* the public for this privilege."[114] Ocular democracy acknowledges and accepts the existence of disequilibrium in power between the governed and the governors and subjects it to the norm of trade that is *do ut des*. In other words, it barters citizens' autonomy for leader's publicity in the very moment it attempts to do away with words.[115]

Ocular democracy claims a normative value and the comparison of gaze and words is the key to grasp it. Rhetoric is responsible for creating more passivity under the pretext of propelling knowledge and reasonable arguments in public discourse. In addition, it violates equality much more systematically than visual appearance does. The case of eloquence seems to prove Green's argument. This public use of persuasive speech is geared to the many and requires equality of some basic potential, like the ability of making moral judgments, but not, however, of any specific kind of intellectual competence or skill or knowledge.[116] The public use of words does not presume a direct response or a dialogical exchange: the audience of a speaker, like that of an actor on stage, is for the most part more inclined to listen than to talk. As a matter of fact, eloquence cannot exist without an audience, and attention-getting words are more important than are logical inferences because aesthetics can move the emotions. The audience thus plays an important role because it determines the quality of arguments and the behavior of the orator.[117] Hence, Plato in *Republic* compared eloquence to poetry because it presumes an audience and a sympathetic relationship between author and speaker and reader and listener.[118] Yet its aim is to affect the audience members' will by touching their emotions and inspiring their decisions to act, not to make them equal participants or capable of control.

Reversing the idea that lies at the core of the linguistic foundation of deliberative democracy, Green concludes that words do not protect the people from interference and manipulation more than images do, nor do they allow for more participation, nor are they more egalitarian. In sum, there seems to be no reason to believe that a public of words makes for a better democracy than a public of images. The comparison becomes even more compelling if we consider the controlling potential of these two forms of democratic public. Although plebiscitarian democracy starts with the acceptance of a relation of inequality between political leaders and everyday citizens' gaze, it allows for a "corrective" strategy as deliberative theory does not, which makes democracy a philosophical ideal (characterized by the normative values of autonomy, reciprocity, and universalizability) but has nothing to say about the way in which democracy operates. The hiatus between ideal and real makes the deliberative theory of democracy ineffective and toothless.

The "remedial" strategy that plebiscitarian democracy proposes is not inspired by the goal of augmenting people's power, or opposing one positive power (participation) against another one (decision). It is instead based on the idea that revealing arcana is equivalent to taking away from them the arbitrary component which lies in secrecy. Green is in perfect agreement with Schumpeter that decision stays with the few because it cannot be the domain of the unorganized many. But he then gives "the People" a power that the few do not have: that of unveiling. The remedy to the unavoidable unbalance of power that politics entails (democracy is no exception) comes from a power of a *"negative* type: one that imposes special ocular burdens on the selected few whose voices have been specially empowered to represent others, to deliberate with fellow elites, and to engage in actual decision." Candor imposes "extra burdens on public figures" while equalizing the viewers and the viewed in something important: public exposure of their deeds, or the ocular power.[119]

Green exalts the democratic and egalitarian potentials of gaze by referring to, among other things, the existential aspect of control and agency that the spectator exercises on the leader. Despite the unpleasant and even perverse implications that the power of gaze may have, it is certain that it sets up a direct confrontation between the viewers and the viewed, and this, as opposed to hearing, adds to its more egalitarian implications. The

disciplinary power of gaze recognizes "the spectator as potentially occupying a position of power vis-à-vis the individual who is being seen."[120] The
Bentham/Foucault paradigm of a viewer that increases its power in proportion to its invisibility inspires Green's model of ocular democracy, in which
the masses have the same all-powerful invisibility as the guardian of a prison
whose architecture is predisposed so as to make its presence unseen (Bentham, whose defense of representative government earned him Schmitt's
accusation of being a "fanatic of liberal rationality," proposed to make the
people powerful in judgment, much like the prison guardian, when he
defined public opinion as "the power of a tribunal").[121]

In relocating people's power of judgment from words to visions Green
wants to make "the tribunal of opinion" truly effective and thinks that the
revolution of the means of information and communication supports his
case because it gives the People its own function, which is not that of acting (a mass, as Weber showed, cannot act without a leader) but that of
observing and judging. Plebiscitary democracy reconfigures the diarchic
structure by creating two actors: people as voters (with ideologies, interests, and the intention and desire to compete for power) and the People as
an impersonal and totally interest-free unity that inspects the game of
politics by imposing publicity. Citizens' political participation is minimal
and consists in the electoral selection of the elite. The real place of the
People is the forum, in which, however, it does not play the role of forming opinions because it is not in the form of a plurality of interests or
views but rather in the form of an anonymous mass of viewers. The
People is the supreme inspector that "only watches" but "does not win"
because it does not participate in the competing game of politics, a task
only for the few.[122]

The Cost of Publicity

Becoming a political leader in plebiscitarian audience democracy must
be made a costly business: this is the only resource of control the audience
has. The cost a leader pays in exchange for holding the tools of state power
in his hands is the renunciation of most of his individual freedom. The
leader is wholly in the hands of the people because he is permanently
under the people's eyes. This is the "extra burdens on public figures" that
ocular plebiscitarian democracy provides. Green's proposal is compelling
because it is undeniable that those who compete for power should be

aware they do not enjoy nor can they claim the same latitude of negative liberty as ordinary citizens. More power entails more responsibility and thus less liberty of concealment. Political power longs for the ring of Gyges, or the power to be invisible in order to be able to do what it otherwise could not.[123] Secrecy is a basic good in the private life of the individual but may be an intractable obstacle in the case of public officials. Of course, a minister or a prime minister is protected in his basic rights as anybody else is; however, in order for his private life to be proved transparent and lawful, some extra inspection may be needed. In this case, trust does not come *ex ante* as a blank check but entails and actually requires corroboration of evidence. As a matter of fact, running for a political post is a free choice of the candidate whose outcome comes with a mix of honor and burdens.

What is less convincing in Green's peroration for making the leader the object of the viewers is the assurance that putting the leader on stage will *eo ipso* entail making his power more constrained or checked; that in substance, the public can substitute for the constitution in limiting power, thus fulfilling the goal of making politics more democratic because it is less subjected to the control of nondemocratic institutions. But the "politician's motive for wearing a socially acceptable mask did not disappear with the advent of modern democracy,"[124] and Green's argument for the controlling power of an ocular public is unconvincing and unwarranted. It is based on abstract considerations of the role of the ocular public that the actual experiences seem to disprove.

Prime Minister Silvio Berlusconi was permanently under the eyes of the media, who intruded in his life not necessarily for revealing his lawless behavior but for satisfying the public's thirst for scandalous news, which in turn created the market of scandals and made public opinion into tabloid format.[125] Putting the private life of the prime minister under people's eyes did not serve either to control or limit his power; moreover, it did not even deter him from living his life as he preferred. The fact that Berlusconi owned or controlled six national television stations was of course an aggravating factor, but it was not the only reason that made Italian audience democracy a passive democracy that could hardly control him. Indeed, even more than the ownership of the means of information, the empire of the ocular or the inflation of images is the factor that makes vision an especially inept power of inspection.

The paradox of exasperating the aesthetic factor of public opinion at the expense of understanding and participating in the making of political judgment is that it does not consider that images are the source of a kind of judgment that evaluates tastes more than political or moral facts. Taste, Kant explained, exalts rather than contains the rhetorical potentialities of vision, and moreover isolates but does not foster communication. Indeed, while it is possible "to argue about taste" it is impossible "to dispute" about it because no beyond-disputation conceptual determination is available in the domain of taste. The most we can do is to have *faith* that "there must be hope of coming to mutual agreement" and to work for making it possible. Taste is a subjective opinion and can hardly be a vehicle for mutual agreement among viewers. To the contrary, it is hypothetical reasoning (imagination in Kant's words) that has the power and capability to arouse the will and does so by leading our reason to devise strategies that could attract consent: "there must be hope of coming to mutual agreement; hence one must be able to count on grounds for the judgment that does not have merely private validity and thus are not merely subjective, which is nevertheless completely opposed to the fundamental principle *Everyone has his own taste.*"[126] Ideology is the daughter of hypothetical reasoning and imagination; it makes us prefigure the future so as to mobilize our will to action in the present in order to fulfill it. Giving ideological accounts is a rational behavior in a domain that, like politics, deals with future-oriented behavior or decisions that are supposed to make things happen. But what is the outcome of images and taste? "The upshot is this: that the priorities of television are the scoop, the shoot (a good image), and the ratings (the largest possible audience)."[127] The predictable outcome is that information does not in and by itself empower the faculty of judgment.

The hegemony of the ocular would drive the public in exactly the opposite direction as intended by Green. The audience does not control the leader but suggests to the leader what he should do or avoid doing in order to meet with people's favor (which is not necessarily identical to the interest of society), and actually to forge their favorable opinion. Moreover, the empire of the visual inevitably ruins the tenor and style of political discourse. The Italian experience confirms this diagnosis because in the years Berlusconi reigned as a de facto plebiscitarian leader of an audience democracy, the issues of political conversation were dictated by the logic of commercial marketing and publicity. Political issues that the mass media led were expunged from the public discourse simply because they were not attractive to television assets or to the viewers.[128] The paradox of the total video public, or putting an "extra burden" on public figures, is that political decisions do remain unseen and unrevealed because they are most of the time unattractive to the aesthetic taste and the spectacular desires of the televised crowd. Knowing very little of what elected politicians were doing was the cost Italian citizens paid by becoming an all-powerful ocular audience that was fed with a kind of information that was driven by the goal of impressing people's minds with images that stirred compassion or anger. "The effect is not the function where the mass media seems to lie; this functions seems to lie in the reproduction of non-transparency through transparency, in the production of *non-transparency of effects* through *transparency of knowledge*."[129] Thus, making the life of the leader visible and an object of spectacle may engender new opacity under the pretense of publicity.

The Italian case proves that the transformation of the base of politics from party programs to audience has made the People not only less in control but actually unable to watch and the domain of politics more vulnerable to corruption. Years ago, Alessandro Pizzorno interpreted the paradox unfurled by this transformation as a sign of the decline of political language and judgment and its replacement with the language and judgment of subjective morality and taste. The centrality of symbols over programs, of the personality of the leader over the collective of party supporters, translates into the centrality of moral qualities over political qualities in the formulation of political judgment by citizens. Political virtues (prudence, competence, etc.) decline and personal virtues (aesthetic, sexual, etc.) become central. A proved outcome of this transformation is the increase of corruption, because what should be an object of public visibility is not as interesting to the viewers and the media experts as the person of the leader. Politics becomes more professional in the sense that it becomes an activity that lives from concealed exchanges. In fact, the plebiscite of the audience facilitates corruption.[130]

What Is the Point of Watching?

Giving the People an exclusive ocular power does not give them any guarantee that what they are going to see are the most important things government and the politicians deal with or what the society needs and wants.[131] For opinions to be public it is not enough that they are diffused among the public; it is also necessary that they pertain to "public things," to the *res publica*, and the judgment on this pertinence is something that the citizens develop freely when they participate in the making of their will and judgments as citizens, not simply as viewers.[132] They do so when they do other things besides watching, such as participating in movements, associations, and elections; making their representatives aware of their problems and interests; contesting them; and voting them in and out. It is not, however, only the content and the doer that make a fact a public fact but also the form in which it was achieved. Citizens contribute in making the public when they induce the state to do what Kant thought it should do: submitting its deeds to the citizens' judgment in order to be evaluated according to the principles of the public use of their reason, which is equality of consideration and liberty. The public use of citizens' reason demands that the state's acts are public. But at what point does the publicity of a public deed start? Does it start when it is still in the form of a plan in the mind of the politicians,[133] or when it is under debate in public institutions, like an assembly?[134]

In commenting on the Kantian maxim of public reason, Noberto Bobbio asked the following questions: If a government's concealment of its deeds is in and by itself an admission that those deeds are grounds for a scandal, "what is it that constitutes a scandal?" and "at what point is a scandal born?" How exposed to the public must a deed be in order to count as being under people's eyes? In other words, no decision can be made in a fully transparent way, particularly when, as in a democracy, individual freedom is the principle that guides political behavior (not only private), because it is the condition thanks to which bargaining and compromise among plural parties and interests can be achieved.[135] The way in which public deeds are made public (when? in what form? by means of what kind of images? etc.) is in and of itself not a transparent issue.

The answer of plebiscitarian democracy does not seem to take away opacity: "Candor is useful because it seeks to regulate this secondary set of concerns: not the policies that are legislated, but the leaders empowered to legislate."[136] The ocular power of the People operates on the person of the leader rather than policies. This is what makes it a chapter in plebiscitarianism. "Presidential debates, public inquiries, and press conferences" are the strategies of ocular democracy, which pertains essentially to the "watchability" of behavior.[137] But as Luhmann argued convincingly, opacity is implied in the paradigm of the public as total viewer because "being offered from the outside, entertainment aims to activate that which we ourselves experience, hope for, fear, forget—just as narrating of myth once did."[138] The ocular public stimulates identification and empathy, two phenomena that are hardly conducive of a critical or controlling attitude.

Thus, although the visual transformation of the public generates a "constant presence" of the public, this may not be a controlling presence. Seeing more and constantly does not necessarily imply seeing all and seeing what is important to see in order to judge or hold accountable the leaders for their decisions. Most of all, it does not make the citizens more powerful than when they vote in a political election, as Green thinks. "The plebiscitarian approach to democratic reform is valuable precisely because it deprivileges both the specific act of voting and the general conception of the everyday citizen as a decider."[139] But elections, which are the opposite of a "constant presence," have the power of kicking an unpleasant leader out of office; on the other hand, watching the leader through the information or images provided by the mass media and the press agents every day may make the citizens feel powerless—unless ocular democracy is interpreted as a tool for more participation, or even the breaking of ordinary politics. Yet this is not what Green's plebiscitarian people are supposed to aim at or do because audience is meant to substitute for participation rather than inspire participation.[140]

At this point a question comes up spontaneously: Since the People is assumed to be only a visual audience that has no role whatsoever in the process of decision, which only the few have, what is the point for it to watch? Stripping the people of its "capacity to author norms and laws" entails making the public sphere play merely an aesthetic role, the impact of which is more entertaining than it is controlling. The statement according to which "in modern democracy *minorities* rule" would thus need to be completed with the statement that they rule after the people have elected them. Without including the moment of participation or "the will" in the definition of the People, ocular democracy has no goal, or more precisely, it has no other goal than watching. The diarchy of will and judgment is what makes the democratic people a controlling actor because it contemplates a structural communication (regulated by procedures and constitutional norms and operated by intermediary associations like parties and civil society organizations) between political action and political judgment. This diarchy is disfigured if the will is given to the few that make the procedural and institutional game (as elected elite), and the judgment is given to the people, but in the sole form of visual or aesthetic.

Thus, I would propose we reverse the plebiscitarian argument and stress that being under the people's eyes may be a cunning strategy the leader or simply media experts use to diminish the people's control over the power of the leader if some provisions are not made that do not simply pertain to the regulation of his or her appearance in public. As we just saw, Green suggests that for the executive or the president to hold regular press conferences or for candidates to engage in a frank and open debate on television—in sum, to make the arena of politics a gladiatorial experience—is enough to expose him or her to people's ocular power. These events, he surmises, are in tune with the identity of the People as a unity that is not fragmented in partisan parts. Elections give the verdict of the majority and reflect partisan battles. They are means in the hands of political groups, not a procedure the democratic sovereign uses to create, control, and limit state power. In Green's rendering, elections or the authoritative voice is outside of the People's competence, which is only one: watching and judging from a position that is above all partisan views and with no active goal ahead. The political sovereignty of the people disappears. The sovereign is only an audience.[141] The aesthetic and theatrical public forum replaces both the political and the deliberative function.

Audience Democracy

It has been said that video politics registers the end of the citizen in mass society, a transformation whose consequences are not yet wholly clear to us because "television is in the process of reshaping our way of being" and the Internet adds to this change.[142] The acceptance of this fact is propaedeutic to a new theory of democracy made "in light of the specific pathologies and dysfunctions" that mass communication technologies, and especially television, have produced, yet not in order to find remedies against those pathologies and dysfunctions.[143] Democracy of the audience marks the acknowledgment of the decline of the ideal of political autonomy. In a classical work on mass society, William Kornhauser asked many years ago the question of how we can distinguish between good and bad plebiscitarianism in a democracy in which the masses play the role of a receptive engine of leadership. Kornhauser proposed an answer that is still valuable (and worrisome): the crucial factor we have to pay attention to is how the leaders relate to the masses and to other leaders. In plebiscitarian politics, the factor of control is situated in the person of the leader rather than in procedures and the institutions. The reference point for judging whether we have a good or bad plebiscitarian leader is the character of the leader himself, thus an accident or a condition that can hardly be controllable by the audience. Audience democracy is a politics open to hazards.

This finds a confirmation in Green's argument that candor and transparency are the only containing strategies we dispose of in mass democracy. Yet candor and transparency cannot be fully enforced through institutions and norms unless the basic rights to privacy and individual freedom of speech are not blatantly violated. Thus, although, as I said above, being accountable to the audience entails the leader enjoys less privacy, his acceptance of exposing his life to the audience depends mostly on his morality or the calculus of prudence he and his staff make.[144] Hence, the renaissance of plebiscitarianism confirms the relationship proposed by Kornhauser of mass society as easily manipulatable and mobilizable by the decline of the citizen.[145] In addition, as authors in the liberal tradition from Mill and Tocqueville to Walter Lippmann have abundantly warned us, the "mass man" is not only vulnerable to the leaders but to the masses themselves. To these warnings, Green answers that this intricacy of dependence shows that all the power of the democratic masses is in opinion, an opinion that, moreover, has been gradually transformed in images and visual attention. The mass media place the government under a permanent inspection by the people who do not for this reason need to vindicate participation in politics to be active like a sovereign. Plebiscitarian democracy completes the transformation of the political people in the public and fulfills the promise of the government by means of opinion as one that pivots on the negative power of judgment, a form of political participation that wants to check rather than make decisions, that has no longing for making things happen and is not very much concerned with delegated powers. The power of the viewer is the only power the People retain, and moreover the only checking power.

Mass media and the electronic system of direct communication are an unprecedented support to the democracy of the audience and the collapse it entails of the distinction and mediation between the private person and the citizen.[146] The disappearance of the general actor (or the artificiality of the political identity of the citizen) means that judgment itself is going to change by becoming more adherent with the point of view or the idiosyncratic taste of the individual person and in direct reaction to the events or occurrence of facts the person sees. "The citizen who converses with other citizens on the Internet does not exist."[147] As Lippmann anticipated some decades ago, the perfection of the democracy of the public corresponds to the creation of a world that has no external reference point to the mind and life of the private person, in which the evidentiary perspective is no longer possible.[148] The world created by the mass media is the world itself, a total and only reality. According to Luhmann it is not a world of communication to begin with because with these instruments interaction between senders and receivers of images is ruled out. And it is precisely this interruption of direct contact that ensures a high level of freedom of the media, with the implied coda that the receivers are truly passive recipients.[149] Yet this is likely to change the meaning of publicity and the public sphere, while undermining Bentham's idea of the public as a tribunal. The diarchy of will and judgment empowers the public thus because it incorporates a regulative idea (the citizen as an identity that belongs to all equally and is not identical to the social reality of the private person) that makes judgment itself a "public" act because it is a parameter that every citizen knows how to use, and thanks to which state actions and decisions are judged as right and wrong.

As we have seen above, Schmitt reinterpreted plebiscitarian democracy from the perspective of the change in the meaning of the "public" from something that is defined in a juridical-normative sense (what pertains to the civil state) into something that is exposed to vision or exists in a theatrical sense (what is done in front of others' eyes). This is the view of the public that returns in contemporary plebiscitarianism. The resurrection of the ideas that piloted the criticism of parliamentarianism in early twentieth-century Germany is an interesting indication of a new worrisome trend in democratic theory. Bernard Manin's book on representative government is perhaps the most important document of this trend. A central theme of Manin's book is a diagnosis of the decline of party democracy and the emergence of the democracy of the public in which trust in the leader and the acceptance of an increasing call for discretionary power by the executive meet with a change in the organization of political elections from party leaders and militants to experts in communication. "Audience democracy is the rule of the *media expert*,"[150] or the celebration of the ocular power, as Green observes in completing Manin's diagnosis. Although during party democracy elections were heavily based on the vocal and the volitional aspect of politics—participation was the central marker of popular sovereignty—appearance in public now defines the art of politics. Words, discussion, and conflicts between ideas and interests are central in the one case and candor or transparency in the other, in which the organ of popular power is "the gaze rather than the decision, and the critical ideal of popular power [is] candor rather than autonomy."[151] Manin's audience democracy is an insightful and influential step toward participation as spectatorship.

Manin did not intend to sponsor the movement in that direction. Indeed, his diagnosis was based on the idea that the spectating audience is a sovereign judge, hence presumed the traditional idea that consent and discussion are essential to legitimacy, but that judgment alone is not a mark of self-government. Thus, Manin evaluated the transition from party democracy to audience democracy in terms of a decline of sovereign power of the people because it was a disempowerment of the decision-making power of the citizens. When people used to vote for parties with a platform they exercised their judgment on future politics; their votes did not contain simply their trust in the person of a notable, as it used to happen at the beginning of representative government, when the candidate-notable was the figure of representation. In party democracy, the image of the candidate did not substitute for the future expectation of the voters as in plebiscitarian democracy, in which elections occur on the basis of the image of the candidate, and reference to programs and platforms is almost irrelevant. The consequence is that accountability itself becomes meaningless since electors do not have any control on issues and policies, not even during the electoral campaign. Clearly, Manin judged the transition from debating and participating to attending and gazing as a sign of "malaise," not an improvement. Indeed, he concluded his book with discomforting words: "representative government appears to have ceased its progress towards popular self-government."[152]

But once we drop Manin's evaluative judgment on the transition from party democracy to audience democracy and take the latter to be a fait accompli to cope with, we see that the normative scenario changes. What a consistent audience perspective propels, Green argues, is the final overcoming of the "hegemonic status of the vocal model" and its idea that peoples' participation is "an active, autonomous, decision-making force."[153] The plebiscitarian project consists in overturning this hegemony and liquidating deliberative and procedural democracy, which considers plebiscitarian democracy a "profanity" because of the passive role it ascribes to the people. The arguments that deliberativists and proceduralists advance against it are mainly ethical and moral; they are made either in the name of the universalizability of rational arguments or in the name of preference aggregation and the periodical change of the elected as the only pragmatic way to resolve the lack of rationality that the government by opinion contains. Habermasian theorists and proceduralist theorists conceive democracy as a political order that is based on autonomy and voting, a view of political activity that is centered on decision and voice. They treat the opinion of the private individual as a matter that cannot enter the political domain without going through a transformation. The former do so by filtering opinions through rational deliberation, the latter by extracting from those opinions the numerical unit of calculus. This is what ocular democracy wants to confute and change when it opposes intermediation of judgment with visual reaction to images.

A Roman Model

Lawrence K. Grossman wrote several years ago that telecommunication technology has reduced the traditional barriers of time and space and redirected politics back to direct democracy. The decline of the Madisonian model, he surmised, goes hand in hand with this process of narrowing distance and blurring the traditional checks and balances and separation of power that accompanied the first two centuries of constitutionalism. A new season of direct democracy seems to be awaiting the moderns if it is true that even the judges of the Supreme Court feel the pressure of the audience instead of defending their independence.[154] However, the scenario I have been painting in this chapter is not that of direct democracy but of a new form of oligarchy that develops from the centrality of vision over voice. Indeed, when the norms of political autonomy give way to those of spectatorship, democratic procedures are demoted to methods for elite selection, with the understanding that this does not give any power to citizens. It is possible to say that in exchange for the power of influencing politics, ordinary citizens exit the space that institutions and procedures organize. Recovering the visual role of *doxa* is in this case for vindicating the irrational power of the people through gaze, rumors, cheers, and boos. The distance from the cognitive myth of the public as the space for the formation of an enlightened public opinion cannot be greater. Equally great is the distance from the political role of opinion as verisimilar judgment that, to paraphrase Aristotle, characterizes an isonomic democracy in which reasoned arguments and votes are the tools (and rights) that all citizens have and can use. The tradition in which plebiscitarian democracy belongs is thus neither the enlightenment nor Athenian direct democracy. It is instead the Roman forum in which the plebiscitarian presence of the masses acted functionally in support of the leading role of the few. In this concluding section of the chapter I would like to suggest the renaissance of the plebs and their audience activity as the best representations of the new figures or characteristics of democracy in the age of technological and mass media.

As we saw in the previous chapter, the *Populus Romanus* was *both* a crowd and the lawmaker that shared in the sovereign power with the Senate. The crowd in the forum was not identical to the *populus*, which acted inside of the tribes (*tributa curiata* and *tributa centuriata* according to the different gatherings made for voting on laws or for magistrates).[155] The crowd was active in its own way, and "not limited to demonstration of public opinion" (that is, *extimatio* or voting). It was the active protagonist (as a whole, not a sum of individuals) of the political functions held in the forum, which was judging and on some occasions voting by plebiscite for candidates or on laws. The crowd "functioned as a public political theater" that all public figures recognized, appreciated, and feared.[156] It was its presence en masse that exercised its powerful influence on the leaders; gaze, shouting noise, and rumors were the weapons branded in the forum. The effect on the leaders had to be certainly stronger than that of today's televised public, which is performed in collective isolation, if I may say so, or within private homes. The ocular was in Rome a stronger and more direct power in comparison to which our power of television attendee pales. Although the differences are enormous, the analogy with the forum is important in order to better understand the consequence for democracy that comes from exalting the function of the informal audience or the public over the citizen. To anticipate my argument, the Roman experience shows us that the crowd acquires more relevance in proportion to the decline of the relevance of the people's voting power, at the twilight of the republic.

The physical presence of the Roman public and the visual spectacle it performed was a force that strongly impressed the "eyes and mind" of the performer.[157] To paraphrase Bentham, the forum was the most frightening judging tribunal in the republic. It was hard to discern who led and who was led because emotions ruled the forum. Emotions, which Cicero described as the agents of a contagious disease, were the irrational factor that made all the Romans recognize and feel the forum as a unique place. Le Bon's analysis of the crowd in mass society translated Cicero's description into a language that fits modern plebiscitarianism.

The crowd, Le Bon explained, has an "invincible" power because it is not a power that can be translated into quantity. It is "invincible" because it is not the sum of individual wills but a surplus value, so to speak, that exists only when the people become an indistinct unit. It is characterized by a lack of individual responsibility for one's decision that makes it all the freer to act and produces a contagious phenomenon that makes people act by imitation and think in a way they cannot, if interviewed later on, explain. It is finally run by the power of suggestion which comes from the fact that each individual feels the presence of the others and cannot resist them. Le Bon described a crowd as a falling back to the spontaneity of the tribe: possessing the "spontaneity, the violence, and the enthusiasm" and even "heroism" of "primitive beings."[158] Aggregative calculus but also strategic rationality was wholly inept to represent the power of the forum or the crowd. Le Bon used the argument of the invincible power of the crowd, its contagiousness and emotional power of suggestion, to explain how it was that the nobles in France renounced their privileges and decided against both their class and their individual interests. "The renunciation of all its privileges which the French nobility voted in a moment of enthusiasm during the celebrated night of August 4, 1789, would certainly never have been consented in by any of its members taken singly."[159] "Inferior" to the "insulated individual" (and to the individual-citizen thinking in the solitude of his or her mind as when he or she votes) in terms of rationality, according to Le Bon, the crowd is well superior to the individual in terms of feelings, and above all in terms of emotions. The strength of the public sight or the style in which opinions are voiced is what makes the crowd, ancient and modern, so unique and special.

The Roman crowd also had a checking function. This was the important power of being under the people's eyes, or being in public. Jon Elster wrote that the effect of public debate (of being before an audience) on assemblies in which decisions are to be made is that of inducing the speakers to replace the language of interests with the language of reason or an impartial reason.[160] This does not of course imply that proposals under consideration are cleansed of partial motives or interests, since it is the skill of a good speaker to be able to employ words that cover his or her intention. That the presence of the public makes it difficult for orators to appear motivated merely by self-interests does not mean that orators or politicians are unable to succeed if they appear sincere without being so, if they are purely hypocrites.[161] Machiavelli spent important pages to show precisely this possibility, which means indeed turning the public from a controlling devise into a spectacle and an engine of legitimacy.

This is the sense in which Miller speaks of "the ideology of publicity that pervaded every aspect of Roman communal life."[162] Publicity entailed first of all that all actions or proposals or events that pertained to the functions of the republic were made and shown in public so as to give all the *populus* an effective chance to be informed, to judge, and to make decisions. Law proposals, the names of jurors or Tribune candidates, and all other kinds of information were daily updated in public on boards or hung on lists. Publicity meant making "the details" of any prospective action available to all citizens who passed or stood by in the forum. "Writing, public action, and spoken words all played a part if guaranteeing publicity."[163]

The use of the public was thus more important for the symbolic character it had than for the actual effect it might have had on decisions. Thus, withdrawing from the public, acting behind closed doors marked an extraordinary change in Roman politics, which traditional republicans opposed and feared. The reconstruction in Cicero's speech of how Verres conducted his electoral campaign is an important document because "for the first time in Roman politics, we hear of *divisiores* meetings [party meetings] at the home of a candidate, with the aim of distributing bribes from him to different tribes."[164] Before it was "privatized," political influence was exercised in the open, in the forum.

Yet public exposure was able to protect the republic from bribery and corruption because political leaders *felt* the burden of appearing dishonest (not necessarily being so). The public was able to deter corruption for as long as the city was virtuous. Transparency held an effective power of surveillance as long as the Roman citizens felt the sense of shame in showing their vices to their fellow citizens. Clearly, procedures that regulated the law-making power of the *populus* were not perceived as enough protection, and virtue needed to be mobilized to strengthen them. Acting in public was a supplement of protection in a city in which the ordinary currency was honor and virtue—the risk of being seen by the public of

Rome and being publicly denounced was a deterrent power that both constrained and stimulated the leaders. "Public" was thus an adjective that entailed "being under the eyes of the crowd." For it to have a checking function, some ethical factors needed to be presumed and effectively working.

Corruption deterrence on human weakness is certainly one of the most important legacies of the Roman republic. As a matter of fact, all those who ran for offices, if elected and then once they stepped back from their offices, had to take an oath in the forum, and if "they would not take such an oath, they had to resign."[165] In the logic of Bentham's idea of the public as tribunal, we may say of the Roman case that whereas the tribunal of sorted judges judged, the crowd judged the judges with the invisible power of opinion. The formal judge felt the pressing influence of the informal judge. To be *under the eyes of the people* was thus both a condition for competent participation on the part of those who so wanted (and assembled in the comitia to vote) and a condition for controlling political deeds (in the forum). The check on the performers did not need to be in the form of speech or words. The *passive* activity of attending, seeing, and hearing was also very influential on decisions; it was a powerful form of passivity insofar as it could induce a public officer or a jury or an orator or a candidate to say or desist from saying something. The crowd, we read in Sallust, was "active" even when "apathetic and listless."[166]

Reflecting upon the Roman forum, we might say that the crowd or the indistinct public has two powers: a containing power and a releasing power. It exercises the function of chastising and instigating—at any event, directing those who have the power to act (in Rome, the citizens in their voting function and the candidates). It is important to understand this double function if we want to assess the complexity of procedural democracy, which, although it may have a plebiscitarian moment, is not plebiscitarian.

Speech in the Forum

Why can the Roman forum alone not figure as a model of democracy, although it is a model of popular presence, and even a strongly egalitarian one, when considered in its dynamic relation to the leaders? In order to answer this question I will be focusing on the right to free speech the Romans enjoyed in the forum. A subsequent question to be posed is whether the Roman people in their sovereign capacity had the right to speak also in public or if, like the Athenians when assembled in the *ekklēsia*, they could speak when gathered in the voting assemblies or the comitia. *Isēgoria* and *parrhēsia* were the names of the individual right to speak that each Athenian citizen enjoyed when gathered in the assembly: the former "a positive, procedural freedom that guaranteed Athenian citizens an equal opportunity to address the *ekklēsia*," and the latter "a positive, substantive freedom that shaped the content of each *rhētor*'s speech."[167] As explained in Chapter 1, freedom of speech as an equal opportunity of the citizen to take part directly or indirectly in the process of decision has been at the core of political liberty since the inception of democracy. According to Roman historians, *isēgoria* and *parrhēsia* was not an opportunity the Roman citizens enjoyed equally: some enjoyed it in the forum (the few who ran for political posts), while none enjoyed it when met in their assemblies (the comitia).[168] This does not mean, however, that the Roman citizens did not enjoy the right to influence the decisions and to speak in the open or in public (as they did in the forum). It means that their influence in the forum was exercised by them as private individuals, not sovereign citizens. Let me try to explain this important distinction.

Holding an office (by election) or belonging to the senatorial class and thus having the right to run for office gave to only some Roman citizens the individual right to address the people and talk.[169] *Isēgoria* was only for the few in Rome. Ordinary Romans did not enjoy it. It is impossible to say that in Rome there existed "a formal right for every citizen to speak" in the place in which decisions were made.[170] When acting as a sovereign, "any citizen who wished to do so could hear opposing views on any topics, either at different *contiones* held by different officeholders or, sometimes, at the same *contio*."[171] Electoral campaigns were extremely lively, more than they are today. All persons in the forum enjoyed the right to free speech, but the Roman citizens did not enjoy it when meeting in the comitia within which they voted or acted as sovereign *populus*. They enjoyed it as private citizens and thus in the form of a right to "private speech"—a right that was extended also to the noncitizens or all those individuals who traveled to Rome and went freely to the forum. Both ordinary citizens and noncitizens enjoyed the right to free speech in the forum. What they did not enjoy—not all of them—was the equal right to public speech or the right to address the people or discuss in the comitia, a right that only the patricians or the potential magistrates enjoyed.

When Green observes that vision, not voice, is the sense that makes the People as one crowd that "only watches" but does not "compete for power," he means to stress precisely the power not of making decisions but of influencing by acting as spectators. The kind of right to free speech that the spectator enjoys is in the form of a private right. To elaborate from the argument I made in Chapter 1 concerning the meaning of free speech in a democratic society, two different rights to free speech entail two different kinds of people: one that speaks but does not decide, and one that speaks and also decides. This distinction is at the core of the mixed government model that scholars use to describe contemporary representative government in order to stress the fact that, although ordinary citizens can hope to influence their representatives by voicing their opinions freely, they have no certainty that their voice will be listened to (the separation between assemblies that vote without talking and senates or councils that only talk without voting was endorsed by modern republicans in the Roman tradition, from Harrington to Rousseau). As citizens in the decision-making function, the Romans had "passive" kinds of rights: for instance, the right to hear and see and to be sensed as a judging audience by "active" leaders. In order to make that right effective, the Roman system made sure that all oppositional views were always expressed in public by the leaders and that all the information on candidates, magistrates, law proposals, and passed laws were divulged and made known to the public. But in their sovereign function, the citizens talked through their shouted votes (plebiscite) and, when in the forum, through the words of the speakers. The debates and *conciones* they attended daily in the forum were made by speakers (candidates and magistrates) with whom people would identify and, in this empathetic sense, participate or identify with, as according to Schmitt's plebiscitarian notion of representation.

At any event, the Roman people could exercise a *reactive* kind of power: the power of impeding or exalting, of judging or chastising, in the forum as well as in the voting tribes. They did not have the right of being *fully* active like the patricians (who, however, did not have the right to vote). In sum, a clear-cut division between speaking and voting, proposing and resolving (which Harrington would then theorize as an argument for

223

bicameralism) dominated Roman political life. Along with a silent voting in the tribes, the Roman people also had a vociferous presence in the forum, yet not as citizens who debated *and* voted (as in Athenian democracy) but as a collective public that influenced and constrained the speakers en masse.

In contemporary parlance, it is the individual right to speak as a private right (not as a right of the citizen) that is for us important to consider. Ordinary Roman citizens talked freely and directly as private individuals in the forum and everywhere they wished, but not in the voting assemblies or comitia. It was as private individuals that they made up the crowd. The crowd was thus a public (as visible) actor made of private individuals. This was true in Rome as it is true in today's audience democracy. The citizens who converse with me and other citizens on the Internet or watch the television do not exist, properly speaking, as citizens; we interact as private individuals who utter personal views and see the same images in the immediacy of the time that informal communication allows, when we want and like.

In Rome, the crowd, not the sovereign people, had the right to talk in public forum. Precisely because of this, public talk was not in the form of a rational argument or a deliberative kind of speech but of a *collective reaction* to what the candidates or leaders said: a shout against a speaker, a noise of approval, and silence itself, as we saw. This was the *populus* against which Cicero launched his disparaging words when he compared it to a storming sea with the tribunes as the winds agitating it.[172] Cicero gave this people the name of *democratic people* against which he threw his invectives. In the eighteenth century, that image of "democratic" turbulence and folly of the populace in the forum would inspire the fear of democracy in the speeches of revolutionary republicans seated in the constitutional assemblies of Philadelphia and Paris.[173] On the other hand, it would inspire antiliberals to mock (or exalt) democracy as a mass regime.

In the Roman scenario, within which plebiscitarian democracy found its nourishment, the public was a theater, and like in a theater, it acted as a "group" (to use the appropriate word of Cicero) whose members had the right to voice loudly, yet they did not have the same rights that the actors had. Indeed, a theater is not a place for individual discussions or reasoned speeches but a gathering of attendees who can voice their views in the form of a reaction to what they hear or see. But only the actors speak and perform. "This theater was available at a fixed traditional location to those who were interested, and in it the crowd (which itself could be described as a *contio*) was not necessarily a passive audience but could intervene with shouts or an explicit dialogue with the speaker or could show its opinion simply by drifting away. The same crowd could moreover be transformed into a sovereign assembly of voters simply (in principle) by being instructed by the presiding magistrate to separate *(discernere)* into its voting *tribus*."[174] Thus, in Rome (as in plebiscitarian democracy) the public was not an abstract "public opinion" but a physical context in which magistrates shaped their words anticipating the reaction of the crowd. As with a play, all Romans knew the rules of that game, whose performance was also a form of amusement.

Conclusion

While populism blurs democratic diarchy because it wants to make the opinion of the larger majority the will of the whole people, plebiscitarianism keeps the function of decision (the few) and that of visual judgment (the people) separate and ascribes them to two groups of citizens. Here, the negative or reactive character of politics is the only determinant factor that counts as democratic. It was Schmitt more than Weber who opened the path to this radical revision of democratic politics when he acknowledged that acclamation is the voice of the collective (the many), the only act that proves the empowerment of the people, while decision is the prerogative of the few. Contemporary theorists of the plebiscite of the audience embrace Schmitt's definition of democracy in which the People is the "nonpolitical part [of the state], keeping within the protection and shadow of political decisions."[175] As a matter of fact, Schmitt's view is excessively decisionist when compared with this new rendering of plebiscitary politics as fully consonant with the paradigm of "a nonvocal, ocular ideal of candor."[176] Whereas Schmitt took reason and individual participation in deliberation away from democracy, Green takes away from it, as we saw, the last vestige of a discursive character by making opinion no longer the sphere of discourse but that of vision and ocular judgment. Autonomy is no longer part of the democratic vocabulary, not even in the form of a mass that shouts its collective will.

The democracy of the audience has the Roman model of the forum as its reference point. The difference between a plebiscitarian gathering and a democratic citizenry resides essentially in the character and function of speech. In the latter, speech is a prerogative of the individual citizen as a political right that the person exercises together with others in the view of influencing, proposing, and evaluating decisions. Speech is the organ of political autonomy, whether in the form of direct or indirect participation. In the plebiscitarian gathering, speech is instead the prerogative of the crowd that is made of private persons who react to what they see and are made to see, and is not for the sake of forming a political view or taking part in a debate but observing the doers act. This is the freedom of the audience. It captures the difference between the action of a crowd that can follow or stimulate a speaker or several speakers and the action of citizens who speak through their voting power and their diverse political opinions and interests.

A crowd practices free speech as a private right because its members are a public of bystanders or individuals who can drift away if not amused, not yet a public of citizens whose behavior is guided by procedures. The rule of the street, like that of the Internet or television, is the rule of the crowd; its freedom is unleashed, but this does not make it in and of itself the freedom of an autonomous people. The force of the crowd does not yet testify to political freedom, although it is a manifestation of individual freedom. When the Roman people were stripped of their right to vote on laws after Sulla's push against the power of the tribunes, the crowd did not lose its visual and effective influence in the forum: "it may seem paradoxical to argue that crowd politics in the Forum was at its most effective precisely in the only period when the unconditional power to legislate had been lost."[177]

The contemporary theory of plebiscitarian democracy is an illustration of the renaissance of the power of rumors in a forum that is shaped by the means of mass communication. Yet in the Roman republic (when it was not yet in decline) the forum and the comitia, the opinion and the will, were equally strong powers. Contemporary representative democracy faces instead a decline of electoral and political participation to which corresponds the growth of the aesthetic and theatrical function of the public, a voyeuristic machine that serves to gratify people's longing for political spectacle more than their liberty from arbitrary power. Indeed, the diarchic feature of representative democracy entails not only that the sovereign is made of two functions but also that these functions communicate so that opinion does not remain ineffective and the will does not remain unchecked. A public sphere that plays an essentially aesthetic role can hardly be a means for control and critical judgment, even less so if it is complemented by a disaffected citizenship and the decline of the meaning of the political right to vote. This illustrates the paradox of today's democracy in which movements of protest arise that are as strong in their appearance as they are weak and powerless in their impact on political decisions.

Conclusion

In this book I have detected some mutations of democracy and examined them as disfigurements of the democratic diarchy of will and opinion. In its representative form, I argued, democracy is a system in which the power of authorizing the use of force as a last resort is exercised in the name of and on behalf of the people by virtue of the procedure of elections, which entails that institutions and political leaders cannot ignore what citizens think, say, and want outside the voting booth. In this government, the sovereign power is not simply the authorized will contained in the civil law that magistrates and institutions implement but a twin power in which the decision is one component. The forum of opinions partakes of democratic sovereignty although it does *not* have any formal authoritative power and its force lies external to the institutions. The challenges awaiting contemporary democracies are twofold. First, although they can never be truly separated, these powers need to operate separately and remain different: we do not want the opinion of the majority to become one and the same thing as the will of the sovereign, and we do not want our opinions to be simply a passive reaction to the spectacle leaders put on stage. Second, that representative democracy is government by means of opinion also means that the public forum keeps state power under scrutiny and should be ruled according to the same egalitarian principle that is embodied in citizens' right to be self-governing. From here the following maxim: once the forum becomes part of our understanding of political presence, democracy must attend to the question of the circumstances of opinion formation. Citizens' right to an equal share in determining the political will (one person, one vote) ought to go to-gether with citizens' equal opportunity to be informed but also to form, express, voice, and give their ideas public weight and influence. The func-tioning of the forum of opinion is thus an issue that pertains to political justice, and although influence can hardly be equal and estimated with rigorous calculation, the opportunity to exercise it can and should tend to be so. Although we can hardly prove beyond any reasonable doubt that there is a causal relationship between media content, public opinion, and political results or decisions, the barriers to equal opportunity to partici-pate in the formation of political opinions should be kept low and their level permanently monitored. The same logic that governs the decision-making power holds with the forum of opinion: economic power must not translate into political power.

Representative democracy is thus government by *doxa* in the fullest sense: because the chance of contesting and controlling power rises to the extent that citizens' opinions are not confined within their inward minds or held as private opinions; because it is consonant with the character of democ-racy as a political system that is based on and engenders dispersion of power; and because it makes possible the formulation of multiple political options in relation to which citizens make their choices. Thus, while elec-toral power is no doubt the basic condition of democracy, its guarantee is given by the conditions under which citizens get the information and are exposed to the pressure of opinion makers. Elections are truly the means to a government of opinion as a government responsive to, and responsible toward, the public.

In relation to democracy's diarchy I argued that there are three roles that *doxa* plays in the public forum: cognitive or information require-ment; political or agenda formation and contestation; and aesthetic or a call for transparency and the subjection of the work of politics to the pub-lic. In relation to them I have identified three forms of disfigurement, which are not merely theoretical possibilities but detectable phenomena in existing democracies. Epistemic interpretation of democracy and popu-list and plebiscitarian phenomena each radicalizes one of these three roles of *doxa* and they all emerge from within representative democracy as its internal yet extreme borders. Indeed, although these radicalizations are not meant to bring about any regime change (in fact, they announce themselves as a perfection or even a norm of democracy) because they do not question the "will" (do not disenfranchise the citizens), they modify the external figure of democracy in ways that are visible and, I maintain, unpleasant and problematic.

The target of these disfigurements is *doxa*, although for reasons and according to ends that are different. Epistemic theory proposes to depoliticize democratic procedures and make them a method for achieving "correct outcomes" or neutralizing partisan as majority-based decisions, rather than outcomes that are simply procedurally and constitutionally valid. They want to rescue democracy from its cacophonic, noisy, and at times demagogical partisanship but end up narrowing it rather than respecting the political nature of its process. If successful, the epistemic and unpolitical correction would change the opinion-based character of democracy and make it an expression of the power of knowledge. I called this disfigurement democratic Platonism, as it revives the myth of the philosopher-king although dressed in collective and egalitarian garb. I contend that a crowd that is made of people that, given some data and procedures of deliberation, are supposed to achieve a correct outcome is still not necessarily a democratic gathering, although it is egalitarian. The missing component is political liberty.

In focusing on the content of the outcome, the epistemic translation of democratic politics judges the work of procedures from the perspective of their ability to channel the knowledge of the many toward decisions that satisfy reasons that exceed their opinion (and the majority they get) rather than from the perspective of the principle of equal political liberty, the good that procedures are supposed to promise, reflect, and promote. Of course, there are many important ways of employing knowledge in politics, for instance, in the executive, the bureaucracy, the judiciary, and the legislative committees that assist the work of the lawmakers. Knowledge and competence are surely essential as ancillary to political judgment and decisions. Yet putting value in the "correct outcomes" over or instead of political procedures is something different than invoking competent politicians and good policies, and is problematic since it may prepare the terrain for a sympathetic welcome to technocratic revisions of democracy, as is already happening in European countries.

If procedures deliver good outcomes or educate citizens morally and cognitively, I have argued, they do all of that without premeditation. We do not choose democracy with the understanding it can make us good philosophers but because we want to remain free even while obeying laws we disagree with (which is something procedures presume). This is the sense in which I used the expression "democratic proceduralism": in order to stress that what makes procedures the spine of political legitimacy is the fact that they make the process happen in the way it is supposed to, not so that it delivers some substantive (or desirable) outcomes, which, if they come, come with no premeditation on the part of the procedures, although the actors may want to use them for that goal. A bad decision is equally legitimate as a good one, when made according to democratic rules and procedures. This seemingly unpleasant conclusion is an invitation to think of democracy as a system for regulating political conflicts in a way that fosters liberty and consolidates civil peace although with no promise to make us achieve the last word on them.

Populist theorists may thus have some good reasons against Platonists, although they reach a conclusion that is not preferable and is in fact another kind of disfigurement. I have analyzed populism in its multiple components, from the polarization and radicalization of political opinions it fosters to the Caesarist embodiment of the representative power it tends to produce. A mirrorlike image of the former one, this disfigurement answers to the traditional accusation of the ignorance and incompetence of the masses not by giving them the epistemic quality of the few but by questioning altogether the idea of extending to the collective the character of individual rationality. Populism claims that the masses are indeed rational in their political presence, and that they are so not because of the rules and procedures they create but because they make a strategic use of myths, symbols, and rhetoric in view of creating a hegemonic narrative that is meant to reinstall the excluded many (the plebs) at the center of democracy. The masses do not achieve this end by themselves but rather by relying on some intellectuals and gifted leaders who can create a winning narrative and exploit procedures to conquer power and bring democracy to what populists consider its most genuine form, which reduces the diversity of the forum and approaches consensual decisions. *Doxa* loses its autonomous status while the democratic procedures are instrumentally curbed so as to allow strong majorities to rule. This solution is primed to facilitate centralization of power, weaken checks and balances and the division of powers, disregard political oppositions, and transform election in a plebiscite of the leader. I have acknowledged contextual differences in the implementation and interpretation of populism. However, of a populist transformation of representative democracy I suggested we say what Aristotle said of demagoguery in relation to direct democracy: it is an extreme form of democracy, so close to its far borders to be able to provoke a regime change, and in fact an authoritarian government. Populist actors in some European and Latin American countries have recently used the media to merge the opinion of the majority with public opinion; have acquired large consensus and used state power to favor and strengthen their constituency; have thus weakened institutional control of government and furthered corruption; and finally have used the state to promote their majority in clear violation of democracy's diarchy.

The last disfiguration I discussed seems to be close to populism but is different in many important respects. Plebiscitarianism promises us to restore the notion of "the People" as a "meaningful concept of collective identity" and does so by rendering it a "mass spectator of political elites."[1] Visual audience becomes the only collective capacity of the people. This disfiguration is even graver than the previous ones because it does not question the diarchic structure of representative democracy but rather reinterprets it in a way that defies the very principle of citizenship as political autonomy. While historically it was possible to adapt political autonomy to indirect forms of participation like representation (modern democracy did it by making equal suffrage or the right to vote central), it seems hard to reconcile democracy with a view of politics that makes the condition of "being ruled" and watching leaders act into a norm or the figure of "the People." Contemporary theorists of plebiscitarian democracy bring the instrumental reading of proceduralism to its extreme consequence, namely, the realistic recognition that politics is a business of the few even when the many elect them. Their hint in stressing that decisions are the domain of the elite is that democratic theory should redirect its attention from political procedures to what is most congenial to the people, which is not acting (no collective can be autonomous, only individuals can) but watching. Procedures are for the ruling elites; ocular presence is for the masses. The scheme of the Roman politics as a mix of patrician acting and plebeian attending is the model of plebiscitarianism, which violates diarchy by distributing the function of will and opinion to two separate groups and moreover taking away from opinion any political or deliberative implication. Audience democracy is the proper name of this new form of plebiscitarianism, which makes the given into a norm insofar as it accepts the subjection of the citizens to the ruling creativity of leaders and their media experts and concludes that the core activity of the citizens is visual and spectatorial only, neither discursive nor participation oriented. Plebiscitary democracy is a presidential mass democracy that downplays a liberal conception of power limitation and the division of powers, the classical legal strategies of constitutionalism.

While populism has been a recurrent object of study, the end of totalitarian regimes has made plebiscitarianism a forgotten relic. However, things seem to be changing both in theory and practice. In the United States, for instance, political theory scholarship is witnessing a renaissance of interest in and sympathy for plebiscitary democracy as a result of a more favorable inclination toward majoritarianism and an idea of democracy that is less concerned with legal and institutional controls and limitations and more with forms of popular activity that rely upon both a call for transparency and president-leaders' identification with the masses bypassing Congress. In some Western democracies, calls for transparency, information intrusion in the life of leaders, and direct appeal to the audience proved unable to be effective checking powers, notwithstanding the clamor of supervision that media claim. Concerning the Italian case, perhaps the most interesting in this regard, the fact that a prime minister owned or controlled six national television stations was of course an aggravating factor, but it was not the only reason that made Italians a passive crowd of viewers that could hardly control Berlusconi's power. Indeed, even more than the ownership of the means of information, the empire of the ocular or the inflation of images seems to be the factor that makes vision an especially inept power of inspection and control, contrary to what plebiscitarian theorists seem to believe.

The plebiscite of the audience can be used to prove *a contrario* that the defense of democracy's diarchy passes today through the emancipation of proceduralism from the strictures of the Schumpeterian theory, the idea that democracy is a method for selecting leaders with practically no influencing action on the part of the citizens, save voting. This book is not devoted to pursuing this task, although its entire structure relies upon an interpretation of democratic proceduralism as normative, as I have clarified in Chapter 1. The recovery of the political worth and value of democratic procedures is the most radical and consistent answer against these disfigurations. To make political proceduralism normative in its own right it means to see it in the service of the basic good that democracy claims and advances: an equal distribution of political liberty. Democracy promises nothing else besides this, which is very much indeed because it is a good that is all too easily devalued by a poor implementation and performance of rules and institutions, the meaninglessness of citizens' electoral participation, and the increasing infiltration of economic power in the forum of opinion. Yet as effectively argued by C. Edwin Baker, the "democratic distribution principle is an end in itself, not a means predicted to lead empirically to some desirable result," and it holds both for the function of making decisions (voting) and the function of forming and questioning them.[2] Only within this normative view of political procedures is it possible to make sense of democracy as a government that is based on *doxa* and in which the decision making process relies in its entirety upon citizens' equal right to vote and judge. This is the diarchic figure that makes us recognize a government as democratic.

The proponents of the three disfigurements I discussed are dissatisfied with this view of democracy, which they discard as merely procedural, empty of any ideal and only formal. Against it, they propose we judge or evaluate or praise the democratic process from the perspective of some specific outcome, be it a correct decision, a realignment of the diverse components of the people under a hegemonic unity, or visual transparency. Against them I have argued that democracy is its procedures and that in this our liberty as citizens rests. Contrary to perfectionistic plans that situate democracy's value in what its procedures should allow the citizens to achieve, democracy does not have any ideal society to promise or any specific goal to make us achieve. Its procedures do not guarantee to improve our decision-making capacity (we do not learn how to vote by voting) nor do they promise to guide us toward outcomes that are correct according to criteria that transcend them.

Proceduralism in its seemingly realistic but in fact Schumpeterian rendering bore most of the responsibility for its bad reputation when it opposed method against ideal. As a method for regulating the distribution of power among a group of citizens, democracy can hardly be an ideal. Giving proceduralism a pure instrumentalist meaning has been the goal of Schumpeter's revision against consensual and fascist popular governments. Its consequence on the normative value of democratic proceduralism, however, is negative. The implications of disassociating ideal and method was already foreseen by Hans Kelsen in 1929: "In arguments over democracy, a lot of misunderstanding is repeatedly created by the fact that one side only talks about the idea, while the other side only talks about the reality of this phenomenon. The two sides disagree because neither manages to capture the phenomenon in its entirety, whereas ideology and reality must be understood in reference to one another."[3]

In this book I tried to object to content- and outcome-oriented approaches by advocating and proposing a normative emancipation of political proceduralism. I sought two things: questioning the antidemocratic vilification of this method that makes it another name for the circulation of elites, and questioning the idea that to make it noble or normative we need to ascribe to it an external goal that it is able to make us achieve. I argued that in order to be able to resist content- or outcome-oriented views of democratic procedures we do not need to divest them of principled value, and that in order to ascribe them a normative value we do not need to make them serve a goal that is preselected (by whom?) as good according to criteria external to them.

Democracy has something to promise besides electing lawmakers (a function that is, however, a crucial indication of political liberty and is still subjected to resistance in consolidated democracies, where citizens encounter unjustifiable obstacles when they decide to go to vote and their votes are too many times made a contested good). What democracy promises is a process of regulated participation, direct and indirect, in the construction of political authority (civil laws) based on equal conditions of political power and performed in view of devising proposals and making decisions that hold for all but without making political power pursue any other specific goal except endlessly reproducing itself and its conditions. Democratic citizens make themselves three promises:[4]

a) that all can freely and publicly disagree on the interpretation of what it means that they should participate as political equals in the construction of the law (for instance, on the meaning and extension of equality; on the interpretation of freedom of speech, whether only an individual right or also a political right; or on whether political equality should rely upon some socioeconomic conditions);

b) that they resolve temporarily their disagreements with decisions that are made by counting each individual vote according to majority rule (they recognize the majority/minority political divide, not unanimity, as foundational, and moreover select counting of votes because they presume dissent, not consent);

c) and that they will not accept considering any decision to be the last one or to be unquestionable (because they interpret democracy primarily as a way to change previously made decisions rather than to reach a point of goodness or correctness that ends the process of change).

The organizing principle of this constitutionalized process of promises is equal political liberty, which is a purposefully general term that leaves citizens free to interpret in different ways on the condition that the basic rights that define and protect it (the rights to suffrage and freedom of speech, press, and association) are not revocable. This is what makes procedures valuable and it is the promise that a "mere" procedural conception of democracy makes. Democracy does not have any utopia to deliver and seems in fact to be the consumption of all utopias insofar as it is a political system that erodes messianic visions or Platonist plans of justice and epistemic actualization in the moment it allows them to compete for consent and seek majority approval. Democracy may be described as a process of permanent secularization of politics, given that new visions always emerge that claim to be its true or more faithful interpreter. The unpremeditated work of this system is to direct the citizens to look for objectives that are meant to make their equal political liberty more secure or better preserved. The value of the democratic process makes its maintenance a political task that is anything but a vile and minor goal. One may hazard to say that it is a utopian work of its own, because to be performed its actors, the citizens, have to esteem the worth of the rules and norms of democracy despite their bad performance, recognize their malfunctioning or disfigurations, yet also recognize the possibility of redressing them. Thus, this method of political participation is open to all possible contents insofar as it allows for a strategy of political confrontation and compromise among the parties that compete on the interpretation of democracy's conditions. The limits on the contents are in the rules of the game they use.

This method is very demanding, and the first thing it asks of its citizens is that they respect it in its conditions and principles because in this respect all the advantages of the democratic method reside.[5] This involves not only an equal distribution of the basic political power of making decisions but also a not-futile participation by freely expressing one's mind, trying to influence the system, imposing responsiveness to representatives and making them accountable, and doing so under conditions of equal opportunity.[6] The protection of civil, political, and basic social rights is essential to a meaningful equal participation of this kind. Whenever these conditions are respected, the democratic procedures regulate a political system that is open to all possible contents and makes it possible that those who exercise power are controlled by those who are the basic repositories of that power, the citizens. The power of control is diarchic and composed of both the power of making decisions and the power of expressing and associating openly and freely in order to question, check, and change decisions and representatives alike.

Clearly, institutions and procedures are exposed to distortion. In a democratic society distortions come from the violation of equality or the escalation of inequality in the conditions that determine a fair use of those procedures. "One could hardly take seriously one's status as an equal citizen, for example, if owing to a lack of resources one was precluded from advancing one's views effectively in the public forum."[7] The good work of procedures requires that the overall political system takes care not only of its formal conditions but also of the perception citizens have of its effectiveness and value. The criterion orienting this maintenance should be in agreement with the procedural interpretation of democracy: it should aim to block the translation of socioeconomic inequalities into political power (social and redistributive justice is justifiable for the sake of preserving political equality). This task looks like Tantalus's job because the insulation of the political system from socioeconomic power must be achieved without blocking the communication between society and institutions, which is, as we saw, one of the most important features of representative government and what makes it diarchic. In this book I insisted on one aspect in particular of this task, namely, the maintenance of the forum of opinion formation and expression, the terrain in which today democracy's disfigurements originate.

Whereas in ancient times, risks to democracy came mostly from the side of the decision-making power (depriving the many of their right to sit in the assembly and the popular juries), today, risks come mostly from within the forum. The technological means that freedom of opinion requires in modern society make economic power enter politics and even occupy it in quite a direct and muscular manner. *Doxa* can become, and actually has become in several democratic countries, a commodity that money can buy and sell with the unavoidable consequence of making inequality in politics a consolidated condition against which lawmakers have to constantly devise new strategies. Empirical research proves this concern is well posed when it demonstrates how economic inequality and political inequality "are mutually enforcing with the result that wealth tends to entrench, rather than distribute, power over time."[8] Thanks to the ownership or the control of the means of communication, those citizens who dispose of more economic power may have more chances to elect the representatives they prefer and facilitate decisions that favor their interests. This is a breach of legal and political equality that is primed to cause domination of some over the rest and to jeopardize democratic procedures by lowering the barrier against arbitrariness. Owen M. Fiss elaborated perhaps the most effective argument for why private money is a grave constraint on political equality and why the state cannot simply be seen as the enemy on issues of opinion formation. "Protecting autonomy by placing a zone of noninterference around the individual . . . is likely to produce a public debate that is dominated, and thus constrained, by some forces that dominate social structures, not a debate that is 'uninhibited, robust, and wide-open.'"[9] Hence, an important implication of the diarchic character of democracy is that free speech is a Janus-faced right, with a negative or individual face (protection against power) and a positive or political one (formation of political opinions).

Students of politics take this as evidence that in representative democracy citizens may suffer from a new kind of corruption, a "duplicitous corruption" that consists in excluding those who have equal citizenship from a meaningful presence in the forum, and doing so in a way that the excluded cannot prove their exclusion because they retain the right to throw a "paper stone" in the ballot box, which is factual evidence of their equal citizenship.[10] In democracy though, protecting political institutions from corruption is protecting political equality, which entails protecting "the integrity of the system of political representation," and ensuring, for instance, "fair access to the public arena at each stage of political competition for those candidates entitled to participate at that stage."[11] These are issues of political justice that arise from the concern shaping the controversies over campaign finance reform in the United States and the political debates within European countries on the protection of pluralism of the media and the system of information from private potentates. As I have shown in Chapter 1, legal and political scholars have used the argument of corruption to describe the "corrosive influence" of corporate wealth or the "undue influence" that an unequal "political presence" in the forum is primed to have, even though corporations or wealthy citizens have no explicit plan or intention to exercise it and even though talking is not identical to voting. I rely upon this argument to outline at the end of this book some guidelines for maintaining and protecting democracy's diarchic figure. They descend from the three above-mentioned promises that democratic citizens make to themselves and pertain to the regulation of the relationship between the domain of the will and of opinion.

The first guideline aims at containing the opacity in the process of interdependence between elected representatives and the citizens. Because in a representative democracy the right to vote entails both the right to form a majority and that of being represented (on which the claim of accountability and responsiveness rests), the mode of selection of candidates and the formation of political agendas and the channels of communication between representatives and citizens throughout the electoral mandate are seminal factors in the making of a decent democratic practice of voting rights. Political parties' leadership should not be allowed to steal from the citizens the right to voice their claims and reduce them to plebiscitarian choosers of yes-no preferences that some electoral and media experts concoct.

This brings us to the second guideline, which pertains to the *vexata questio* of the regulation and limitation of the use of private economic resources in electoral campaigns and the political sphere more generally. The issue is a sensitive one because while the disposal of money in politics is an expression of one's freedom to compete or contribute in the political process, there is empirical evidence that money also has a direct negative impact on citizens' equal opportunity to make themselves heard, although, to paraphrase Justices Stevens's and O'Connor's words, the secret ballot prevents us from producing "concrete evidence" that "money buys influence." Since its liberal inception in the seventeenth century, property rights and freedom of expression have been mutually supporting allies of political liberty. Yet in a representative democracy in which people's political presence occurs through layers of indirectness, the public check on private money in the political sphere can hardly be avoided. As a matter of fact, since ancient Athens, although democracy does not promise economic equality, it *does* promise to break the continuity between the power of wealth and political power. Seen from this perspective, the U.S. Supreme Court's decision to allow corporations full freedom of financing politics and electoral campaigns legalizes and justifies a serious break in democratic equality, because in treating private corporations as juridical persona endowed with civil and political rights, it opens the door to a new conception of the citizen that is primed to overturn the egalitarian foundation of democracy, the guarantee that each citizen's vote counts as one.

The final remark pertains to the protection of the independence and pluralism of the public forum of information from both the power of political majorities and the power of private potentates.[12] In both cases, guarding and defending pluralism may entail updating existing constitutions. Written before the technological revolution of the means of communication and information, most of them are not effectively equipped to protect the right of information and the pluralism of the sources of information.[13] In recent years, legal innovation has proceeded toward the affirmation of the political right to fair access to the relevant information both as personal freedom to express opinions and as a right that belongs to the citizen. The Charter of Fundamental Rights of the European Union is landmark on this issue. Article 11 is explicitly devoted to "Freedom of expression and information." Part 1: "Everyone has the right to freedom of expression. This right shall include freedom to hold opinions and to receive and impart information and ideas without interference by public authority and regardless of frontiers." Part 2: "The freedom and pluralism of the media shall be respected."

The Madisonian strategy of impeding the growth of monopolies through pluralism seems to be the most consistent in dealing with the private system of media and the press since dispersion of power is in and of itself a form of control and a check on those who hold power.[14] The question that is at the center of contemporary controversies pertains not so much to the validity of this strategy but to its implementation, which entails revisiting what a consolidated liberal tradition is (in the United States in particular), namely, the disdain of any intrusion of the public in the "marketplace of ideas." Yet "the market" is not a spontaneous self-regulating domain, let alone a natural setting of human relations; it is an institution that relies on a quite strong system of norms and rules without which it can generate its own negation, monopoly. As Fiss has convincingly argued, the paradigm of the market of ideas would need to contemplate an equal attention to and a careful maintenance of the *pluralist requisite*, all the more so because in this specific case the idea of it as a jungle in which only the fittest survive runs against the democratic principle, which, as we saw, accords to everyone, not only the majority, the right to be heard.

I conclude by returning to the implication of treating democracy as a diarchy of will and opinion, namely, that a democratic answer to the disfiguring proposals of changing the meaning and function of *doxa* or substituting it with truth consists in making the forum a public good, with free speech as a fundamental component of the political right of the citizen. The forum is a public good that among other things allows citizens to acquire other goods, such as monitoring the constituted power, disclosing what it tends to conceal and thereby risking facilitating corruption, and finally enabling citizens to make and voice their political choices. Democracy's maintenance today requires tackling the complex issue of "undue influence" in the forum so as to reassess the diarchic power of will and opinion and make the latter play its complex function (the cognitive, the political, and the aesthetic). Epistemic and unpolitical interpretations and populist and plebiscitarian proposals cast doubt on the capacity of democracy to solve these problems while remaining procedural in its character or without the succor of extra factors. In this book I intended to bring to the fore this argument and contest it. The sense of futility that disadvantaged citizens may have of democratic institutions should be interpreted not as a denunciation of the latter's deficit or inability to amend themselves but as a recognition that in order to be preserved their conditions require being persistently monitored and reasserted, because social inequality does translate into unequal political power.

NOTES

Introduction

1. Bernard Manin has rendered this idea with the spatial metaphor of a split be-tween "the higher will" and the "lower will" in *The Principles of Representative Government* (Cambridge: Cambridge University Press, 1997), p. 205. The image of diarchy I use to convey the idea of this distance is similar although avoids reference to a hierarchical order.

2. *Demosthenes: I Olynthiacs, Philippics Minor Public Orations I–XVII and XX* (Loeb Classical Library), ed. J. H. Vince (Cambridge, MA: Harvard University Press, 1930), p. 563; Niccolò Machiavelli, *Discourses*, ed. Bernard Crick, trans. Leslie J. Walker (London: Penguin Books, 1970), 1:58; Alexander Meiklejohn, *Free Speech and Its Relation to Self-Government*, in *Political Freedom: The Consti-tutional Power of the People* (New York: Harper, 1960), p. 27.

3. Plato thought that there was "more freedom of speech [in Athens] than every-where else in Greece"; Plato, *Gorgias*, trans. Walter Hamilton (London: Penguin, 1960), p. 42; Euripides, *Hippolytus*, trans. Gilbert Murray, vol. 8, pt. 7, Harvard Classics (New York: P.F. Collier & Son, 1909–1914), Bartleby.com, 2001 (accessed September 3, 2013). See Josiah Ober, *Athenian Legacies: Essays on the Politics of Going on Together* (Princeton, NJ: Princeton University Press, 2005), particularly pp. 4, 99; Robert W. Wallace, *The Power to Speak—and Not to Listen—in Ancient Athens*, in *Free Speech in Classical Antiquity*, ed. Ineke Sluiter and Ralph M. Rosen (Leiden: Brill 2004), pp. 221–25.

4. John Stuart Mill, *Considerations on Representative Government*, ed. John M. Robson (Toronto: University of Toronto Press, 1977), in *The Collected Works*, 19:432. "Thanks to broadcasting," Lindsay argued in 1929, "the whole world might become in some sense a public meeting. . . . And long before radio was invented, skillful

reporting and a cheap Press had done something of the same thing. They had transformed the representative assembly into the platform of a public meeting. On it men talked only partially to one another and increasingly to the invisible public behind." A. D. Lindsay, *The Essentials of Democracy* 2nd ed.(London: Oxford University Press, 1930), p. 24.

5. Jürgen Habermas, *The Structural Transformation of the Public Sphere: An Inquiry into a Category of Bourgeois Society,* trans. Thomas Burger, with the assistance of Frederick Lawrence (Cambridge, MA: MIT Press, 1991), in particular pp. 211–22.

6. John Dunn, *Democracy: A History* (New York: Atlantic Monthly Press, 2005), p. 175; and Giovanni Sartori, *Comparative Constitutional Engineering: An Inquiry into Structures, Incentives and Outcomes* 2nd ed. (New York: New York University Press, 1997), p. 133. The same can be said of communication networks more generally, which are "largely owned and managed by global multimedia corporate networks," and although states are parts of these networks, "the heart of global communication network is connected to, and largely dependent on financial investors and financial markets." Manuel Castells, *Communication Power* (Oxford: Oxford University Press, 2009), p. 424.

7. C. Edwin Baker, *Media Concentration and Democracy: Why Ownership Matters* (Cambridge: Cambridge University Press, 2007), p. 18.

8. The fact that Mr. Silvio Berlusconi is no longer prime minister does not make my early inspiration null, because the fact that he was able to acquire such a powerful position through the forum reveals that the problem exists in representative democracy. The locus of this problem lies in the way opinion is organized, performed, and expressed. The Berlusconi phenomenon is internal to the diarchic structure of democracy, a challenge from "within," as I argue in this book.

9. Cass R. Sunstein, *Infotopia: How Many Minds Produce Knowledge* (Oxford: Oxford University Press, 2006), pp. 5–19.

10. Giovanni Sartori, *Homo videns: Televisione e post-pensiero* (Roma-Bari: Laterza, 1997).

11. Cass R. Sunstein, *On Rumors: How Falsehoods Spread, Why We Believe Them, What Can Be Done* (New York: Farrar, Strauss and Giroux, 2009).

12. I discuss these views in Chapter 2.

13. Bruce Ackerman, *The Decline and Fall of the American Republic* (Cambridge, MA: Harvard University Press, 2010), p. 26.

14. I borrow this expression from one of the works I am going to discuss extensively in Chapter 3: Jeffrey Edward Green, *The Eyes of the People: Democracy in the Age of Spectatorship* (Oxford: Oxford University Press, 2010).

15. In the tradition of Habermas, Klaus Eder proposed an interesting analysis of each of these three aspects of the public sphere in "The Transformations of the Public Sphere and Their Impact on Democratization" in *La democrazia di fronte allo Stato: Una discussione sulle difficoltà della politica moderna,* ed. Alessandro Pizzorno (Milano: Feltrinelli, 2010), pp. 247–79.

16. David Estlund, *Democratic Authority: A Philosophical Framework* (Princeton, NJ: Princeton University Press, 2007), chap. 1.

17. I would like to adapt to epistemic egalitarians the words Kelsen used to criticize socialist egalitarians: "The demand for universal, and therefore equal, freedom requires universal, and therefore equal, participation in government. . . . Insofar as the idea of equality is meant to connote anything other than formal equality with regard to freedom (i.e., political participation), that idea has nothing to do with democracy. This can be seen most clearly in the fact that not the political and formal, but the material and economic equality of all can be realized just as well—if not better—in an autocratic-dictatorial form of state as it can in a democratic form of state." Hans Kelsen, *Vom Wesen und Wert der Demokratie* (1929, rev. vers. of the first 1920 ed.), in English with the title, *The Essence and Value of Democracy*, trans. by Brian Graf and to be published by Rowan and Littlefield; I am citing from the manuscript, p. 86.

18. For a persuasive analysis of the "democracy's actual failures and symptoms of malfunctioning," see Claus Offe, "Crisis and Innovation of Liberal Democracy: Can Deliberation Be Institutionalized?," *Sociologiký časopis/Czech Sociological Review* 47 (2011): 447–72.

19. John Rawls, "The Idea of Public Reason Revisited" (1997), in *Collected Papers*, ed. Samuel Freeman (Cambridge, MA: Harvard University Press, 1999), pp. 579–80.

20. Ibid.

21. Stephen Holmes, *Passions & Constraint: On the Theory of Liberal Democracy* (Chicago: University of Chicago Press, 1995), p. 196.

22. Margaret Canovan, "Taking Politics to the People: Populism as the Ideology of Democracy," in *Democracies and the Populist Challenge*, ed. Yves Mény and Yves Surel (Oxford: Palgrave, 2002), p. 33.

23. Michael Kazin, *The Populist Persuasion: An American History* (New York: Basic Books, 1995), p. 2.

24. Green, *Eyes of the People*, p. 38.

25. Cf. Gerry Mackie, "Schumpeter's Leadership Democracy," *Political Theory* 37 (2009): 128–53.

26. Cf. Paul A. Taylor, "From Hackers to Hacktivists: Speed Bumps on the Global Superhighway?," *New Media & Society* 7 (2005): 640.

27. Green, *Eyes of the People*, p. 36.

28. Manin, *Principles of Representative Government*, pp. 218–28.

1. Democracy's Diarchy

1. Vilfredo Pareto, *The Mind and Society*, 4 vols., trans. Andrew Bongiorno and Arthur Livingston (New York: Harcourt, 1935), vol. 4, § 2244. Pareto's view rephrased David Hume's, which claimed that it is "on opinion only that government is founded;

and this maxim extends to the most despotic and most military governments, as well as to the most free and most popular." "Of the First Principles of Government," in *Political Essays*, ed. Knud Haakonssen (Cambridge: Cambridge University Press, 1994), p. 16.

2. As Sartori explained, "information is not knowledge," and while knowledge presumes information, "it does not go by definition that he who is informed is knowledgeable." This means two things: first, that the exposition of people's opinions to information does not translate into their betterment or even transformation; second, that no matter how many times we vote we do not learn how to vote (or vote more "competently" or "rationally"). Giovanni Sartori, *The Theory of Democracy Revisited: Part One: The Contemporary Debate* (Chatman, NJ: Chatman House, 1987), pp. 117–18.

3. *New York Times Co. v. Sullivan*, 376 U.S. 270 (1964).

4. Robert C. Post, *Democracy, Expertise, Academic Freedom: A First Amendment Jurisprudence for the Modern State* (New Haven: Yale University Press, 2012), p. 9 (citing *Hustler Magazine, Inc. v. Falwell*).

5. "Private opinion may be highly unfavorable to a regime, policy, or institution without generating a public outcry for change. The communist regimes of Eastern Europe survived for decades even though they were widely despised. They remained in power as long as public opinion remained overwhelmingly in their favor, collapsing instantly when street crowds mustered the courage to rise against them." Timur Kuran, *Private Truths, Public Lies: The Social Consequences of Preferences Falsification* (Cambridge, MA: Harvard University Press, 1995), p. 57.

6. Baker, *Media Concentration and Democracy*, p. 8. Political scientist Larry Diamond expresses more or less the same view in *The Spirit of Democracy: The Struggle to Build Free Societies Throughout the World* (New York: Henry Holt and Co., 2008), p. 24.

7. Sartori, *Theory of Democracy Revisited*, pp. 86–87.

8. Mackie, "Schumpeter's Leadership Democracy," p. 129.

9. Charles Louis de Secondat, Baron de Montesquieu, *The Spirit of the Laws*, trans. Anne M. Choler, Basia Carolyn Miller, and Harold Samuel Stone (Cambridge: Cambridge University Press, 1989), p. 157 (bk. 11, chap. 6).

10. Norberto Bobbio, *Eguaglianza e libertá* (Turin: Einaudi, 1995), p. xii (my translation).

11. Charles Beitz asked years ago the important question on whether we should retain this expression—"political equality"—or simply abandon it, because "it confuses matters of institutional design with deeper questions about their justification" on actual distribution. Thus, Beitz proposed to interpret it as fairness or the stipulation of treating citizens equally when basic political power is distributed, equality not of outcome but of condition and opportunity. I think this is a reasonable argu-

ment, consistent with a procedural interpretation of political equality. Charles R. Beitz, *Political Equality: An Essay in Democratic Theory* (Princeton, NJ: Princeton University Press, 1989), p. 18.

12. "Contrast with this [kingship] the rule of the people: first, it has the finest of all names to describe it—equality under the law; and, secondly, the people in power." *Herodotus*, 4 vols., bk. 3, trans. A. D. Godley, Loeb Classical Library (London: Heinemann, 1928–1930), 80; Moses I. Finley, "The Freedom of the Citizens in the Greek World," in *Economy and Society in Ancient Greece*, ed. Brent D. Shaw and Richard P. Saller (University of California: Chatto and Windus, 1981), pp. 77–84.

13. Emily Greenwood, "Making Words Count: Freedom of Speech and Narrative in Thucydides," in *Free Speech in Classical Antiquity*, ed. Ineke Sluiter and Ralph M. Rosen (Leiden: Brill, 2004), 175–76; Josiah Ober, "The Original Meaning of 'Democracy': Capacity to Do Things, not Majority Rule," *Constellations* 15, no. 1 (2008): 3.

14. See Joseph A. Schumpeter, *Capitalism, Socialism, and Democracy* (New York: Harper & Row, 1942); Adam Przeworski, "Minimalist Conception of Democracy: A Defense," in *Democracy's Value*, ed. Ian Shapiro and Cassiano Hacker-Cordón (Cambridge: Cambridge University Press, 1999), pp. 23–55.

15. "Proceduralism is not the problem, but the effort to rely on nothing but proceduralism is. Democratic authority and legitimacy could never be understood without relying to some extent on the idea of retrospective," namely, that proceduralism is the "tendency to produce decisions that are better or more just by standards that are independent of the actual temporal procedure that produced them." Estlund, *Democratic Authority*, p. 97. To which a proceduralist would answer: "It is voting that authorizes coercion, not reason behind it." Przeworski, "Minimalist Conception of Democracy," p. 48.

16. Hans Kelsen, *General Theory of Law and State* (1945), trans. Anders Wedberg (Union, NJ: Lawbook Exchange, 1999), pp. 287–88.

17. ". . . the aspect more cherished by the Athenian democrats was *isegoria*, not *isonomia*. Now, whereas *isonomia* implies natural equality as well as equality of opportunity, *isegoria* is really about equality of opportunity. No Athenian expected that every one of the 6000 citizens who attended a meeting of the Assembly could—or would—address his fellow citizens. *Isegoria* was not for everyone, but for anyone who cared to exercise this political right. Each citizen must have equal opportunity to demonstrate his excellence, but he deserved reward according to what he actually achieved." Mogens Herman Hansen, *The Athenian Democracy in the Age of Demosthenes*, trans. J. A. Crook (Oxford: Blackwell, 1993), pp. 83–84.

18. "On this view, the First Amendment signifies what Michel Foucault has called a 'parrhesiastic contract,' through which the sovereign people acquire the truth they need for self-government, in exchange for a promise not to punish speakers who

speak the truth, 'no matter what this truth turns out to be.'" Keith Werhan, "The Classical Athenian Ancestry of American Freedom of Speech," *The Supreme Court Review* 2008, no. 1 (2008): 16.

19. Hansen, *Athenian Democracy*, p. 84.

20. An excellent elucidation and critical discussion of the meaning and implications of a political conception of proceduralism can be found in Valeria Ottonelli, *I principi procedurali della democrazia* (Bologna: Il Mulino, 2012), in particular chap. 6 titled "Equal Respect and Political Agency" (author's translation).

21. Manin, *Principles of Representative Government*, pp. 188–90.

22. Noberto Bobbio, *Which Socialism? Marxism, Socialism and Democracy*, trans. Roger Griffin (Cambridge: Politiy Press, 1987), p. 74.

23. Beitz, *Political Equality*, p. 192.

24. Athens, which was a genuine democracy, is the touchstone for a procedural interpretation of democracy. Born as a compromise between the newly empowered "common people" and the already powerful wealthy ("a strong shield around both parties"), it took several revolutions to become the rule of the many (poor or "ordinary"). Democracy meant that poverty was neither something the people had to be ashamed of, nor a reason for political and civil disempowerment; from Solon's Fragments, in *Early Greek Political Thought: From Homer to the Sophists*, ed. Michael Gagarin and Paul Woodruff (Cambridge: Cambridge University Press, 1995), p. 26, and Pericles's "Funeral Oration," in Thucydides, *History of the Peloponnesian War*, trans. Rex Warner, ed. M. I. Finley (New York: Penguin Classics, 1972) pp. 145–47.

25. Jean Bodin and Robert Filmer strictly distinguished between the legislative act and the debate that preceded it; the former only consisted in the sovereign act of promulgation; the latter was held by the "counselors" whose opinion or judgment the king decided to listen to or ignore: cf. Jean Bodin, *On Sovereignty: Four Chapters from the Six Books of the Commonwealth*, ed. Julian Franklin (Cambridge: Cambridge University Press, 1992), p. 23; Robert Filmer, *Patriarcha*, in *Patriarcha and Other Essays*, ed. Johann P. Sommerville (Cambridge: Cambridge University Press, 1991), p. 47.

26. Norberto Bobbio, *The Future of Democracy*, trans. Roger Griffin, ed. Richard Bellamy (Minneapolis: University of Minnesota Press, 1984), p. 93.

27. Baker, *Media Concentration and Democracy*, p. 7.

28. One of the most substantial themes in twentieth-century political science has been precisely that of distinguishing public opinion from the initiatives of government—on this distinction communication between the two was deemed possible. This is technically speaking the meaning of "government by means of opinion," which was systematically studied (particularly in the United States) in the years in which Europe experienced despotic and plebiscitarian mass regimes. See the classical works of Emil Lederer, "Public Opinion," in *Political and Economic*

Democracy, ed. Max Ascoli and Fritz Lehmann (New York: Norton, 1937), in particular pp. 284–93, and Harold D. Lasswell, *Democracy through Public Opinion* (Menasha, WI: George Banta Publishing Company, 1940), in particular pp. 19–31.

29. "Elections are not only instruments for choosing governments; they are also media for sending messages about the democratic process," which means that although we accept that people decide not to exercise their right to vote, this should not make "neglect a salient empirical fact," that the opportunity to exercise the right to vote and voice messages are not equal; sometimes this inequality is felt by citizens as a reason for futility in voting. Thus, paying attention to the conditions in which opinions are formed is an essential component of our respect for procedures and rules. Dennis F. Thompson, *Just Elections: Creating a Fair Electoral Process in the United States* (Chicago: University of Chicago Press, 2002), p. 28.

30. Bernard Yack, "Democracy and the Lover of Truth," in *Truth and Democracy*, ed. Jeremy Elkins and Andrew Norris (Philadelphia: University of Pennsylvania Press, 2012), p. 171.

31. Thus, Hobbes defined democracy an "aristocracy of orators" because popular consent is consent on arguments or speeches that citizens make in view of persuading the larger number. Thomas Hobbes, *The Elements of Law Natural and Politic*, ed. J. C. A. Gaskin (Oxford: Oxford University Press, 1994), p. 120. See also on this issue Michael Walzer, *Spheres of Justice: A Defense of Pluralism and Equality* (New York: Basic Books, 1983), p. 304.

32. Przeworski, "Minimalist Conception of Democracy," pp. 34–35.

33. Ibid.

34. Cf. John Dewey, "The Ethics of Democracy," in *The Early Works, 1882–1898*, vol. 1: *1882–1888*, ed. J. A. Boydston (Carbondale-Edwardsville: Southern Illinois University Press, 1969), pp. 232–33, and Ronald Dworkin, *Sovereign Virtue: The Theory and Practice of Equality* (Cambridge, MA: Harvard University Press, 2000), p. 207. Dworkin writes that participation requires specific structures and institutions of which the vote is one component. "The symbolic goals [of egalitarian politics] argue for equal votes within the district, the agency goals for liberty and leverage, and the choice-sensitive accuracy goal for a large degree of equality of impact."

35. On the "punctuated" short-term logic implied in direct votes on issue, see Yannis Papadopoulos, "Analysis of Functions and Dysfunctions of Direct Democracy: Top-Down and Bottom-Up Perspectives," *Politics & Society* 23 (1995): 438–39.

36. I discussed these oppositional views of election and representation in *Representative Democracy: Principles and Genealogy* (Chicago: University of Chicago Press, 2006), chap. 1.

37. "To deliver an opinion is the right of all men; that of constituents is a weighty and respectable opinion, which a representative ought always to rejoice to hear"

and "use a respectful frankness of communication." Edmund Burke, "Speech at Mr. Burke's Arrival in Bristol" (1774), in *The Portable Edmund Burke*, ed. Isaac Kramnick (London: Penguin Books, 1999), p. 156.

38. James Wilson, *Commentaries on the Constitution of the United States of America* (London: Debrett, Johnson, and Jordan, 1792), pp. 30–31.

39. Hume, "Of the First Principles of Government," p. 16.

40. The expression "paper stones" was coined by Friedrich Engels; I borrow it from Przeworski, "Minimalist Conception of Democracy," p. 49. I discussed this aspect in *Representative Democracracy*, pp. 30–33. The problem of "circularity" between opinion and government was studied early on by Charles E. Lindblom, *Politics and Markets: The World's Political Economic System* (New York: Basic Books, 1977), chap. 15.

41. Pierre Rosanvallon, *La légimité démocratique: Impartalité, réflexivité, proximité* (Paris: Seuil, 2008), pp. 47–53.

42. Yasmin Dawood, "The New Inequality: Constitutional Democracy and the Problem of Wealth," in *Maryland Law Review* 67 (2007): 147. On the growth of economic inequality in the last decades and its negative effects on democracy, see Joseph M. Schwartz, *The Future of Democratic Equality: Rebuilding Social Solidarity in a Fragmented America* (New York: Rutledge, 2009); Kay Lehman Schlozman, Benjamin I. Page, Sidney Verba, and Morris P. Fiorina, "Inequality of Political Voice," in *Inequality and American Democracy*, ed. Lawrence R. Jacobs and Theda Skocpol (New York: Russell Sage Foundation, 2005), pp. 19–87.

43. Mark Warren, "What Does Corruption Mean in a Democracy?," in *American Political Science Review* 48 (2004): 328–33.

44. I made this claim in *Representative Democracy*, pp. 226–28.

45. Thompson, *Just Elections*, p. 22.

46. The debate in the United States and other democratic societies over the effects of political campaigns and television news is rich and its analysis would require a research of its own; I limit myself to mention some representative tracts in American scholarship, such as James B. Lemert, *Does Mass Communication Change Public Opinion After All?: A New Approach to Effects Analysis* (Chicago: Nelson Hall, 1981); Benjamin I. Page and Robert Y. Shapiro, *The Rational Public: Fifty Years of Trends in Americans' Policy Preferences* (Chicago: University of Chicago Press, 1992); and Susan Herbst, *Reading Public Opinion: How Political Actors View the Democratic Process* (Chicago: University of Chicago Press, 1998).

47. For an excellent analysis on the role of Ciceronian eloquence in the modern conceptualization of free speech and toleration, cf. Garry Remer, *Humanism and the Rhetoric of Toleration* (University Park: Pennsylvania State University Press, 1996).

48. Plato, *The Republic*, trans. G. M. A. Grube, rev. C. D. C. Reeve (Indianapolis: Hackett, 1992), p. 156 (479e–480).

49. Walter Lippmann, *Public Opinion* (1922), with a new foreword by Robert Steel (New York: Free Press, 1997), pp. 252–56. For a critical overview of this representation of public opinion, see Robert Y. Shapiro and Yaeli Bloch-Elkon, "Do The Facts Speak for Themselves? Partisan Disagreement as a Challenge to Democratic Competence," in *Critical Review* 20 (2008): 115–18.

50. As we read in the opening statement of Mill's *The Subjection of Women*, an opinion is stronger in proportion as people perceive it as uncontroversial, like a natural given.

51. Tocqueville explained with the argument of silence induced by social impotence the decline of the French church in the ancient regime: "Those who retained their belief in the doctrines of the Church became afraid of being alone in the allegiance and, dreading isolation more than error, professed the opinion of only a part." Alexis de Tocqueville, *The Old Régime and the French Revolution*, trans. Stuart Gilbert (New York: Doubleday, Anchor, 1955), p. 155.

52. "Observations made in one context spread to another and encouraged people either to proclaim their views or to swallow them and keep quiet until, in a spiraling process, the one view dominated as its adherents became mute. This is the process that can be called a 'spiral of silence.'" Elisabeth Noelle-Neumann, *The Spiral of Silence: Public Opinion—Our Social Skin* (Chicago: University of Chicago Press, 1993), p. 5.

53. Marcus Tullius Cicero, *Letters to Atticus*, ed. D. R. Shackleton Bailey (Cambridge, MA: Harvard University Press, 1999), 4:193–99 (n. 371A).

54. Plato, *The Republic*, p. 156 (479e–480), where Socrates also added: "We won't be in error, then, if we call such people lovers of opinion rather than philosophers or lovers of wisdom and knowledge?."

55. Terence Ball, *Transforming Political Discourse: Political Theory and Critical Conceptual History* (Oxford: Blackwell, 1988), p. 121.

56. Plato, *Gorgias*, pp. 76–82; cf. Thomas C. Brickhouse and Nicholas D. Smith, *Plato's Socrates* (New York: Oxford University Press, 1994), pp. 138–39.

57. Plato inaugurated a tradition of political philosophy that sees disagreement as transitory and considers collective assemblies—thus, multiplicity of opinions—as either able to become like one mind (unanimity) or else doomed to produce foolish governments; the dualism between "one mind" like decisions and multiplicity has been excellently analyzed by Jeremy Waldron, *The Dignity of Legislation* (Cambridge: Cambridge University Press, 1999), pp. 28–35. The matrix of Plato's argument can be detected in the main theorists of modern sovereignty within the contractarian and individualistic tradition, from Hobbes to Rousseau.

58. Aristotle, *The Art of Rhetoric*, trans. John Henry Freese, Loeb Classical Library (Cambridge, MA: Harvard University Press, 1994), p. 3 (354a1).

59. Ball, *Transforming Political Discourse*, p. 121.

60. Aristotle, *The Art of Rhetoric*, pp. 5–7 (354a4–6; 354b7–8).

61. Richard Kraut, *Aristotle* (Oxford: Oxford University Press, 2002), p. 195.

62. Aristotle, *Topics* 104b1–8 (from the edition published by Clarendon Press, 1997) and *Eudemian Ethics* in *Athenian Constitution, Eudemian Ethics, Virtues and Vices*, trans. H. Rackhman, Loeb Classic Library Cambridge, MA: Harvard University Press, 1935), 1227a13.

63. Aristotle, *The Nicomachean Ethics*, trans. David Ross (Oxford: Oxford University Press, 1990), pp. 189–90 (bks. 7, 14).

64. Kraut, *Aristotle*, pp. 229–34.

65. "But we only deliberate about things which seem to admit of issuing in two ways; as for those things which cannot in the past, present, or future be otherwise, no one deliberates about them, if he supposes that they are such; for nothing would be gained by it." Aristotle, *The Art of Rhetoric*, p. 23 (1357a12–13).

66. Cf. Yack, "Democracy and the Love of Truth," pp. 167–69.

67. Aristotle, *The Art of Rhetoric*, p. 5 (354a4–5).

68. I use the word "epistocracy" (essentially an enlightened despotism or rule by experts) in a way similar to that of Terence Ball, who used "epistemocracy" instead. The way I use "epistocracy" pertains to the rule by experts in a form of government that is not necessarily democratic, while Ball's term adapts specifically to what in the next chapter I will illustrate as a case of disfigurement of democracy. Ball, *Transforming Political Discourse*, pp. 115–20.

69. John Locke, *An Essay Concerning Human Understanding*, ed. Alexander Campbell Fraser, 2 vols. (New York: Dover, 1959), 1:361 (chap. 14). *Sensus communis*, Kant wrote, "does not say that everyone *will* concur with our judgment but that everyone *should* agree with it. Thus . . . it is a merely ideal norm, under the presupposition of which one could rightfully make a judgment that agrees with it." Immanuel Kant, *Critique of the Power of Judgment*, trans. Paul Guyer and Eric Matthews (Cambridge: Cambridge University Press, 2000), p. 123 (§ 22).

70. Locke, *An Essay Concerning Human Understanding*, 1:477 (bk. 2, chap. 28).

71. Hence, Albert Venn Dicey wrote, in agreement with David Hume, that it is "public opinion that governs a country" whether "the sovereign be a monarchy, an aristocracy, or the mass of the people" (see in particular David Hume's "Of the First Principles of Government" and "Whether the British Government Inclines More to Absolute Monarchy, or to a Republic" in *Political Essays*, nos. 3 and 6). Dicey's argument was meant to criticize the radicals, the Benthamites *in primis*, who presumed the existence of an objective interests in relation to which they spoke of "sinister interest" and finally devaluated political deliberation itself. Albert Venn Dicey, *Lectures on the Relationship Between Law & Public Opinion in England during the Nineteenth Century* (London: MacMillan, 1905), pp. 10–16. Dicey's view has been endorsed by theorists like Sartori who resist interpreting democratic decisions as a

matter of preferences and interests. Interests and preferences are themselves government by opinion and actually the outcome of opinions. Sartori, *The Theory of Democracy Revisited*, 1:86–130). This view has the merit of explaining the force and power of ideology in democratic politics, the fact that, for instance, citizens vote all too often "against" their own interests, as Przeworski observes in "Minimalist Conception of Democracy."

72. Locke, *An Essay Concerning Human Understanding*, 1:477 (bk. 2, chap. 28, § 10).

73. "For though men uniting into politic societies, have resigned up to the public the disposing of all their force . . . yet they retain still the power of thinking well or ill." Ibid.

74. Habermas, *The Structural Transformation of the Public Sphere*, p. 90.

75. Paul A. Palmer considered Rousseau to be the first prominent thinker to employ the expression *l'opinion publique* in "The Concept of Public Opinion in Political Theory," in *Essays in History and Political Theory, in Honor of C. H. McIlwain*, ed. Carl Wittke (Cambridge, MA: Harvard University Press, 1936), p. 236. Baker showed, however, that the term appeared in the work by Saint Aubin published in 1735 with the title of *Traité de l'opinion, ou Mémoires pour servir à l'histoire de l'esprit humain*, and was used a few years later in the *Encyclopédie méthodique* as equivalent of the universal tribunal by an enlightened reason; the term was not unknown in the ancient regime, and Montesquieu had an important role in the circulation of this idea. Keith Michael Baker, *Inventing the French Revolution* (Cambridge: Cambridge University Press, 1990), pp. 167–68; see also Mona Ozouf, " 'Public Opinion' at the End of the Old Regime," *Journal of Modern History* 60 supplement (1988): 1–21, and Colleen A. Sheehan, *James Madison and the Spirit of Republican Self-Government* (Cambridge: Cambridge University Press, 2009), pp. 57–83.

76. In this sense Rousseau could write that "the closer opinions come to unanimity, the more dominant too is the general will" (*On the Social Contract*, bk. 4, chap. 2). James Bryce, *The American Commonwealth*, 2 vols. (Indianapolis: Liberty Fund, 1995), 2:909–28. But see also Jeremy Waldron, "Rights and Majorities: Rousseau Revisited," in *Majorities and Minorities, Nomos XXXII*, ed. John W. Chapman and Alan Wertheimer (New York: New York University Press, 1990), p. 58.

77. Steven Lukes, *Power: A Radical View*, Second edition (London: Palgrave MacMillan, 2005), p. 34.

78. This is, I would say, the Hegelian aspect of Rousseau; the same aspect can be found in Rawls when he distinguishes between three levels of publicity and justification of the public conception of justice and concludes that the first principles (of justice) are "embodied in political and social institutions and in public traditions of their interpretation. . . . The full justification [of the public conception of justice] is present in the public culture, reflected in its system of law and political institutions, and in the main historical traditions of their interpretation."

John Rawls, *Political Liberalism* (New York: Columbia University Press, 1983), pp. 71, 67.

79. George Wilhelm Friedrich Hegel, *Philosophy of Right*, trans. T. M. Knox (Oxford: Oxford University Press, 1967), pp. 204–05 (§§ 316, 317, 318).

80. James Curran, "Crisis of Public Communication: A Reappraisal," in *Media, Ritual and Identity*, ed. Tamar Liebes and James Curran (London: Routledge, 1998), p. 175; Baker, *Media Concentration and Democracy*, p. 9.

81. Noelle-Neumann, *The Spiral of Silence*, p. 221.

82. "[I]n cultivating the art of convincing we lost the art of arousing," and turned to "reasoned" discursive forms of interaction that persuade us without convincing. Jean-Jacques Rousseau, *Essai sur l'origine des langues où il est parlé de la mélodie et de l'imitation musicale*, in *Oeuvres complètes*, ed. B. Gagnebin and M. Raymond (Paris: Gallimard, 1964), 5:425; in the same volume, see also his *De l'imitation théâtrale*.

83. He preferred the language of music to that of theater and rhetoric because it would guide the mind to turn its attention inward, away from the fictitious world of representation and theatrical performance. Cf. C. N. Dugan and Tracy B. Strong, "Music, Politics, Theater, and Representation in Rousseau," in *The Cambridge Companion to Rousseau*, ed. Patrick Riley (Cambridge: Cambridge University Press, 2001), pp. 342–44.

84. Jean-Jacques Rousseau, *Émile*, trans. Barbara Foxley (New York: Everyman Library, 1993), p. 179. The model for the kind of (civic) education that Rousseau proposes for the citizens is Emile, who has to go through a "solitary education" (p. 82).

85. I elucidated this tradition among others in "Competing for Liberty: The Republican Critique of Democracy," *American Political Science Review* 106 (2012): 607–21.

86. Jean-Jacques Rousseau, *On the Social Contract, or Principles of Political Rights*, in *Basic Political Writings*, trans. Donald A. Cress (Indianapolis: Hackett, 1987), bk. 2, chap. 12.

87. See respectively, Rousseau, *On the Social Contract*, p. 219; Judith Shklar, *Men and Citizens: A Study of Rousseau's Social Theory* (Cambridge: Cambridge University Press, 1969), p. 201; and Jean-Jacques Rousseau, *Du contract social (première version, Manuscrit de Genève)*, in *Oeuvres completes*, 3:294. Yet institutional action is not the people's prerogative. Delegated politics is the site of both the life and the death or corruption of the body politic, because while it keeps it alive, united, and strong, it can also make it sick, dismembered, and weak. The source of the republic's life can also be the source of its death.

88. Henry St James Bolingbroke, *A Dissertation upon Parties*, in *Political Writings*, ed. David Armitage (Cambridge: Cambridge University Press, 1997), p. 101.

89. Ibid., p. 88.

90. Ibid., p. 85.

91. Ibid., p. 86.

92. Habermas, *The Structural Transformation of the Public Sphere*, p. 93. On the innovative role Bolingbroke played in understanding the place of political action and parties in parliamentary politics, see Quentin Skinner, "The Principles and Practice of Opposition: The Case of Bolingbroke versus Walpole," in *Historical Perspectives: Studies in English Thought and Society in Honor of J. H. Plumb*, ed. Neil McKendrick (London: Europa Publisher, 1974), pp. 93–128.

93. Hannah Arendt, *Origins of Totalitarianism* (New York: Meridian Books, 1958), pp. 64–65; and *On Revolution* (1963) (London: Penguin Books, 1990), pp. 271–80. For an analysis of this transformation, see Jean L. Cohen and Andrew Arato, *Civil Society and Political Theory* (Cambridge, MA: MIT Press, 1995), pp. 186–88.

94. Edmund Burke, "Speech on a Committee to Inquire into the State of the Representation of the Commons in Parliament," in *The Portable Edmund Burke*, pp. 174–82 (in the same collection, see also "Speech on Economic Reform," p. 160). On the same line, Hegel and Tocqueville would also defend political parties and the kind of "partisanship" that in their minds served to strengthen the unity in a society that was deeply divided along the line of class and economic interests. See, respectively, George Wilhelm Friedrich Hegel, "The English Reform Bill," in *Political Writings*, trans. T. M. Knox (Oxford: Clarendon Press, 1964), pp. 295–330, and *Philosophy of Right* § 303; Alexis de Tocqueville, *Democracy in America*, trans. J. P. Mayer (New York: Harper Perennial, 1969), pp. 174–75.

95. Waldron, *The Dignity of the Legislation*, p. 16. For a mapping of the antipartisanship arguments, see Rosenblum, *On the Side of the Angels*, chaps. 1 and 2.

96. Green, *The Eyes of the People*, p. 25.

97. "Unlike all physical forces, the power of thought is often actually increased by the small number of those expressing it. The word of a strong-minded man which alone reaches to the passions of a mute assembly has more power than the confused cries of a thousand orators." Tocqueville, *Democracy in America*, p. 181.

98. Ibid., p. 180.

99. Manin, *Principles of Representative Government*, pp. 168–69.

100. Machiavelli, *The Prince*, in *Selected Political Writings*, ed. and trans. David Wootton (Indianapolis: Hackett, 1994), chap. 18.

101. Cass R. Sunstein, *Designing Democracy: What Constitutions Do* (Oxford: Oxford University Press, 2001), pp. 222–23.

102. Owen M. Fiss, "Free Speech and Social Structure," *Iowa Law Review* 71(1986): 786.

103. John Locke, "A Letter Concerning Toleration" (1685), in *Political Writings*, ed. and intro. by David Wootton (New York: Merton, 1993), p. 396. Cf. Reiner Forst, "Pierre Bayle's Reflexive Theory of Toleration," in *Nomos XLVIII*, pp. 78–113; Jeremy

Waldron, "Locke: Toleration and the Rationality of Persecution," in *Justifying Tolera-tion: Conceptual and Historical Perspectives*, ed. Susan Mendus (Cambridge: Cam-bridge University Press, 1988), pp. 61–86; and Ira Katznelson, *Liberalism's Crooked Circle: Letters to Adam Michnik* (Princeton, NJ: Princeton University Press, 1996), p. 145.

104. Cf. Paul Starr, *The Creation of the Media: Political Origins of Modern Com-munications* (New York: Basic Books, 2004), particularly pp. 23–46.

105. "This is the radically untraditional idea that *public disagreement is a creative force.*" Holmes, *Passions & Constraint*, p. 33.

106. John Milton, *Areopagitica*, in *Areopagitica and Other Works*, ed. C. E. Vaughan (London: Dent and Dutton, 1950), p. 2.

107. In explaining how the commonwealth men used the notion of civil liberty in a "strict political sense," Skinner has called attention on the fact that they generally included among those liberties "freedom of speech, freedom of movement and free-dom of contract, and they often summarized them in the form of the claim that all citizens have an equal right to the lawful enjoyment of their lives, liberties and es-tates." Quentin Skinner, *Liberty before Liberalism* (Cambridge: Cambridge Univer-sity Press, 1998), pp. 17, 20.

108. The rights that are required for the democratic procedure to operate properly (i.e., to comply with its basic procedural traits of anonymity, neutrality, positive re-sponsiveness, and decisiveness) should be considered intrinsic to democracy. Jürgen Habermas, *Between Facts and Norms: Contribution to a Discourse Theory of Law and Democracy* (1992), trans. William Rehg (Cambridge, MA: MIT Press, 1996), pp. 82–131 (chap. 3). Although, by being enshrined in the Constitution, they impose limits on democracy's operation and outcomes, they ensure the process's democratic *nature* and its continuity. For this type of argument, see John Hart Ely, *Democracy and Distrust: A Theory of Judicial Review* (Cambridge, MA: Harvard University Press, 1980); Stephen Holmes, "Precommitment and the Paradox of Democracy," in *Constitutionalism and Democracy*, ed. Jon Elster and Rune Slagstad (Cambridge: Cambridge University Press, 1988), pp. 195–240.

109. Kelsen, *General Theory of Law and State*, pp. 287–88.

110. Baker, *Media Concentration and Democracy*, p. 9.

111. Walzer, *The Spheres of Justice*, p. 304.

112. John Rawls, *Theory of Justice* (Cambridge, MA: Harvard University Press, 1971), p. 225.

113. Jane J. Mansbridge, *Beyond Adversary Democracy*, with a rev. preface (Chi-cago: University of Chicago Press, 1983), pp. 234–35.

114. Rousseau's general will relies upon a deterministic use of the norm that re-sembles Montesquieu's use of the concept of *esprit* or the Constitution. For an excel-lent analysis of the hypothetical foundation of Rousseau's general will, see Bruno

Leoni, *Scritti di scienza politica e teoria del diritto,* ed. Mario Stoppino (Milan: Giuffré, 1980), pp. 70–72.

115. Mansbridge, *Beyond Adversary Democracy,* p. 235.

116. Adam Przeworski, *Capitalism and Social Democracy* (Cambridge: Cambridge University Press, 1985), pp. 218–21.

117. Theodore Roosevelt, *The New Nationalism,* with an introduction by Ernest Hamlin Abbott (New York: The Outlook Company, 1910), pp. 13–14.

118. Dworkin, *Sovereign Virtue,* pp. 351–54.

119. Manin, *Principles of Representative Government,* p. 190.

120. James Madison, "Speech in the Federal Convention on Suffrage" (1787), in *Writings* (New York:: Library of America, 1999), pp. 132–33; and "Property and Suffrage: Second Thoughts on the Constitutional Convention (1821)" in *The Mind of The Founder: Sources of the Political Thought of James Madison,* ed. Marvin Meyers (Indianapolis: Bobbs-Merrill, 1981), pp. 399–400.

121. Beitz, *Political Equality,* p. 203.

122. Yasmin Dawood, "Democracy, Power, and the Supreme Court: Campaign Finance Reform in Comparative Context," in *International Journal of Constitutional Law* 4 (2006): 278. Dawood refers in particular to *Bukley v. Valeo* and *McConnell v. FEC* decisions by the U.S. Supreme Courts and to other decisions by state courts in cases concerning corporate wealth in politics.

123. "The system of financing campaigns through private contributions disadvantages already disadvantaged citizens." Amy Gutmann and Dennis F. Thompson, *Democracy and Disagreement* (Cambridge, MA: Belknap Press of Harvard University, 1996), p. 134.

124. Beitz, *Political Equality,* pp. 194–95. Beitz dissected in detail the implications coming from two different approaches to the protection of equality of political influence: one that is consistent with the "insulation" of institutions from social interests and one that wants to contrast the formation of social inequality so as to block at the start the potential for an unequal political influence. A procedural conception of democracy, he rightly concludes, is more consistent with the former than the latter. Yet once we follow the former, we have to choose between establishing an equilibrium between the candidates so that they can compete on a fair base, and giving the voters the chance to enter the competition, if they so choose. The debate over electoral campaign finance in the United States focuses on the former, although a more radical conception of political equality in representative government is interested also in the latter. Ibid., pp. 196–97.

125. Baker, *Media Concentration and Democracy,* p. 7.

126. Ibid.

127. Jerome Barron, "Access to the Press—A New First Amendment Right," *Harvard Law Review* 80 (1966–1967): 1643.

128. Based on this reflection on the flow in modern constitutionalism because more sensitive to place constraints only to the many poor than the affluent few, John P. McCormick has insisted on the need to devise new institutional forms like the Tribunate that protect the former not so much from the power of public officials but from that of wealthy citizens; see his "Contain the Wealthy and Patrol the Magistrates: Restoring Elite Accountability to Popular Government," in *American Political Science Review* 100 (2006): 143–47.

129. Robert E. Goodin, *Reflective Democracy* (Oxford: Oxford University Press, 2003), p. 14. As it has been proved in thought-provoking research on the role of public opinion in the increase of equality in the United States, the argument that the American public is against inequality-reducing programs is unwarranted. In fact, in a study on senators' votes in relation to constituency demands, Larry Bartles has shown that both Republican and Democratic senators are overwhelmingly more responsive to high-income groups than middle- and low-income ones: "there is no evidence of any responsiveness to the views of constituents in the bottom third of the income distribution, even from Democrats." Larry M. Bartels, "Economic Inequality and Political Representation," in *The Unsustainable American State*, ed. Lawrence Jacobs and Desmond King (Oxford: Oxford University Press, 2009), p. 181.

130. See David Plotke, "Representation Is Democracy," *Constellations* 4 (1997): 19; and Iris Marion Young, "Deferring Group Representation," in *Ethnicity and Group Rights: Nomos XXXIX*, ed. Ian Shapiro and Will Kymlicka (New York: New York University Press, 1997), p. 352.

131. *New York Times*, March 26, 2012 (editorial).

132. Beitz, *Political Equality*, p. 205.

133. *Citizens United v. Federal Election Commission* (2010): 44. Among the earlier critical comments on this decision are Ronald Dworkin, "The Decision that Threatens Democracy," *New York Review of Books*, May 12, 2010; Jeffrey Toobin, "Annals of Law: Money Unlimited: The Chief Justice and Citizens United," *The New Yorker*, May 21, 2013, p. 36; Randall P. Bezanson, "No Middle Ground? Reflections on the *Citizens United* Decision," *Iowa Law Review* 96 (2011): pp. 649–67. The Court referred several times to the *Austin* Court, which bypassed *Buckley v. Valeo* (1976) and *First National Bank of Boston v. Bellotti* (1978) and "identified a new governmental interest in limiting political speech: an antidistortion interest." *Austin* found indeed a compelling government interest in preventing "the corrosive and distorting effects of immense aggregations of wealth that are accumulated with the help of the corporate form and that have little or no correlation to the public's support for the corporation's political ideas" (pp. 31–32).

134. Beitz, *Political Equality*, p. 205.

135. Dennis F. Thompson, *Restoring Responsibility: Ethics in Government, Business, and Healthcare* (Cambridge: Cambridge University Press, 2005), p. 162.

136. Cf., for instance, John R. Hibbing and Elizabeth Theiss-Morse, *Stealth Democracy: Americans' Beliefs about How Government Should Work* (Cambridge: Cambridge University Press, 2002).

137. Dara Strolovitch, *Affirmative Advocacy: Race, Class, and Gender in Interest Group Politics* (Chicago: University of Chicago Press, 2007), pp. 200–12. On the formulation of elections as enabling citizens to *control* policy makers and to *influence* them, see G. Bingham Powell Jr., *Elections as Instruments of Democracy: Majoritarian and Proportional Visions* (New Haven, CT: Yale University Press, 2000), pp. 4–7.

138. Rawls, *A Theory of Justice*, p. 225.

139. Ibid., pp. 7–8.

140. Ibid., p. 8.

141. *Citizens United v. Federal Election Commission* (2010), p. 23.

142. Lippmann, *Public Opinion*, p. 10.

143. The necessary material resources as the base for any public sphere, and thus the issue of a new form of inequality that economic advantages introduce in public opinion formation, was already underlined by Habermas in *The Structural Transformation of the Public Sphere*. In this rests the importance of his distinction between the public sphere and both the state and the market. As observed by Garnham, we are forced to ask us "what new political institutions and new public sphere might be necessary for the democratic control of a global economy and polity." Nicholas Garnham, "The Media and the Public Sphere," in *Habermas and the Public Sphere*, ed. Craig Calhoun (Cambridge, MA: MIT Press, 1997), p. 362.

144. Cf. Ronald Dworkin, "What is Equality? Part 4: What is Political Equality?," *University of San Francisco Law Review* 22 (1987): 1–30.

145. John Rawls, *Justice as Fairness: A Restatement*, ed. Erin Kelly (Cambridge, MA: Harvard University Press, 2001), p. 149. Cf. Corey Brettschneider, "When the State Speaks, What Should It Say? The Dilemma of Freedom of Expression and Democratic Persuasion," in *Perspectives on Politics* 8 (2010): 1014.

146. "It is fairly well established that the political contents of the mass media— especially the reported views of ostensibly nonpartisan commentators and 'experts'— tend to affect the priorities and policy preferences of the public. . . . At minimum, it seems important to bear in mind the possibility that the wealthier and more powerful members of American society have been able to influence the opinions of the less affluent, reducing public support for policies that would combat economic inequality and adding to inequalities of political voice." Schlozman, Page, Verba, and Fiorina, "Inequalities of Political Voice," p. 27.

147. Although this is not the only factor that makes economically unequal citizens feel their voice is "likely to be futile" because representatives are more willing to be responsive and listen to those citizens who are socially more powerful. Thus, Bartels and others have explicitly argued that elected officials attach "more weight to

preferences of affluent and middle-class constituents than of low-income constituents," as if voice counts in proportion to the economic power of the social class where from it comes. Larry M. Bartels, *Unequal Democracy: The Political Economy of the New Gilded Age* (New York: Russell Sage Foundation; Princeton: Princeton University Press, 2008), pp. 285–88.

148. Niklas Luhmann, *The Reality of the Mass Media*, trans. Kathleen Cross (Stanford, CA: Stanford University Press, 2000), p. 4. To Eco and Baudrillard technological and mass communication escape our control completely, and this makes us less in communication with others because we are less able to put ourselves in a critical distance; communication absorbs more than it makes us participate. Umberto Eco, *Travels in Hyperreality* (London: Picador, 1967), pp. 140–51; Jean Baudrillard, *For a Critique of the Political Economy of the Sign*, trans. Charles Levin (New York: Telos Publishing, 1981), pp. 171–82.

149. Immanuel Kant, "What is Orientation in Thinking?," in *Political Writings*, ed. Hans Reiss (Cambridge: Cambridge University Press, 1991), p. 247.

150. In *Kleindienst v. Mandel* (1972), which scholars consider a landmark case for the interpretation of the First Amendment as implying the consideration of communication as a right, although the "protection" of this right did not hold "great influence with the Court." Mary Elizabeth Bezanson, *"Kleindienst v. Mandel,"* in *Free Speech on Trial: Communication Perspectives on Landmark Supreme Court Decisions*, ed. Richard A. Parker (Tuscaloosa: University of Alabama Press, 2003), p. 181.

151. Sunstein, *Designing Democracy*, p. 155.

152. In Bezanson, *"Kleindienst v. Mandel,"* p. 180.

153. Aristotle, *The Politics*, trans. H. Rackham (Cambridge, MA: Harvard University Press, 1977), p. 262. See also Moses I. Finley, *Democracy Ancient and Modern* (New Brunswick, NJ: Rutgers University Press, 1985), pp. 17–18; and Josiah Ober, *Mass and Elite in Democratic Athens: Rhetoric, Ideology, and the Power of the People* (Princeton, NJ: Princeton University Press, 1989), pp. 118–19, 123–27, 134.

154. Chris Demaske, *Modern Power and Free Speech: Contemporary Culture and Issues of Equality* (Lanham, MD: Rowman & Littlefield, 2009), pp. 39–41 (also for the citation of *Miami Herald v. Tornillo*). The argument that free speech is a right of the citizen and has a direct conncetion with the principle of self-determination has been made already by Justice Louis Brandeis in 1920, and revised recently by Robert C. Post, "Recuperating First Amendment Doctrine," *Stanford Law Review* 1249 (1995).

155. Finley, *Democracy Ancient and Modern*, p. 19.

156. Direct democracy was a politics of personality because it was a politics based on direct knowledge and direct hearing; the only mediation was the quotidian interaction among citizens and their exchange of opinions on issues and leaders. Moses

I. Finley, *Politics in the Ancient World* (Cambridge: Cambridge University Press, 1996), p. 97.

157. Mill, *Considerations on Representative Government*, pp. 457–60.

158. *Red Lion Broadcasting Company v. FCCC* (1969), cited in Bezanson, *"Kleindienst v. Mendel,"* p. 176.

159. Cf. the majority report by Justice Black in the case *Marsh v. Alabama* (1947) in a case involving the distribution of literature in a company-owned town: "To act as good citizens they must be informed." And the property rights of that corporation could not overcome the political right of the citizens to receive information. Bezanson, *"Kleindienst v. Mendel,"* p. 174.

160. Ellen P. Goodman, "Media Policy and Free Speech: The First Amendment at War With Itself," in *Hofstra Law Review* 35 (2007): 1211–17.

161. An excellent theoretical and historical analysis of the foundation of the communication right in the interpretation of the First Amendment was the core of Robert C. Post's Tanner Lectures at Harvard University, May 1–3, 2013. The final version of these lectures is under press by Harvard University Press.

162. Cf. Owen M. Fiss, *Liberalism Divided: Freedom of Speech and the Many Uses of State Power* (Boulder, CO: Westview Press, 1966), pp. 9–12.

163. Ronald Dworkin, "The Course of American Politics," *New York Review of Books* 43, no. 16 (October 1997). Pettit's idea of control and contestation is also consistent with this view, although inspired by a bias toward representative institutions. Philip Pettit, *Republicanism: A Theory of Freedom and Government* (Oxford: Clarendon Press, 1997), pp. 171–205.

164. Larry M. Bartels found evidence that the government fails to weigh interests of the lower sections of the population and that its overall arbitrariness grows in proportion to the number of the citizens who are not heard or simply excluded from the means of communication that could make their voice louder. Bartels, *Unequal Democracy*, pp. 252–82.

165. See in paeticular Nicolas de Condorcet, *Rapport sur l'instruction publique*, eds. C. Coutel and C. Kintzler (Paris: Edilig, 1989).

166. John Dewey, "The Challenge of Democracy to Education" (1937), in *Problems of Men* (New York: Philosophical Library, 1946), pp. 48–49.

167. Guillermo O'Donnell, *Democracy, Agency, and the State: Theory with Comparative Intent* (Oxford: Oxford University Press, 2010), pp. 105–9. Dawood wrote on the issue of which branch of government is more apt to tackle the question of inequality in wealth translating into political inequality in "Democracy, Power, and the Supreme Court," p. 272.

168. Stephen Holmes, "Lineages of the Rule of Law," in *The Rule of Law*, ed. José Maria Maravall and Adam Przeworski (Cambridge: Cambridge University Press, 2003), pp. 21–22. On the impact of economic inequality on the performance of state

institutions and the laws, see the review essay by Alfred Stepan and Juan J. Linz, "Comparative Perspectives on Inequality and the Quality of Democracy in the United States," in *Perspectives on Politics* 9 (2011): 841–56.

169. Jeffrey A. Winters, *Oligarchy* (Cambridge: Cambridge University Press, 2011), p. 4.

170. Lee C. Bollinger, *The Tolerant Society* (Oxford: Oxford University Press, 1986), pp. 215–18.

171. On the progression of power concentration in media in the United States, see the first and second eds. of Ben H. Bagdikian, *The Media Monopoly* (Boston: Beacon Press, 1983 and 2004). For a comparative view on the situation of Europe, see Peter J. Humphreys, *Mass Media and Media Policy in Western Europe* (New York: Manchester University Press, 1996); and moreover the highly informative research of Daniel C. Hallin and Paolo Mancini, *Comparing Media Systems: Three Models of Media and Politics* (New York: Cambridge University Press, 2004).

172. Bagdikian, *Media Monopoly* (2004), p. 3.

173. Commission on Freedom of the Press, *A Free and Responsible Press: A General Report on Mass Communication* (Chicago: University of Chicago Press, 1947), pp. 1, 5, 17, 37–44, 83–86.

174. Robert Y. Shapiro and Lawrence R. Jacobs, "The Democratic Paradox: The Waning of Popular Sovereignty and the Pathologies of American Politics," in *Oxford Handbook of the American Public Opinion and the Media*, ed. Lawrence R. Jacobs and Robert Y. Shapiro (Oxford Handbooks Online: September 2011), intro. Yet this argument is weak or incomplete because Internet freedom is itself an object of contention and a problematic issue. The dominance of private companies in the software and hardware industries as well as in web-based services gives those companies and the government huge advantage in inspection and control, while on the other hand is not in itself a sign of diffuse power; see Evgeny Morozov, *The Dark Side of Internet Freedom: The Net Delusion* (New York: Public Affairs, 2011), p. 236.

175. See, for instance, Zachariah Chafee Jr., *Government and Mass Communication: A Report from the Commission on Freedom of the Press* (Chicago: University of Chicago Press, 1947), 2:647–77; and C. Edwin Baker, *Advertising and a Democratic Press* (Princeton, NJ: Princeton University Press, 1994), pp. 15–20.

176. Under some specific circumstances, Steiner wrote some decades ago, a monopoly is likely to provide perhaps more content diversity events or views precisely because it wants to win all possible competitors. Peter O. Steiner, "Program Patterns and Preferences, and the Workability of Competition in Radio Broadcasting," *Quarterly Journal of Economics* 66 (1952): 194–95.

177. Baker, *Media Concentration and Democracy*, p. 15. On the impact of media on the quality of deliberation, see, among others, Benjamin Barber, "The New Telecommunications Technology: Endless Frontier or the End of Democracy?," *Constel-*

lations 4 no. 2 (1997): pp. 208–38; and, in the same issue, Hubertus Buchstein, "Bytes the Bite: The Internet and Deliberative Democracy," pp. 248–63.

178. Baker, *Media Concentration and Democracy*, p. 16.

179. In New York State, the law requires political parties to place their ads equally in TV and local papers; a similar strategy is followed in European countries; cf. Hallin and Mancini, *Comparing Media System*.

180. On the value of cognitive difference (from an epistemic perspective), see more recently Hélène Landemore, "La raison démocratique: Les mécanismes de l'intelligence collective en politique," in *La saggesse collective*, special issue of *Raison Publique* no. 12 (April 2010): pp. 35–39. On the relationship between dispersed information and viewpoints diversity, see also Sunstein, *Infotopia*, pp. 46–55.

181. Alexander Meiklejohn, *Free Speech and Its Relation to Self-Government* (Clark, NJ: Lawbook Exchange, 2004 [1st ed. 1948]), p. 77. For a perspicacious commentary of the positions of Holmes and Maiklejohn, see Bollinger, *The Tolerant Society*, pp. 145–74.

182. Meiklejohn, *Free Speech*, p. 23.

183. Ibid., pp. 24–25.

184. Ibid., p. 70.

185. He was thus able to defend free speech in the years of Communist witch hunts with the argument that no wrong ideas must be barred from the public forum. Ibid., 44–46.

186. Schumpeter, *Capitalism, Socialism, and Democracy*, p. 250.

187. Ibid., p. 272.

188. Dawood, "The New Inequality," p. 147.

189. Winters, *Oligarchy*, p. 16.

190. Owen M. Fiss, "Building a Free Press" (1995), in *Liberalism Divided*, pp. 143–44.

191. Isaiah Berlin, "Two Concept of Liberty" (1958), in *Four Essays On Liberty* (Oxford: Oxford University Press, 1992), pp. 29–30.

192. On the difference between nondomination and noninterference and on the republican argument of a nonarbitrary interference, see in particular Philip Pettit, *A Theory of Freedom: From the Psychology to the Politics of Agency* (Oxford: Oxford University Press, 2001), pp. 125–51; and Skinner, *Liberty Before Liberalism*, pp. 1–57.

193. Rawls, *Justice as Fairness*, pp. 149–50.

194. Norberto Bobbio "Della libertá dei moderni comparata a quella dei posteri" (1954), in *Politica e cultura* (Turin: Einaudi, 2005), p. 144 (my translation).

195. Yet this was also Madison's view, who understood quite clearly that "[i]n proportion as government is influenced by opinion, it must be so, by whatever influence. This decides the question concerning a *Constitutional Declaration of Rights*, which

requires an influence on government, by becoming part of the public opinion." James Madison, "Public Opinion" (1791), in *Writings*, p. 501.

196. Kelsen, *General Theory of Law and State*, pp. 287–88.

197. Jürgen Habermas, *The Inclusion of the Other: Studies in Political Theory*, ed. Ciaran Cronin and Pablo De Greiff (Cambridge, MA: MIT Press, 1998), pp. 260–61.

198. John Dewey, *The Public and Its Problems* (Athens, OH: Swallow Press/Ohio University Press, 1991), p. 148.

199. For an interesting reading of a procedural conception that is not minimalist because it contemplates participatory rights of voting and opinion making, see O'Donnell, *Democracy, Agency, and the State*, pp. 13–29.

200. Claude Lefort, *Democracy and Political Theory*, trans. David Macey (Cambridge: Polity Press, 1988), p. 225.

201. Mill, *Representative Government*, chap. 10. Mill proposed also plural voting (distributing number of voting ballots in relation to social and intellectual prominence), although he resolved to abandon this strategy (chap. 8). For an excellent criticism of exchanging political equality with some social benefits, see Rawls, *A Theory of Justice*, pp. 232–34.

202. Lippmann, *Public Opinion*, pp. 19–20.

203. Brian Barry, *Justice as Impartiality* (Oxford: Clarendon Press, 1996), p. 111.

204. Kelsen, *General Theory of Law and State*, pp. 259–60.

2. Unpolitical Democracy

1. Ball, *Transforming Political Discourse*, p. 119.

2. In this vein, see Sylvie Goulard and Mario Monti, *La democrazia in Europa: Guardare lontano* (Milan: Rizzoli, 2012), in which the argument is made that the salvation of the European Union rests on the determination of its member states to find new venues for decisions that are less subjected to electoral checks and public opinion, the opposite of what democratic representation prescribes.

3. In the process of writing the republican constitution of France, Condorcet called attention on the risk laying in the argument that a headless system of collective decision making is an obstacle to quick and competent decisions; thus, he thought that the regulation of time becomes an essential factor of liberty. Nadia Urbinati, *Representative Democracy* (Chicago: University of Chicago Press, 2006) pp. 201–7.

4. Thomas Mann, *Reflections of a Nonpolitical Man*, trans. with an intro. by Walter D. Morris (New York: Frederick Ungar, 1983), p. 16.

5. For a critical discussion of the several facets of relativism, see Steven Lukes, *Moral Relativism* (New York: Picador, 2008).

6. Mann, *Reflections of a Nonpolitical Man*, pp. 169–70.

7. Massimo Cacciari, *The Unpolitical: On the Radical Critique of Political Reason*, ed. and with an intro. by Alessandro Carrera, trans. by Massimo Verdicchio (New York: Fordham University Press, 2009), p. 94.

8. It echoes Ratzinger's criticism of democracy's presumption of making law sub-stitute for the ethical good: "the majority principle always leaves open the question of the ethical foundations of the law. This is the question of . . . whether there is something that is of its very nature inalienably law, something that is antecedent to every majority decision and must be respected by all such decisions." "That Which Holds the World Together: The Pre-political Moral Foundations of a Free State," in Joseph Ratzinger and Jürgen Habermas, *The Dialectic of Secularism: On Reason and Religion* (San Francisco: Ignatius Press, 2007), p. 60.

9. Yack, "Democracy and the Love of Truth," p. 166.

10. Waldron, *The Dignity of Legislation*, p. 29.

11. Marie Jean Antoine Nicolas, marquis de Condorcet, "Sur la nécessité de faire rati-fier la constitution par les citoyens" (1789), in *Oeuvres: Nouvelle impression en facsimilé de l'édition Paris 1847–1849*, 12 vols., ed. M. F. Arago and A. Condorcet-O'Connor (Stuttgart-Bad Cannstatt, Germany: Friedrich Frommann, 1968), 9:427–28; "Aux amis de la liberté," 10:178–79; "Project de Déclaration de Droits" (art. 28), 10:16; "Sur la né-cessité d'établir en France une constitution nouvelle" (March 1793), 12:353.

12. He then added: "The following distinction must be made: restrictions im-posed by the majority must not go so far as to create conditions which the minority might find oppressive, contrary to its rights and incompatible with justice." Marie Jean Antoine Nicolas Caritat, marquis de Condorcet, "On Freedom: On the Meaning of the Words Freedom, Free, a Free Man, a Free People" (1793–1794), in *Political Writings*, ed. Steven Lukes and Nadia Urbinati (Cambridge: Cambridge University Press, 2011), p. 184.

13. For a critical overview of the counterrevolution ideology and its manifestation with different streams of antiliberal thoughts, cf. Stephen Holmes, *The Anatomy and Anti-Liberalism* (Cambridge, MA: Harvard University Press, 1993).

14. Joseph de Maistre, *Considerations on France* (1797), ed. Richard A. Lebrun (Cambridge: Cambridge University Press, 1994), chap. 7; Edmund Burke, *Reflec-tions on Revolution in France* (1790), in *The Portable Burke*, pp. 438–44.

15. Terence Ball, "Manipulation: As Old as Democracy Itself (and Sometimes Dangerous)," in *Manipulating Democracy: Democratic Theory, Political Psychology, and Mass Media*, ed. Wayne Le Cheminant and John M. Parrish (New York: Rout-ledge, 2011), pp. 42–46.

16. In a democracy, manipulation may stimulate activism at least because it drives people to denounce and search out truth, which is what does not happen in an undemocratic regime. Ball, "Manipulation," p. 46.

17. Post, *Democracy, Expertise, Academic Freedom*, p. 31.

18. Max Weber, *From Max Weber: Essays in Sociology*, ed. H. H. Gerth and C. Wright Mills (New York: Oxford University Press, 1958), pp. 231–34.

19. Pierre Rosanvallon, *Counter-Democracy: Politics in an Age of Distrust*, trans. Arthur Goldhammer (Cambridge: Cambridge University Press, 2012); Philip Pettit,

"Depoliticizing Democracy," *Ratio Juris* 17 (March 2004): 52–65; Phillip Pettit, "Deliberative Democracy, the Discursive Dilemma, and Republican Theory," in *Debating Deliberative Democracy*, ed. James S. Fishkin and Peter Laslett (Oxford: Blackwell, 2003), pp. 138–62; and Estlund, *Democratic Authority*.

20. I made this argument in "Unpolitical Democracy," *Political Theory* 38, no. 1 (2010): 65–92.

21. Estlund, *Democratic Authority*, pp. 23, 27.

22. Rosanvallon, *Counter-Democracy*, pp. 14–15.

23. Pettit, "Depoliticizing Democracy," p. 64.

24. Rosenblum, *On the Side the Angels*, pp. 25–26.

25. Ball, *Transforming Political Discourse*, pp. 115–20. J. S. Mill designed parliamentary commissions made of deliberating experts as a strategy to make the assembly simply voting on issues, a task that required some disciplinary and special competence. Mill, *Considerations on Representative Government*, chap. 5.

26. Young was among the first to criticize the rationalist vocation of deliberation. Iris Young, *Justice and the Politics of Difference* (Princeton, NJ: Princeton University Press, 1990), chap. 4. But see also Bernard Yack, "Rhetoric and Public Reasoning: An Aristotelian Understanding of Political Deliberation," *Political Theory* 34 (2006): 417–38; Bryan Garsten, *Saving Persuasion* (Cambridge, MA: Harvard University Press, 2006); and Linda L. Zerilli, "Response To Jon Simons," *Political Theory* 28, no. 2 (April 1, 2000): 279–84.

27. Chantal Mouffe, "Deliberative Democracy or Agonistic Pluralism?" *Social Research* 66 (1999): 745–58; and *The Democratic Paradox* (London: Verso, 2000), in particular chap. 4.

28. Pettit, "Depoliticizing Democracy," p. 59.

29. The inspiration and main theme of this section comes from the paper I wrote with Maria Paula Saffon, "Procedural Democracy: The Bulwark of Equal Liberty," *Political Theory* 41, no. 3 (June 2013): 441–81 (in particular pp. 445–50).

30. Habermas, *Facts and Norms*, pp. 292–95; on the identification of procedural democracy with Schumpeterianism and how this compromised the normative understanding of this interpretation and in fact facilitated a distorted idea of what democratic procedures do, see Mackie, "Schumpeter's Leadership Democracy."

31. Jürgen Habermas, *Moral Consciousness and Communicative Action*, trans. Christian Lenhardt and Shierry Weber Nicholson (Cambridge, MA: MIT Press, 1993), pp. 71–72. Bringing this mode to its extreme, Bohman has thus objected against proceduralism because it is self-referential: "merely following a procedure, no matter how fair, will not influence the quality of the agreement reached or the reasons that support it." James Bohman, *Public Deliberation: Pluralism, Complexity, and Democracy* (Cambridge, MA: MIT Press, 2000), p. 51.

32. Habermas, *The Inclusion of the Other*, p. 19.

33. Habermas, *Facts and Norms*, p. 294.

34. This criticism has been made early on by Bernard Manin, "On Legitimacy and Political Deliberation," *Political Theory* 15, no. 3 (1987): p. 338–68.

35. "Thus, as we have seen, normative democratic theory has largely proceeded on the assumption that the most that can be said for a legitimate democratic decision is that it was produced by a procedure that treats voters equally in certain ways." Estlund, *Democratic Authority*, p. 98.

36. Joshua Cohen, *The Arc of the Moral Universe and Other Essays* (Cambridge, MA: Harvard University Press, 2010), pp. 188–91; Goodin, *Reflective Democracy*, chap. 5.

37. Estlund, *Democratic Authority*, pp. 27, 29. Cf. Pettit, *Republicanism*, pp. 180–82. As Estlund puts it, if antagonism is at the center of political values, "there is predictable ambivalence about appeals to truth in political discourse," and "nihilism" would be the predictable "price." Estlund, *Democratic Authority*, pp. 23, 27.

38. The fortune of the term "wisdom of the crowd" comes from James Surowiecki's *The Wisdom of Crowds* (New York: Anchor Books, 2005), which argues, with empirical and experimental evidence, that a group made of diverse individuals, more or less smarter and unequally uninformed, is better at making decisions than a small group of equally informed individuals holding similar opinions (in particular, see chap. 1). Defense of the "many-brains" is based on two arguments: that "the group's 'competence' or chance of being correct can exceed that of the group's most competent members" and that "a large enough number of fairly poor (but better than random) guessers can easily prove more competent than a small panel of highly competent experts." The "corollary" is that "diversity—here, the statistical independence of the guesses—makes a big difference in group performance, holding competence constant." Adrian Vermeule, "Many-Minds Arguments in Legal Theory," in *The Journal of Legal Analysis* 1 (2009): 5. More recently Hélène Landemore used this theorem to prove against the oligarchic usage of "good" deliberation that large crowds are more diversified since they are more numerous than small groups of few intelligent individuals in "Democratic Reason: The Mechanism of Collective Intelligence in Politics," in *Collective Wisdom: Principles and Mechanisms*, ed. Hélène Landemore and Jon Elster (Cambridge: Cambridge University Press, 2012), pp. 251–89.

39. Estlund, *Democratic Authority*, p. 7.

40. Ibid., p. 29.

41. Ibid., p. 97.

42. Ibid., p. 27; Saffon and Urbinati, "Procedural Democracy," p. 6.

43. Estlund, *Democratic Authority*, pp. 8, 98.

44. Ibid., p. 98.

45. Proceduralists "see the goodness or rightness of an outcome as being wholly constituted by the fact of its having emerged in some procedurally correct manner." Goodin, *Reflective Democracy*, p. 92.

46. Estlund, *Democratic Authority*, p. 18.

47. Archon Fung, "Varieties of Participation in Complex Governance," *Public Administration Review* 66 (2006): pp. 66–75; Bruce Ackerman and James Fishkin, *Deliberation Day* (New Haven, CT: Yale University Press, 2004), pp. 179–84.

48. Habermas, *Between Facts and Norms*, p. 106.

49. "It is true that a democratic regime runs the risk that the people will make mistakes. But the risk of mistakes exists in all regimes in the real world. . . . Moreover, the opportunity to make mistakes is an opportunity to learn. . . . At its best, only the democratic vision can offer the hope, which guardianship can never do, that by engaging in governing themselves, all people, and not merely a few, may learn to act as morally responsible human beings." Robert Dahl, *Controlling Nuclear Weapons: Democracy vs. Guardianship* (Syracuse, NY: Syracuse University Press, 1985), p. 51.

50. Albert O. Hirschman, "On Democracy in Latin America," in *New York Review of Books*, May 10, 1986, but see also his "Doubt and Antifascist Action in Italy, 1936–1938," in *A Propensity to Self-Subversion* (Cambridge, MA: Harvard University Press, 1995), pp. 118–19.

51. Albert O. Hirschman, *Shifting Involvements: Private Interest and Public Action* (Princeton, NJ: Princeton University Press, 1982), p. 123.

52. Cf. Josiah Ober, *Democracy and Knowledge: Innovation and Learning in Classical Athens* (Princeton, NJ: Princeton University Press, 2008), pp. 31–33.

53. Hence, Plato made Callicles say that philosophers have "no knowledge of the legal code of the city," in *Gorgias*, p. 80.

54. Marcus Tullius Cicero, *Tusculan Disputations*, with an English trans. by J. E. King, Loeb Classic Library (Cambridge, MA: Harvard University Press, 1945), p. 335.

55. See Remer, *Humanism and the Rhetoric of Toleration*, pp. 16–26.

56. Marcus Tullius Cicero, *De natura deorum*, ed. Arthur Stanley Pease, Loeb Classic Library (Cambridge, MA: Harvard University Press, 1955–1958), chap. I.1.

57. In mid-twentieth century, Kelsen wrote that attempts to justify democracy on the basis of the "epistemic" quality of its political decisions equates making it resemble a "donkey in a lion's skin" because the whole of the political community is *not* the most qualified body for discovering and applying an objective standard of political "truth," nor should it be expected to be. Grounding political legitimacy on the principle of autonomy only (obey the laws we make) really makes sense of the supposition that an objective standard of *political* truth is not available. Hans Kelsen, *The Essence and Value of Democracy*, p. 90. On his argument that democracy cannot operate with dogmatic creeds, see also Hans Kelsen, "Absolutism and

Relativism in Philosophy and Politics" *American Political Science Review* 42 (1948): 906–14.

58. For an excellent overview of an exemplar of abortion of the colloquium for reconciliation among Catholics and Calvinists in France (which occurred ten years before the massacre of the Huguenots), see Donald Nugent, *Ecumenism in the Age of the Reformation: The Colloquy of Poissy* (Cambridge, MA: Harvard University Press, 1974).

59. As Mario Turchetti wrote, the room for compromise was broader when post-Reformation Christians did not know each other's positions well; contrary to the hope of the spiritual guide of *concordia*, Erasmus of Rotterdam (which was a theoretical inspiration of both Catholics and Calvinists for some decades), the "fundamentals of faith," which were supposed to be basic truth not open to disputation and shared by all Christians qua Christians, became the main object of discord and disagreements among the different Christian denominations. To overcome disagreement would mean to overcome differences among Christians and belong to one and the same church. Yet it was precisely in the name of difference that the break with the "fundamentals of faith" occurred. Mario Turchetti, *Concordia o Tolleranza? François Bauduin (1520–1573) e i 'Moyenneurs'* (Milan: Franco Angeli, 1984), pp. 102–8.

60. Supporters of Concordia, Catholics and Protestants, opposed their idea of unity against models of empire that were based on religious pluralism, like the Ottoman Empire or the old Roman empire. Joseph Lecler, "Liberté de Conscience: Origins et sens divers de l'expression," *Recherches de Science religieuse* 54 (1966): 394.

61. The association of "strongly held beliefs" with intolerance and, vice versa, of a more skeptical outlook with toleration is widely echoed in contemporary analysis. Quentin Skinner, *The Foundations of Modern Political Thought*, 2 vols. (Princeton, NJ: Princeton University Press, 1978) 2:244–54; Preston King, *Toleration* (London: Allen and Unwin, 1976), pp. 122–31. For a critical reading that stresses instead the "treacherous" and relativist implication of skepticism, see Richard Tuck, "Scepticism and Toleration in the Seventeenth Century," in *Justifying Toleration: Conceptual and Historical Perspectives*, ed. Susan Mendus (Cambridge: Cambridge University Press, 1988), pp. 21–35; for a challenge of the "modernist" assumption that links toleration to skepticism, see Cary Nederman, "Toleration, Skepticism, and the 'Clash of Ideas,'" in *Beyond the Persecuting Society: Religious Toleration Before the Enlightenment*, ed. John Christian Laursen and Cary J. Nederman (Philadelphia: University of Pennsylvania Press, 1998), pp. 66–67.

62. As Rawls says, "Holding a political conception as true, and for that reason alone the one suitable basis of public reason, is exclusive, even sectarian, and so likely to foster political division." Rawls, *Political Liberalism*, p. 129.

63. Ober observes: "Condorcet's jury theorem is limited to binary judgment. . . . Yet Condorcet's theorem is incapable of explaining the decision-making processes of the

Athenian Assembly, where a very large body of persons, some of them expert in various domains relevant to the issue of the day, often decided among a variety of possible policy options after listening to a series of speeches." Ober, *Democracy and Knowledge*, p. 109.

64. Condorcet, "Sur la nécessité de faire ratifier la constitution par les citoyens," pp. 427–28.

65. Condorcet, *Lettres à M. le Comte Mathieu de Montmerency*, pp. 375, 371 (my translation).

66. "As soon as the philosopher submitted his truth, the reflection of the eternal, to the polis, it became immediately an opinion among opinions." Hannah Arendt, "Philosophy and Politics," *Social Research* 57, no. 1 (Spring 1990): 78.

67. Frank Michelman, "How Can the People Ever Make the Laws? A Critique of Deliberative Democracy," in *Deliberative Democracy: Essays on Reason and Politics*, ed. James Bohman and William Rehg (Cambridge, MA: MIT Press, 1997), p. 148.

68. To contain the emendation of constitutions by representative assemblies, super-majority rule has been adopted in many modern democracies. Yet while this method is in the view of protecting the Constitution from the representatives (who cannot use it as they think fit), it is not a violation of equality because it does not preselect the minority. Kelsen, a staunch supporter of the principle of majority, thought that the only way of making rights juridically effective was to inscribe them in the Constitution and make them not immediately accessible to the possibility of being changed or nullified by the elected majority. For this reason, he concluded that the proper institutionalization of the majority principle requires the introduction of certain "super-majoritarian" constraints that constitute the basis for a distinction between different "levels" of legislation. "The protection of the minority is the essential function of so-called freedoms and fundamental rights or human and civil rights, which are guaranteed by all modern parliamentary-democratic constitutions. . . . The typical way of qualifying constitutional laws vis-à-vis conventional laws is the requirement of a higher quorum and of a special— possibly two-thirds or three-quarters—majority." Kelsen, *The Essence and Value of Democracy*, p. 50.

69. The more multitudinous an assembly, Madison argued, the more susceptible the decisions are to passions and sectarian interests: "Ignorance will be the dupe of cunning, and passion the slave of sophistry and declamation," *Federalist* No. 58, in James Madison, Alexander Hamilton, and John Jay, *The Federalist Papers*, ed. Isaac Kramnick (Marmondsworth: Penguin, 1987).

70. Estlund, *Democratic Authority*, pp. 208–9; Waldron, *The Dignity of Legislation*, pp. 33–34.

71. See Melissa Lane, "Aristotle as Schumpeterian? The Multitude's Claim to "Rule" as a Claim to Election and Inspection Only," forthcoming in *The Cambridge Companion to Aristotle's Politics*.

72. Ober has proposed a kind of theorem for this functional collective doing that recuperates Hayek's theory of diffuse expertise through socially communicated information: "The key to successful democratic decision making is the integration of dispersed and latent technical knowledge with social knowledge and shared value." Ober, *Democracy and Knowledge*, p. 18.

73. Cf. Kurt A. Raaflaub, "II. Democracy, Oligarchy, and the Concept of the 'Free Citizen' in Late Fifth-Century Athens," *Political Theory* 11 (1983): 517–24; Hansen, *Athenian Democracy in the Age of Demosthenes*, pp. 71–78.

74. "As Aristotle insisted, we do not deliberate about things that we believe cannot in the nature of things be otherwise." Stuart Hampshire, *Innocence and Experience* (Cambridge, MA: Harvard University Press, 1989), pp. 56–57. The point has been made by Rostbøll, although against theorists of minimalist democracy, to stress that preferences are not to be treated as "given" because the meaning of deliberation is precisely that of creating institutions and social conditions that are conducive of "free opinion and will formation." Christian F. Rostbøll, *Deliberative Freedom: Deliberative Democracy as Critical Theory* (New York: State University of New York Press, 2008), p. 22.

75. Post, *Democracy, Expertise, Academic Freedom*, p. 34.

76. Przeworski, "Minimalist Conception of Democracy," p. 29.

77. Holmes, *Passions & Constraint*, pp. 196–98.

78. Kelsen, *The Essence and Value of Democracy*, chap. 6.

79. *Vigilance, dénounciation*, and *notation* are the three forms of the "pouvoirs de surveillance" that negative power puts in action. Rosanvallon, *Counter-Democracy*, pp. 12–18.

80. Early on Gauchet suggested a parallel between the judge (in the court) and opinion (in civil society) because both of them put in action a "permanent representation" of the sovereign while none of them wants to substitute to the ordinary powers of the sovereign, but rather wants simply to recall them that they must remain within the constitutional limits. Michel Gauchet, *La révolution des pouvoirs: La souveraineté, le peuple et la représentation 1789–1799* (Paris: Gallimard, 1995), pp. 36–43. I thank Jennifer Hudson for her useful insights on the place of bureaucracy in French thought.

81. "Une telle défiance démocratique s'exprime et s'organise de multiples façons. J'en distinguerait trois modalités principales: les pouvoirs de surveillance, les formes d'empêchement, les mises à l'épreuve d'un jugement." Rosanvallon, *La contre-démocratie: La politique à l'âge de la défiance* (Paris: Seuil, 2006). ["Democratic distrust can be expressed and organized in a variety of ways, of which I shall emphasize three main types: power of oversight, forms of prevention, and testing of judgment." Rosanvallon, *Counter-Democracy*, p. 8.]

82. Rosanvallon, *Counter-Democracy*, pp. 214–220.

83. Rosanvallon, *La légitimité démocratique*, pp. 338–40.

84. Rosanvallon, *La contre-démocratie*, p. 354.

85. Arendt captured the political implications deriving from being a spectator and being an actor: the former entails impartial judgment, but the later is unavoidably partial; "only the spectator occupies a position that enables him to see the whole; the actor, because he is part of the play, must enact his part—he is partial by definition." Hannah Arendt, *Lectures on Kant's Political Philosophy*, ed. with an interpretative essay by Ronald Beiner (Chicago: University of Chicago Press, 1992), p. 55.

86. For a critical analysis of the myth of the independent citizen (not partisan), see Rosenblum, *On the Side of the Angels*, in particular chap. 7.

87. "Le populisme peut être appréhendé dans ce cas comme une forme d'expression politique dans laquelle le projet démocratique se laisse totalment aspirer et vampiriser par la contre-démocratie: il est la forme extréme de l'anti-politique." Rosanvallon, *La contre-démocratie*, p. 276. Translation available in Rosanvallon, *Counter-Democracy*, p. 268.

88. Ibid.

89. Damian Tambini, *Nationalism in Italian Politics: The Stories of the Northern League, 1980–2000* (London: Routledge 2001), chaps. 3 and 4; Tom Gallagher, "Rome at Bay: The Challenge of the Northern League to the Italian State," *Government and Opposition* 27, no. 4 (2007): 470–85.

90. According to Manin, video democracy represented a new stage in the evolution of representative government, one in which partisanship would be replaced by more objective information. Manin, *Principles of Representative Government*, pp. 228–29.

91. Rosanvallon, *Counter-Democracy*, pp. 259–64.

92. Ibid., p. 299.

93. Philip Pettit, "Republican Freedom and Contestatory Democracy," in *Democracy's Value*, ed. Ian Shapiro and Casiano Hacker-Cordón (Cambridge: Cambridge University Press, 1999), pp. 163–90.

94. Xavier De Souza Briggs, *Democracy as Problem Solving: Civic Capacity in Communities Across the Globe* (Cambridge, MA: MIT Press, 2008), pp. 302, 305.

95. Gene Rowe and Lynn J. Frewer, "Public Participation Methods: A Framework for Evaluation," *Science, Technology & Human Values* 25 (2000): 3–29. For an excellent critical overview of citizens' panels, see Mark B. Brown, "Survey Article: Citizen Panels and the Concept of Representation," *Journal of Political Philosophy* 14 (2006): 203–25; Archon Fung, "Varieties of Participation in Complex Governance," *Public Administration Review* 66 (2006): 66–75; and James Fishkin, *The Voice of the People: Public Opinion and Democracy* (New Haven, CT: Yale University Press, 1995).

96. Nadia Urbinati and Mark E. Warren, "The Concept of Representation in Contemporary Democratic Theory," *Annual Review of Political Science* 11 (2008): 387–412.

97. Bruce Ackerman, *We the People: Foundations* (Cambridge: Cambridge University Press, 1991), p. 181.

98. Mansbridge, *Beyond Adversary Democracy*, pp. 248–51.

99. Russell Muirhead, "Can Deliberative Democracy Be Partisan?" *Critical Review* 22 (2010): 129–57.

100. Brown, "Survey Article," p. 8.

101. Fishkin wrote that deliberative polls are a modern version of the ancient Athenian selection by lot in *Voice of the People*, p. 169; for a counterargument, see Brown, "Survey Article," pp. 9–10.

102. Pettit, "Depoliticizing Democracy," pp. 56–57.

103. Ibid., p. 54.

104. An interesting comparison has been proposed by Miller, who shows how the deliberative ideal fulfills the promises of liberal-democratic institutions because, while it starts from the "premise that political preferences will conflict" and that the democratic institutions must resolve them, "it envisages this occurring through an open and uncoerced discussion of the issue at stake with the aim of arriving at an agreed judgment." Informal processes of discussion make procedural and institutional factors less central. David Miller, "Deliberative Democracy and Social Choice," in *Debating Deliberative Democracy*, ed. James S. Fishkin and Peter Laslett (Oxford: Blackwell, 2003), p. 183.

105. Pettit, "Depoliticizing Democracy," p. 57.

106. Ober, "Original Meaning of 'Democracy,'" p. 3.

107. Pettit, *Republicanism*, p. 174.

108. Ibid., p. 167.

109. Dunn, *Democracy*, p. 54.

110. Cf. Giuseppe Cambiano, *Polis: Un modello per la cultura europea* (Roma-Bari: Laterza, 2000), in particular chaps. 1 and 2; J. G. A Pocock, *The Machiavellian Moment: Florentine Political Thought and the Atlantic Republican Tradition* (Princeton, NJ: Princeton University Press, 1975), pp. 100–3.

110. Pettit, *Republicanism*, p. 166.

111. Ibid., p. 176.

112. Philip Pettit, *On the People's Terms: A Republican Theory and Model of Democracy* (Cambridge: Cambridge University Press, 2012), p. 15.

113. Pettit, *Republicanism*, p. 176.

114. Hence, liberal theorists of democracy from Joseph Schumpeter to William Riker have insisted in giving suffrage a mainly negative function that involves removal of leaders more than guiding politics.

115. Richard Bellamy, *Political Constitutionalism: A Republican Defense of the Constitutionality of Democracy* (Cambridge: Cambridge University Press, 2007), pp. 163–71.

116. Pettit adds an important caveat to his criticism: the enemy of liberty as non-domination and republican good government was born in the nineteenth century, with the theory of national sovereignty and the centrality of public opinion and parliamentary democracy. Pettit, *Republicanism*, p. 182.

117. Ibid., pp. 54–55.

118. In the nineteenth century this ancient idea delivered for instituting parliamentary committees, as Mill conceived in the same line of thought as Pettit's. Yet Mill's goal was to make the parliament not into a silent yes-no voting body but into an agora that was supposed to stage in front of the entire nation the great political debates. Mill's strategy of discharging the assembly of technicalities (hence the constitution of committees) was in order to make the assembly a truly talking body, which is exactly what Pettit would not like because the talking of a representative assembly is unavoidably an exercise of rhetoric and partisan arguments that would not help impartial decisions.

119. Machiavelli, *Discourses*, 1:18, 58.

120. James Harrington, *The Commonwealth of Oceana*, in *The Commonwealth of Oceana and a System of Politics*, ed. J. G. A. Pocock (Cambridge: Cambridge University Press, 1996), pp. 143, 32–33, 24–25, 29; Rousseau, *On the Social Contract*, bk. 4, chap. 2.

121. The enmity of republicanism to democracy became particularly strong after and as a consequence of the French Revolution; an antidemocratic republican was certainly Jean Charles Léonard Simonde de Sismondi (1773–1842), as one can see from his *Recherches sur les Constitutions des Peuples libres*, written between 1796 and 1800, and whose first complete edition was edited by Marco Minerbi (Genève: Droz, 1965).

122. Pettit, "Deliberative Democracy," pp. 144–45.

123. But also in the *Leviathan* the subjects have the legal right to sue the sovereign in a controversy over property, debt, or criminal law "as if it were against a Subject." Although the content of the law, the scope of what the law "requireth," is under the control of the sovereign (and this gravely contradicts the neorepublican principle of making liberty secure, not simply legally defined), it is, however, certain that Hobbes argued that when the sovereign oversteps these bounds or can no longer fulfill its role, it is no longer legitimate. Thomas Hobbes, *The Leviathan*, ed. Richard Tuck (Cambridge: Cambridge University Press, 1991), chap. 21.

124. Pettit, *Republicanism*, p. 196.

125. In *Counter-Democracy*, Rosanvallon reconstructs the history and institutional characteristics of the main controlling strategy, from the ancient tribunate to modern constitutional courts and central banks.

126. For a clarification on the role of the theory of liberty as nondomination in relation to democracy, see Pettit, *Republicanism*, pp. 164–72. On the antidemo-

cratic implications of neo-Roman republicanism, see John McCormick, "Machiavelli against Republicanism: On the Cambridge School's 'Guicciardinian Moments,'" *Political Theory* 31 (2003): 615–43; and Urbinati, "Competing for Liberty."

127. Pettit, *Republicanism*, p. 166. For some recent critical appraisals of Pettit's theory of liberty, see Bellamy, *Political Constitutionalism*, pp. 154–62; and Patchen Markell, "The Insufficiency of Non-Domination," *Political Theory* 36, no. 1 (2008): 9–36.

128. Pettit "Deliberative Democracy," p. 154.

129. Pettit, *Republicanism*, p. 179. Thus, the target of Pettit's neo-roman model of good government is not merely democracy but post-eighteenth-century representative democracy, a hybrid embodiment of several components, all of which potentially hostile to liberty: popular sovereignty, suffrage and the electoral appointment of representatives, the law-making power of the parliament, party competition, and the manipulation of public opinion (pp. 182, 198). Pettit's concern reminds us of Friedrich Hayek's regarding the natural tendency of democracy to become "unlimited" and the conviction that the conditions of liberty can be met "only by taking the powers of the decision out of the hands of democratic assemblies," whether representative or plebiscitarian.

130. Pettit, *Republicanism*, p. 174.

131. Pettit, "Deliberative Democracy," p. 156.

132. Pettit, *Republicanism*, p. 185.

133. Samuel Freeman, "Deliberative Democracy: A Sympathetic Comment," *Philosophy and Public Affairs* 29, no. 4 (2000): p. 375. (Freeman argues, convincingly, that the contrast between aggregative or interest-based voting and deliberative judgment is wrongly posed because, as Rousseau and Rawls have shown, assessing one's interests is not necessarily opposite to making judgments in the general interest, pp. 376–77.) For a version of deliberation less unfavorable to party advocacy, see Gutmann and Thompson, *Democracy and Disagreement*, p. 135.

134. I discussed this issue at length in *Representative Democracy*, chap. 3.

135. This is the scheme followed by Rawls in depicting the mind of the individuals behind the veil of ignorance. Manin, *Principles of Representative Government*, p. 349.

136. The judge cannot be representative of (the opinion of) the sovereign *because* he does not have himself the power to make the law and thus to resist the law—wherein it is evident that *opinion* is directly related to sovereignty or the sphere of political deliberation. This was in Tocqueville's correct opinion the main source of the difference between the American and European systems and the fact that the former gave to judges an "immense political power," as the latter did not. Tocqueville, *Democracy in America*, pp. 100–1. On the negative impact of political

judgment (thus election) on "judicial integrity" of trial judges, see Gregory A. Huber and Gordon C. Sanford, "Accountability and Coercion: Is Justice Blind when It Runs for Office?," *American Political Science Review* 28, no.2 (2004): 247–63.

137. Montesquieu, *Spirit of the Laws*, bk. 11, chaps. 4 and 6.

138. Rawls, "Idea of Public Reason Revisited," p. 577.

139. Hanna Fenichel Pitkin, *The Concept of Representation* (Berkeley: University of California Press, 1967), p. 212.

140. Frank R. Ankersmit, *Aesthetic Politics: Political Philosophy beyond Fact and Value* (Stanford: Stanford University Press, 1997), p. 47.

141. Different as they were, both Jean-Jacques Rousseau and James Madison agreed that lawmaking is a work that consists in finding the *minimum common denominator* among partial views or interests in order to dilute the extremes, rather than erasing or ignoring them. Rousseau, *On the Social Contract*, pp. 155–56; *Federalist* No. 10, in *The Federalist Papers*, p. 57.

142. Jon Elster, "Deliberation and Constitution Making," in *Deliberative Democracy*, ed. Jon Elster (Cambridge: Cambridge University Press, 1998), p. 104. For an extremely useful analysis of the forms of judgment and rhetorical reasoning, see Chaim Perelman, *Justice, Law, and Argument: Essays on Morals and Legal Reasoning* (Boston: Reidel Publishing Company, 1980), pp. 59–66.

143. "The grammar of egalitarian societies seems to accentuate predicates, evaluations by the subject, whereas the language of hierarchic societies would be evocative, its grammar and syntax would have a magic quality. . . . In an equalitarian society language belongs to everybody and evolves quite freely; in a hierarchic society it congeals. Its expressions and formulas become ritual and are listened to in a spirit of communion and total submission." Chaim Perelman and L. Olbrechts-Tyteca, *The New Rhetoric: A Treatise on Argumentation*, trans. John Wilkinson and Purcell Weaver (Notre Dame, IN: University of Notre Dame Press, 1971), p. 164.

144. I interpret "ideology" in the way Skinner suggested: to designate the use of beliefs and values in order to legitimize behavior and the active function of political ideas in the interpretation of social and cultural beliefs and interests, and to advance social visions. Quentin Skinner, "Retrospect: Studying Rhetoric and Conceptual Change," *Visions of Politics*, 3 vols. (Cambridge: Cambridge University Press, 2002), 1:175–87.

145. On the "perspectival" nature of political judgment, see Norberto Bobbio, *Left and Right: The Significance of A Political Distinction*, trans. with an intro. by Allan Cameron (Cambridge: Polity Press, 1996), pp. 1–17.

146. The issue of opinion and truth in politics opens to the fundamental question of the role of hypocrisy and thus authenticity in democratic politics, which I can only mention here. Runciman proposes an interesting definition that supports the case

for a procedural conception of democracy: "we need politicians who are sincere, but that does not mean we should wish them to be sincere believers in everything they do. Instead, we need them to be sincere believers about the system of power in which they find themselves, and sincere in their desire to maintain the stability and durability of that system. . . . Democratic politicians should be sincere about maintaining the conditions under which democracy is possible, and should place a higher premium on that than on any other sort of sincerity." David Runciman, *Political Hypocrisy: The Mask of Power, From Hobbes to Orwell and Beyond* (Princeton, NJ: Princeton University Press, 2008), p. 213.

147. Manin, *Principles of Representative Government*, pp. 183–92.

148. Aristotle, *The Art of Rhetoric*, pp. 33–47.

3. The Populist Power

1. Jan-Werner Mueller, "Getting a Grip on Populism," *Dissentmagazine.org*, September 23, 2011.

2. For an excellent, rich, and well-documented analysis of the Tea Party, see Vanessa Williamson, Theda Skocpol, and John Coggin, "The Tea Party and the Remaking of Republican Conservatism," *Perspectives on Politics* 9, no. 1 (2011): 25–43.

3. The Tea Party has some clear proposals (from Social Security to taxation) and seeks to revitalize or reshape the Republican Party: "we should regard the Tea Party as a new variant of conservative mobilization and intra-Republican party factionalism, a dynamic, loosely-knit, and not easily controlled formation of activists, funders, and media personalities that draws upon and refocuses longstanding social attitudes about federal social programs, spending, and taxation." Ibid., p. 37.

4. I would like to express my gratitude to Ian Zuckerman for inviting me to reflect upon this distinction.

5. Cf. Cas Mudde, "The Populism Zeitgeist," in *Government & Opposition* 39 (2003): 541–63; as Sunstein writes, an effective way to create a radical group is to separate its members from the large society and the other groups (*Rumors* and *Infotopia*).

6. Robert Dahl, *Democracy and Its Critics* (New Haven, CT: Yale University Press, 1989), pp. 112–15.

7. Claude Lefort, "The Question of Democracy," in *Democracy and Political Theory*, pp. 13, 19–20.

8. On the paradox of politics as that of making the democratic subject (the people) by democratic means, see Bonnie Honig, "Between Deliberation and Decision: Political Paradox in Democratic Theory," in *American Political Science Review* 101 (2007): 17–44.

9. Jason Frank, *Constituent Moments: Enacting the People in Postrevolutionary America* (Durham, NC: Duke University Press, 2010).

10. Lefort, "Question of Democracy," pp. 13–20; Ernesto Laclau, *On Populist Reason* (London: Verso, 2007), pp. 164–68. For a comprehensive analysis of Lefort's conception of populism, see Andrew Arato, "Political Theology and Populism," *Social Research* 80, no. 1 (Spring 2013): 156–59.

11. Norberto Bobbio, *Saggi sulla Scienza Politica in Italia* (Bari: Laterza, 1969); *Democracy and Dictatorship: The Nature and Limits of State Power*, trans. Peter Kennealy (Cambridge: Polity Press, 1989); and *Autobriografia*, ed. Alberto Papuzzi (Roma-Bari: Laterza, 1997).

12. Canovan, "Taking Politics to the People," p. 39; "'Trust the People!' Populism and the Two Faces of Democracy," *Political Studies* (1999): pp. 2–16.

13. Benjamin Arditi, *Politics on the Edge of Liberalism: Difference, Populism, Revolution, Agitation* (Edinburg: Edinburg University Press, 2008).

14. Yves Mény and Yves Surel, "The Constitutive Ambiguity of Populism," in *Democracies and the Populist Challenge*, pp. 1–21.

15. I take this definition of a parasite from Jacques Derrida, *Limited Inc.*, trans. Samuel Weber (Evanston, IL: Northwestern University Press, 1988), p. 90: "The parasite then 'takes place.' And at the bottom, whatever violently 'takes place' or occupies a site is always *something* of a parasite. *Never quite* taking place is then part of its performance, or its success, as an event, or its 'taking place.'" Populism is a permanent possibility within representative democracy, and the "never taking place" refers to its being a permanent mobilizing possibility even when it is strong enough to manifest its power. If all the populist potentials were actualized it would replace representative democracy altogether and this would be a regime change (like fascism did when it "took place").

16. Otto Gierke, *Political Theories of the Middle Age*, trans. Frederic William Maitland (Cambridge: Cambridge University Press, 1958), p. 61.

17. Pitkin, *Concept of Representation*, chap. 4. Pitkin located the transition in the terminological meaning of the word "representation" from "standing for" to "acting for" between the second half of the sixteenth century and the first half of the seventeenth century.

18. Cf. my *Representative Democracy*, chaps. 1 and 2.

19. Laclau, *On Populist Reason*, pp. 157–58.

20. Carl Schmitt, *Constitutional Theory* (1928), trans. and ed. by Jeffrey Seitzer, foreword by Ellen Kennedy (Durham: Duke University Press, 2008), p. 370.

21. Ibid.

22. Canovan, "Trust the People!," p. 5; Arato, "Political Theology and Populism," pp. 160–62.

23. As Lane writes, the word "demagogy" did not have pejorative meaning in classical democratic practice: "there is no pejorative meaning of the words *dēmagōgos*, *dēmēgoros*, or their cognates, in any of the dramatists, orators, or historians whose

works survive." Melissa Lane, "The Origins of the Statesman: Demagogue Distinction in and after Ancient Athens," in *Journal of the History of Ideas* 73 (2012): 180. And Ober clarified that the former "derives from *dēmos* and the verb *agō* (to lead), while the latter derives from *dēmos* and the verb *agoreuō* (to speak in public assembly)," but "the two root verbs are themselves closely related." Ober, *Mass and Elite in Democratic Athens*, p. 106, footnote 7. "The words," Lane adds, "do sometimes have a partisan meaning, associating a political speaker or leader with the popular party, but they are not inherently condemnatory." Lane, "Origins of the Statesman," p. 180).

24. Aristotle, *Politics*, 1304b1–10.

25. Ibid., 1304b20–25.

26. Ibid., 1304b1–10.

27. Laclau, *On Populist Reason*, p. 169.

28. Bernard Crick, "Populism, Politics and Democracy," in *Democratization* 12 (2005): 626.

29. Przeworski made a similar argument in his comparative analysis of class conflicts, capitalism, and democratic stability (or uneasiness) in *Capitalism and Social Democracy*, pp. 207–21.

30. Both a negative and a neutral meaning of the term can be found in Finley, who, writing in a time in which bad demagogues proliferated, was, however, more prone to stress the former one. Finley, *Democracy Ancient and Modern*, pp. 38–75.

31. "In other words, the noun [demagoguery] itself is neutral: it is the change in qualities of those occupying the neutral position of political leader that bears the pejorative weight." Lane, "Origins of the Statesman."

32. Aristotle, *Politics*, 1305a30–35, which is what the few always do. Przeworski, "Minimalist Conception of Democracy," pp. 40–41.

33. Schwartz, *Future of Democratic Equality*, p. 178.

34. Machiavelli, *Discourses*, 1:16.

35. The Roman people had little interest in the law instituting the ballot as long as they were free. This law was "demanded only when they were tyrannized over by the powerful men in the State." Marcus Tullius Cicero, *De legibus*, in *De re publica: De legibus*, trans. C. W. Keyes, Loeb Classical Library (Cambridge, MA: Harvard University Press, 1928), p. 499.

36. Aristotle, *Politics*, 1305a30–35.

37. Kazin, *Populist Passion*, p. 2.

38. Ralph Waldo Emerson, "Power," in *The Complete Writings* (New York: Wise & Co., 1929), p. 541.

39. Harry S. Stout, *The New England Soul: Preaching and Religious Culture in Colonial New England* (New York: Oxford University Press, 1986), pp. 193–94; Richard

Hofstadter, *Anti-Intellectualism in American Life* (New York: Vintage Books, 1962), chaps. 3 and 4.

40. Alan Heimert, *Religion and the American Mind* (Cambridge, MA: Harvard University Press, 1966), pp. 12–15.

41. Richard Hofstadter, "North America," in *Populism: Its Meaning and National Characteristics*, ed. Ghita Ionescu and Ernest Gellner (London: Weidenfeld and Nicolson, 1969), pp. 16–18.

42. Frank, *Constituent Moments*, pp. 4–18.

43. Gino Germani, *Authoritarianism, Fascism, and National Populism* (New Brunswick, NJ: Transaction Books, 1978); Christopher Lasch, *The True and Only Heaven: Progress and Its Critics* (New York: Norton, 1991).

44. Hofstadter, *Anti-Intellectualism*, pp. 117–36.

45. Peter Worsley, "Populism," in *The Oxford Companion to Politics of the World*, ed. J. Krieger (New York: Oxford University Press, 1993), pp. 730–31; and "The Concept of Populism," in *Populism*, p. 247.

46. Canovan, "Trust the People!," pp. 8–9.

47. Ernesto Laclau, *Politics and Ideology in Marxist Theory: Capitalism-Fascism-Populism* (London: Verso, 1979), p. 18. Not so differently from fascism, Peronism was marked by a strong antiliberal character, whose populist-nationalist language served as a strategy for empowering and homogenizing civil society against the existing economic and political oligarchy (pp. 182–91), even though it also made alliances with the military and landlord elites. Yet, see also Laclau, *On Populist Reason*, in particular pt. 2. For a democratic reading of Latin American populism, see also Cristóbal Rovira Kaltwasser, "The Ambivalence of Populism: Threat and Corrective for Democracy," in *Democratization* (available online May 24, 2011): pp. 1–25.

48. John P. McCormick, *Machiavellian Democracy* (Cambridge: Cambridge University Press, 2011).

49. "In the spring of 1804, the officer corps and the troops they commanded set up an insistent clamor for the designation of Napoleon Bonaparte as emperor. . . . The petition that poured into Paris from the military made the proclamation of the Empire seen as an irresistible proposition. It is difficult to reconstruct with exactitude how this campaign of pen and ink was orchestrated, but a few markers survived in the archives." Isser Woloch, "From Consulate to Empire: Impetus and Resistance," in *Dictatorship in History and Theory: Bonapartism, Caesarism, and Totalitarianism*, ed. Peter Baehr and Melvin Richter (Cambridge: Cambridge University Press, 2004), pp. 29 and 45.

50. Karl Mannheim, *Ideology and Utopia: An Introduction to the Sociology of Knowledge*, trans. L. Wirth and E. Shils (New York: Harcourt, Brace & World, 1964), p. 74.

51. On the total unity of the leader and the people in Italian fascism, see the recent work of Jan-Werner Mueller, *Contesting Democracy: Political Ideas in Twentieth-Century Europe* (New Haven, CT: Yale University Press, 2011), p. 117.

52. For an analysis of the various forms of populist strategies that emerged in the years after the collapse of traditional political parties in Italy, see Alessandro Lanni, *Avanti popoli! Piazze, tv, web: dove va l'Italia senza partiti* (Venice: Marsilio, 2011). The Internet movement Beppe Grillo initiated between 2005 and 2007 in Italy (then named the Five Star MoVement) would deserve an analysis of its own. The use of the Internet in the making of populism is the topic of the study edited by Piergiorgio Corbetta and Elisabetta Gualmini, *Il partito di Grillo* (Bologna: Il Mulino, 2013).

53. More recently and per effect of a widespread mistrust in the political elite and the "indignation" for its corrupted system of power, populist movements have attracted leftist sympathizers and militants; Pierre-André Taguieff, *Le nouveau national-populisme* (Paris: CNRS Éditions, 2012), pp. 67–92.

54. For the view of populism as malaise and pathology of democracy, see Pierre-André Taguieff, "Le populisme et la science politique: Du mirage conceptuel aux vrais problèmes," *Vintième siècle* 56 (1997): 4–33. An invaluable resource is the mentioned collection edited by Ionescu and Gellner, *Populism*.

55. Carl Schmitt thought that mass democracy was more antithetical to liberalism than fascism and bolshevism. Schmitt, *Crisis of Parliamentary Democracy*, trans. Ellen Kennedy (Cambridge, MA: MIT Press, 1994), p. 25.

56. Jan-Werner Mueller, "Towards a Political Theory of Populism," *Politeia* 28, no. 107 (2012): 23.

57. Paul Taggart, *Populism* (London: Open University Press, 2000); see also his "Populism and the Pathologies of Representative Politics," in *Democracy and the Populist Challenge*.

58. http://archives.politicususa.com/2010/08/05/gingrich-obama-elite.html (accessed September 3, 2013).

59. Ernest Preston Manning, *The New Canada* (Toronto: Macmillan, 1992).

60. Laclau, *On Populist Reason*, pp. 129–56.

61. Canovan, "Taking Politics to the People," pp. 26–28.

62. "Under autocratic rule the mass of the people are completely excluded from power." Canovan, "Taking Politics to the People," p. 26.

63. Ibid., pp. 26–30.

64. Michael Freeden, *Ideologies and Political Theories: A Conceptual Approach* (Oxford: Oxford University Press, 1996), pp. 76–77.

65. Worsley, "Concept of Populism," p. 247; Canovan, "Taking Politics to the People," pp. 25–44.

66. In *Principles of Representative Government*, Manin's definition of contemporary democracy as postparty and audience democracy, thus more plebiscitarian than

representative, has clearly helped the renaissance of this stream of thought within democratic theory; see, for instance, Green, *Eyes of the People*, pp. 109–12; and Arditi, *Politics on the Edges of Liberalism*, pp. 51–52.

67. Rosanvallon, *La contre-démocratie*, p. 276; Bobbio, *Autobiografia*, p. 199.

68. Kurt Weyland, "Clarifying a Contested Concept: Populism in the Study of Latin American Politics," *Comparative Politics* 34 (2001): 14.

69. Cas Mudde, "Populism: Reflections on a Concept and Its Usage," paper delivered at Princeton University on February 19, 2012; see also Lanni, *Avanti popoli!*, pp. 102–5.

70. Reflections on Caesarism are in chap. 8 of his *On Populist Reason*.

71. This is the argument made by Slavo Žižek, "Against the Populist Temptation," *Critical Inquiry* 32 (2006): 554.

72. Antonio Gramsci, *Quaderni del carcere*, ed. Valentino Gerratana (Turin: Einaudi, 1975), pp. 1604, 1618–22.

73. Ibid., pp. 1194–95.

74. Benedetto Fontana, "The Concept of Caesarism in Gramsci," in *Dictatorship in History and Theory*, p. 177. On the conservative and radical interpretation of plebiscitarian or Caesaristic leader in the age of World War I, see Luisa Mangoni, "Cesarismo, bonapartismo, fascismo," *Studi storici* 3 (1976): 41–61, and for the birth of the myth of Caesar and of Caesarism in the nineteenth century, see Peter Baehr, *Caesar and the Fading of the Roman World: A Study in Republicanism and Caesarism* (New Brunswick, NJ: Transaction Publisher, 1998), pp. 89–164.

75. Gramsci, *Quaderni*, p. 1195.

76. In modern society, thus, because of pluralism (social and political) and of political "technicalities" associated with the growth of the social state, the individualistic despot would be destined to fade. Ibid.

77. Even in parliamentary regimes there was the chance of a Caesaristic leader in cases of dramatic need of overcoming partisan divisions, and in the case of parliamentary England during the cabinet of Ramsey MacDonald. Representative leader was Gramsci's equivalent of Weber's plebiscitarian leader within parliament (ibid., pp. 1194–95, 1619–22; cf. Fontana, "The Concept," pp. 180–82). I will return to the plebiscitarian leader in Weber's work in the next chapter.

78. Fontana, "The Concept," pp. 184–85.

79. Ibid., pp. 181, 191–92.

80. Gramsci, *Quaderni*, pp. 1145–46.

81. This is the problem that Žižek pointed to when he showed the switch from structural argument to ideological creation of the unifier: for populists (and Laclau) "the cause of the troubles is ultimately never the system as such but the intruder who corrupted it (financial manipulators, not necessarily capitalists, and so on); not a fatal flaw inscribed into the structure as such but an element that doesn't play its role

within the structure properly. For a Marxist, on the contrary . . . the pathological (deviating misbehavior of some elements) is the symptom of the normal, an indicator of what is wrong in the very structure that is threatened with 'pathological' outbursts." Žižek, "Against the Populist Temptation," pp. 555–56.

82. Laclau thus criticizes Lefort's idea of democracy as disembodiment of power, or the permanent empty space in which all can compete and participate. His criticism is very interesting because it pertains to Lefort's failure of explaining the "production" of emptiness, which according to Laclau is the revolutionary moment or the "operation of hegemonic logic." Laclau, *On Populist Reason*, p. 166. The place of the "supreme judge," wrote Lefort, belongs to no one and remains always "indeterminate" in modern democracy. Lefort, *Democracy and Political Theory*, p. 41.

83. Laclau, *On Populist Reason*, p. 18.

84. Ibid., p. 13.

85. Canovan, "Taking Politics to the People," p. 35.

86. William H. Riker, *Liberalism against Populism: A Confrontation between the Theory of Democracy and the Theory of Social Choice* (San Francisco: Freeman Press, 1982), p. xviii.

87. For an excellent critique of Riker's identification of democracy with populism (a position Riker derived from Pareto and Burnham) as a strategy that sponsors a "plebiscitarian" view in which an elite "flatters" the people who do nothing more than elect it, see Gerry Mackie, *Democracy Defended* (Cambridge: Cambridge University Press, 2003), pp. 418–31.

88. Schmitt, *Crisis of Parliamentary Democracy*, pp. 16–17.

89. Sartori, *Theory of Democracy Revisited*, 1:21–23.

90. *Archives Parlementaires de 1787 à 1860. Recueil Complet des Débats Législatifs et Politiques des Chambres Françaises imprimé par ordre de l'Assemblée Nationale sous la direction de M. Mavidal et de MM.E. Laurent et E. Clavel. Première Série (1787 à 1799)*, Tome VIII, du 5 Mai 1789 au 15 Septembre 1789 (Paris: Librairie administrative de Paul Dupont, 1875), p. 118.

91. For an overview of the different meanings of the term "the people," see Sartori, *Democratic Theory Revisited*, 1:21–28.

92. "Communities are to be distinguished, not by their falsity/genuinely, but by the style in which they are imagined." Benedict Anderson, *Imagined Communities* (London: Verso, 1991), p. 6.

93. Giuseppe Mazzini, "Nationalité: Quelques idées sur une Constitution Nationale," in *Scritti editi e inediti*, 100 vols. (Imola: Cooperativa Galeati, 1906–1943), 6:125. A translated version of the essay has been printed in *Giuseppe Mazzini on Nation Building, Democracy, and Intervention*, ed. Stefano Recchia and Nadia Urbinati (Princeton, NJ: Princeton University Press 2009).

94. Kurt A. Raaflaub, "Equalities and Inequalities in Athenian Democracy," in *Dēmokratia*, ed. Josiah Ober and Charles Hedrick (Princeton, NJ: Princeton University Press, 1996), p. 147; Christian Meier, *Athens: A Portrait of the City in Its Golden Age*, trans. Robert and Rite Kimber (London: Murray, 1999), pp. 162–88.

95. Thucydides, *History of the Peloponnesian War*, 2.37.1.

96. Raaflaub, "Equalities and Inequalities," p. 153.

97. Paul Cartledge, "Comparatively Equal," in *Dēmokratia*, p. 180.

98. Plutarch, "Lycurgus," in *Life of the Noble Grecians and Romans*, trans. John Dryden (New York: Modern Library, n.d.), p. 54.

99. John Dewey, "Creative Democracy—The Task Before Us" (1939), in *The Later Works, 1925–1953*, vol. 14, *1939–1941*, ed. Jo Ann Boydston (Chicago: Southern Illinois University Press, 1988), p. 226.

100. Aristotle, *Politics*, 6:2.

101. James Harrington, *The Commonwealth of Oceana* (1656), in *The Political Writings of James Harrington*, ed. with an intro. by Charles Blitzer (Westport, CT: Greenwood Press, 1980), p. 141.

102. Rousseau, *Social Contract*, bk. 4, chaps. 1 and 2.

103. Hence, Rousseau preferred the language of music to that of theater and rhetoric because it would guide the mind to turn its attention inward, away from the fictitious world of representation and theatrical performance. Dugan and Strong, "Music, Politics, Theater, and Representation in Rousseau," pp. 342–44.

104. Kelsen, *General Theory of Law and State*, pp. 287–88.

105. In this sense Castoriadis has argued, referring to Athens and more generally to democracy, for a distinction between the notion of "politics" and that of "the political"; indeed, the "democratic movement is not confined to the struggle around explicit power, it aims potentially at the overall reinstitution of society." Cornelius Castoriadis, "Power, Politics, Autonomy," in *Philosophy, Politics, Autonomy: Essays in Political Philosophy* (New York: Oxford University Press, 1991), p. 159.

106. Laclau, *On Populist Reason*, p. 81.

107. Ibid., p. 200.

108. Laclau's example of a nonpopulist politics is Ataturk, who not only aimed at but attained the elimination of all groups or classes in Turkish society in order to build the Turkish nation (Ibid., p. 209).

109. Cf. Andrew Lintott, *The Constitution of the Roman Republic* (Oxford: Oxford University Press, 2004), chap. 5.

4. The Plebiscite of the Audience and the Politics of Passivity

1. Green, *The Eyes of the People*, pp. 27–28.

2. See on this an old yet still timely study by Samuel Kernell, *Going Public: New Strategies of Presidential Leadership* (Washington, DC: CQ Press, 1986), chap. 1.

3. Carl Schmitt, *Legality and Legitimacy*, trans. Jeffrey Seitzer with an intro. by John P. McCormick (Durham, NC: Duke University Press, 2004), pp. 61–62. This finds a confirmation in the words Bonaparte used to comment on the plebiscite of 1802 that made him consul for life: "the plebiscite has the advantage of legalizing my extension of office and placing it on the highest possible basis," cited in Woloch, "From Consulate to Empire," p. 33.

4. The dualism between will and reason was used to invoke Caesarism in France in 1850 and sponsor the coup of Louis Napoleon); see Melvin Richter, "Tocqueville and French Nineteenth-Century Conceptualization of the Two Bonapartes and Their Empires," in *Dictatorship in History and Theory*, p. 87.

5. Rosanvallon, *La légitimité démocratique*, pp. 45–46.

6. Green, *The Eyes of the People*, p. 21.

7. For an interesting sociological analysis of the "vanity" of action in a political system of communication that has ushered away all externality of judgment, see Luc Boltanski, *Distant Suffering: Morality, Media and Politics*, trans. Graham D. Burchell (Cambridge: Cambridge University Press, 1999), pp. 170–81 in particular.

8. Schmitt, *Constitutional Theory*, p. 271.

9. Schumpeter, *Capitalism, Socialism, and Democracy*, pp. 284–85.

10. Green, *The Eyes of the People*, chap. 2.

11. Max Weber, "Parliament and Government in Germany under a New Political Order" (1918), in *Political Writings*, ed. Peter Lassmen and Ronald Speirs (Cambridge: Cambridge University Press, 1994), p. 221.

12. Ibid., p. 222.

13. Meanwhile Chavez "attacked the Internet as 'a battle trench' that was brining 'a current of conspiracy.'" Morozov, *The Dark Side of Internet Freedom*, p. 113.

14. Weber, "Parliament and Government," p. 220.

15. Jeffrey K. Tulis, *The Rhetorical Presidency* (Princeton, NJ: Princeton University Press, 1987), p. 133.

16. In relation to Weber, the link between plebiscitarian leadership and populism has been envisaged by Rune Slagstad, "Liberal Constitutionalism and Its Critics: Max Weber and Carl Schmitt," in *Constitutionalism and Democracy*, pp. 122–23; and Sven Eliaeson, "Max Weber and Plebiscitarian Democracy," in *Max Weber: Democracy and Modernization*, ed. Ralph Schroeder (New York: St. Martin's Press, 1998), pp. 47–60.

17. Nicos Poulantzas, *State, Power, Socialism*, with an intro. by Stuart Hall (London: Verso, 2000), pp. 203–16.

18. Tulis, *The Rhetorical Presidency*, chap. 5.

19. Green, *The Eyes of the People*, p. 32. See Fergus Millar, *The Crowd in Rome in the Late Republic* (Ann Arbor: University of Michigan Press, 2005), pp. 13–14; and Lintott, *The Constitution of the Roman Republic*, pp, 53–55.

20. Schmitt explained the difference between the type of referendum that belongs to the system of parliamentary legislative state (i.e., abrogative or propositional of laws that the parliament decided or will decide) and the other type in which "'the people' emerge as the exclusive, definite figure of a democratic-plebiscitary system." Schmitt, *Legality and Legitimacy*, p. 62.

21. Bonaparte himself framed the proposition to be voted by the French people: "Shall Napoleon Bonaparte be named first consul for life?" Woloch, "From Consulate to Empire," p. 32.

22. Ibid., p. 44.

23. Robert A. Young, *The Breakup of Czechoslovakia*, Research Paper no. 32, Institute of Intergovernmental Relations (Kingston, Ontario, Canada: Queen's University, 1994), p. 14.

24. Ernest Renan, *Qu'est-ce qu'une nation?* (1882), in *Discours et Conférences* (Paris: Calmann-Lévy, 1887), pp. 278, 285, 295–96, 299.

25. In the French plebiscite of 1802 official concern did not center on the prospect of "no" but on abstention. Woloch, "From Consulate to Empire," p. 34.

26. Max Weber, *General Economic History*, trans. Frank H. Knight (Glencoe, IL: Free Press, 1950), pp. 325–26 (chap. 28).

27. On the creation of the Tribune, see Livy, *The Rise of Rome*, trans. B. O. Foster (Cambridge, MA: Harvard University Press, 1922), pp. 33–34 (III, ix.6–12); on the prerogatives of the Tribune, see Lintott, *The Constitution of the Roman Republic*, pp. 120–28.

28. When after the Treaty of Amiens, the Senate and the Tribunate were looking for the better way to show the "gratitude" of the French nation to Napoleon, they did not think that a vote of confidence would be appropriate because the voting in the Senate was regarded as a work of intrigue and impure; Woloch, "From Consulate to Empire," p. 30. On the individualist meaning of the right to vote (by the citizens as well as their representatives), see Pierre Rosanvallon, *Le sacre du citoyen: Histoire du suffrage universel en France* (Paris: Gallimard, 1992), p. 167.

29. Bolingbroke, *A Dissertation upon Parties*, pp. 85–86.

30. Elections that are based more on ex ante considerations (trust or faith) than ex post judgment are said to be more consonant to "delegative democracies," which are an "inferior" form of representation, one that fits better plebiscitarian and popu-

list democracies; see Susan C. Stokes, "What Do Policy Switches Tell Us about Democracy?," in *Democracy, Accountability, and Representation,* ed. Adam Przeworski, Susan C. Stokes, and Bernard Manin (Cambridge: Cambridge University Press, 1999), p. 100; on the inverse proportion between ideological identification of electors and candidates and the function of accountability, see also Jane J. Mansbridge, "Rethinking Representation," *American Political Science Review* 97 (2003): 515–28.

31. For an interesting case of destruction of faith and trust, see Antony Pagden, "The Destruction of Trust and Its Economic Consequences in the Case of Eighteenth-century Naples," in *Trust: Making and Breaking Cooperative Relations,* ed. Diego Gambetta (Dept. of Sociology, University of Oxford, electronic edition 2000), pp. 127–14.

32. Thomas C. Schelling, "Strategic Analysis and Social Problems," in *Choice and Consequence* (Cambridge, MA: Harvard University Press, 1984), p. 211.

33. Schmitt, *Constitutional Theory,* p. 270.

34. Woodrow Wilson, *Leaders of Men,* ed., with intro. and notes by T. H. Vail Motter (Princeton, NJ: Princeton University Press, 1952), p. 29.

35. Weber, "Parliament and Government," p. 221.

36. Cf. Peter Baehr, "Max Weber and the Avatars of Caesarism," in *Dictatorship in History and Theory,* pp. 163–64.

37. Weber's "Parliament and Government" was "an effort to influence opinion on the constitutional question" in the view of "outlining the precondition for effective parliaments" but also a "call in favor of a system which allows room for a considerable degree of plebiscitarian leadership. Ernest Kilker, "Max Weber and Plebiscitarian Democracy: A Critique of the Mommsen Thesis," in *Politics, Culture, and Society* 2 (1989): 446.

38. Max Weber, *The Protestant Ethics and the Spirit of Capitalism,* trans. Talcott Parsons (London: Routledge, 1992), p. 182; cf. Andreas Kalyvas, *Democracy and the Politics of the Extraordinary: Max Weber, Carl Schmitt, and Hannah Arendt* (Cambridge: Cambridge University Press, 2008), pp. 17–21.

39. On the irrationalism and Romantic Niezschianism of Weber, see, among others, Luciano Cavalli, *Carisma: La qualità straordinaria del leader* (Roma-Bari: Laterza, 1995).

40. Baehr, "Max Weber and the Avatars," p. 164.

41. See Max Weber's chapter on "Bureaucracy" (1922) in *From Max Weber: Essays in Sociology,* pp. 216, 220, 224–27. This parliamentary interpretation can be found in Wolfgang J. Mommsen, *The Age of Bureaucracy: Perspectives on the Political Sociology of Max Weber* (New York: Harper Torchbooks, 1974), pp. 72–94.

42. Contra Mommsen, David Beetham argued in *Max Weber and the Theory of Modern Politics* (Oxford: Oxford University Press, 1985) that Weber's thought evolved

toward a more individual notion of the leader who tended to separate himself from the parliament, a transition that registered the tragic trajectory of German history. Equally critical of the benign interpretation of Mommsen is Kilker, "Max Weber and Plebiscitarian Democracy."

43. For a prescient parallel between Marx and Weber on the blocking effect of alienation and normalcy on creativity, see Karl Lövith, *Max Weber and Karl Marx* (London: Allen and Unwin, 1982).

44. Cf. Lane, "Origins of the Statesman." "Charisma knows only inner determination and inner restraint." Weber, *From Max Weber*, p. 246.

45. Theodor Mommsen, *The History of Rome*, trans. with the sanction of the author by William Purdie Dickson (London: Bentley, 1900), 5:325, chap. 11. For an interesting discussion on the potential and risk of charismatic leadership in times of international crisis and the distinction between "democratic leadership" (Roosevelt and Churchill) and "ideological leadership" (Mussolini, Hitler, and Stalin), see, respectively, Arthur Schlesinger, "Democracy and Heroic Leadership in the Twentieth Century," and Carl J. Friedrich, "Political Leadership and the Problem of Charismatic Power," in *Journal of Politics* 23 (1961): 16. Whatever we make of it, the political conception of charismatic leadership presumes the irrational nature of the masses.

46. Mommsen, *History of Rome*, 5:324.

47. Weber, "Parliament and Government," pp. 220–21.

48. Hence, Weber criticized "the popular view amongst our littérateurs" who interpreted the question of the effect of democratization as true manipulation that the demagogue perpetrates unscrupulously. Weber, "Parliament and Government," p. 219.

49. The function of elections is "not to make a democracy more democratic, but to make democracy possible. Once we admit the need for elections, we minimize democracy for we realize that the system cannot be operated by the *demos* itself." Giovanni Sartori, *Democratic Theory* (New York: Praeger, 1965), p. 108, and the restatement of this characterization in his *Theory of Democracy Revisited*, 1:102–10.

50. Schumpeter, *Capitalism, Socialism, and Democracy*, pp. 284, 287.

51. The interpretation of the role of plebiscitarianism in Weber's political thought is the object of a ponderous literature. I simply cite the protagonists of two representative interpretations: David Beetham, according to whom Weber's endorsement of plebiscitarianism coincided with a break in his thought toward an irrationalist and Nieztschean solution, and Mommsen, according to whom, rather than being a turning point, the endorsement by Weber coincided with his deep concern with the decline of German national might in European politics. See, respectively, Beetham, *Max Weber and the Theory of Modern Politics*; and Mommsen, *The Age of Bureaucracy*.

52. Weber, "Parliament and Government," p. 221, cf. Baehr, "Marx Weber and the Avatars," pp. 164–66.

53. Tulis, *Presidential Rhetoric*, p. 4.

54. Dunn, "Situating Democratic Political Accountability," in *Democracy, Accountability, and Representation*, p. 330.

55. Tulis, *Presidential Rhetoric*, p. 46; see Stephen Holmes, "Precommitment and the Paradox of Democracy," pp. 225–35; the dualistic conception of political life relies on an electoral notion of representative democracy, as in Bruce A. Ackerman, "Neo-federalism?," in *Constitutionalism and Democracy*, pp. 155–93.

56. Dunn, "Situating Democratic Political Accountability," p. 332.

57. On Schmitt's relationship to Weber's political thought, and in particular plebiscitarian and charismatic leadership, see Wolfang J. Mommsen, *Max Weber and German Politics, 1890–1920* (Chicago: University of Chicago Press, 1984), pp. 381–89; Slagstad, "Liberal Constitutionalism and Its Critics," pp. 103–30; and John McCormick, *Carl Schmitt's Critique of Liberalism: Against Politics as Technology* (Cambridge: Cambridge University Press, 1997), p. 135.

58. Schmitt, *Constitutional Theory*, pp. 102–3, 127–32. Thus, the form of the *presence* of the "sovereign people" in the public is what makes the difference, as we shall see. Plebes-demos is characterized by the convergence of the presence of the people and the opinion of the people. The diarchic structure is overcome in the monoarchic nature of the collective sovereign, which is proclaimed yet not in the institutional organization (as in the case, for instance, of Sieyès) but in the actual assembling of the people so that "the rule of opinion" only designates "democracy" (ibid., pp. 272–75). For an analysis of Schmitt's constitutional theory, see Ellen Kennedy, *Constitutional Failure: Carl Schmitt in Weimar* (Durham, NC: Duke University Press, 2004), pp. 119–53.

59. Schmitt, *Constitutional Theory*, p. 274.

60. I analyzed this phenomenon in relation to the English debate in the mid-nineteenth century in *Mill on Democracy: From the Athenian Polis to Representative Government* (Chicago: University of Chicago Press, 2002), pp. 104–22.

61. Schmitt, *Crisis of Parliamentary Democracy*, pp. 10–11.

62. The identification of popular sovereignty with mass democracy has been well captured by Kalyvas, *Democracy and the Politics of the Extraordinary*, pp. 96–100.

63. Schmitt, *Crisis of Parliamentary Democracy*, p. 37.

64. For an interesting example of the clash over the interpretation of the Eucharist and religious symbols in the debates that followed the Reformation, see the analysis of the exemplary case of the Colloquy of Poissy (1560–1561) made by Nugent, *Ecumenism in the Age of the Reformation*.

65. The source of Schmitt's analogy of the sovereign power and Catholic theology was Joseph de Maistre and moreover Donoso Cortes, two central figures of

antimodernism and antiliberalism in post–French Revolution age; see in particular Schmitt's *Political Theology: Four Chapters on the Concept of Sovereignty*, trans. George Schwab (Cambridge, MA: MIT Press, 1985).

66. Pierre Bordieu, *In Other Words: Essays Towards a Reflexive Sociology*, trans. Matthew Adamson (Stanford, CA: Stanford University Press, 1990), p. 133.

67. The antithesis to Schmitt's idea of open ballot is of course Kelsen's theory of electoral democracy as he exposed it during the debates on the Weimar republic, and, precisely in order to oppose Schmitt's vision of mass democracy, in his *The Essence and Value of Democracy* (see in particular chap. 8 on the "choice of leaders").

68. Michael Foucault, *Discipline and Punish: The Birth of the Prison* (1975), trans. Alan Sheridan (New York: Vintage, 1977), p. 47.

69. Schmitt, *Crisis of Parliamentary Democracy*, p. 39.

70. Ibid., pp. 38–39.

71. Immanuel Kant, "An Answer to the Question: 'What Is Enlightenment?,'" in *Political Writings*, ed. Hans Reiss (Cambridge: Cambridge University Press, 1991), p. 55.

72. Indeed, Schmitt wrote that bolshevism and fascism were opposite to liberal democracy, not democracy in *Crisis of Parliamentary Democracy*, p. 16; cf. McCormick, *Carl Schmitt's Critique of Liberalism*, p. 314; and William Scheuerman, *Carl Schmitt: The End of Law* (Lanham, MD: Rowman & Littlefield, 1999), pp. 251–55.

73. Schmitt, *Constitutional Theory*, p. 275.

74. Ibid., p. 272.

75. Ibid., pp. 270–71.

76. Fergus Millar, *The Roman Republic in Political Thought* (Hanover, NH: University Press of New England, 2002), pp. 18–22, 154–56.

77. Gustave Le Bon, *The Crowd: A Study of the Popular Mind*, with an intro. by Robert K. Merton (New York: Viking Press, 1960), p. 187; and Laclau, *On Populist Reason*, p. 23–29.

78. See his defense of transcendence and the attack on immanentism that representative government entailed in *Political Theology*, pp. 49–52.

79. As Beetham writes, after a Marxist beginning, in which social classes were the foundation of political parties, Weber ended as a Nietzschean, and pivoted state politics mainly on great individuals. Beetham, *Max Weber*, pp. 215–49.

80. This is one of the themes of Rosanvallon's *La contre-démocratie*.

81. On this point, see Schumpeter, who listed pluralistic public opinion and "a considerable amount" of free press as essential condition of the competitive struggle "for" power in *Capitalism, Socialism and Democracy*, p. 272.

82. Le Marquis de Condorcet, "On Despotism: Thoughts on Despotism" (1789), in *Political Writings*, p. 163. In his article "Despotism" for the *Encyclopédie*, Louis de

Jacourt characterized it as the "tyrannical, arbitrary, and obsolete government of one man"; the same individualistic approach can be found in Diderot, d'Holbach, and Rousseau; cf. Leonard Krieger, *An Essay on the Theory of Enlightened Despotism* (Chicago: University of Chicago Press, 1975), pp. 29–31.

83. Condorcet, "On Despotism," p. 163. A historical confirmation of Condorcet's theory came a few years after from Napoleon's Caesarism, a system that relied upon "a host of good citizens" who sought through his power for life, their own stability as a class born in the year of Thermidor and enriched with Napoleon's military campaigns; cf. Woloch, "From Consulate to Empire," pp. 39, 34. A similar view can be found in Weber himself: "The danger does *not* lie with the *masses*. . . . The deepest core of the *socio*-political problem is not the question of the *economic* situation of the *ruled* but of the *political* qualification of the *ruling and rising classes*." Max Weber, "The Nation State and Economic Policy," in *Political Writings*, p. 26.

84. Describing the two types of despotism, Condorcet depicted the indirect one as follows: "but the despotism of janissaries is only indirect. It is not on account of a specific law, or an established tradition, that the sultan is obliged to bow to their will. In some countries people living in the capital exercise indirect despotism; in others, the nation's leaders have surrendered their independence to the moneyed classes; government activity depends on the case with which loans can be obtained from these people; they compel [the government] to appoint ministers who meet with their approval, and the nation then is subjected to the despotism of the bankers." Condorcet, "On Despotism," pp. 164–65.

85. Gianfranco Pasquino, "Plebiscitarismo," in *Enciclopedia Treccani* (my translation).

86. Green, *Eyes of the People*, p. 14.

87. Mommsen, *Age of Bureaucracy*, p. 19.

88. Gaetano Mosca, *The Ruling Class*, ed. and rev. by Arthur Livingston, trans. by Hannah D. Kahn (New York: McGraw-Hill Book Company, 1939), p. 487; Sartori, *Comparative Constitutional Engineering*, pp. 86–91; and Bruce Ackerman, *We the People: Transformations* (Cambridge MA: Harvard University Press, 1998), 2:135–36, 388–89. On this issue, see the classical work of Juan J. Linz and Alfred Stepan, eds., *Breakdown of Democratic Regimes* (Baltimore, MD: Johns Hopkins University Press, 1978); and Juan J. Linz, *Totalitarian and Authoritarian Regimes* (Boulder, CO: Lynne Rienner Publishers, 2000).

89. As C. Wright Mills wrote, those theorists who have supposed the masses to be in their way to triumph are wrong, because it is the case that in our time the influence of the masses is diminished, and when it seems they have some influence their influence is "guided" because they do not show any autonomous public acting. Mills, *The Power Elite* (New York: Oxford University Press, 1957), p. 309.

90. Green, *Eyes of the People*, pp. 17–29.

91. Eric A. Posner and Adrian Vermeule, *The Executive Unbound: After the Madisonian Republic* (Oxford: Oxford University Press, 2011), pp. 60–61.

92. Ibid., p. 7.

93. Ibid., p. 42.

94. Ibid., p. 8.

95. William Scheuerman, *Liberal Democracy and the Social Acceleration of Time* (Baltimore, MD: Johns Hopkins University Press, 2004), p. 124.

96. Posner and Vermeule, *Executive Unbound*, pp. 11–12.

97. Luhmann, *The Reality of the Mass Media*, p. 82.

98. Ibid., p. 65.

99. Posner and Vermeule, *Executive Unbound*, p. 13.

100. Ackerman, *We the People: Foundations*, p. 249.

101. Sartori, *Comparative Constitutional Engineering*, p. 134.

102. Weber, "Parliament and Government," pp. 160–66.

103. Ibid., pp. 201–2, 204.

104. Green, *Eyes of the People*, p. 207.

105. Ibid., p. 120.

106. Emmanuel-Joseph Sieyès, "Pour ma dispute avec Payne," in *Les Manuscrits de Sieyès: 1773–1799*, ed. Christine Fauré (Paris: Honoré Champion, 1999), p. 445. "Thus, monarchy . . . is established in order to preserve a kind of equality that cannot be obtained in the republics; it is a true limit on inequality because it tells you that no matter how high the social position you have reached, you will always have the interest of society above you. There is but one *legal inequality*, that of all over each; this is represented by the person of the prince. It is not the *superiority* of the magistrate, but a true personal *inequality*, the only one. 'We want a prince in order to avoid the risk and evil of having a master,'" repeated Sieyes with Rousseau (ibid., p. 421.)

107. Thucydides, *History of the Peloponnesian War*, pp. 163–64.

108. Arnaldo Momigliano, The *Classical Foundations of Modern Historiography*, Sather Classical Lectures (Berkeley: University of California Press, 1990); Jacqueline de Romilly, *Problèmes de la démocratie grecque* (Paris: Herman, 1975); and Luciano Canfora, *La democrazia di Pericle* (Roma-Bari: Laterza, 2008).

109. Weber, "Parliament and Government," p. 222.

110. Green, *Eyes of the People*, p. 130. Not by chance, the Roman plays by Shakespeare, *Coriolanus* and *Julius Caesar*, are among Green's selected document of plebiscitarian theory.

111. Luhmann, *Reality of the Mass Media*, p. 84.

112. Ibid.

113. Sartori, *Comparative Constitutional Engineering*, p. 148.

114. Green, *Eyes of the People*, p. 26.

115. "The elementary political process is the action of mind upon mind through speech," not images. Bernard de Jouvenal, *Sovereignty: An Inquiry into the Political Good*, trans. J. F. Huntington (Chicago: University of Chicago Press, 1957), p. 304.

116. Perelman and Olbrechts-Tyteca, *The New Rhetoric*, pp. 14–19.

117. Ibid., p. 24.

118. Plato, *Republic*, pp. 23–24. While "eloquence is *heard*, poetry is *overheard*" Mill observed on the same line in "Thoughts on Poetry and Its Varieties" (1833), *Collected Works*, 1:348, 363.

119. Green, *Eyes of the People*, p. 23.

120. Ibid., p. 11.

121. Schmitt, *Crisis of Parliamentary Democracy*, p. 38.

> The public compose a tribunal, which is more powerful than all the other tribunal together. An individual may pretend to disregard its decrees—to represent them as formed of fluctuating and opposite opinions, which destroy one another; but every one feels, that thought this tribunal may err, it is incorruptible; that it continually tends to become enlightened; that it unites all the wisdom and the justice of the nation; that it always decides the destiny of public men; and that the punishments which it pronounces are inevitable. Those who complain of its judgments, only appeal to itself; and the man of virtue, in resisting the opinion of to-day— in rising above general clamour, counts and weighs in secret the suffrage of those who resemble himself.

Jeremy Bentham, *An Essay on Political Tactics*, or *Inquiries Concerning the Discipline and Mode of Proceeding Proper to Be Observed in Political Assemblies . . .* in *The Works of Jeremy Bentham published under the superintendence of his Executor, John Bowring* (1843) (Elibron Classics Series: 2005), p. 310.

122. Green, *Eyes of the People*, p. 29.

123. For an excellent reflection on secrecy and opacity as an invaluable good of the person and the new risk coming from the obsession with coverage and technology of watching and knowing everything, see George Kateb, "On Being Watched and Known," in *Patriotism and Other Mistakes* (New York: Yale University Press, 2004), pp. 93–113. On the domain in which publicity is valuable and the domain in which its limit is valuable, see Gutmann and Thompson, *Democracy and Disagreement*, pp. 95–127; on the promises of publicity in democratic state, cf. Bobbio, *Il futuro della democrazia*, pp. 85–113.

124. Green, *Eyes of the People*, p. 29.

125. An interesting study of the politics of scandals is that of Nicolas Dirks, *Scandal of Empire: India and the Creation of Imperial Britain* (Cambridge, MA: Belknap

Press of Harvard University Press, 2006), which argues that the various media-driven moral scandals of eighteenth- and nineteenth-century British imperialism in fact served to buttress and justify the project of empire rather than criticize it (in particular pp. 87–132).

126. Kant, *Critique of the Power of Judgment*, pp. 214–17 (§§ 56–57); cf. Peter J. Steinberger, *The Concept of Political Judgment* (Chicago: University of Chicago Press, 1993), pp. 138–53.

127. Sartori, *Comparative Constitutional Engineering*, p. 149.

128. Commenting on President Clinton's extramarital affairs that occupied the American public for half of its second mandate, Gutmann and Thompson rightly argued that the quality of deliberation would be less "strained if we talked less about the private immoralities of public officials" in *Democracy and Disagreement*, p. 124.

129. Luhmann, *Reality of the Mass Media*, p. 103.

130. Alessandro Pizzorno, *Il potere dei giudici: Stato democratico e controllo della virtù* (Roma-Bari: Laterza, 1998), pp. 45–63.

131. Sartori, *Comparative Constitutional Engineering*, pp. 149–50.

132. Sartori, *Theory of Democracy Revisited*, 1:87.

133. Cf. Michael Walzer, "Political Action: The Problem of Dirty Hands," *Philosophy and Public Affairs* 2 (1973): 160–180; and Thomas Nagel, "Ruthlessness in Public Life," in *Public and Private Morality*, ed. Stuart Hampshire (Cambridge: Cambridge University Press, 1978), pp. 75–91.

134. This question is particularly relevant when it involves religion: How should religious belief enter the public sphere? And should the citizens translate their private religious view in the language of public reason always? Cf. in particular Rawls, "The Idea of Public Reason Revisited;" and Jürgen Habermas, "Religion in the Public Sphere," *European Journal of Philosophy* 14, no. 1 (2006): 1–25; Habermas's article has been recently republished with minor changes and the title "Cognitive Presuppositions for the 'Public Use of Reason' by Religious and Secular Citizens," in *Between Naturalism and Religion* (London: Polity Press, 2008), pp. 114–47.

135. Bobbio, *Il futuro della democrazia*, p. 93.

136. Green, *Eyes of the People*, p. 203.

137. Ibid., pp. 203, 200.

138. Luhmann, *Reality of the Mass Media*, p. 58.

139. Green, *Eyes of the People*, p. 199.

140. Ibid., p. 28.

141. Ibid., chap. 7.

142. Sartori, *Comparative Constitutional Engineering*, p. 148.

143. Green, *Eyes of the People*, p. 5.

144. It is striking that Green sees the leader's acceptance to curtail his privacy as a core feature of political control and surveillance. But it seems like increased public surveillance of a leader's personal life and private activities feeds into the kind of endlessly distracted, celebrity-culture videocracy that has nothing to do with surveillance of political decision making and the *arcana imperii* behind the closed doors. Inversely, it is not clear why properly functioning institutions of public transparency would require politicians' private lives to become public.

145. William Kornhauser, *The Politics of Mass Society* (Glencoe, IL: Free Press, 1959).

146. Cf. the excellent and prophetic work of Lawrence K. Grossman, *Electronic Republic: Reshaping Democracy in the Information Age* (New York: Penguin Books, 1995).

147. Barbara Becker and Joseph Wehner, "Electronic Networks and Civil Society: Reflections on Structural Changes in the Public Sphere," in *Culture, Technology, Communication: Toward an Intercultural Global Village*, ed. Charles Ess and Fay Sudweeks (Albany: State University of New York Press, 2001), p. 74.

148. Walter Lippmann, *The Public Philosophy* (New York: Mentor Book, 1955), pp. 22–24.

149. Luhmann, *Reality of the Mass Media*, p. 2.

150. Manin, *Principles of Representative Government*, p. 221.

151. Green, *Eyes of the People*, p. 15.

152. Manin, *Principles of Representative Government*, p. 233.

153. Green, *Eyes of the People*, pp. 111–12.

154. Grossman, *Electronic Republic*, pp. 4–6.

155. Cicero captured the distinction between the *populus* and the *crowd* very effectively when set out to distinguish between "a group" and the *populus Romanus*: "Do you think that that group is the *populus Romanus* which is made up of those who are hired to pay, who are incited to use force against the magistrates, besiege the Senate, and hope every day for slaughter, fire, and devastation—that *populus* whom you could not have got together except by having the *tabernae* closed? . . . But *that* was the beauty of the *populus Romanus*, that its true shape, which you saw in the Campus at the moment when even you had the power to speak against the authority and the will of the Senate and of the whole of Italy. *That* is the *populous* which is the master of kings, the victor and commander of all peoples" and who judge and make laws; cited in Millar, *Crowd in Rome*, p. 38.

156. Ibid., p. 57.

157. Cited in Millar, *Crowd in Rome*, p. 72.

158. Le Bon, *The Crowd*, p. 32.

159. Ibid., p. 33.

160. Jon Elster, "Deliberation and Constitution Making," in *Deliberative Democracy*, p. 111.

161. Cf. the description of the perfect hypocrite politician in Runciman, *Political Hypocrisy*, pp. 85–90.

162. Millar, *Crowd in Rome*, p. 45.

163. Ibid.

164. Ibid., p. 68.

165. Ibid., p. 46.

166. Ibid., p. 59.

167. Werhan, "Classical Athenian Ancestry of American Freedom of Speech," pp. 14–15.

168. See, in particular, ibid., p. 19; Millar, *Roman Republic in Political Thought*, pp. 197–226; Janet Coleman, *A History of Political Thought*, 2 vols. (Oxford: Black-well, 2000), 1:285; Lily Ross Taylor, *Party Politics in the Age of Caesar* (Berkeley: University of California Press 1949), pp. 26, 3; Ober, *Masses and Elite*, p. 109; Raaf-laub, "Democracy, Oligarchy, and the Concept of the 'Free Citizen' in Late Fifth-Century Athens," pp. 517–44; and Charler Wirszubski, *Libertas as a Political Idea at Rome During the Later Republic and Early Principate* (Cambridge: Cambridge University Press, 1968), pp. 11–17.

169. Citizens belonging in the *populus* had no right to run for public posts (nor thus to harangue the crowd); for a nonsenator to attain that goal, wealth or the acquisition of a reputation as a professional (this was Cicero's case as a great lawyer) was needed, or one must marry a patrician women (as in Caesar's case).

170. Millar, *Crowd in Rome*, p. 46.

171. Ibid., p. 47.

172. Ibid., p. 63.

173. Jon Elster, *Ulysses Unbound* (Cambridge: Cambridge University Press, 2000), p. 130, footnote 93. But the image of democracy in eighteenth-century constitutional assemblies, French and American as well, were nourished by a literature that had the Roman, not the Athenian, writers at its core. The democratic element in the Roman plebiscitary republic is what they meant by democracy.

174. Millar, *Crowd in Rome*, p. 47.

175. Ibid., p. 251.

176. Ibid., p. 167.

177. Ibid., p. 49.

Conclusion

1. Green, *Eyes of the People*, pp. 27–28.

2. Baker, *Media Concentration and Democracy*, p. 8.

3. Kelsen, *Essence and Value of Democracy*, pp. 12–13.

4. On the promises of democracy and their permanent unfulfilled status, cf. Bob-bio, *Il futuro della democrazia*, pp. 3–31.

5. Bobbio, *Il futuro della democrazia*, p. 23.

6. Cf. Gerry Mackie, "The Values of Democratic Proceduralism," *Irish Political Studies* 26, no. 4 (2011), pp. 441–44.

7. Beitz, *Political Equality*, p. 192.

8. Dawood, "New Inequality," p. 147.

9. Fiss, "Free Speech and Social Structure," p. 786.

10. Warren, "What Does Corruption Mean in a Democracy?" pp. 328–33.

11. Beitz, *Political Equality*, p. 203.

12. On the "democratic safeguards" in relation to public and inclusive systems of communication, cf. Baker, *Media Concentration and Democracy*, pp. 6–19.

13. Some constitutions are better equipped than others. For instance, article 5 of the German constitution declares that "any body has the right to freely express and diffuse its opinions with words, written materials, and images and to be informed without impediment through sources that should be accessible to all."

14. The argument according to which pluralism is a dissatisfying strategy because it inclines opinions toward fragmentation and their supporters toward sectarian identification, and thus impedes rather than facilitates public conversation, seems to reify actual phenomena and underrate the fact that, as said, political competition for achieving consent that democratic procedures promote is able to neutralize these negative potentials in the moment they induce them to compete for majority.

ACKNOWLEDGMENTS

I wrote this book during months of formidable changes in Western societies and democracies, while the second great depression started incinerating triumphant dreams of endless economic growth for all, and rating agencies put into question the ability of elected parliaments and democratic procedures to make competent and prompt decisions. Increase of economic inequality and the escalation of political ambition to power by the well-off, with either technocratic credentials or populist rhetoric or plebiscitarian consensus, are the phenomena that challenge today's democratic system and that this book is intended to study. A continuation of my previous work on representative democracy, it detects and subjects to a critical inquiry some of the most visible contemporary metamorphoses of democracy. My greatest debt of gratitude is to my students at Columbia University and Scuola Superiore Sant'Anna of Pisa, to whom this book is dedicated. I owe a special debt of gratitude to some of them in particular: Ian Zuckerman, Luke MacInnis, Maria Paula Saffon, Carlo Invernizzi Accetti, Alexander Gourevitch, Giulia Oskian, and David Ragazzoni. They read parts of this book while it was still in manuscript, discussed passionately with me some of its main topics, and compelled me to a greater understanding of democracy as a diarchy of procedures and *doxa*. I also had the chance to discuss chapters of the book at Princeton University's Center for Human Values and their workshop on populism, as well as at Oxford University, the University of Louvain, Northwestern University, Collegio Moncalieri of Turin, University of Bologna, Bocconi University and the University of Bicocca in Milan, the 36th annual meeting of Anpocs, Brazil, The Straus Institute at NYU Law School, and the Centre de Recherches Politiques at Sciences Po, Paris. I thank the participants of these seminars, lectures, and symposia for their comments. I record my sincere thanks to Juan González Bertomeu, Jan-Werner Müller, Michele Battini, Terence Ball, Steven Lukes, Danielle Allen, Maria

Salvati, Nancy Rosenblum, John McCormick, Gil Delannoi, Pierre Rosanvallon, and Salvatore Veca; the conversations I had with them on specific topics at different stages of the composition of the book were illuminating and precious. Lastly, I owe a final recognition to the anonymous readers of Harvard University Press whose suggestions and critical observations were an excellent guide to the final revision of the manuscript.

INDEX

Acclamation: versus voting, 24, 160, 163, 179, 187; and plebiscitarianism, 179, 181, 183, 189; and democracy of the audience, 189, 192. *See also* Caesarism; Leadership; Schmitt, Carl

Accountability, 130, 136–137, 176, 179, 182–183

Ackerman, Bruce, 114, 196

Advocacy, 55, 109, 126, 136–137

American Founding Fathers, 26

Antiparliamentarianism, 82, 181

Arcana, 108, 184, 186, 188

Arcana imperii, 43, 49, 184, 295n144

Arditi, Benjamin, 134

Arendt, Hannah, 45, 171

Aristotle, 23, 29, 43, 44, 64, 79, 80, 99, 102, 103–104, 124, 157, 163–164, 218; *Art of Rhetoric*, 23, 33, 127, 252n65; on functions of government, 31–33; on verisimilitude in lawmaking, 31–33; on constitutional conception of the polis, 31–33, 43, 102, 103, 138–142; on forms of political judgment, 31–33, 127; on opinion, 31–34, 35; *Nicomachean Ethics*, 33; on deliberation, 33–34; on communication, 62–63; on demagoguery, 138–144, 154, 231

Athenian democracy, 75, 79, 89, 104, 117–118, 138, 175, 201, 202, 222, 239; and the procedures of the assembly, 3, 13, 20, 21; and the individual foundation of voting, 20, 21, 162–163; and political equality, 20–21, 163; dealing with the tyranny of the assembly, 25; compared to modern, 63. *See also* Roman republic; Sparta

Augustus, 144

Baker, C. Edwin, 50, 54, 59, 69, 234

Ball, Terence, 30, 80

Barron, Jerome, 58

Barry, Brian, 78

Beccaria, Cesare, 187

Beitz, Charles R., 53

Bentham, Jeremy, 44, 207, 215, 218, 221

Berlin, Isaiah, 72, 74, 121

Berlusconi, Silvio, 4, 14, 28, 110, 148, 174, 208, 209, 233

Bobbio, Norberto, 18, 21, 69, 75, 134, 152, 211

Bodin, Jean, 22

Bolingbroke, Henry St. John, 43–44, 178

Bollinger, Lee C., 68

Bonaparte, Napoleon, 148, 176, 179, 182, 189, 285n3

Bourdieu, Pierre, 185

Brandeis, Louis, 65

Brennan, William, 17

Bryce, James, 38

Bureaucracy, 106–107

Burke, Edmund, 26, 35, 45, 87